revise philosophy
FOR AS LEVEL

Revise Philosophy for AS Level is the definitive revision guide for students of the AQA Advanced Subsidiary Level syllabus. Following the syllabus, and using past exam questions, it covers all three units of the AS Level syllabus:

Unit 1: Theory of Knowledge

Unit 2: Moral Philosophy and Philosophy of Religion

Unit 3: The set texts.

The authors dedicate a whole chapter to each of the four set texts; Plato's *The Republic*, Descartes's *Meditations*, Marx and Engels's *The German Ideology* and Sartre's *Existentialism and Humanism*.

All chapters are helpfully subdivided into short digestible passages, and include:

* Quiz questions to test core knowledge.
* Discussion questions to deepen understanding.
* 'Going further' sections for advanced study.
* Cross-references to help students make connections.

In addition, a chapter on exam preparation contains a wealth of helpful hints and tips on revision and exam techniques.

Essential reading for all students of AS Level .... the textbook *Philosophy for AS and A2*, also publis........

Michael Lacewing is a Lecturer at Heythrop College, ...thor of *Philosophy for AS and A2*, founder of the company .... nt on philosophy at A Level for the British Philosophical A........

Jean-Marc Pascal is Master of Philosophy at Sherborne School, Dorset. He has over twenty years experience as a philosophy teacher and has worked as an examiner for various examining boards.

ALP

www.alevelphilosophy.co.uk

MICHAEL LACEWING

WITH JEAN-MARC PASCAL

revise
philosophy
FOR AS LEVEL

 Routledge
Taylor & Francis Group

LONDON AND NEW YORK

First published 2007
by Routledge
2 Park Square, Milton Park, Abingdon, Oxon OX14 4RN

Simultaneously published in the USA and Canada
by Routledge
270 Madison Ave, New York, NY 10016

Routledge is an imprint of the Taylor & Francis Group, an informa business

© 2007 Michael Lacewing
Chapter 6 'Marx and Engels' *The German Ideology* © 2007 Jean-Marc Pascal
Chapter 7 'Sartre's *Existentialism and Humanism*' © 2007 Jean-Marc Pascal

Typeset in Berling by
M Rules
Printed and bound in Great Britain by
Bell and Bain Ltd, Glasgow

British Library Cataloguing in Publication Data
A catalogue record for this book is available from the British Library

Library of Congress Cataloging in Publication Data
Lacewing, Michael, 1971–
Revise philosophy for AS level/Michael Lacewing with Jean-Marc Pascal.
     p. cm.
  Includes index.
     1. Philosophy.   I. Pascal, Jean-Marc.   II. Title.
  B72.L28 2006
  107.6–dc22   2006014632

ISBN10: 0–415–39997–1 (hbk)
ISBN10: 0–415–39998–X (pbk)
ISBN10: 0–203–96855–7 (ebk)

ISBN13: 978–0–415–39997–5 (hbk)
ISBN13: 978–0–415–39998–2 (pbk)
ISBN13: 978–0–203–96855–0 (ebk)

CONTENTS

6 MARX AND ENGELS'S *THE GERMAN IDEOLOGY* (UNIT 3)   Jean-Marc Pascal

7 SARTRE'S *EXISTENTIALISM AND HUMANISM*

˙introduction

HOW TO USE THIS BOOK

Revising for a philosophy exam involves two things: developing what you remember about the theories and arguments you have studied; and deepening your understanding of these theories and arguments, so that you can discuss them critically. This book is designed to help you do both. Because it is a revision book, it takes a certain familiarity with doing philosophy for granted. The main focus is on presenting and evaluating the theories and arguments.

Remembering the theories

Each chapter follows the AQA syllabus very closely. Headings and subheadings from the syllabus are used to structure the discussion, and each section is further divided by the main ideas, arguments and objections. So if there is a particular area of the course you want to revise, you can find it very quickly and concentrate on just that issue. You can use either the table of contents or the index to find what you're looking for.

Philosophical terms are explained when they are first introduced, and there is a glossary providing definitions of the most important ones, so that wherever you start to read from, you can always look up the words you don't understand (words that appear in the glossary are in **bold**).

At the end of each discussion, we've included Quiz Questions (the sort that you'll find in parts a and b on the exam paper; some are actual past exam questions). These test your knowledge of the issue and your understanding of the section. We've also added a list of Key Points, putting clearly the main issues the section has covered. Both will help prepare you for the exam.

In a book of this size, we haven't been able to cover *everything* that you might want to talk about when answering questions on the exam paper. But we've covered everything that we think is most central, using the syllabus and mark sheets as a guide in deciding what to include.

Deepening understanding

To help you deepen your understanding, we've included **Going further** sections, which provide discussions of the more difficult ideas or take the arguments further. They will broaden your knowledge and help you 'go further' in your evaluation of the theories and arguments.

Understanding is also about being able to make connections. So we've put in lots of CROSS-REFERENCES to other discussions so that you can follow up the links and see how arguments and issues connect up.

We've also provided Discussion Questions (the sort you'll find in part c questions in the exam) at the end of each section to test and strengthen your understanding and evaluation of the issues.

Exam focus

In writing this book, we have used the syllabus to guide our discussions, and we have also looked carefully at past papers, mark schemes and examiners' reports to make sure that the book is as relevant as possible to the exam.

We've included all actual part (b) and part (c) exam questions, and all part (a) questions for Units 1 and 2, from 2001 to 2006 at the end of those sections that are relevant to the question. We decided not to include part (a) questions for Unit 3, since these depend on having the text extract in front of you. If you want to look at these, you can

- download past exam papers from www.aqa.org.uk/qual/gceasa/phi.html (click on Examination materials at the top of the page); or
- buy exam papers from the AQA; or
- ask your teacher!

Although we haven't included actual part (a) questions for Unit 3, many of our own Quiz Questions are similar in style and will help you to develop the skills of comprehension you need to answer part (a) questions well.

The final chapter provides advice on how to revise for the exam and how to perform well on the day.

The AS examination

Assessment Objectives

The examiners mark your answers according to three principles, known as 'Assessment Objectives' (AOs). They are:

AO1 *Knowledge and understanding*: how well do you know and understand the central debates for a particular issue, the theoretical positions philosophers have defended and the arguments they use to defend them? For Unit 3, how well do you understand the extract of text and its place in the philosopher's thought?

AO2 *Selection and application*: how well do you select relevant ideas, concepts, examples and arguments that you encountered in the material or text you studied? How well do you use these ideas and examples to construct an answer that is coherent and relevant to the question asked?

AO3 *Interpretation and evaluation*: how well do you do interpret, evaluate and analyse the arguments that you have read? Do you understand whether an argument succeeds or fails, and why? How well do you compare arguments and counter-arguments to weigh up what the most plausible position is? Are you able to present a good example that illustrates the point you wish to make?

In addition, you will be marked on the clarity and pertinence of your terminology and expression.

The structure of the exams

Each of the exams lasts for one hour. The questions for Unit 3 have a different structure from those of Units 1 and 2. The examples below show the structure of the questions and how marks are assigned to each part.

For Units 1 and 2, you must answer one question from a choice of two in the area you studied. In Unit 1, this is Theory of Knowledge: there are just two questions on the exam, and you must answer one. In Unit 2, this is either Moral Philosophy or Philosophy of Religion: there are four questions on the exam, two in Moral Philosophy and two in Philosophy of Religion; you must answer one question. The structure and the way the marks are divided up are the same for each question. Here is an example from Unit 1 Theory of Knowledge (from 2001):

1   Total for this question: *45 marks*

(a) Explain and briefly illustrate the meaning of *a priori* **and** *a posteriori* knowledge. (*6 marks*)

(b) Identify and explain **two** reasons why empiricism may lead to scepticism concerning the *extent* of our knowledge. (*15 marks*)

(c) Assess the view that all of our *concepts* are derived from experience. (*24 marks*)

The questions for Unit 3 (set text) are slightly different. First, only one question is asked on each set text; if, like most students, you have studied just one set text, you do not have any choice, you have to answer that question. Each question gives a quotation from the set text, and then asks a series of questions all structured the same way. Here is an example (2001):

2 *Text: Descartes's 'Meditations'*   Total for this question: *45 marks*

Study the following passage and then answer **all** parts of Question 2.

[. . .]

(a)   With close reference to the passage above:
     (i)   Identify what Descartes understands by 'God'. (*2 marks*)
     (ii)   To what conclusion does a consideration of divine attributes lead Descartes? (*2 marks*)
     (iii) Briefly explain how a consideration of 'infinity' leads Descartes to conclude that God exists. (*6 marks*)
(b)   Describe how Descartes distinguishes intellect from the imagination. (*10 marks*)
(c)   Critically discuss Descartes's attempt to show that his mind is independent of his body. (*25 marks*)

The marks

In all three AS Units, the marks for AO1 (knowledge and understanding) are distributed throughout parts (a), (b) and (c). The marks for AO2 (selection and application) are distributed in parts (b) and (c). All the marks for AO3 (interpretation and evaluation) are in part (c). In total, there are 18 marks available for AO1, 18 marks available for AO2, and 9 marks available for AO3.

Units 1, 2

(a)   6 marks for AO1
(b)   6 marks for AO1, 9 marks for AO2
(c)   6 marks for AO1, 9 marks for AO2, 9 marks for AO3

Unit 3 (the mark allocation is not as rigid, but commonly as follows)

(a)   (i) 2 marks for AO1; (ii) 2 marks for AO1; (iii) 4 marks for AO1, 2 marks for AO2
(b)   4 marks for AO1, 6 marks for AO2
(c)   6 marks for AO1, 10 marks for AO2, 9 marks for AO3

● FURTHER RESOURCES

You can find further resources, including book lists and helpful weblinks, on the Resources page of the A Level Philosophy website:
www.alevelphilosophy.co.uk/index.php?s=content&p=resources&tn=alp.

● ACKNOWLEDGEMENTS

In preparing this book, I have drawn on two excellent reference works: the Stanford Encyclopedia of Philosophy: http://plato.stanford.edu/contents.html and the *Routledge Encyclopedia of Philosophy*: http://www.rep.routledge.com. Thanks to Routledge for providing me with free access during this time.

Thanks also to Priyanka Pathak and Tony Bruce at Routledge for encouraging this project, and to my colleagues at Heythrop College, for supporting my work with A Level philosophy. In particular, thanks to Janice Thomas, Peter Gallagher and Tom Crowther for reading and commenting on drafts of chapters. Finally, thanks to Stephen Law for our many discussions over the last few years and his unfailing encouragement.

● AQA ACKNOWLEDGEMENT

All examination questions reproduced in this book are by kind permission of the Assessment and Qualifications Alliance.

1

theory of knowledge

UNIT 1

● I EMPIRICISM AND RATIONALISM

A priori and a posteriori knowledge

A priori knowledge is knowledge of **propositions** that do not require (sense) experience to be known to be true. Knowledge that can be established only through experience is **a posteriori**. The a priori–a posteriori distinction is about how to check or establish knowledge. It is not about how we acquire the concepts or words of the proposition. Babies are not born knowing that all bachelors are unmarried! Yet this is a truth that clearly doesn't need testing against experience: we know it is true just by knowing what it means. Of course, we first have to *learn* what it means, but that is a different issue from how we check if it is true.

This contrast between a priori and a posteriori knowledge should be distinguished from another contrast, that between **analytic** and **synthetic** propositions. A proposition is analytic if it is true or false just in virtue of the meanings of the words. Many analytic truths, such as 'All bachelors are unmarried', are obvious, but some are not, e.g. 'Your mother's brother's father's niece's sole female cousin is your mother' (think about it!). A proposition is synthetic if it is not analytic, i.e. it is true or false not just in virtue of the meanings of the words, but in virtue of the way the world is, e.g. 'snow is white'.

❓ QUIZ QUESTION

Explain and briefly illustrate the meaning of a priori **and** a posteriori knowledge. (AQA, 1a, 2001, *6 marks*)

Defining rationalism and empiricism

Philosophers do not agree on precisely how to define rationalism and empiricism. Obviously, rationalism gives an important role to reason, and empiricism to experience, but the terms range across theories of knowledge, theories of concept acquisition, theories of justification and historical schools of thought. Thinking of them just in terms of 'reason' versus 'experience' is much too simple – why should we think that we have to choose? Most rationalists (the exception is Plato) do not deny that experience can provide us with knowledge under certain circumstances; and empiricists clearly use reasoning, based on experience, to construct arguments about what we know. Furthermore, we need to qualify just what is meant by 'reason' and 'experience'.

Nevertheless, there is a way of contrasting rationalism and empiricism that makes them exclusive (no one is both a rationalist and an empiricist), and which goes to the heart of the historical debate. Stephen Law puts it like this: *rationalism claims that we can have synthetic a priori knowledge of how things are outside the mind; empiricism denies this.*

In other words, rationalists argue that it is possible for us to know (some) synthetic propositions about how the world outside our own minds is – e.g. about mathematics, morality or even the material world – without relying on sense experience. Empiricists argue that it is not. Notice that they don't deny *all* a priori knowledge – no empiricist claims that you have to check whether all bachelors are unmarried to see if it is true! They simply claim that all a priori knowledge is of analytic propositions. If we don't know if a proposition is true or false just by the meaning of the words, we have to use sense experience to find out whether it is true or false.

(The clause 'how things are outside the mind' is necessary. Many propositions about my mental states are synthetic, e.g. 'I feel sad' or 'I am thinking about unicorns'. But they don't require *sense* experience to be known; in fact, does knowing my own thoughts involve *experiencing* them at all? We don't need to worry about this. Rationalists and empiricists alike do not deny that we *just do* know that we have certain impressions and ideas, thoughts and feelings. The argument is about knowledge of things other than our own minds.)

 KEY POINTS

- Rationalism claims that we can have synthetic a priori knowledge of how things are outside the mind.

● Empiricism denies this. It claims that all a priori knowledge is only of analytic propositions.

Rationalism: reason as the source of our knowledge, as justification for our beliefs and as the source of our conceptual apparatus

Rationalists claim that we have synthetic knowledge that does not depend upon sense experience. How do we gain such knowledge? Rationalists argue either that we have a form of rational 'intuition' or 'insight' which enables us to grasp certain truths intellectually; or that we know certain truths innately, as part of our rational nature; or both. Rationalists may also argue that some of our concepts are innate – that although it might take sense experience to make us aware of these concepts, the content of the concept is not given by experience.

Many rationalists add that the knowledge we gain through reason or have innately cannot be had in any other way. They may also argue that such knowledge is superior, e.g. by being more certain, to the knowledge or beliefs we gain through the senses.

Plato

Plato argues that we can have knowledge only of the Forms, which are abstract entities we can know through reason, but not through sense experience. He argues that we can never have knowledge through sense experience, we can form only opinions. His theory of knowledge is discussed in the first four sections of Ch. 4 (THE THEORY OF FORMS p. 194; KNOWLEDGE, BELIEF AND IGNORANCE p. 196; THE SIMILES OF THE CAVE AND THE DIVIDED LINE p. 198; EPISTEMOLOGICAL IMPLICATIONS OF THE THEORY OF THE FORMS p. 201). Since that discussion of knowledge and reason is self-contained, I discuss only Plato's theory of concepts here.

Plato doesn't just argue that we can have knowledge only of the Forms. He also argues that our concepts are derived from the Forms. In the *Phaedo*, he argues that learning must be a kind of recollection. When we learn, we become able to apply concepts to what we experience, which involves knowing what 'equality' or 'beauty' or 'rose' means. Where do these concepts come from? If all we have are many and various experiences, how are we able to classify experiences? We might argue that we classify experiences, and so form concepts, through similarities and differences between our experiences. But in order to know what is 'the same' or 'different', we must already be able to classify our experiences. But we can't do so unless we already have concepts! So we can't form concepts by classifying experiences.

So, Plato argues, we have concepts innately. Concepts are our recollection of the Forms, which we (our souls) experienced before birth. Unless we have this innate knowledge, we could never learn anything. We are able to classify our experiences by comparing them with our innate concepts (memories of the Forms). (Plato doesn't argue that we *realize* this is what we are doing.)

A second argument against thinking that concepts derive from experience is that because we all have different experiences, we'll all form different concepts. But then how can we talk to each other and share ideas? Yet we do mean the same thing by the same word, so our concepts can't be formed by our different experience, but by something we all share, viz. innate knowledge of the Forms.

Descartes

Unlike Plato, Descartes does not deny that we can have knowledge of the objects of sense experience. But we only gain that knowledge through the use of reason; it is reason which justifies our beliefs about the world. Descartes's theory is discussed at length in Ch. 5 (see especially SCEPTICAL DOUBT AND ITS USE IN THE QUEST FOR CERTAINTY, p. 222; THE WAVES OF DOUBT, p. 224; ABSOLUTE CERTAINTY OF THE COGITO AND ITS IMPLICATIONS, p. 227; THE ESSENTIAL NATURES OF MIND AND BODY, p. 235; THE PROOF OF MATERIAL THINGS, p. 240; DESCARTES'S RATIONALISM, p. 242; and THE ROLE OF GOD IN DESCARTES'S SYSTEM, p. 250). I give a brief overview here.

Descartes begins his investigation into what we can know by attacking sense experience as untrustworthy. Most of what we think we know we have acquired this way, he says. However, appearances can be deceptive; e.g. objects far away look small. So what sense experience presents to us is too unreliable to count as knowledge. You can doubt even those sense experiences that seem most certain – e.g. that you are now reading a book – because you could be asleep, and, if you were, you wouldn't know that you were (see Ch. 5, THE WAVES OF DOUBT, p. 224). So sense experience, at least on its own, can't give us knowledge.

Descartes then questions what we think material objects are. He notices that when he melts a piece of wax it loses all of its original sensory qualities (taste, smell, tactility, shape); yet he believes it is the same wax. So the wax is not equivalent to its sensory qualities. So when he thinks of the wax, he is in fact thinking about something that is extended and changeable. This is the essence of our idea of material objects, but it is given by *reason*, not sense experience. The idea of the wax as something defined by its sensory properties is muddled. When we realize that we comprehend the wax through *understanding*, as something extended and changeable, our idea of the wax has become clear and distinct (see Ch. 5, THE ESSENTIAL NATURES OF MIND AND BODY, p. 235).

Descartes goes on to argue that what is clearly and distinctly conceived is true (see Ch. 5, DESCARTES'S RATIONALISM, p. 242). So if material objects exist, then they *really are* extended. And he has shown this using reason. He then argues that we can know that material objects do exist (see Ch. 5, THE PROOF OF MATERIAL THINGS, p. 240). We have experiences which appear, very forcefully, to be experiences of a world external to our minds. There are only two options for what might cause these experiences: a real external world; or God. If the cause was God, this would mean that God was a deceiver because he would have created us with a very strong tendency to believe something false. However, Descartes has also argued that God exists and is perfect by definition (see Ch. 5, THE TRADEMARK ARGUMENT and THE ONTOLOGICAL ARGUMENT, p. 245 and p. 248). Because we know that God is perfect, we know that God is not a deceiver. So there must really be an external world.

In establishing what we know about material things, Descartes has relied on reason, and not sense experience, in three places:

1 in the argument that our idea of material objects as extended derives not from the senses, but from the understanding;
2 in his assertion that our experiences must have a cause, which for Descartes is a matter of logic (Hume rejects this claim – unless we already know that our experiences are *effects*, we can't know by logic alone that they have causes);
3 in invoking God, since proving the existence of God depends on reason alone.

The first point is also the basis of Descartes's claim that material objects are *only* extended; they don't have, essentially and in themselves, those properties of colour, smell and so on that we seem to detect through our senses. So what we can know about material objects in general is completely dependent on reason. Having established this, Descartes is quite happy that our senses inform our understanding about particular objects, which then judges whether they exist or not.

Descartes also shows his rationalism in his claim that the idea of God is innate, rather than acquired from experience (see Ch. 5, THE TRADEMARK ARGUMENT, p. 245).

● **KEY POINTS**

● Plato argues that we can have knowledge only of the Forms, not of objects of sense experience, and that we gain this knowledge through reason.

● He also argues that our concepts are innate memories of the Forms. Unless we had such innate memories, we wouldn't be able to classify experience using concepts.

● Descartes argues that reason is needed to establish the nature and existence of material objects in general and the existence of God. Sense experience provides only information about particular material objects, and even then our understanding judges whether they exist or not.

● Descartes also argues that the idea of God is innate.

❓ QUIZ QUESTIONS

Explain and illustrate the rationalist view that some concepts are **not** drawn from experience. (AQA, 1b, 2003, *15 marks*)

Outline Plato's argument that we cannot have knowledge about the objects of sense experience.

Outline Descartes's argument that we know the nature of material objects using reason not sense experience.

Outline Descartes's argument for the claim that we can know that material objects exist.

Empiricism: experience as the source of our knowledge of concepts and propositions, and the means by which we justify our beliefs

Hume argues that we can have knowledge of just two sorts of things: the relations between ideas; and matters of fact. His distinction was developed by later philosophers, and is now understood in terms of the two distinctions, mentioned above: **analytic–synthetic** and **a priori–a posteriori**. Hume argued that all a priori knowledge must be analytic, while all knowledge of synthetic propositions is a posteriori. In other words, anything we know that is not true by definition, every 'matter of fact', we must learn and test through our senses.

The relations of ideas don't depend on matters of fact, so we can know these a priori, through rational proof. By relations of ideas, Hume means propositions such as 'All sons have fathers' (about the ideas 'son' and 'father') and 'If A is longer than B, and B is longer than C, then A is longer than C' (about the idea of length). This seems uncontroversial so far. But an area of knowledge that has proved problematical for empiricists is *mathematics*, which I discuss further in THE LIMITATIONS OF EMPIRICISM (p. 17).

All knowledge of matters of fact, by contrast, relies on experience. We gain it by using observation, and by employing induction and reasoning about probability. The foundation of this knowledge is what we *experience* here and now, or can remember. Hume argues that all our knowledge which goes beyond what is present to our senses or memory rests on *causal inference*. If I receive a letter from a friend with a French postmark on it, I'll believe that my friend is in France – because I *infer* from the postmark to a place. I do this because I think that where something is posted causes it to have the postmark of that place; and if the letter was posted by my friend then I believe that he must be in France.

And how do I know all this? I rely on past *experience* – in the past, I have experienced letters being posted, I have seen different postmarks, I have found that postmarks relate to where you post something, and so on. I can't work out what causes what just by thinking about it. It is only our experience of effects following causes that brings us to infer from the existence or occurrence of some cause to its effect, or from some effect to its cause.

Going further: empiricists on moral and religious knowledge

The debate between empiricists and rationalists has historically focused on knowledge of the material world. As a result, empiricists concentrated on sensory experience. But knowledge of the material world may not be all the knowledge we can have. So how have empiricists dealt with the question of moral knowledge and knowledge of God's existence?

Empiricists deny that there is any synthetic a priori knowledge of how things stand outside the mind. So for any area of knowledge, they have three options:

1 to deny that we have any knowledge in that area;
2 to say that any knowledge we do have is based on experience; or
3 to say that any knowledge we have is analytic.

John Locke, somewhat surprisingly, argues that truths of morality and the existence of God can be established by reason because they are truths by definition. He uses a form of THE COSMOLOGICAL ARGUMENT (Ch. 3, p. 144) to derive the idea of God and to prove that we can know God exists. We need only the fact, from experience, that we exist, and some truths that Locke claims are analytic: we know that we exist and that something cannot come from nothing; so something must always have existed, and everything else which exists must have come from this. As we have knowledge and intelligence, we may deduce that this original being is a knowing intelligence.

He argues that we can know moral truths in a similar way. From our knowledge of the existence and nature of God, and of ourselves as creations of God, we can deduce what our moral duties are. It is only because it is not obvious, and we don't reason well, that people have ever disagreed on such matters.

John Stuart Mill, by contrast, argues for moral knowledge on the basis of 'observation and experience'. He defends the claim that what is good, to be aimed at, is the greatest happiness. He argues that the only evidence we have for what is good is what we desire. Everyone desires happiness, and so there is no better final aim for action than happiness. This argument doesn't establish that we should desire and aim at *each other's* happiness, since each person desires his or her own; but Mill assumes that morality is concerned with all persons equally, and that this is an analytic truth. So we know that everyone's happiness is what we should aim at.

Empiricists on acquiring concepts

Locke and Hume have very similar theories of how we acquire concepts; we'll concentrate on Hume's. Hume believes that we are immediately and directly aware of 'perceptions'. 'Perceptions' are divided into 'impressions' and 'ideas'. Impressions are divided into impressions of 'sensation' and those of 'reflection'. Impressions of sensation derive from our senses, e.g. seeing a car; impressions of reflection derive from our experience of our mind, e.g. feeling emotions.

Ideas differ from impressions in 'forcefulness' and 'vivacity'. Ideas are 'faint copies' of impressions. Think what it is like to see a scene or hear a tune; now what it is like to imagine or remember that scene or tune. The latter is weaker, fainter. Hume argues that ideas are also *copies* of impressions. And so there are ideas of sensation (e.g. the idea of red) and ideas of reflection (e.g. the idea of sadness). *Concepts* are a type of idea. So his theory of how we acquire ideas, viz. by copying them from impressions, is a theory of how we acquire concepts.

Hume's claim that ideas are *copies* of impressions may seem implausible. There are many ideas we have for which we have had no corresponding impression, e.g. unicorns and God. Hume agrees, but says we are capable of forming *complex* ideas for which we have no corresponding impression. But all such complex ideas are derived from *simple* ideas, which *are* copies of impressions. Ideas can work only with the materials which impressions provide; no idea, no matter how abstract or complex, is more than a putting together, altering or abstracting from impressions. Hume presents two arguments for this claim.

First, all ideas can be analysed into simple ideas which each correspond to an impression. Consider the idea of God. Hume claims that the idea of God, based on ideas of perfection and infinity, is extrapolated from ideas of imperfection and finitude. (Descartes argued that the idea of infinity in God is not the negation of finitude, but a more 'positive' conception; which he thought established that God must exist to have caused this idea – see Ch. 5, THE TRADEMARK ARGUMENT, p. 245.) Second, Hume argues there is a correspondence between an experience (or type of experience) and the ability to form an idea of that experience. Thus, a blind man does not know what colour is and a mild man cannot comprehend the motive of revenge.

● **KEY POINTS**

- Empiricists deny that we have any a priori knowledge of synthetic propositions about how the world is outside our mind.

- Hume argues that all a priori knowledge is of relations of ideas, and so is analytic. All knowledge of synthetic propositions, matters of fact, is a posteriori. It depends either on present experience or causal inference, which relies on past experience.

- Empiricists must claim that moral and religious knowledge is a priori and analytic (Locke), *or* that, if it is synthetic, it depends on experience (Mill), *or* that there is no such knowledge.

- Empiricists claim that *all* concepts are derived from impressions of sensation or of reflection.

- Simple concepts are copies of impressions; complex concepts are created out of simple concepts by combining and abstracting from them.

❓ QUIZ QUESTIONS

Briefly explain and illustrate Hume's division of knowledge into two kinds.

Outline and illustrate the empiricist theory of concept acquisition.

DISCUSSION QUESTION

Assess the view that all of our **concepts** are derived from experience. (AQA, 1c, 2001, *24 marks*)

The limitations of rationalism: scepticism concerning the nature and extent of rational knowledge

Material objects

Hume challenges Descartes's argument that our knowledge of material objects as extended comes from understanding, not the senses. He argues that the only way to form an idea of extension is by abstraction from particular sensory experiences. We have no conception of extension that is neither visible, and therefore derived from sight, nor tangible, and therefore derived from touch.

Descartes explicitly rejects this claim. He argues that we don't get the idea that the wax is essentially extended from any particular sense experience. We also think that the possible changes it can go through outstrip what we can imagine: we can't imagine all the changes I know the wax can undergo. So the idea of extension outstrips what the senses can provide. But his claim that our concept of extension therefore derives from the understanding instead does not mean extension is neither visible nor tangible: the wax conceived by the understanding is the same wax that is perceived through the senses.

However, Hume may reply that Descartes's argument overlooks the possibility that we form our concept of extension by *abstraction* (rather than imagination). Of course, this can be seen as a process of reasoning; but the origin of the concept is still sensory experience.

God

Hume similarly argues against Descartes's claim that our concept of God is innate because it could not have been formed from experience. Hume claims that it is formed from experience by abstraction and negation: we are familiar with things being finite and imperfect, so we can form an idea of something that is not finite (infinite) and not imperfect (perfect). Descartes's response is that our idea of God is not negative but positive. For further discussion, see objections to THE TRADEMARK ARGUMENT (Ch. 5, p. 245).

Given that Descartes (thinks he) needs to prove the existence of God in order to know that there is a material world beyond his mind, if Hume is right, this is very damaging to Descartes's rationalist project.

Going further: rational intuition

Both Plato and Descartes argue that knowledge requires certainty, and sensory experience cannot deliver it. But empiricists can reply that reason may not deliver certainty either. Hume argues that many of the so-called 'truths' which previous philosophers claimed were known by 'rational intuition' were actually just assumptions, propositions unjustifiably taken for granted. For example, it is not an analytic truth that every event must have a cause. It is very difficult for us to believe otherwise, but this does not mean that we are *rationally justified* in that belief. Reason doesn't do 'insight', says Hume, it does just analytic truths.

So rationalists owe us an account of what intuition is and exactly *how* it can provide knowledge. Knowledge needs to be secure, it needs justification, it needs to be reliable. Our senses are a reliable basis for beliefs because sense experiences are caused by material objects. But what justifies the claim that rational intuition is reliable? Plato didn't claim that the Forms *cause* our intuitions of them.

However, rationalism's best form of defence may be attack. As I explain in the next section, empiricism has struggled to show that all our knowledge is either analytic or comes from the senses. If there are good arguments against empiricism, then rationalism can claim that if we are not to fall into scepticism, we must accept that we have rational intuition, even if we don't know what it is or how it works.

● **KEY POINTS**

- Hume challenges Descartes's claim that we know material objects are extended through reason, arguing that the concept of extension is derived from sensory experience.

- He also argues that the concept of God is not innate, but formed by abstraction.

- Finally, he argues that reason can provide knowledge only of analytic truths. Rationalists owe us an account of *how* reason is supposed to provide the knowledge they claim it does. However, rationalists may respond that the only alternative to rationalism is scepticism, so even if we cannot account for how reason works, if we think we have knowledge at all, we should accept that it does.

❓ QUIZ QUESTION

Explain and briefly illustrate **two** objections to rationalist claims of knowledge.

DISCUSSION QUESTION

Assess the claim that it is possible to have knowledge of synthetic truths that does not depend on sense experience.

The limitations of empiricism: scepticism concerning the nature and extent of empirical knowledge

We saw that empiricists have just three options regarding any knowledge claim:

1 to deny that the claim is knowledge;
2 to say that the claim is based on experience; or
3 to say that the claim is analytic.

Hume, although an empiricist himself, presents some of the strongest challenges to empiricist knowledge. He argues, along with many rationalists, that sensory experience is not enough to secure knowledge; but instead of turning to rationalism, he looks for other solutions.

Matters of fact

We saw that Hume argues that much of our knowledge about the external world depends on causal inference; and that depends on our assumption that the present and the future will be like the past. If, in the past, French postmarks on letters were the result of a letter being posted in France, I assume that to be so again on this occasion.

But Hume points out that this is, indeed, an *assumption*. What is the basis of inferring from past experience to the present or the future? We have experience that, in the past, whenever a cause of a particular type occurs, e.g. a billiard ball striking another, it was followed by an effect, the second ball moving; but why think that this succession will occur again? Suppose I say that I know the billiard ball will move because it has always moved in the past; on what basis do I think that the future resembles the past? It's true that in the past the billiard ball always moved. But why think it will move again now? Past experience can give me '*direct* and *certain* information of those precise objects only, and that precise period of time, which fall under its cognizance'. We reason that the billiard ball will move on the basis of the principle that 'the future will be like the past'. But this is what we're trying to prove, so we can't assume it.

Hume's solution is to say that we draw the inference *without reasoning or argument*, but on the basis of a principle of the 'imagination' that has bound the two ideas – of the cause and of the effect – together in our minds. When we experience something that has been a cause in the past (one billiard ball striking another), we immediately believe that its usual effect is about to occur (the second ball moving). Or when we experience an effect (receiving a letter with a French postmark), we believe that its usual cause has occurred (the letter was posted in France). This principle of the imagination Hume calls 'Custom', without pretending that such a label explains it at all. Custom is a natural instinct of the mind, a disposition we simply have in the face of experience of the same effects repeatedly following the same causes. Without custom, we would be unable to draw causal inferences, and so we would have no knowledge of anything beyond what was present to our senses and memory.

Philosophers thought that Hume's argument produced scepticism. Since there is no 'reason' to believe the future will be like the past, then *any* belief about what the future will be like, and what will happen on this occasion, is equally unsupported. But recently some philosophers have argued that Hume did not embrace this scepticism: he clearly claimed we do have knowledge as a result of causal inference. One resolution to the tension in Hume's work is to say that he works with more than one model of 'knowledge'. He is content to grant the status of knowledge in a 'practical sense' to beliefs that rest on custom and other instincts (such as belief in the external world). But if one requires all knowledge to be firmly grounded in reason (which, at times, Hume understands to be restricted to deductive proof), then we know only analytic truths, what we are experiencing now and what we can be certain of in memory.

Morality

In the area of morality, Hume makes a different sort of move. He attacks Locke's argument, claiming that the 'analytic truths' Locke relies on to establish God and morality, such as 'something cannot come from nothing', are not analytic truths at all, but unjustified assumptions. And, Hume argues, we cannot have moral knowledge through our senses. So there is no moral knowledge. But Hume argues that this is because morality isn't about *truth* at all. Sentences such as 'Abortion is wrong' don't state **propositions** (which can be true or false); they express attitudes. There can be no moral knowledge because there are no moral *facts* that we can know or not know (see Ch. 2, EMOTIVISM, p. 112).

Mathematics

It is difficult to argue that mathematical knowledge is a posteriori, so Locke and Hume argue that mathematical propositions are analytic. All mathematical knowledge is reached by developing a series of definitions. But then how are mathematical 'discoveries' possible? How can we 'discover' something that is true *by definition*? Empiricists reply that analytic knowledge doesn't need to be obvious; mathematical truths are very complex, so it takes work to establish that they are true. But that doesn't mean they are not true by definition.

This reply is difficult to believe. For example, truths of geometry don't seem to be true by definition. The fact that it takes at least three lines to enclose a space in two dimensions seems to be a truth about the *nature* of space, rather than the *concept* of space. Yet it has mathematical certainty, and can be proved by mathematical geometry. How could such certainty come from sensory experience alone?

In the twentieth century, empiricists such as Bertrand Russell argued that although mathematical truths are not analytic, they are nevertheless 'logical' truths. His argument depended on technical developments in logic and in mathematics. For our purposes, it is enough to note that many philosophers believe that Russell's arguments showed that in order to account for mathematics, we don't need to turn to 'rational insight': we just need to develop a more sophisticated account of how logic can produce new truths.

● **KEY POINTS**

● For any knowledge claim, empiricists must argue that either it is based on experience, or it is analytic, or it is not knowledge.

● Hume claims that knowledge of matters of fact is based on experience. However, much of it depends on inferring from cause to effect or effect to cause. This inference is not rationally supported, and we have no *reason* to think events will cause the same effects in the future as they have done in the past. We are simply led to believe this by 'custom'. Whether this leads to scepticism depends on whether we believe causal inferences must be based on reason to count as knowledge.

● Hume argues that there is no moral knowledge, not because he is sceptical, but because morality is not about truth at all, but is an expression of feelings.

● Empiricists argue that mathematics is analytic. We may object that the truths of geometry seem to be synthetic, e.g. about the nature of space. Russell developed a new theory of logic to argue mathematical truths are logical truths.

❓ QUIZ QUESTION

Identify and explain **two** reasons why empiricism may lead to scepticism concerning the extent of our knowledge. (AQA, 1b, 2001, *15 marks*)

❓ DISCUSSION QUESTION

Assess empiricism. (AQA, 1c, 2003, *24 marks*)

● II KNOWLEDGE AND JUSTIFICATION

Believing-that and knowing-that: evidence and degrees of justification

Belief and knowledge

There are different types of knowledge: acquaintance knowledge (I know Oxford well), ability knowledge (I know how to ride a bike) and propositional knowledge (I know that eagles are birds). The first two types of knowledge are very interesting, but we are concerned only with the third: what it is to know some **proposition**, *p*.

We intuitively make a distinction between belief and knowledge. People can believe propositions that aren't true; but if you know that *p*, then *p* must be true. You can't know something false; if it is false, then you don't know it. You have made a mistake, believing it to be true when it is not. For example, if you claim that flamingoes are grey, and you think you know this, you are mistaken. If flamingoes are not grey, but pink, then you can't know they are grey. Of course, you *believe* that they are grey; but that's the difference – beliefs can be false.

There is another distinction between beliefs and knowledge. People can believe propositions for all sorts of reasons. They can have true beliefs without having any *evidence* or *justification* for their beliefs. For example, someone on a jury might think that the person on trial is guilty just from the way he dresses. The jury member's belief that the person is guilty might be true; but how someone dresses isn't evidence for whether he is a criminal! So belief can be accidentally true, relative to the evidence the person has; if it is, it isn't knowledge. Someone can hold a belief that is, in fact, true, even when he or she has evidence to suggest it is false. For example, there is a lot of evidence that astrology does not make accurate predictions, and my horoscope has often been wrong. Suppose that on one occasion I read my horoscope and believe a prediction, although I know there is evidence against thinking it is right. And then this prediction turns out to be true! Did I *know* it was right? It looks more like my belief is irrational. I had no reason, no evidence, no justification, for believing that prediction was true. Knowledge, then, needs some kind of support, some reason for thinking that the proposition believed is true. Knowledge needs to be *justified*.

But what is justification? Some philosophers argue that justification is about having evidence. To have evidence, some argue, is to have a mental state, apart from the belief, that represents *p* as true. For example, you might have a sensory experience – you believe the rose is red because you see the rose, and it looks red. Or the mental state could be a memory – you remember where you left your keys, you remember putting them down. Or it could be that *p* is 'self-evident' – you just 'see' the truth of 'if the dog is behind the cat, the cat is in front of the dog'. However, we will later discuss a theory which claims that justification is not about having evidence for your belief, but about how reliable the *source* of your belief is (RELIABILISM, p. 35).

Infallibilism and certainty

How strong does justification need to be to turn true belief into knowledge? How is it related to certainty? The strongest claim we could make is that knowledge has to be *infallible*. A weaker view would say that evidence needs only to make the belief *more probable*.

Infallibilism seems plausible because if I know that *p*, then I can't be mistaken about *p*, because no one can know what is false. And so if I know that *p*, *p must* be true. This makes knowledge very difficult, since it is rare that our evidence rules out the *possibility* of error. A consequence of infallibilism, then, is that it opens the door to scepticism.

Descartes takes a different approach. He understands knowledge in terms of what is 'completely certain and indubitable'. To establish this certainty, he seeks to test his beliefs by doubt. Doubt, then, is the opposite of certainty. If we can doubt a belief, then it is not certain, and so it is not knowledge. The sort of doubt Descartes employs is 'hyperbolic'. Descartes does not test his beliefs, e.g. that the external world exists, by whether there is good evidence against them; but by whether it is *possible* that his beliefs are mistaken. In other words, doubt as the test for knowledge is not a matter of what *is doubtful* in the light of the available evidence; the test is what *can* be doubted.

So, in effect, Descartes assumes that in order to know that *p*, I must be certain of my belief that *p*, i.e. I *cannot* doubt that *p*. What he means by 'cannot doubt' is that, when I consider *p* carefully, I am unable not to believe it. Using my best, most careful judgement, I judge that it is impossible that it should be false: the proposition 'is necessarily true each time it is expressed by me, or conceived in my mind'. We can say that in order for my belief that *p* to be justified I must be certain of it in this way. And by this Descartes means I am unable to doubt it.

Plato also argued that knowledge required certainty, but he thought this meant that *what* you know mustn't change (see Ch. 4, KNOWLEDGE, BELIEF AND IGNORANCE, p. 196 and EPISTEMOLOGICAL IMPLICATIONS OF THE THEORY OF THE FORMS, p. 201).

Going further: rejecting the argument for infallibilism

Knowledge is more than just true belief, because it shouldn't be accidental or unsupported in the way that true belief can be. But that doesn't mean we have to say that knowledge is *infallible*.

The first argument for infallibilism rests on a logical error. Infallibilism is the claim 'If I know that *p*, then I can't be mistaken about *p*'. But this claim is ambiguous, i.e. it has more than one possible meaning, depending on how one understands the 'can't'. Here are two ways of understanding the claim:

Reading 1: 'It can't be the case that if I know that *p*, I *am* mistaken that *p*.'

We should agree with this; in fact, it is analytically true. By definition, you cannot know what is false.

Reading 2: 'If I know that *p*, (I am in the position that) I *can't possibly* be mistaken that *p*.'

This is what infallibilism claims. It is a much stronger claim that reading 1, because it says that not only am I *not* mistaken, but I *can't possibly be* mistaken that p. Obviously, there are many cases in which I *could* be mistaken that *p*, but in fact I am not. Furthermore, if my true belief rests on evidence, there are good reasons why I am not mistaken. Nevertheless, I *could be*; this isn't impossible.

The first argument for infallibilism used reading 1 to support reading 2. But this is a mistake. The two claims are distinct, since one is a claim about whether I *am* mistaken, and the other is a claim about whether I *could be* mistaken. So if we are going to accept infallibilism, we need some other, independent, reason for believing reading 2. Descartes offers us such a reason when he claims that knowledge requires certainty, and certainty requires that I can't be mistaken.

Knowledge and certainty

Descartes's understanding of knowledge, certainty and the place of doubt can be criticized. First, Descartes's idea of certainty appears to be psychological: he is after beliefs that *he* is certain of. And this is not the same thing as a belief *being certain*, i.e. indubitable. After all, we can make mistakes; we can be certain of a belief that can be doubted. Descartes has an answer to this, but for further discussion see SCEPTICAL DOUBT AND ITS USE IN THE QUEST FOR CERTAINTY (Ch. 5, p. 222).

Second, once we recognize the distinction between my being certain and a belief's being certain, we can argue that certainty is not relevant to knowledge; what is really relevant is justification. 'Being certain' is not the same as 'being justified'. We can be certain of beliefs that are not justified – and because the belief is not justified, it is not knowledge. What Descartes assumes is that if we are not certain of a belief, it is not justified. But perhaps this is wrong; perhaps we can be uncertain of beliefs that are justified. This is, at least, a question worth discussing. Is certainty necessary for knowledge? If we can provide an account of justification that doesn't mention certainty, then maybe not. If it is enough for a belief to be justified that the evidence makes it more probable (how much more, though?), then we don't need certainty for justification.

In part, this is a question about what we are willing to call knowledge. Infallibilism claims that to know that *p*, we can't possibly be mistaken that *p*. A different objection to infallibilism is that it leads to scepticism: on this account of justification, we will very rarely be justified in what we believe. A weaker notion of justification will say that we need *good* grounds for believing that *p*, but not grounds that are so strong the belief is infallible. This will allow for more beliefs to count as knowledge. But the infallibilist will reply that this is no objection. If it turns out we don't know much, then that's that. If infallibilism results in scepticism, this isn't an objection, it's just what the situation is.

Infallibilism appeals to our sense that knowledge, unlike true belief, cannot be accidental. The less we demand of justification, the more 'accidental' justified beliefs can be. The question of whether infallibilism is true will arise repeatedly in the following sections. Even if infallibilism is wrong, we still need to come up with some alternative theory of justification.

For more on infallibilism in justification, see FOUNDATIONALISM (p. 28).

- There are different types of knowledge: acquaintance, ability and propositional knowledge. Theories of knowledge discussed here are about propositional knowledge.

- Knowledge is not the same as belief. Beliefs can be mistaken, but no one can know what is false.

- Knowledge is not the same as true belief, either. True beliefs may not be justified, but can be believed without evidence. To be knowledge, a belief must be justified.

- Many philosophers have argued that justification is about evidence. To have evidence is to have some mental state, other than the belief, that represents the proposition to be true, e.g. an experience or a memory. Some philosophers argue that justification is not about evidence, but about how reliable the source of the belief is.

- Infallibilism argues that to be knowledge a belief must be certain. It argues that if I cannot know what is false, if I know that *p*, *p* must be true, so I *can't be* mistaken. But this argument is wrong. If I know that *p*, then it can't be that I *am* mistaken. But it can happen that I am not mistaken even though I *could* be.

- Descartes argues that what we can doubt is not certain enough to be knowledge. A justified belief is one I cannot doubt. However, we can argue that certainty and justification are not the same thing: e.g. I can be certain of beliefs that are not, in fact, justified. We need to think more about whether justification requires certainty.

- Infallibilism leads to scepticism, because most beliefs are not certain.

❓ QUIZ QUESTIONS

Explain and illustrate how knowledge differs from true belief. (AQA, 1b, 2005, *15 marks*)

Explain **two** reasons for thinking that knowledge requires certainty.

❓ DISCUSSION QUESTION

Assess whether knowledge requires the impossibility of doubt. (AQA, 1c, 2005, *24 marks*)

The tripartite definition of knowledge: truth, belief and justification

The tripartite definition of knowledge applies only to propositional knowledge, knowing 'that *p*'. Some philosophers argue that a complete analysis of a concept such as propositional knowledge ought to state conditions that are together 'equivalent' to knowledge. In other words, if someone knows some proposition, he or she should fulfil exactly those conditions that the analysis of knowledge states. The 'justified true belief' theory of knowledge is like this. It claims that to know that *p* involves exactly these three things:

1   The proposition *p* is true.
2   You believe that *p*.
3   Your belief that *p* is justified.

It claims these are the *necessary* and *sufficient conditions* for knowledge.

Necessary and sufficient conditions

Necessary and sufficient conditions are related to conditional statements, which take the form 'If x, then y'. Such statements relate the truth of two propositions, e.g. 'It is raining' and 'I am getting wet', e.g. 'If it is raining, I am getting wet'. The conditional asserts that if the first statement (known as the antecedent) is true, then the second statement (the consequent) is also true.

Suppose the conditional is true – that *if* it is raining, I am getting wet. It follows that if the antecedent is true (it is raining), then the consequent is true (I am getting wet). It also follows that if the consequent is false (I am not getting wet), then the antecedent is false (it is not raining).

The justified true belief theory of knowledge claims that *if* all the three conditions it lists are satisfied – if *p* is true, and you believe that *p*, and your belief is justified – then you know that *p*. You don't need anything else for knowledge: the three conditions, together, are *sufficient*.

But the theory says more than this. It also says that *if* you know that *p*, then you have a justified true belief that *p*. There is no other way to know that *p*, no other analysis of knowledge. So, it claims, each of the three conditions is *necessary*. You can't have knowledge without meeting exactly these three conditions. If *p* is false, or you don't believe that *p*, or you believe that *p* is not justified, then you don't know that *p*.

So the theory puts forward *two* conditionals: if all three conditions are satisfied, then you know that *p*; and if you know that *p*, then all three conditions are satisfied. This means whenever you have one, you have the other. And so, the theory claims, we can say that knowledge and justified true belief *are the same thing*. Justified true belief is necessary for knowledge (you can't have knowledge without it), but it is also sufficient for knowledge (you don't need anything else).

Justified true belief

The claim that knowledge is justified true belief matches many of our intuitions. First, we cannot know what is false. Of course, we can *think* we know something and it turns out that we don't. But that isn't knowledge – we were just wrong to think we knew it. No one disputes this.

Second, it is intuitively plausible to think that we must believe that *p* in order to know that *p*. Some philosophers have certainly challenged this, claiming that knowledge is an entirely different mental state from belief. They say either you believe something or you know it;

but you don't know something by believing it. The usual reply to this is to point to those occasions on which we make mistakes. Suppose I think I know something, but it turns out that I didn't. We would usually say that I had, nevertheless, *believed* it. I believed it, but I thought I knew it; this shows that we can mistake belief for knowledge. If knowledge isn't a kind of belief, this would be puzzling.

Finally, as we saw in BELIEVING-THAT AND KNOWING-THAT (p. 19), we want to make a distinction between knowledge and true belief. The distinction seems to be a matter of justification.

Justified true belief theory is a theory about knowledge. It doesn't tell us what *justification* is or how strong it must be. We discussed the strength of justification in BELIEVING-THAT AND KNOWING-THAT (p. 19); we'll discuss what justification is in the sections on FOUNDATIONALISM (p. 28), COHERENTISM (p. 33) and RELIABILISM (p. 35).

● **KEY POINTS**

● The justified true belief theory of knowledge claims to give necessary and sufficient conditions for knowledge. If you have a true belief that *p* which is justified, you know that *p* (the conditions are sufficient for knowledge); if you know that *p*, you have a justified true belief that *p* (the conditions are necessary for knowledge).

● If justified true belief is both sufficient and necessary for knowledge, it is the same thing as knowledge.

● The claim that knowledge is justified true belief initially matches many of our intuitions. However, the theory tells us nothing about justification.

❓ QUIZ QUESTIONS

Explain and illustrate how knowledge differs from true belief. (AQA, 1b, 2005, *15 marks*)

Explain the claim that knowledge *is* justified true belief.

Problems in the application of this definition

If infallibilism is true, justification *entails* truth. If your belief is justified, you *can't possibly* be mistaken. But if you *can't possibly* be mistaken about *p*, then *p* must be true. So if your belief that *p* is justified, then *p* must be true. So if infallibilism is correct, then knowledge is simply justified belief – and the 'truth' clause is redundant.

However, we noted that infallibilism also makes knowledge extremely rare. So many philosophers have adopted a weaker notion of justification, one related to evidence. With *enough* 'good' evidence, our beliefs are justified and count as knowledge. Let us suppose this weaker theory of justification is true. How does the justified true belief theory of knowledge stand up?

Gettier: justified true belief is not enough for knowledge

Edmund Gettier famously presented cases in which we want to say that someone has justified true belief but *not* knowledge. These cases became known as 'Gettier cases'.

Here's a typical example: I awake in the middle of the night and, wanting to know what time it is, I reach to where I believe my watch to be. My belief that it is there is justified, as I always put it in the same place, and I remember putting it there before sleeping. However, while I was asleep, a thief stole into my room and knocked my watch from its usual position, but replaced it – as it happens, just where I had put it. Although my belief regarding where my watch is is both true and justified, it does not amount to knowledge, says Gettier.

It's obvious that my belief is true: my watch is where I believe it is. Is it justified? Well, I have all the evidence that I usually have. If you think that my memory of where I put my watch, and my habit of always putting it in the same place, are not enough justification, then you have to say that I *never* know where my watch is when I wake up at night. You move back towards infallibilism – and the scepticism that results. Gettier is assuming we don't want to adopt this type of scepticism. If we can't use memory as good evidence, there is a great deal we don't know (what you had for breakfast, what your name is . . .)! So, usually, I do know where my watch is. But in the case in which the thief knocks off my watch and replaces it, I'm still relying on exactly the same evidence – so my belief is justified on the same grounds. But, says Gettier, *it isn't knowledge*. The connection between the reasons why I have my belief (its justification) and my belief's being true is, in this case, too *accidental*.

Gettier cases all have the same structure: they portray situations in which we have justified true belief, but not knowledge, by demonstrating how the fact that our belief is true is accidental, relative to our evidence, even though the belief is justified by that evidence. So justified true belief is not *sufficient* for knowledge. But that means it is not the *same* as knowledge. If knowledge isn't justified true belief in these cases, then knowledge is *never* justified true belief. Something else must be required to turn justified true belief into knowledge.

Gettier cases show that for knowledge we need to connect the belief and its justification to the truth of the proposition believed. The result we want is that in normal cases I know (where my watch is), but in Gettier cases I don't, even though I have exactly the same evidence in each case. We'll consider two theories which give this result, one immediately below and the other in RELIABILISM (p. 35).

Going further: 'fully justified belief'

My belief about where my watch is is justified by my memory of where I put it and my habit of always putting it in the same place. In normal cases, there is nothing that makes this justification inadequate. In the Gettier case, it is 'defeated'. The facts in this case – that the thief came in, knocked my watch and replaced it –

make my usual justification insufficient. But, of course, in the normal situation I'm not in a Gettier case. And so my justification is, in fact, not defeated. This has inspired philosophers to add a fourth condition to the three for justified true belief:

4   My justification for believing that *p* is not defeated by the facts.

If my justification is not defeated by the facts, it is 'fully justified'. In a normal situation, my belief is fully justified, so I know that *p*. In a Gettier case, my belief is justified but not 'fully justified', since it *is* defeated by the facts; so I don't know that *p*. This was the result we wanted.

However, maybe *I don't know* if I'm in a Gettier situation or not! I don't know whether a thief has been in or not. In a Gettier situation, there isn't any *subjective* difference from normal cases: I still believe what I do (where my watch is) for exactly the same reasons. My justification for my belief is the same in both cases. According to the fully justified true belief theory, whether I know where my watch is depends not *just* on my evidence, but also on the situation I am in. So it makes knowledge dependent on something that is not available to me (since I can't tell which situation I am in).

Some philosophers, and especially sceptics, have argued that this can't be a good account of knowledge. If I know where my watch is, then I am not in a Gettier situation. But if I am in a Gettier situation, I don't know where my watch is. Surely in order to know where my watch is, I should know whether I'm in a Gettier situation or not. We will look at this argument again in SCEPTICISM CONCERNING KNOWLEDGE AND BELIEF (p. 4).

● **KEY POINTS**

- A Gettier case is a situation in which a person has justified true belief but not knowledge because their belief, even though it is justified, is only *accidentally* true relative to their evidence. So, Gettier concluded, justified true belief is not knowledge.

- One response to Gettier cases is the 'fully justified true belief' theory, which adds the fourth condition that the person's justification is not 'defeated' by the facts. However, this means that whether my belief is knowledge depends not just on my evidence, but on my situation.

❓ **QUIZ QUESTION**

Briefly explain and illustrate Gettier's objection to the justified true belief theory of knowledge.

❓ DISCUSSION QUESTION

Assess the claim that knowledge is justified true belief.

Foundationalism as grounds of justification and the problem of an infinite regress

What is it for a belief to be justified? We have talked about the importance of evidence; but how does evidence support a belief? Does evidence lead 'down' to some basic, certain beliefs? What is the *structure* of justification? Foundationalism claims that all knowledge rests on a foundation which is justified 'immediately' or (more accurately) 'noninferentially'. It is easiest to understand this claim by looking at the most famous argument offered for it, viz. the regress argument.

The regress argument

For very many beliefs, I have the belief on the basis of believing something else, which is usually my evidence for my belief. For example, I believe that Napoleon was Corsican because I also believe that the historical sources that make this claim can be trusted. Now if my belief that Napoleon was Corsican is *justified*, it seems that my belief that the historical sources are trustworthy also needs to be justified. If my *only* source of evidence that Napoleon was Corsican is a letter from a madman that made a number of wild allegations about Napoleon, then my belief that the historical sources can be trusted in this case would be unjustified, and therefore so would my belief that Napoleon was Corsican. We can draw the general principle: to be justified in believing some proposition *p* on the basis of evidence, one must be justified in believing the evidence.

However, it is now clear that if every belief is justified only on the basis of some other belief, we have an infinite regress. If I'm justified in believing one belief only on the basis of believing some other belief, and justified in believing that second belief only on the basis of some third belief, and so on, then am I ever justified in believing anything? The justification for my beliefs must come to an end somewhere, with beliefs that are not justified on the basis of other beliefs.

This is what foundationalism claims. The *foundations* of justification, and therefore of knowledge, are beliefs that are not justified *inferentially*, i.e. on the basis of further beliefs and evidence, but in some other way, 'noninferentially'. There are, therefore, two types of justified belief: those whose justification depends on other beliefs and those whose justification does not.

Noninferential justification

Foundationalists disagree about noninferential justification. One theory of noninferential justification is infallibilism (see BELIEVING-THAT AND KNOWING-THAT, p. 20). Descartes argued that the foundations of knowledge are beliefs in propositions that cannot be false, such as his clear and distinct ideas. If a belief is certain in this way, then it does not need to be inferred from some other belief to be justified. Its justification rests in its certainty. However, we have already discussed a number of objections to infallibilism, so what other options are there?

An alternative to certain beliefs is experience. Many empiricists, including Locke and Hume, have argued that all knowledge is founded on what we experience immediately in consciousness. Sensory experience isn't belief – just seeing a table isn't yet to believe anything, e.g. that there is a table in front of you or that you are seeing a table. But you can infer these beliefs from what you see. This version of foundationalism claims that what we experience justifies all our other beliefs.

Because experience, or what is immediately available to consciousness, isn't a belief-that anything, then the knowledge we have of what we experience isn't 'knowing-that'. It is a different kind of knowledge. Bertrand Russell called this relation between us and the contents of our experience or consciousness 'acquaintance' and this type of knowledge 'knowledge by acquaintance'. Russell argued that I can't be acquainted with *p* unless *p* is actually true. *What* we are 'acquainted' with depends on which theory of perception is correct. Locke and Hume both argued that we are immediately conscious only of **sense-data** (see REPRESENTATIVE REALISM, p. 49). But philosophers who argue for NAIVE REALISM (p. 54) claim we are immediately acquainted with aspects of the world.

The important point for foundationalism is that acquaintance is immediate, not inferential. What we are 'directly and immediately' acquainted with, therefore, can serve as the noninferential foundation of knowledge.

Objections to foundationalism

Objections to foundationalism can take two forms:

1 There is something wrong with the foundation.
2 Foundationalism will lead to scepticism, because although we have knowledge of the foundation we can't move beyond it.

1 Objections to the foundation

We have already seen objections to the idea that the foundation is infallible beliefs (see BELIEVING-THAT AND KNOWING-THAT, p. 20). But can experience serve as a foundation for the rest of knowledge? The first beliefs we infer on the basis of experience are beliefs about *what* we experience. If there is a problem with this first inference, there will be problems with any inferences.

One objection argues that experience isn't an *infallible* justification of beliefs. To say that experience is an infallible ground to beliefs about what we perceive is to say that we can't make mistakes moving from one to the other. But this isn't true. If a car passes me quickly, I can believe I saw something blue when it is actually green. I can believe I saw you smile when you didn't. I can believe there is a bit of dust on my shirt when it is actually a stain. If experience can't even give me knowledge about how the world is now, when I'm experiencing it, this version of foundationalism produces scepticism. However, there is a worse problem, viz. that even my beliefs about my experience itself don't seem infallible. They can be uncertain – I can be unsure whether that passing car *looks* blue or green; and they can be partial – while looking at a pattern of dots, I don't know how many dots I see.

But this is only an objection that experience isn't an *infallible* justification of beliefs. However, foundationalists don't have to be infallibilists. If experience isn't infallible, at least it seems that it provides good grounds or evidence for beliefs.

Going further: concepts and experience

A second objection to using our immediate acquaintance with experience as a foundation was given by Wilfrid Sellars, who asked how I *infer* my belief from my experience. Beliefs are structured by concepts – table, brown, loud, car and so on. Is experience also structured by concepts? Do I see a brown table or hear a loud car? Or do I have certain 'unstructured' sensory experiences and then apply concepts to them? Whichever way we go, Sellars argues, we have a problem.

Suppose we say that experience is structured by concepts. This can't always have been true, because children need to *learn* concepts. If a small child doesn't know what a car is or what blue is, he or she can't experience 'a blue car'. The child experiences something, what we adults call 'seeing a blue car', but his or her experience can't be structured by these concepts. Children are taught concepts, and they learn them through being taught judgements about what is the 'same' and what is 'different'. Whenever we use concepts, therefore, we are depending on judgements about similarities between 'this' and other things. But this knowledge is *not* noninferential: it depends on other beliefs and other experiences we had in the past when learning the concepts. So if experience is structured by concepts, experience can't be the foundation, because it would depend on inferential knowledge.

Suppose, then, we say that experience is not structured by concepts. But now the problem is that we can't move from experience, on its own, to any beliefs about experience, because *beliefs* are structured by concepts. So to move from experience to beliefs, we need to apply concepts to our experience. But this makes use of inferential knowledge. Now experience can't be the foundation, because we can't infer any beliefs from it (without using the inferential knowledge of concepts).

One response is to argue that our experience is of *facts*, which are themselves structured, but *not by us*. This claims that my (conceptual) belief that, e.g., the car is blue corresponds to the fact that the car is blue. When I perceive the car, I have direct and immediate acquaintance with this fact, unmediated by *my concepts* of 'blue' and 'car'. And this acquaintance justifies my belief. The world is structured and our concepts mirror that structure. But *this seems so unlikely*, because concepts change. For example, different cultures have different colour concepts. It's hard to say that one set of concepts is *the* way the world is and the others are somehow mistakes.

2 Foundationalism and scepticism

Even if the foundations were sound, we can object that we end up knowing very little apart from the foundation itself. Descartes may be able to know the truth of his foundation 'I think, I exist' (see Ch. 5, ABSOLUTE CERTAINTY OF THE COGITO, p. 227) but many philosophers argue that this doesn't help us to know much else (see THE LIMITATIONS OF RATIONALISM, p. 15). Again, if the foundations of knowledge are what we are immediately acquainted with, we may not be able to infer much at all from this (see THE LIMITATIONS OF EMPIRICISM, p. 17).

To understand this better, we should ask 'When (and how) is an inferred belief a justified belief?' For instance, infallibilism requires not only that the foundation is infallible but also that the relationship between my foundation and my other beliefs is such that I *can't possibly* be mistaken about my other beliefs. This would seem to require that nonfoundational beliefs are *logically entailed* by foundational ones. But there is very little that is logically entailed by truths such as 'I think' or 'I am now aware of a white square with black squiggles'. Descartes uses the existence of God to move further, e.g. to infer that the external world exists. Hume abandons the idea that such beliefs are logically entailed.

But infallibilism isn't a plausible theory, we might claim. Foundational beliefs don't need to logically entail for nonfoundational ones; they simply need to provide evidence for them or make them more probable. But this raises another problem, viz. how we ever got to know what 'evidence' is. The principles of evidence and probability, which allow us to form inferences from the foundation to other beliefs, *are not noninferentially known*. We have to infer these principles on the basis of experience and reasoning. But that means that these principles, by which we infer anything from the foundation, aren't part of the foundation. But in that case, we cannot use them to move beyond the foundation. In other words, we have to *already know* the principles of evidence and probability to move beyond the foundation; but we *don't know* these principles until we *are able* to move beyond the foundation.

Going further: a defence

The foundationalist may respond that this isn't such a problem. The beliefs I infer from the foundation are justified if the principles of evidence and probability I have used are sound. But I don't have to *know* that these principles are good, I don't have to *know* that my inferred belief is in fact justified, for the belief to *be* justified. It needs only to be true that the foundation actually justifies my belief.

But a foundationalist cannot say this, because foundationalism is the claim that all knowledge rests just on the foundation. But it seems that a lot of knowledge rests on principles of evidence and probability, and these aren't part of the foundation, and we can't infer them from the foundation without already assuming them. If I am allowed to use the principles of evidence and probability without knowing them, then whatever I infer doesn't rest on the foundation, and foundationalism is false.

● **KEY POINTS**

- Foundationalism claims that all knowledge rests on a foundation of beliefs that are noninferentially justified. All other justified beliefs are justified by inferential support (e.g. logical entailment, evidence, probability) from the foundation.

- The regress argument supports foundationalism. If there were no beliefs that are noninferentially justified, then every belief would depend on some other beliefs to be justified, and these would depend on some others, and so on. How could justification ever really get going?

- Some foundationalists claim the foundation comprises certain beliefs, beliefs in propositions that could not be false, such as 'I think'. Others claim the foundation is acquaintance with experience.

- One objection to foundationalism is that the foundation is inadequate. For example, beliefs about what I am experiencing can be false. Sellars argues that *either* we cannot infer beliefs from experience, because experience is not conceptually structured while beliefs are, *or* that experience is not the foundation, because it is conceptually structured but concepts require inferential knowledge.

- Another objection is that we cannot infer from the foundation to other beliefs, so foundationalism leads to scepticism. If the inference uses logical entailment, then because there is very little the foundation entails, we don't know much. If the inference uses evidence and probability, then a different problem arises: these principles are inferentially known, so they are not part of the foundation. So either we don't know them or any belief that relies on them, or foundationalism is false.

❓ QUIZ QUESTIONS

Briefly explain what foundationalism involves. (AQA, 1a, 2005, *6 marks*)

Explain and illustrate the regress argument for foundationalism.

❓ DISCUSSION QUESTION

Assess foundationalism.

Coherentism as grounds of justification

Like foundationalism, coherentism accepts that the regress argument poses a problem. However, rather than attempting a solution, it disputes an assumption the argument makes, viz. that a belief cannot be justified unless its justification stops at some point, that justifications that go on forever aren't any good. Coherentism is often portrayed as arguing that justification *in a circle* is acceptable. In fact, very few coherentists adopt this position. Rather, they argue that justification *isn't linear*, it doesn't take the form of a series of inferences, all eventually leading to the 'foundation'. There are no privileged beliefs that underlie all knowledge.

Coherentism claims that a belief is justified if and only if it is coherent with other members of a system. Traditionally, coherentists thought this was a system of beliefs; more recently, some have argued that we need coherence between beliefs and experiences as well. Different theories have different accounts of exactly what coherence is. Everyone agrees that it involves logical consistency, but that it is more than that. Two beliefs about completely different subjects, e.g. 'elephants are grey' and 'flamingos are pink', are logically consistent. But they don't lend each other evidential support. Coherence involves providing support in terms of evidence or explanation. A belief is justified if it 'fits in' with a structure of evidence or explanation, e.g. if it explains other propositions we believe or if it is explained by them.

Objections to coherentism

Coherentism has faced several important objections. First, we need to be able to make a distinction between

1 a situation in which a person holds a belief and has good evidence for it, but doesn't hold the belief *because* of the evidence; and
2 a situation in which the person *does* hold it on the basis of the evidence.

In (1), we wouldn't usually say the person's belief is justified; to be justified, you must believe what you do *on the basis of* the evidence (2). But the difference between (1) and (2) isn't coherence. In (1), it looks like the belief still *coheres* with the other beliefs (about the evidence). So the belief is coherent with the system of beliefs, but we don't want to say it is justified. Holding a belief on the basis of evidence, which is necessary for justification, isn't the same as coherence.

Second, if coherence is about relations between members of a system of beliefs, it doesn't depend on the relation between those beliefs and anything which isn't a belief, such as the way the world is. A whole system of beliefs could be coherent, and so justified, while being completely out of contact with the world. But surely justification and *truth* are more closely connected than this.

If we accept that justification and truth are closely connected, then unless we are very strong rationalists like Plato we need to make room for *experience* of the world in our account of justification. This is because the world is what we have beliefs about, and experience is how we have access to the world. So experience can guide us towards truth.

But do we need to accept that justification *is* a good guide to truth? It is possible to have *inconsistent justified beliefs*. For example, the chances of any one ticket winning the lottery are so small that we are justified in believing, of any ticket, that it won't win. But we can then infer that no ticket will win. Yet we are also justified in thinking that some ticket will win. Yet both of these beliefs cannot be true.

However, pointing out the possibility of inconsistent justified beliefs doesn't help the coherentist. Coherence involves consistency. So if the two beliefs are both justified and *inconsistent* coherence can't be the measure of justification.

Going further: coherentism and experience

Some coherentists do take experience into account. There are two different responses possible here, relating to whether they think experience is structured by concepts or not (as discussed above).

Some have argued that experience is not structured by concepts, and so it can't 'cohere' with beliefs – coherence requires conceptual structure, so coherence is still a relation just between beliefs. However, experience of the world will have an *impact* on the system of beliefs, e.g. the spontaneous formation of new beliefs. The system would need to be coherent with these constantly forming new beliefs to remain justified; but they are informed by experience.

Other coherentists claim that experiences are conceptually structured, and the 'system' that should be coherent is not a system of just beliefs, but of beliefs + experiences. This successfully allows the world to play some role in justifying our beliefs.

In both cases, experience doesn't form the foundation of knowledge, though, since we may not form new beliefs at all if we reject the experiences, e.g. as illusions, because they don't fit with our beliefs. More importantly, experiences (or the beliefs we form as a result of experiences) must be interpreted in light of our existing beliefs (in the form of concepts).

● **KEY POINTS**

- Coherentism rejects the assumption of the regress argument that justifications which do not come to an end somewhere are no good. It argues that justification is not linear, and that a belief is justified if and only if it coheres with other members of a system (of beliefs or beliefs + experience).

- One objection to coherentism is that to be justified, a belief must be believed on the basis of evidence. But this is not coherence, as a belief can be coherent with the evidence without being held because of the evidence.

- A second objection is that coherence isn't a good guide to truth – a whole coherent system of beliefs could be untrue. But justification should be a guide to truth. Coherentists have responded by arguing that beliefs must be coherent with experience or the beliefs that experience naturally causes.

❓ QUIZ QUESTIONS

Outline and illustrate **two** theories of justification.

Briefly explain what coherentism involves.

❓ DISCUSSION QUESTION

Assess coherentism.

Reliabilism as grounds of justification

In its simplest form, the reliabilist theory of justification claims that S's belief in p is justified if and only if it is produced by a reliable process, i.e. one that produces a high percentage of true beliefs. Usually, what makes a process reliable is a causal connection between p and the belief that p. For example, it is that fact that the rose is red, or more accurately, the rose's redness, that causes me to believe that the rose is red. It is Descartes's writing the *Meditations* which – through a chain of causes – causes me to believe that he wrote the *Meditations*.

Reliabilism has three important implications. First, and most importantly, reliabilism rejects the view, accepted by foundationalism and coherentism, that justification requires *evidence*. It is not the grounds that the person is able to produce that make a belief knowledge; it is the source of the belief. Second, reliabilism doesn't require the person to *know* that the process is reliable. The fact that a process is reliable is not evidence the person needs to have that the belief is true; again, justification isn't about evidence. Third, according to reliabilism, sometimes a belief can be false, but still justified, because it was produced by a reliable process (of course, a false belief still can't be knowledge). So justification doesn't require infallibility or certainty, just reliability.

Objections to reliabilism

Some philosophers have objected to reliabilism's separation of knowledge from evidence. Suppose someone is a clairvoyant in that, every so often, she forms a belief about some event happening elsewhere in the world. For example, she suddenly believes that the head of McDonald's is in a secret meeting about the recipe for burger sauce. She's never checked up on these beliefs, and has no idea how she comes by them. But, in fact, they are usually correct; but she doesn't know or even believe this. In other words, she has *no evidence* for her beliefs. She even has evidence *against* her beliefs, given what she knows about science and how we normally come to know things. Does she *know* the head of McDonald's is in a secret meeting?

Some reliabilists say 'yes', even though this is counter-intuitive, just because, however it is that her beliefs are being caused, they are in fact reliable. But reliabilists who accept the objection add a condition: not only must the process be reliable for her belief to be justified, but the person must not have evidence that her belief is *unreliably* caused. That the belief is caused in a very unfamiliar way, going against a general scientific understanding of how the world works, is evidence that the belief is unreliably caused (even though, in fact, it is reliable). So it is not knowledge. Justification does depend on evidence, but only in this way.

A different objection argues that reliability isn't enough to rule out accidentally true belief. Of course, on the whole, a belief won't be *accidentally* true if the process that produces it is *reliable*. But consider this Gettier case: you see and recognize someone as a friend, Judy, and wave to her. Unknown to you, Judy has a twin sister, Trudy, who lives nearby. If it *had been* Trudy across the street, you *would* have believed it was Judy. So your belief that it is Judy is only accidentally true. However, the process which produced that belief – seeing and recognizing – is reliable. Should we say that you know it is Judy, even though you would have thought it was Judy even if it was Trudy? A generally reliable process might produce a true belief in circumstances in which things might easily have been otherwise, and the belief not true. Is that enough for knowledge?

Reliabilists can respond by saying that the objection isn't against reliabilism as a theory of *justification*. Surely your belief that it is Judy is justified, even if it doesn't amount to knowledge; it would be justified even it was false, i.e. if you were waving at Trudy. The problem is in the assumption that knowledge is justified true belief. Your belief that you are waving at Judy is justified (because produced by a reliable process) and true; but it is not knowledge.

Going further: reliabilism and the justified true belief theory of knowledge

We discussed how to improve the justified true belief theory of knowledge above (see PROBLEMS IN THE APPLICATION OF THIS DEFINITION, p. 25), and came up with the 'fully justified belief' theory. It made knowledge, e.g. my knowledge of where my watch is, dependent on the situation. If I'm in a normal situation, my justification 'stands up to the facts', and my belief about my watch is knowledge. But if I'm in a Gettier situation, my justification does not stand up to the facts, and is not knowledge.

Reliabilism offers a different improvement on the justified true belief theory. Some reliabilists have argued that to be knowledge, a belief must be produced by a process that is reliable (this is justification), *and* I am able to use the process to *discriminate between relevant possibilities* in the actual situation. If Judy doesn't have a twin sister, I can discriminate between relevant possibilities, so I know it's Judy. If Judy does have a twin sister, I only know I am waving at Judy if I can tell her apart from her twin sister.

So in normal cases, I know; in Gettier cases, I don't. But I may not know whether I am in a Gettier case or not. So as with the fully justified belief theory, this suggestion means that whether my belief is knowledge is dependent on the situation in ways I might not know about.

A different suggestion defends the *original* justified true belief theory of knowledge. We could say that if I can't use the process to rule out real alternative possibilities, then it isn't sufficiently reliable, and so the belief *isn't justified*. In other words, we could say that whether a process counts as reliable is relative to the actual situation. In the normal case, the process by which I come to believe where my watch is is reliable. When there are thieves about, this process is not reliable enough to justify my belief. The justified true belief theory is right, and in Gettier cases my beliefs aren't justified, which isn't why I don't know.

However, this means that whether my belief is *justified*, not just whether it is knowledge, is dependent on the situation in ways I might not know about. But reliabilism claims that I do not need to *know* my belief is justified for it to be justified, so it is happy to accept this consequence.

● **KEY POINTS**

- Reliabilism claims that a belief is justified if and only if it is produced by a reliable process, i.e. one that produces a high percentage of true beliefs.

- Reliabilism rejects the view that justification requires evidence or certainty.

- Philosophers object that if I have no evidence at all for my belief, or strong evidence against it, then my belief is not knowledge. Some reliabilists accept that I must not have strong evidence that my belief was not caused reliably for it to be knowledge.

- Gettier cases suggest that a belief caused by a reliable process can still be accidentally true, so won't be knowledge. Reliabilists reply that, since the belief is still justified, reliabilism is true, and the problem lies with the justified true belief theory of knowledge.

- However, reliabilism also suggests an improvement to that theory – that to have knowledge I must be able to use the reliable process to discriminate between real alternative possibilities.

❓ QUIZ QUESTIONS

Briefly explain what reliabilism involves.

Outline **one** objection to reliabilism's claim that justification does not depend on evidence.

❓ DISCUSSION QUESTION

Assess reliabilism.

● III KNOWLEDGE AND SCEPTICISM

The difference between ordinary doubt and philosophical doubt. What is the role of doubt in the search for knowledge?

Philosophical doubt can get started by reflecting on *how* we know what we think we know. We discover judgements it seems silly to doubt, but for which we seem to have no clear justification. Take the belief that I have two hands. Why do I believe this? Well, I can feel them, I can see them. But couldn't my experience – what I feel and what I see – be just the same even if I were dreaming, and had been dreaming all my life? Or if I were a brain in a vat being 'fed' experiences by some super-computer? Do I know that I haven't been dreaming all my life, that I'm not wired up to a computer? If I don't know this, do I really know that I have two hands? In fact, do I know that a world exists outside my mind at all? But if I don't know *that*, how can I know anything? Raising these doubts as a challenge to be answered is known as scepticism.

Philosophical doubts are peculiar. They don't make sense in everyday circumstances. Of course, if I've just been in an accident, and can't feel my left arm, doubting whether I have two hands does make sense! But the sceptic is not interested in these propositions when we have an 'everyday reason' to doubt them. The sceptic's reason for doubting them does not arise from a particular context – it is a general doubt about their justifiability. The sceptic admits that there is no everyday reason to doubt whether I have two hands or whether there is an external world. But that doesn't mean there isn't *any* reason to doubt these things. For example, 'I see that this is a hand' is not good grounds for 'I know this is a hand' in the light of the sceptical challenge. How do I know that what I see is a good guide to how things really are? I can say that it *appears* that I have two hands. But how do I know that appearance is a reliable guide to reality?

We may wonder whether this sort of sceptical doubt is *doubt*; it has no practical consequences, after all. A philosophical sceptic is not a very cautious person! Yet the sceptic insists that sceptical doubts are relevant; the standards of 'knowing' are not being changed here – we *should* know that we are not wired up to a super-computer or being deceived by an evil demon to know that 'This is a hand'. Yes, sceptical doubt is peculiar. But this is not because it isn't legitimate doubt. It's because we are not usually reflective in this way.

Yet we might still think that it is 'unreasonable' to have such doubts. But this misunderstands the role or purpose of doubt. Philosophical doubts aren't introduced in an attempt to persuade us that sceptical possibilities are *true*. The sceptic doesn't suggest that there is any reason to *believe* in sceptical possibilities, but requests that we *rule them out* as possibilities. Doubt based on challenging us to rule out the *possibility* of very unlikely situations is called 'hyperbolic' doubt. And the purpose of this doubt is to help us find what we *can* know, if anything. In other words, the sceptic presents his challenge in order to help us discover what we know and how we know it. (See also Ch. 5, SCEPTICAL DOUBT AND ITS USE IN THE QUEST FOR CERTAINTY, p. 222.)

Again, the sceptical challenge isn't an attempt to make us less *sure* of our everyday claims of knowledge. The effect of sceptical doubts is not 'We can't be *certain* of our everyday judgements, although they are *probably* true'. It is to put the whole idea of our usual justifications into question. If these sceptical possibilities were true, we would have *absolutely no reason* to hold on to our usual beliefs. If I was wired up to a super-computer, things *seem* exactly the same, but the reality is completely different. Sceptical arguments aim to completely undercut our usual justifications.

Scepticism is sometimes taken as the claim that nothing is known. But this is not a good definition, for it must then defend the claim that we can know nothing, which is trivially self-defeating anyway (because then we would know that we know nothing – so there is something we know). Likewise, scepticism is not the claim that all our beliefs are false, for this is not logically coherent. For instance, my beliefs that 'I am not at the South Pole' and that 'I am not at the North Pole' can't both be false (obviously, both can be true). Scepticism is best understood as the claim that our usual justification for claiming our beliefs amount to knowledge is inadequate. It focuses on very fundamental beliefs, such as the existence of the external world, which it claims form the basis for many other beliefs.

● **KEY POINTS**

- Scepticism challenges whether our usual justifications for what we think we know are adequate. For example, it points out that we assume that appearance is a reliable guide to reality – but how do we know this?

- Sceptical doubt is odd: it is not interested in everyday reasons for doubting a proposition; it has no practical consequences; and it invents very unlikely situations that we have no reason to think are actually true. But it insists that it is legitimate – we should know that sceptical possibilities, e.g. that I am dreaming, are not true in order to know the things we claim to know.

- Scepticism does not claim that we know nothing, nor that all our beliefs are false. It challenges our justifications and challenges us to say how we know what we claim to know.

QUIZ QUESTIONS

Outline and illustrate the claim that sceptical doubt is distinct from everyday doubt.

Briefly explain what scepticism is.

Sceptical arguments concerning our perceptual knowledge: arguments from illusion, deception, dreaming

Descartes famously gives arguments from illusion, dreaming and deception to support doubt about what we think we perceive. As his arguments are discussed in THE WAVES OF DOUBT (Ch. 5, p. 224), we will discuss only other arguments here. But you should read that section first.

An argument from disagreement

Descartes's argument from illusion points out that we can make mistakes about what we perceive.

A different argument, from Plato's *Theatetus*, points out that people often disagree. The air can seem warm to one person, cold to another; one person may judge the sea to be 'blue', another says it is 'green'. Faced with disagreement, how can I be sure that what *I* experience is how the world is?

First, we can argue that these disagreements apply more to some sorts of perceptions than to others. For example, people agree that air is a gas, not a liquid; and people commonly agree whether there is a breeze (even if they disagree on how strong it is). The disagreements presuppose a lot of agreement in our perceptions, which supports the claim that perception gives us knowledge.

Second, in many cases, we have objective ways of settling the disagreement. We can measure how long something is; and if one person carries on saying 'It is long' and another 'It is short', we just say they are using the terms differently. This works to some extent with 'hot' and 'cold', e.g. someone who has a fever is not a good judge of whether a room is cold or not. We say 'The air *feels* cold to him', even though 'the air is warm'. We reach objectivity by appealing to agreement again: the air is warm, the sea is blue if that is how they seem to normal people under normal conditions.

An argument from illusion

But there are arguments in the theory of perception that temperature and colour are subjective (for a longer discussion, see REPRESENTATIVE REALISM, p. 49). Many philosophers have claimed that we don't perceive the world directly; we perceive it in virtue of perceiving **sense-data**, our subjective experiences of the world. For example, if you put your thumb up against the moon, it looks like your thumb is larger than the moon, but it isn't. If you look at a red rose in sodium street lights, it looks grey, but the rose itself hasn't changed.

But if we only ever perceive sense-data directly, we can never know what the material world is actually like, or even that it exists. All we have 'access' to is our sense-data; who knows what lies beyond them? All that our experience has available to it are sense-data themselves, so we can never know what, if anything, causes them.

This argument at least leaves our knowledge of sense-data intact. It also leaves intact any knowledge that doesn't rely on the senses. Descartes tries to use reason, rather than sense experience, to respond to these sceptical arguments (see Ch. 5, THE PROOF OF MATERIAL THINGS, p. 240).

An argument from deception: the brain in a vat

Descartes's argument from deception appeals to an evil demon. A twentieth-century update of that idea is that we may suppose that we are not walking, talking human beings, but simply brains in vats. Connected to my brain is a super-computer that feeds in just the right impulses to generate the illusion of reality as it is. I'm being deceived. I cannot know that this is not, in fact, the case; because if it is true, things seem *exactly the same* as if I am a walking, talking person. If I can't know I'm not being deceived, then I can't know anything that my senses tell me.

● **KEY POINTS**

- Descartes provides sceptical arguments based on mistakes in perception, the possibility that I'm dreaming and the possibility that an evil demon is deceiving me.

- A different sceptical argument from perception appeals to disagreement. But the argument is only as strong as disagreement, and people agree a great deal about what they perceive.

- Many philosophers have argued that we do not perceive the world directly, but via sense-data. Scepticism argues that, if this is true, then how do we know the world is anything like our sense-data or even that it exists? All we experience are our sense-data.

- A popular sceptical scenario is that we could be brains in vats, and all our perceptual experiences are actually fed to us by a super-computer. If we don't know this is not true, we can't know anything our senses tell us is true.

❓ QUIZ QUESTIONS

Outline and illustrate the sceptical challenge that dreaming poses.

Outline **two** sceptical arguments from perception.

Outline the argument that if I don't know I'm not a brain in a vat, I know nothing through sense experience.

The extent of scepticism, whether global scepticism is possible

Extending scepticism

We have looked at arguments regarding perceptual experience. But we can extend scepticism to memory as well. The arguments from deception (the evil demon, brain in a vat) suggest that we cannot trust our memories, because the computer or demon could create 'memories' of things that never happened. So we cannot know anything about the past, including whether it happened at all. Perhaps I only just came into existence and all my memories are false.

The arguments from deception also threaten our ability to know propositions through reason. If my *thoughts* are being fed to me by a super-computer or a demon, then I can't be certain of them. Isn't it possible that every time I think '2 + 2 = ?', the computer or demon makes me think 4 when the answer is actually 5? So even judgements about logic and mathematics are not certain. If I have no mental *agency*, then the very idea of genuinely making a judgement, whatever that judgement is, is undermined. And if I cannot judge, then I cannot know. This is global scepticism.

Global scepticism

The term 'global scepticism' suggests doubt about *everything*. As discussed in THE DIFFERENCE BETWEEN ORDINARY DOUBT AND PHILOSOPHICAL DOUBT (p. 39), scepticism cannot be the claim that we do not know anything; nor can it be the claim that all our beliefs are false. Neither of these claims is logically coherent.

But scepticism could claim that almost none of our beliefs actually amounts to knowledge, e.g. 'We know nothing except the fact that we know nothing (else)'. But we can object that in order to form coherent doubts we need to know the *meanings of the words* we use (see SCEPTICISM CONCERNING KNOWLEDGE AND BELIEF, p. 47). If nothing else, we need to know what 'knowledge' means in order to know that we know nothing! We could then argue that there is much else we need to know in order for us to know the meanings of words.

But global scepticism, in which even my thoughts are in doubt, makes it very unclear whether I do know what knowledge is in order to be able to say I don't have it. Scepticism does better, then, by not making a positive claim about how little we know at all. It should not say 'we know nothing' or anything like that. Global scepticism should instead claim that no attempt to show that we have any knowledge succeeds.

Going further: global scepticism and analytic truths

However, there is a question whether global scepticism can really include scepticism about **analytic** truths (such as 'All bachelors are unmarried') and basic truths of logic and mathematics (such as '2 + 2 = 4'). Descartes argues that we can know these because we cannot doubt them (see Ch. 5, DESCARTES'S RATIONALISM,

p. 242). An alternative defence would be to say that we can know these truths because it is not possible to think *this* thought and be wrong. For example, if I am thinking about bachelors, then I am *by definition* thinking about unmarried men. It cannot be the case that the demon or super-computer causes the thought 'Bachelors are unmarried' when the truth is that bachelors are married; bachelors cannot be married and still be what I am thinking about when *I* think about bachelors. Analytic truths depend only on concepts. To make a 'mistake' about an analytic truth is to not understand the concepts involved. So if I know what the concepts are, what the words mean, I can know analytic truths.

Can scepticism argue that I can't know what the concepts of my thoughts actually are? Is it possible for me to have a thought using the concept 'bachelor' and not understand it at all? But if I don't understand the concept, in what sense is the thought a thought about *bachelors*? Global scepticism might argue that if I am a brain in a vat, then I don't understand the thoughts I have; or it might agree that we can know analytic truths.

KEY POINTS

- Sceptical arguments from deception attack not only our sense experiences, but our memories and even our thoughts. It seems possible that all my thoughts are caused by a super-computer or a demon, so not even thoughts about logic or mathematics can be known to be true.

- Global scepticism suggests doubt about everything. This is not best understood as the claim that we know nothing (except that we know nothing), since we may object that we must know the meanings of words in order to know that we know nothing. It should be understood as the claim that no attempt to show that we have knowledge succeeds.

- If global scepticism must allow that we know the meanings of words (in order to entertain the hypothesis of global scepticism), it may also have to allow that we know analytic truths since these depend only on the meanings of words.

❓ QUIZ QUESTIONS

Briefly explain what is meant by global (or total) scepticism. (AQA, 1a, 2003, *6 marks*)

Outline and illustrate how the argument from deception supports global scepticism.

Scepticism concerning knowledge and belief

Attempting to refute sceptical arguments one by one does not succeed, for two reasons. First, one sceptical argument will quickly be replaced by another; and, second, scepticism isn't a positive theory. It is a demand for justification, based on arguments as to why our ordinary justification fails. To answer scepticism successfully, we need to understand it. In particular, we need to understand the assumptions about knowledge that it makes. We will then be able to respond to it.

Scepticism, certainty and 'closure'

In claiming that our usual justifications are inadequate, scepticism tends to assume that infallibilism is true. However, we decided that the main argument for infallibilism is flawed (see BELIEVING-THAT AND KNOWING-THAT, p. 21), and we have seen that many discussions of knowledge and justification reject it. Justification doesn't require certainty; it requires only good evidence and probability.

But sceptical arguments suggest that our evidence is worthless unless we can show that sceptical possibilities are false. Sceptics argue for what is known as 'the principle of closure': if I know that p, and I know that if p is true, then q must be false, then I know that q is false. This means that if I don't know that q is false, I *don't* know that p is true.

Many sceptical arguments relating to the external world work this way. For instance, I claim that I know I have two hands. I also know that *if* I have two hands, then I'm not a brain in a vat. So if it is true that I know I have two hands, I know that I'm not a brain in a vat. But the sceptic argues that I *don't* know I'm not a brain in a vat. But that means I don't know I have two hands. In fact, everything I think I know through my senses, I don't actually know, because I don't know that I'm not a brain in a vat.

If the principle of closure is false, this argument doesn't work. Some philosophers have challenged scepticism by rejecting the principle of closure.

Three responses to scepticism

The fully justified belief theory

The fully justified belief theory says that my belief is knowledge if it is justified and my justification stands up to the facts (see PROBLEMS IN THE APPLICATION OF THIS DEFINITION, p. 25). This leads it to reject the principle of closure. The theory claims that if you are not in the Gettier case described, then you know where your watch is. But it accepts that you may not *know* whether or not you are in a Gettier case. So according to the fully justified belief theory, in a normal case I know where my watch is; I know that if I know where my watch is, I'm not in a Gettier case; but maybe I *don't* know I'm not in a Gettier case.

In the case of scepticism: if I am a brain in a vat, my reasons for thinking that I have two hands don't stand up to the facts; but if I am not a brain in a vat, they do, and I know I have two hands. This means that I *don't* have to know that I am not a brain in a vat in order to know that I have two hands. If I'm not a brain in vat, then I do know this, and that's that.

However, we have seen that scepticism argues that my usual justification for my usual beliefs, e.g. that I have two hands, is inadequate. The problem is not (just) whether my justification stands up to the facts, but whether we are right to think that my belief is *justified*. My evidence, it claims, is insufficient, because I would have exactly the same evidence if I was a brain in a vat. For example, I cannot use the fact that I seem to see my hands as evidence, because that presupposes that appearance is a good guide to reality. But we don't have any independent evidence for that claim (independent of how things appear). On its own, the fully justified belief theory isn't enough to respond to scepticism, because it hasn't given us a theory of justification that meets the sceptic's challenge.

Reliabilism

Reliabilism, however, can. A belief is justified if and only if it is produced by a reliable process (see RELIABILISM, p. 35). Reliabilism can accept that we don't know whether we are brains in vats; our ways of knowing are reliable at detecting hands, but are not reliable at detecting whether experience as a whole is veridical or computer-generated. But I don't need to *know* that I'm not a brain in a vat for my beliefs to be justified; they just need to be caused by reliable processes – and if I'm not a brain in a vat, and appearances are in fact a reliable guide to reality, then they are. Similarly with memory and rational thought.

The sceptic may respond that I don't *know* whether appearance is a guide to reality, since I don't know whether I'm a brain in a vat. But this is no objection: I don't need to *know* whether the process that causes my true beliefs is reliable; it just needs to be. (After considering the objection from the clairvoyant, we added that the person must also have no evidence that his or her belief is unreliably caused. But we have no evidence that we are brains in vats, and sceptics don't claim that we do. So this condition is met.)

Reliabilism, then, suggests that if we are not brains in vats, beliefs like 'I have two hands' are justified. But justified true belief isn't yet *knowledge*. So do I know I have two hands even if I don't know that I'm not a brain in a vat?

In the discussion of reliabilism and the example of Judy and Trudy, we concluded that a reliable process isn't enough for *knowledge* unless it is able to rule out relevant alternative possibilities. But, the sceptic argues, reliabilism accepts that the way we acquire our perceptual beliefs can't rule out the possibility that we are a brain in a vat. So although our beliefs are *justified*, they don't amount to knowledge.

The reliabilist can reply that being a brain in a vat isn't a *relevant* alternative possibility. Whether a process is reliable depends on whether it is sensitive to what matters in the context. If I am not a brain in a vat, then this possibility is not relevant to what I perceive. With this move, reliabilism also comes to reject the principle of closure, because I can know I have two hands without knowing I am not a brain in a vat.

Going further: denying the principle of closure

Because the fully justified belief theory and reliabilism both deny the principle of closure, they claim that I can know that I have two hands, while not knowing that I am not a brain in a vat with no hands! If I know I have two hands, that *entails* that I do not have zero hands. And such logic is surely reliable, so I should know that I do not have no hands. On the other hand (so to speak!), I do not know that I am not a brain in a vat, since I have no reliable way of distinguishing veridical experience from computer-generated experience. If I don't know I am not a brain in a vat, I don't know I have no hands. Yet how could I know that I have two hands and not know that I do not have no hands?! Something has gone wrong.

G. E. Moore

Moore accepted the principle of closure, and used it to argue against scepticism. He argued that I know I have two hands; here they are. Since I know I have two hands, then I know an external world exists (I know I am not a brain in a vat).

However, this rebuttal fails. Certainly, it is more *plausible* that I know I have two hands than that I am a brain in a vat. But we saw that scepticism doesn't propose its curious scenarios as plausible. It argues that we must rule them out. If we want to claim that I know I have two hands, we should be able to say *how* I know this, *how* it is that my justification is sufficient, rather than begging the question.

● **KEY POINTS (1)**

- Scepticism usually makes two assumptions about knowledge: (1) that knowledge requires certainty or infallibility; (2) that the principle of closure is true. The principle of closure states that if I know that p, and I know that if p is true, then q is false, then I know that q is false. If it turns out that I don't know q is false, then I can't know that p is true.

- We argued in an earlier section that infallibilism rests on a flawed argument, and that certainty is not necessary for knowledge.

- The fully justified true belief theory and reliabilism both answer scepticism by rejecting the principle of closure. However, this means that they accept that I know I have two hands and that I do not know that I have no hands, which is very problematical.

- Moore argues that because I know I have two hands, I know I'm not a brain in a vat. Sceptics reply that this just begs the question.

Does scepticism make sense?

Another response to scepticism claims that scepticism doesn't in fact make sense, that it contradicts itself in some way; and any claim that is contradictory cannot be true.

Gilbert Ryle

Gilbert Ryle argues that the very idea of 'error' presupposes that we sometimes 'get it right', for 'error' and 'correctness' are complementary concepts, like 'genuine' and 'false'. Without correctness, the idea of error makes no sense, just as counterfeit coins are impossible without real coins.

However, this fails in two ways. First, the sceptic seeks to challenge our belief that we know we've got it right when we have, not the very idea of 'getting it right'. And, second, the fact that we need the *idea* of getting it right to make sense of error doesn't entail that we do ever actually get it right. Compare perfection and imperfection. We need the idea of perfection to make sense of imperfection. But that doesn't mean that anything, ever, needs to be perfect.

Ordinary language

We might argue that what 'knowledge' and 'know' mean is given by how we *usually* use the terms. The sceptic's claim that, say, I don't know I'm reading this page, makes no sense. It is precisely cases like this through which we learn what 'know' means at all.

However, the sceptic's challenge is to point out that even in such paradigmatic cases of 'knowledge', we may be making an unjustified assumption, viz. that appearance is a good guide to reality.

Wittgenstein

Wittgenstein developed a more sophisticated version of the ordinary language approach. He agreed with the sceptic that knowledge and doubt are related, but that the sceptic is wrong in thinking that we can doubt claims like 'There is an external world'. If there is not a way of answering the question 'How do you know?', the question itself makes no sense. 'The external world exists', and other fundamental beliefs or 'background assumptions', are not things we can either doubt or *know*. It is, in fact, a mistake to say 'I know this is a hand' in the contexts which the sceptic is talking about (it makes sense on an archaeological dig!). Knowledge claims require grounds; and to know something is to be able to establish it. But how can we establish 'This is a hand'? What evidence is there we can appeal to? What checks are possible?

Wittgenstein notes that we are *certain* of nothing more than these 'background assumptions'. In fact, they are often used to teach the meaning of words. But the sceptic's situation of doubt is similar to the circumstances under which I learnt 'hand'. So 'If I wanted to doubt whether this was my hand, how could I avoid doubting whether the word "hand" has any meaning?' (369). But if I doubt the meanings of the words I use, I can't put into words what it is I'm doubting. We can argue, then, that sceptical doubts are literally meaningless. They deprive the very words used to formulate the doubt of any meaning. Our background assumptions underpin the meanings of our words.

But Wittgenstein's solution is hard to accept. First, he claims that we do not know such statements as 'This is a hand'. Second, he says these statements do not even *describe* reality, because they provide examples of what words mean: "'I know this is a hand." – "And what is a hand?" – "Well, *this*, for example."' The circularity is clear. If 'this' is a hand by definition, saying 'This is a hand' is not to describe anything. It is more similar to asserting an analytic truth, such as 'Bachelors are unmarried'. Analytic truths help define the meanings of the terms used. Our background assumptions likewise help define the meanings of the words we use. They therefore can't be said to describe the world.

But many of the examples Wittgenstein gives of 'background assumptions', and which he says we cannot know, don't seem to be anything like analytic statements, e.g. 'The world existed before my birth'. And what about 'Appearance is a good guide to reality'? While Wittgenstein's remarks on knowledge, doubt and justification are insightful, on its own his proposal about 'background assumptions' leaves us puzzled.

KEY POINTS (2)

● Ryle argues that scepticism doesn't make sense because we can't understand 'error' without 'getting it right'. We must get it right sometimes in order to get it wrong. But, first, the sceptic argues only that we *don't know* when we get it right; and, second, although we need the *idea* of getting it right to understand error, we don't actually ever need to get it right.

● Another objection claims that what 'to know' means is given by how we usually use the word, so to say I don't know that this is a book makes no sense. But the sceptic argues that even in such cases we may be making an unjustified assumption.

● Wittgenstein argues that sceptical doubts make no sense because they challenge the very situations in which we learnt the meanings of words. We cannot doubt 'This is a hand' without doubting whether we know what 'hand' means. Furthermore, it doesn't make sense to doubt *or to say one knows* unless we can support our claim with grounds. But 'This is a hand' has no grounds we can use as evidence. Wittgenstein's solution, however, means that 'This is a hand' doesn't actually *describe* the world, since it gives the meaning of the word 'hand'. But many claims the sceptic doubts, e.g. appearance is a good guide to reality, do seem to be claims about the way things are.

❓ QUIZ QUESTIONS

Explain and illustrate the principle of closure.

Outline **one** response to scepticism that rejects the principle of closure.

❓ DISCUSSION QUESTION

Assess the claim that sceptical doubts do not make sense.

● IV KNOWLEDGE OF THE EXTERNAL WORLD

Theories of perception can be divided into camps by how they answer the question 'What do we perceive when we experience material objects?' Realists claim that material objects exist as things that are independent of our minds and of our perceptions of them. Naïve realists claim that we perceive the material objects themselves. Representative realists say that we perceive them 'indirectly'; what we perceive 'directly' is a **sense-datum**, a mental image, that exists in our minds but which represents the material object. Idealists argue that material objects, in the sense that realists think of them as independent of our minds, don't exist at all (so we don't perceive them 'indirectly'). The only things we perceive, the only things that exist, are mental; so what we think of as material objects are actually particular sorts of ideas. Phenomenalists argue that material objects exist, and we perceive them, but that their existence is conceptually related to our perceptions of them.

Representative realism: whether our experience of the world is mediated by subjective representations (sense-data) of the external world

It is common sense to think that a world of material objects exists, and that we perceive it through our senses. But a little reflection suggests that what we perceive isn't quite the same as what is 'out there'. For example, if you put your thumb up against the moon, it looks like your thumb is larger than the moon, but it isn't. If you look at a red rose in sodium street lights, it looks grey, but the rose itself hasn't changed. If you half-submerge a straight stick in water and look at it from the side, it looks bent; but it isn't. So *what* we perceive in all these cases isn't the world as it is; but we are still perceiving the world – the moon, the rose, the stick – in some way.

Representative realists argue that they have a good explanation of this. There is a distinction between how the world is and how we perceive the world to be, but it still makes sense to say we perceive *the world*. We perceive it 'indirectly'. What is immediately present to our consciousness, what we perceive 'directly', is a representation of the world. This representation is a mental thing, an 'appearance'; philosophers have called it a 'sense-datum'. If the rose looks grey, but it isn't, what is it we are seeing that *is* grey? If the stick isn't bent, then what is it that is bent? Representative realists say it is the sense-datum of the rose that is grey, the sense-datum of the stick that is bent. Cases of hallucination support this claim still further. If I hallucinate seeing an elephant, there is nothing in the world that I am seeing *as* an elephant. So what is it that looks like an elephant? It can only be something mental, viz. the sense-datum of an elephant.

In these cases in which the world isn't the way we perceive it to be, it looks like we need to say we perceive sense-data. But, argue representative realists, there is really no difference between these cases and cases in which the world *is* the way we perceive it to be. If someone didn't know that straight sticks look bent in water, when he looked at such a stick it would seem to him as though he was looking at a *bent stick*. And when you are in the grip of an hallucination, you don't know you are hallucinating. You can't tell, just by how it seems, whether you are perceiving an illusion, perceiving the world the way it really is or hallucinating. But, then, if we are perceiving sense-data in the cases of illusion and hallucination, yet subjectively we can't tell the difference between these cases and cases in which we perceive the world as it is, we should say we are perceiving sense-data in every case. We don't just perceive sense-data in these cases of illusion; we *always* perceive sense-data. We perceive the world *in virtue of* perceiving sense-data.

Representative realism argues for the existence of sense-data on the basis that there must be *something* that is how things appear to us to be (grey rose, bent stick, etc.). Sense-data, then, are mental things which are the way we perceive them to be. They are 'appearances'. When we are perceiving the world, we perceive it via the sense-data that represent objects in the world. This representation can be accurate or inaccurate in certain ways. (When we hallucinate, we don't perceive the world at all.)

Primary and secondary qualities

There is another argument for representative realism. To understand it, we have to understand the distinction between primary and secondary qualities. The distinction is most famously associated with John Locke. For Locke, primary qualities are those properties of an object that are not related by definition to perceivers. The primary qualities are size, shape, motion, number and solidity. We might say that the object has these properties *in and of itself*. Primary qualities, Locke says, are 'inseparable' from a material object, whatever changes it undergoes. For example, material objects always have *some* shape and size.

By contrast, secondary qualities are related to perceivers by definition. Colour, by definition, is something that is experienced in vision. So it is a property that an object can have only in relation to its being seen by someone. The other secondary qualities are temperature, smell, taste and sound. Secondary qualities aren't possessed by all material objects, e.g. plain glass doesn't have a colour or a smell. And they aren't even possessed by the same material object at different times, e.g. glass is made from sand, and sand does have colour. So sand loses its colour completely when it is made into glass. (See also Descartes's wax argument in Ch. 5, THE ESSENTIAL NATURES OF MIND AND BODY, p. 235.)

Going further: more on secondary qualities

Does colour exist 'in the object' or 'in the mind' of the perceiver? Locke's *official* theory is just that secondary qualities are properties of the object which are related to its being perceived by us. Secondary qualities 'are nothing in the objects themselves but powers to produce various sensations in us'. Here Locke identifies the secondary quality with the *power of the object*. He goes on to argue that this power should be understood in terms of primary properties of the object's 'most minute parts', or, as we would now put it, in terms of its atomic and molecular structure. Secondary qualities can be causally explained in terms of primary properties.

But some philosophers, following an argument in Plato, have claimed that there is another contrast we can draw between primary and secondary qualities. Plato argues that 'heat' *isn't* a real property of an object, since what is hot to one person is not to another. By contrast, we might think that 'being two feet long' *is* a property of an object, since this doesn't vary from one person to another. Likewise, some philosophers, including Bishop Berkeley, claim that secondary qualities vary from person to person – what you see as bluey-green, I see as greeney-blue, what you taste as spicy, I taste as mild, and so on. So we shouldn't say that secondary qualities are properties *of the object*. What shade of colour is it – how you see it or how I see it?? Secondary qualities, they conclude, *exist* only in the mind of the perceiver, whereas primary qualities exist independently of the perceiver. This explains why primary qualities are objective, but secondary qualities are subjective. On this view, secondary qualities are not powers the objects have to cause certain sense-data; they are properties of the sense-data which are caused.

Philosophers still debate which is the better theory of colours, sounds and so on. As our concern is representative realism, we don't need to worry about this debate further.

Resemblance and representation

So what is the argument for representative realism based on the primary–secondary quality distinction? Locke claims that the ideas of primary qualities – our sense-data of shape, size, motion and so on – 'resemble' the primary qualities that the object we are perceiving has. However, the ideas of secondary qualities – our sense-data of colour, smell and so on – don't resemble the object at all. This shows, he argues, that we don't perceive the object 'immediately'. We do so via our sense-data of the object, which resemble it in regard to its primary qualities, but not in regard to secondary qualities.

But the argument faces some strong objections. First, Bishop Berkeley pointed out that Locke was wrong to say that the appearance resembles the object in its primary qualities, but not in its secondary. For example, circles do not *look circular* when viewed from a given angle, they *look oval*. So the lack of resemblance applies to both primary and secondary properties.

Second, Berkeley argued, you can't say that two things resemble each other unless you can compare them. But you can never compare the material object to the sense-data, since you only ever perceive sense-data immediately. We can't say that material objects have *any* of the qualities we perceive, including size and shape, because the only basis for doing so is our experience of the sense-data. We don't know that material objects have size and shape unless we know that our sense-data resemble them; but we don't know whether our sense-data resemble them unless we can say they have size and shape!

To reply to these objections, representative realists dropped the idea of 'resemblance' in favour of 'representation'. They emphasize the other part of Locke's theory, that sense-data are *caused by* material objects; and this causation is very detailed and systematic. For example, if you turn a penny, it looks circular, then increasingly oval, then flat (from the side). But all of these sense-data represent the penny because they are systematically related to it. We can explain representation in terms of this complex causation. What remains central to representative realism is that we perceive the world via sense-data.

Further objections to representative realism

One consequence of representative realism is that the world as it exists *in itself* consists just of primary qualities. But Berkeley argued that we cannot form a conception of a material object that has primary properties alone. For example, we can't conceive of something as merely having size and shape; it must have colour as well. However, Locke agrees that we can't conceive of something as having merely size and shape. But rather than colour, Locke argues the other property we need is solidity, which is a primary property. We can have a coherent conception of something as simply extended and solid without having any further secondary qualities. Colour is not necessary – just ask any blind person!

A second objection relates to scepticism. If we don't perceive material objects directly, on what basis do we think they exist at all? How can we prove that material objects cause our sense-data? Because we only ever experience sense-data *immediately*, if there were no material objects how would we know? It wouldn't seem any different if our sensations were caused by a computer; or were not caused at all, but just 'happened'. In order to know that material objects cause our sense-data, we first have to know that material objects exist. But the only access we have to material objects is through our sense-data. Representative realism gives us no reason to think that material objects exist at all.

Third, sense-data, as mental things, belong to the mind that experiences them. That means that when we look at the *same* table, we actually see different things – I see my sense-data and you see yours. This is counter-intuitive; we want to make sense of the idea that we do, literally, see the same thing, not just that there are *similarities* between what you see and what I see.

Representative realists respond to these last two objections by saying that they misunderstand sense-data. The objections wrongly assume that sense-data *come between* us and the world. In fact, we perceive the world *via* sense-data, which are the 'medium' by which we perceive the world. Compare: we describe the world using words; but words don't get in the way of describing the world. Likewise, sense-data don't get in the way of perceiving the world.

Going further: sense-data are impossible

However, all forms of representative realism are open to two objections according to which sense-data can't really exist. Locke seems to claim that sense-data have the very properties that the objects they represent do. So a sense-datum of a yellow square is itself square and yellow. The object *in itself* is square, so the sense-datum and the object resemble each other; but the object *in itself* isn't yellow, so the sense-datum doesn't resemble it. But how can sense-data be *literally* square or yellow? A sense-datum isn't in space, it doesn't take up space, so how can it be square? And how can something mental actually *be* yellow? Ideas and experiences can't really be coloured. As mental things, sense-data can't resemble what the material objects represent at all.

This is a very strong objection to the argument that representative realism used to establish the existence of sense-data. If the rose looks grey, it said, there must be something that *is* grey. But, the objection claims, how can anything mental actually *be* grey? Certainly, something is *represented as* looking grey. But that 'something' that is represented as grey is *the rose* itself.

Representative realists point out a difficulty with this objection. If the rose isn't grey, and there is no sense-datum which is grey, how is it possible that I *see* a (rose-shaped) patch of grey? Surely it is true that if I see grey, then something must be grey. If it isn't the rose, then it *must* be something mental.

The second objection to the existence of sense-data takes a different approach. Sense-data are said to be exactly how they seem; they are appearances. So it seems that my sense-data can't have properties that I am not aware of. But consider looking at a pile of matches scattered on the table – I don't know how many. How many matches are there in my sense-datum? Is it the same number as on the table? But then why don't I know how many matches there are if my sense-data are exactly as they appear? Alternatively, since I don't know how many matches there are, we could say that there is an 'indeterminate' number of matches in my sense-datum. But how can we say there is a number of matches in my sense-datum, but that that number is not 52 or 54 or 49; it is an 'indeterminate number'? There is no such number as an 'indeterminate number'!

KEY POINTS

● Representative realism claims that the material world exists independently of our minds, and that world we perceive indirectly via sense-data. Sense-data are mental images, appearances, that represent the world (except in the case of hallucination).

● They argue for sense-data by noting that in cases of illusion, the world isn't the way we perceive it to be. But if I perceive something grey or bent, then something must be grey or bent. Since it isn't the world, it must be sense-data. Furthermore, since I cannot tell, just from how the experience seems, whether I am perceiving an illusion or the way the world is, we should say I always perceive sense-data directly and the world indirectly.

● Another argument claims that the world has only primary qualities *in itself*, but we perceive it with secondary qualities. This is another way in which what we perceive is different from how the world is *in itself*. So we perceive the world indirectly.

● Locke argued that sense-data resembled the world in primary qualities, but not in secondary qualities. Berkeley argued that this is not true, and that we can't judge whether two things resemble each other unless we can compare them – but we can't compare the world and sense-data if we only ever perceive sense-data directly. Representative realists abandoned resemblance in favour of representation.

● Berkeley also objects that the idea of a world with just primary qualities makes no sense, e.g. something that has size and shape must also have colour (a secondary quality). Locke argues that something that has size and shape must also have solidity, a primary quality, so a world of just primary qualities does make sense.

● Two further objections argue that representative realism leads to scepticism. If all we perceive are sense-data, how do we know the material world exists at all? And we all, then, perceive our own sense-data. Representative realists reply that this wrongly assumes that we *don't* perceive the world, only sense-data. But the theory claims we *do* perceive the world, only indirectly.

● Two further objections claim that sense-data can't exist. First, as mental objects, they can't have colour, size or other properties that we think material objects have. Second, they seem to be indeterminate – but nothing that exists can be literally indeterminate.

❓ QUIZ QUESTIONS

Identify **two** ways in which sense-data differ from physical objects. (AQA, 1a, 2002, *6 marks*)

Explain and illustrate the distinction, made, for example, in representative realism, between the primary and secondary qualities of objects. (AQA, 2b, 2002, *15 marks*)

❓ DISCUSSION QUESTION

Assess the view that we perceive the world indirectly via sense-data.

Naïve realism: whether our experience of the world is direct

Naïve realists claim that we perceive the world directly, not via sense-data. Either they claim that there are no such things as sense-data, or they claim that we perceive sense-data only in cases of illusion and hallucination, not when we see the world as it is.

Naïve realism is the natural starting point for theories of perception. When we are perceiving the world, it certainly seems to us that we are directly perceiving material objects that exist independently of our minds. Try to describe what you see. We all, automatically, tend to describe what we see in terms of material objects – 'I see a brown deer', not 'I see a brown, deer-shaped patch'. Furthermore, it is virtually impossible to describe what we perceive in terms of sense-data without relying on this appeal to material objects. What is the shape of the brown patch? *Deer*-shaped.

Naïve realism doesn't understand sensory experiences as mental *things*, sense-data. Of course, in perceiving the world, we experience it. But we shouldn't say that we perceive the world in virtue of perceiving sense-data. If we want to say we 'have experiences' of the world, we shouldn't say we *perceive* the experience; we *have* it, thereby perceiving the object. Or better still, experiences aren't 'things'; we *experience*, and in virtue of experiencing, we perceive the object. We do not perceive a mental thing.

Illusion and secondary qualities

But naïve realism needs to answer the arguments given in favour of sense-data. We must admit that in cases of illusion we do not see the object as it is. The argument was that if something looks bent, but the stick isn't bent, then the sense-datum of the stick must be bent. Furthermore, representative realists have argued that if we can't tell the difference between an illusion and perceiving the world as it is, surely we see the *same thing* in both cases, viz. sense-data.

Naïve realists have presented two alternative explanations. The first agrees that if something looks bent, then something is bent, and since the stick isn't, I am seeing a sense-datum. But it objects to the second claim that I see the same thing in cases of illusion and of **veridical** perception. This view is called 'disjunctivism' because it says if it looks to me as if something is *F* (a stick is bent) then *either* there is something that is *F* that I see *or* it is, for me, just *as if* there is something that is *F* (an either/or claim is called a disjunction). In the first case, I see the world as it is; in the second case, I see sense-data. But just because I see sense-data in cases of illusion doesn't mean I see sense-data, rather than the world, in cases of veridical perception.

The second alternative rejects the claim that if it looks to me as if something is *F*, then there is *something* that is *F*. When the stick in water looks bent, there is *nothing* that *is* bent. Instead, the *stick* has the property of *looking bent* when half-submerged in water. The property of 'looking bent' is a distinct property from 'being bent'. It is a relational property, a property the stick has in relation to being seen by us. But because it is a property the *stick* has, we don't need to say that sense-data exist.

What about secondary qualities? Some representative realists argue that these are not properties in the object itself, but properties of the sense-datum. However, naïve realists respond by appealing to Locke's original definition of secondary qualities, viz. that secondary qualities are *powers in the material object* to produce certain experiences in us. Naïve realists say that when we perceive secondary qualities, e.g. colours, we still perceive the objects but *as they appear to us*. Just as a stick can have the property of 'looking bent' under certain conditions, it can have the property of 'looking brown'. In fact, naïve realists argue, to *be* brown is to look brown to normal perceivers under normal conditions.

But then what about the argument that secondary qualities are *subjective*? For example, the sea might look blue to me and green to you; an apple might taste sweet to me and sour to you. But the sea can't be both blue and green; an apple can't be both sweet and sour. It must be, then, that we don't perceive the object directly, that the properties we perceive it to have are actually properties of the sensations that occur in each of our minds.

Naïve realists could insist that whether the sea is blue or green depends on whether it looks blue or green to normal perceivers under normal conditions. But in this example, it is hard, perhaps impossible, to say who and what conditions will count as 'normal'. And in the case of the apple, taste in general seems to differ from one person to another. Naïve realists could say that the taste is still a power in the object to create experiences, but that this power creates different experiences in each of us. So the apple is sweet to me and sour to you; the apple *really is* both of these – so we both perceive the apple when we taste it, not sense-data.

But isn't it simpler just to say we don't perceive the object as *it* is, i.e. we don't perceive the object directly, but in virtue of sense-data?

Going further: what exists in a hallucination?

In the case of hallucinations, there is no material object that *looks* a certain way, because there is no material object at all! Furthermore, representative realists argue, why is it that we can describe both a hallucination, e.g. of an elephant, and a perception of an elephant in exactly the same way unless they have something in common? And the most obvious suggestion for what they have in common is sense-data.

First, all naïve realists argue that we can't generalize from hallucinations to perception generally, i.e. we can't use hallucinations to argue that we always perceive sense-data. Just because they seem similar subjectively doesn't mean the same thing (seeing sense-data) is going on. Hallucination and perception are different types of mental state, because in hallucination, the person isn't connected up to the world.

But this doesn't tell us what we *do* see in cases of hallucination. Disjunctivists can say that in hallucinations, as in illusions, we perceive sense-data. The other naïve realists can't. However, they can compare cases of hallucination with *thoughts* about objects that don't exist. For example, I can think that unicorns are white; but unicorns don't exist. Suppose now I hallucinate seeing a white unicorn. What have I seen that is white? The unicorn; no material object 'looks white' or 'looks like a unicorn' in this hallucination. But then what do I think is white when I think 'A unicorn is white'? Again, just the unicorn. Whatever explains how unicorns can be white without existing will also explain hallucinations of white unicorns.

An objection to this is that it is one thing to *think about* unicorns, quite another to think you are *seeing* a unicorn. In the hallucination, it seems you are confronted, in your consciousness, with an example of something white. The experience is quite different from thinking about something white. Again, the defenders of sense-data will say, in a hallucination of something white, something must *be* white; in a thought of something white, nothing needs to be white. And this difference arises from how different it is to have a hallucination from having a thought.

KEY POINTS

- Naïve realism claims that, at least when we perceive the world veridically, we perceive the world directly, not via sense-data. We experience the world perceptually; there are no mental *things* involved that we perceive.

- Disjunctivists claim that in illusions and hallucinations we do perceive sense-data, but argue that we cannot generalize from these cases to veridical perception.

- Other naïve realists argue that in illusion, nothing *is* the way it looks to you. Rather, the material object has the property of *looking* a certain way. Cases of hallucination are more difficult. They still argue that *nothing* is the way it looks, e.g. nothing *is* white when you hallucinate a unicorn, just as nothing *is* a unicorn when you think of a unicorn. You simply have the visual experience of white.

- Secondary qualities, they argue, are also properties that material objects have, viz. the power to cause certain perceptual experiences. To be red is to look red to normal perceivers in normal light. But then how do we explain that different people have different experiences? We must say that the object is 'sour to you' and 'sweet to me'. But we can object that these are subjective properties of the experience, not properties in the object.

❓ QUIZ QUESTIONS

Identify **one** similarity and **one** difference between naïve and representative realism.

Outline the argument from illusion, as an objection to naïve realism.

❓ DISCUSSION QUESTION

Assess the claim that we perceive the material world directly, not via sense-data.

Idealism: that which is immediately perceived are ideas, which exist only in the mind

Idealism is perhaps more properly described as a doctrine in metaphysics than in the theory of perception. It is a theory about what there is. However, the idealism of Bishop Berkeley, whose theory we shall concentrate on, began with arguments in the theory of perception, and obviously has consequences for our understanding of the nature of perception.

Berkeley rejects the existence of material objects. Exactly what is a material object? It's part of Berkeley's argument that it is difficult to answer this question; we can't make proper sense of the idea, he claims. But we can say this for certain: a material object is something that is *mind-independent*. All forms of idealism claim that reality is, in some important sense, dependent on minds. Berkeley claims that the ordinary objects of perception – tables, chairs, trees and so on – are dependent on minds. They must be perceived in order to exist: *esse est percipi (aut percipere)* – to be is to be perceived (or to perceive). The only things that exist, then, are minds (that perceive) and what minds perceive. Therefore, nothing exists that is independent of mind.

Berkeley's idealism is very counter-intuitive. Berkeley realized this, and many of his arguments, some of which we have already discussed, are objections to representative and naïve realism. If realism doesn't work, perhaps idealism is the answer.

In his objections to naïve realism, Berkeley argued that secondary qualities are subjective: we each perceive objects differently. But in his objections to representative realism, Berkeley argued that primary qualities don't resemble objects any more than secondary qualities do. They can be just as subjective, e.g. the apparent shape of something changes from different angles. So you and I could be looking at a penny, and you see something circular and I see something oval. But if both primary and secondary qualities are mind-dependent, then nothing that we perceive is left to exist independently of the mind. We really do perceive only ideas.

Although an odd result, it should be a welcome one. On the realist understanding, he argues, we can't make sense of material objects and we are in danger of scepticism about them anyway. Idealism claims that what we think of as material objects are bundles of ideas that we have come to associate with each other because they 'are observed to accompany each other'. Ordinary objects of perception exist; but they exist as ideas (bundles of ideas), not as material objects, independent of any mind.

Objections to idealism

We will get a better sense of Berkeley's idealism if we understand his responses to objections.

First, what causes perceptions? Without material objects, what is it that explains why we perceive what we do? There are three options: ideas, my mind and another mind. But ideas themselves don't cause anything, says Berkeley; they are completely passive. Second, perception is quite different to imagining; we are more passive – the sensations just occur to us, and we can't control them. From this difference between (voluntary) imagination and (involuntary) perception, we can rule out my mind. So they must be caused by another mind. When you think of the complexity and systematicity of our perceptions, Berkeley argues, that mind must be God.

If this seems *ad hoc*, Berkeley argues that it is at least no worse than invoking material objects. Realism claims to be able to explain perception by appealing to something outside our minds, material objects, that cause our experiences. But Berkeley argues that material objects provide no explanation at all. No one has been able to say *how* it is that material objects give rise to ideas (even if we can say now how material objects affect processes in the brain, we still have no explanation of how any of this causes an experience). So how our experiences come about remains a mystery.

A second objection: if ordinary ('material') objects are really ideas, how can I distinguish between my 'ideas', just part of my mind, and 'real things', part of the world beyond my mind? Berkeley replies by again pointing out the distinction between perception and imagination. In fact, Berkeley has three criteria for an idea being (part of) an object of perception, rather than *just* my mind: the idea is not voluntary; the idea forms part of the order of nature, the coherent set of ideas that we experience as reality; and the idea is caused by (or part of – see below) the mind of God.

But what about misperceptions and illusions? Misperceptions are no more voluntary than perceptions, and can be perfectly regular and natural: a stick looks bent half-submerged in water, red looks grey under yellow light and so on. Is the stick both bent and not bent?? Berkeley's response is that we aren't misperceiving – the stick is bent when half-submerged. However, this is misleading if we infer that the stick would be bent when pulled out of the water. So we shouldn't *say* 'the stick is bent', since this means it would remain so under normal conditions; the intuitive thing to say is that 'the stick looks bent' – and this is correct, it does look bent.

A third objection to Berkeley's idealism is this: If 'to be is to be perceived' for ordinary objects, that entails that when they are not being perceived, they do not exist. So if I leave a room, and no one else is in it, then everything ceases to exist! This is very counter-intuitive. The objection was put in the form of a limerick:

> There was a young man who said God
> must find it exceedingly odd
> when He finds that the tree
> continues to be
> when no one's about in the Quad.

Berkeley provides two different answers in different books. His first reply comes very close to Ayer's theory of PHENOMENALISM (see p. 62): what the word 'exists' means when applied to an ordinary object of perception is that it is *or can be* perceived. 'The table exists' means the table is being perceived or would be perceived if in the presence of some mind.

However, this reply conflicts with 'to be is to be perceived', which entails not that the table *does* exist if it were perceived, but rather that it *would* exist if it were perceived. So tables do pop in and out of existence. But should we worry about this, as long as they do so with complete regularity?

But Berkeley's second reply is summarized in the second part of the limerick:

> Dear Sir, your astonishment's odd.
> I'm always about in the Quad,
> And that's why the tree
> continues to be
> Since observed by, yours faithfully, God.

According to this response, not only are our ideas of perception *caused* by God, but what we perceive exists *in* the mind of God.

But this is also problematical: *our* ideas of perception couldn't be part of a divine mind, which can't have the sorts of sensations we have. Second, ordinary objects change and go out of existence, but God's mind is said to be unchanging and eternal. But Berkeley may respond that God's ideas which correspond to ordinary objects are not ones God thinks, but what God *wills us* to experience: 'things . . . may properly be said to begin their existence . . . when God decreed they should become perceptible to intelligent creatures'.

Going further: do minds exist?

Berkeley has argued against material substances. But why think there are mental substances, minds? We can no more form an idea of the mind than we can of a material object, because we can never experience mind directly – we experience only ideas. And ideas can't resemble minds, since ideas are passive and minds are (said to be) active. Berkeley first considered the possibility of rejecting minds as well, to adopt the view which Hume later defended, that minds are nothing more than bundles of ideas. But he later argued that we do have a notion of mind, through our own case – the meaning of the term derives from the 'I', we are immediately aware of ourselves as thinking things.

KEY POINTS

- Berkeley's idealism claims that material objects do not exist. To exist is to be perceived or to perceive, so only minds and ideas exist.

- Berkeley objects to naïve realism that secondary qualities are subjective, so we don't perceive material objects directly. He then objects to representative realism that primary qualities are equally subjective.

- Since material objects don't cause perceptions, Berkeley argues that God does.

- We can distinguish between my ideas and the ideas that make up *real things* by the facts that the latter are not voluntary and they are part of a coherent order of nature. Regular illusions are also part of the order of nature, but to mark the fact that the perception is not 'normal', we say that what we see 'looks' a certain way rather than 'is' a certain way.

- If to be is to be perceived, 'material' objects go out of existence when not being perceived. Berkeley can ask whether this matters, if it happens with complete regularity; or he can say that to be is to be perceived or to be able to be perceived in the presence of a mind; or he can say that God always perceives everything.

❓ QUIZ QUESTIONS

Briefly explain two ways in which idealism differs from representative realism.

Identify **one** similarity and **one** difference between idealism and naïve realism. (AQA, 2a, 2004, *6 marks*)

Outline and illustrate the idealist claim that real, as distinct from hallucinatory, experiences involve regularity.

❓ DISCUSSION QUESTION

Assess idealism. (AQA, c, 2004, *24 marks*)

Phenomenalism: whether physical object statements can be analysed in terms of statements describing sensory experience

Phenomenalism claims, intuitively, that we can know about the world of material objects through our sensory experiences; but, counter-intuitively, it is wrong to think of material objects as completely independent causes of our experiences. There are two famous defences of phenomenalism: Mill's 'metaphysical' account and Ayer's linguistic account.

Mill's phenomenalism

John Stuart Mill begins by saying that we have only our experience to go on in establishing what there is. When we interact with material objects, e.g. looking for something on a desk, we are presented with a series of new sensations. Certain sensations which were possible come about. I could move this piece of paper and experience a new shape of the colour beneath it. There are all sorts of possible sensations that would occur under certain conditions. We have come, from experience, to expect this sequence of sensation; you could say that we are certain it will happen. And so we come to think of certain possibilities for sensation as being *permanently* available, under certain conditions. The certainty we have is not unwarranted – it is grounded in our experience. Material objects are 'permanent possibilities of sensation'.

We associate certain sensations, and the possibilities of other sensations, together, since whenever I have one sensation, the conditions of having another associated with it are to hand. These 'clusters' of possible sensations are what material objects are. A piece of paper is the permanent possibility of certain sensations that we associate together. Only some of the sensations in fact occur; but the material object is a collection of those that do and those that could occur. We derive the complexity of the ideas of space, distance, perspective from the complex associations between sensations that we make (automatically – none of this need be thought through!).

We then think of material objects as the cause of the sensations that do occur. This isn't exactly wrong, though perhaps it is peculiar to think of a collection of possibilities causing an actuality. Where we do go wrong, Mill thinks, is if we think this cause is something that could exist quite independently of sensation. This is something we cannot know, and could lead only to scepticism.

Going further: Ayer's linguistic phenomenalism

A. J. Ayer takes a different tack. He defends phenomenalism through his analysis of statements concerning material objects. He claims that the function of philosophy is to give 'definitions in use', showing how the sentences in which a symbol, or type of symbol (such as 'table' or words for material objects generally), occurs can be translated into equivalent sentences which don't contain it or its synonyms. (He contrasts this with dictionary definitions, in which symbols are defined in terms of synonyms.) Philosophical definitions, then, can deepen our understanding of terms in a way dictionary definitions do not, i.e. they can still be informative to someone who already knows what all the terms mean in the dictionary sense. The analysis translates sentences containing the term into sentences that do not.

It can happen that we discover the term is *standing in* for something more complex. What are referred to by terms that do this are 'logical constructions'. Ayer argues that material objects are logical constructions – all propositions about material objects can be *translated without loss* into propositions about sense-data:

> the symbol 'table' is definable in terms of certain symbols which stand for sense-contents, not explicitly, but in use. And this . . . is tantamount to saying that sentences which contain the symbol 'table' . . . can all be translated into sentences . . . which do not contain that symbol, nor any of its synonyms, but do contain certain symbols which stand for sense-contents.

Notice that Ayer doesn't claim that material objects are *constructed*, made out, of sense-data (such a view would be more akin to idealism); but that *propositions* about material objects are in fact *entirely* concerned with features and relations of sense-data. To say that a material object of a certain kind exists is to say that certain sorts of sense-data have been, are being and would be experienced under certain conditions.

Objections to phenomenalism

Phenomenalism argues that it has the edge over representative realism and idealism. Representative realism supposes material objects exist independently of our experience and cause it; but we can't have any knowledge of a realm of causes outside our experience, so this claim is unjustified. But we shouldn't retreat to idealism, because we don't need to be sceptical about the material world. We simply need to understand what it is and how we can talk about it.

But very few philosophers accept phenomenalism now. What objections does it face?

First, experiences of material objects have a logical and reliable pattern. What is the *explanation* for this? Common sense regards claims about material objects as providing such an explanation; phenomenalists can't appeal to anything, they can say only that our experiences do have these patterns. But, first, it isn't obvious that we can actually describe that pattern without referring to material objects; and, second, if there is no independent cause of this pattern, what reason do we have to think that future sense-data will follow the same patterns?

Second, phenomenalism leads to solipsism, for if statements about what is beyond experience are analysed in terms of experience, then statements about *your* experience can be only statements about *my* experience, as I have no experience of your experience.

Going further: sensory routes

Third, phenomenalism's claim that statements regarding material objects can be translated into statements about what was, is and would be experienced under certain conditions invites the challenge: 'Go on, then, prove it!' This challenge may prove insurmountable, for the specification of the conditions under which the various sense-data would be experienced must be in terms of *other sense-data*. The translation of the claim 'There is a table in the next room' must not refer to the room (as a physical space) at any point.

Phenomenalists have responded by appealing to the idea of a *sensory route*, a series of juxtaposed and often overlapping sense-data that would be experienced in *locating* the table. But there are *many* different sensory routes to a given material object, while 'there is a table in the next room' seems to claim just one thing. Furthermore, we can often understand the claim that a certain material object or set of objects exists at a certain location without having any clear idea of the relevant sensory route, e.g. 'Penguins exist at the South Pole'. Finally, the conditionals in which the analysis is given may be falsified by situations that would not falsify the claim referring to the material object, e.g. I won't experience certain sense-data if I suddenly go blind upon entering the room, but the table will still be there.

KEY POINTS

● Phenomenalism claims that material objects are not conceptually independent of our experiences of them.

● Mill claims that material objects are 'permanent possibilities of sensation'.

● Ayer claims that material objects are 'logical constructions', i.e. every proposition containing a word that refers to a material object can be translated into a proposition that contains only words referring to sense-data.

● Phenomenalism argues that it avoids scepticism and idealism. However, philosophers object that it can't *explain* the regularity of our experiences, and possibly can't even describe that regularity without referring to material objects.

● A second objection is that it leads to solipsism, since sense-data logically belong to a mind.

● Third, the project of translating sentences referring to material objects into sentences referring to sense-data is perhaps impossible. In particular, it is difficult to translate sentences that say *where* in space a material object exists.

❓ QUIZ QUESTIONS

Explain and illustrate **one** criticism of phenomenalism. (AQA, 2b, 2004, *15 marks*)

Identify **one** difference and **one** similarity between phenomenalism and idealism.

❓ DISCUSSION QUESTION

Assess phenomenalism. (AQA, 2c, 2002, *24 marks*)

2

·moral philosophy

UNIT 2

● I NORMATIVE ETHICS

Act utilitarianism

Jeremy Bentham defended the 'principle of utility', or 'greatest happiness principle', 'that principle which approves or disapproves of every action whatsoever, according to the tendency which it appears to have to augment or diminish the happiness of the party whose interest is in question'. Or again, 'that principle which states the greatest happiness of all those whose interest is in question, as being the right and proper . . . end of human action'.

If we simplify this a little, we can say that utilitarianism claims that an action is right if it leads to the greatest happiness of all those it affects, i.e. if it *maximizes* happiness. Otherwise, the action is wrong. The greatest happiness should be the goal of our actions, what we hope to bring about. Our actions are judged not *in themselves*, e.g. by what *type* of action they are (a lie, helping someone, etc.), but in terms of what *consequences* they have.

'Greatest happiness' is comparative (great, greater, greatest). If an action leads to the greatest happiness of those it affects, no other action taken at that time could have led to greater happiness. So an action is right only if, out of all the actions you could have done, this action leads to more happiness than any other. Just causing *some* happiness or more happiness than unhappiness isn't enough for an act to be morally right.

Finally, because this theory says an act is right if it, the act, maximizes happiness, it is known as act utilitarianism. Rule utilitarianism presents a different criterion for whether an act is right (see p. 69).

Objections

One objection to act utilitarianism is doubt as to whether it can provide meaningful guidance about what to do. Can we know or work out the consequences of an action to discover whether it maximizes happiness or not? But Bentham does not say that an action is right if it *actually* maximizes happiness. He says it is right according to 'the tendency which it appears to have' to maximize happiness. We don't need to be able to work out the consequences precisely. An action is right if we can reasonably expect that it will maximize happiness.

This still means we must be able to work things out roughly. John Stuart Mill, who defended a different version of utilitarianism, thought this was still too demanding. Happiness is 'much too complex and indefinite' a standard to apply directly to actions. But we don't need to try, he claimed, because over time, people have automatically, through trial and error, worked out which actions tend to produce happiness. This is what our inherited moral rules actually are: 'Tell the truth', 'Don't steal' and 'Keep your promises' are embodiments of the wisdom of humanity that lying, theft and broken promises tend to lead to unhappiness.

A second criticism of act utilitarianism is that no type of action is ruled out as immoral (see DEONTOLOGICAL VIEWS, p. 72). If torturing a child produces the greatest happiness, then it is right to torture a child. Suppose a group of child abusers find and torture only abandoned children. Only the child suffers pain (no one else knows about their activities). But group members derive a great deal of happiness. So more happiness is produced by torturing the child than not, so it is morally right. This is clearly the wrong answer.

Act utilitarians can reply that it is *very probable* that someone *will* find out, and then many people will be unhappy. Because we should do what is *likely* to produce the greatest happiness, we shouldn't torture children. However, the theory still implies that *if* it was very unlikely anyone would find out, then it would be right to torture children. But other people finding out isn't what *makes* torturing children wrong.

Going further: integrity and demandingness

Act utilitarianism does not consider the special relation that obtains between our actions and our lives. My happiness doesn't count any more than anyone else's when I'm considering what to do. Obviously, I am affected more often and more deeply by my actions than are other people. But that's it. My actions, my life, is just a *means* of generating the greatest overall happiness.

One result is that act utilitarianism does not properly take into account the person's own feelings about the action. My conscience and moral integrity may tell me not to do something that act utilitarianism says it is right to do. The only way I am supposed to react to this situation is to calculate how unhappy it would make me to perform the action, and see if that changes what I should do! If it doesn't, I should do the action anyway. This doesn't *respect* the importance of people's integrity.

A second result, some philosophers argue, is that act utilitarianism is too demanding. For example, every time I buy a CD, I could have given the money to charity; and surely that would create more happiness, since other people need food more than I need music. But because people will always need food, it will *never* be right for me to buy myself music. It will never be right, it seems, to do something just for myself if I have more than the bare minimum.

● **KEY POINTS**

- In its simplest form, act utilitarianism claims that an act is right if, and only if, it maximizes happiness, i.e. if it creates more happiness than other act in that situation.

- But how do we know which act will create the most happiness? Bentham replies that an act is right according to the tendency which it appears to have to maximize happiness. Our best idea of what will cause the greatest happiness is enough.

- Mill objected that this is still too difficult, but if we are guided by our common-sense moral rules, we will usually do what maximizes happiness.

- A second objection is that some acts, such as torturing children for pleasure, are wrong even if they cause the greatest happiness.

- Third, act utilitarianism fails to respect people's moral integrity when deciding what to do.

- Finally, it makes morality too demanding.

❓ QUIZ QUESTION

Briefly explain act utilitarianism.

Outline and illustrate **two** criticisms of act utilitarianism.

Hedonistic, ideal, preference and negative utilitarianism

Hedonism

Bentham was a 'hedonist', claiming that happiness is pleasure and the absence of pain, and that happiness is all that matters. He also argued that we can measure pleasures and pains and add them up on a single scale by a process he called the 'felicific calculus'. If a pleasure is more intense, will last longer, is more certain to occur, will happen sooner rather than later or will produce in turn many other pleasures and few pains, it counts for more. In thinking what to do, you also need to take into account how many people will be affected (the more you affect positively and the fewer you affect negatively, the better). The total amount of happiness produced is the sum total of everyone's pleasures produced minus the sum total of everyone's pains.

Mill and ideal utilitarianism

Mill argued that a whole deeper dimension to human experience is missing from Bentham's account. Pleasures and pains are not all equally important; human well-being is more complex than that. Some types of pleasure are 'higher' than others, more valuable, more important to human happiness. But which ones? Mill thought there was an objective test: if almost everyone who knows what they are talking about compares two pleasures and agrees that the first is 'more desirable and valuable' than the second, then the first is a higher pleasure.

But how can we tell if a pleasure is *more valuable* than another, rather than just more *pleasurable*? Anyone who compares a tickle under the chin with a delicious dinner will prefer the dinner because it is more pleasurable! To tell if a pleasure is more valuable, people have to prefer it *even if having that pleasure brings more pain with it*. For example, the pleasure of being in love carries the pain of longing and the possible pain of breaking up. But people still prefer being in love to a delicious dinner. Happiness is distinct from contentment or satisfaction.

Mill argues that, as long as our physical needs are met, people will prefer the pleasures of thought, feeling and imagination to pleasures of the body and the senses, even though our 'higher' capacities also mean we can experience terrible pain, boredom, dissatisfaction. Their pleasures are higher, *not* because, on the Benthamite calculus, such pleasures are greater in *quantity*, but because they are of a different *quality* than other pleasures.

Mill still argues that happiness is the only thing important for human well-being. But we don't know what happiness *is* until we have a theory of well-being. Mill says that 'utility [is] the ultimate appeal on all ethical questions; but it must be utility in the largest sense, grounded on the permanent interests of a man as a progressive being'. These interests, such as freedom of thought, self-expression, creativity, truth, are, Mill claims, actually *higher pleasures*.

But many philosophers object that this is mistaken. These *ideals* are important to human well-being, but not as pleasures. It is not the pleasure the ideal brings which is important, but the ideal itself. This development of Mill's theory is therefore known as *ideal utilitarianism*.

Pleasure and preferences

Other philosophers argue that happiness (or well-being) isn't about pleasure, it is about getting what you want. *Preference utilitarianism* claims we should maximize the satisfaction of people's preferences. Two factors favour this theory. First, it is easier to know whether someone's preference has been satisfied than how much pleasure someone experiences.

So it provides better guidance. Second, it can be right to satisfy someone's preferences even when they don't know this has happened, and so don't derive any pleasure from it. For example, I can want you to look after my ant farm when I die. Suppose you don't derive any pleasure from looking after ants, but you don't mind either. According to preference utilitarianism, you should still look after my ants, rather than kill them, even though no one gets any pleasure from it.

Happiness v. suffering

According to Bentham, decreasing suffering and increasing happiness are the same thing. But we often think it is more important not to hurt someone than it is to please them. *Negative utilitarianism* counts suffering more heavily than happiness. Our main priority, in acting morally, is to minimize the suffering in the world, rather than maximize happiness.

KEY POINTS

- Bentham defends hedonism, claiming that happiness is pleasure and the absence of pain, and all that matters for human well-being is the quantity of happiness.

- Mill argues that some pleasures ('higher' pleasures) are more valuable than others.

- Higher pleasures are more important to happiness. However, we don't know what happiness is until we have a theory of human well-being.

- Philosophers object that human well-being involves more than pleasure, even higher pleasures. The ideals that give us 'higher' pleasure are important as ideals, not just as pleasures.

- Preference utilitarianism argues that we should maximize preference satisfaction.

- Negative utilitarianism argues we should minimize suffering.

❓ QUIZ QUESTIONS

Explain and illustrate **two** differences between hedonistic and ideal utilitarianism.

Briefly explain what preference utilitarianism involves. (AQA, 2a, 2004, *6 marks*)

Outline Mill's argument for rejecting Bentham's theory of happiness.

Rule utilitarianism

We saw that Mill appealed to common-sense moral rules to help us know what to do. Mill called these moral rules 'secondary principles'. It is only in cases of conflict between secondary principles (e.g. if by telling the truth you break your promise) that we need to apply the greatest happiness principle directly to an action. Some philosophers argue that Mill's secondary principles are *rules of thumb*, i.e. not strict rules that we must follow, but helpful guidance in our thoughts about what to do. Mill is still an act utilitarian, because he believes that an action is right if, and only if, it maximizes happiness.

By contrast, *rule utilitarianism* claims that an action is right if, and only if, it complies with those rules which, if everybody followed them, would lead to the greatest happiness (compared to any other set of rules). Rule utilitarianism has some advantages over act utilitarianism (see p. 66). First, we don't have to work out the consequences of each act in turn to see if it is right. We need to work out which rules create the greatest happiness, but we need to do this only once, and we can do it together. Second, the rule forbidding torture of children will clearly cause more happiness if everyone followed it than the rule allowing torture of children. So it is wrong to torture children. Third, it is much less likely that my conscience will prohibit an action that is in accordance with rules that promote happiness. In fact, the rule that we should usually allow people to act on integrity is a rule that will promote more happiness than any other. Finally, morality is not so demanding: I am required only to act in a way that, *if everyone acted like that*, would promote the greatest happiness. In the case of charity, I need only to give as much to charity as would be a 'fair share' of the amount needed to really help other people.

However, act utilitarians object that this means many people will not be helped, because we know that not everyone will give what they should to charity. Surely, knowing this, I ought to give much more to charity; spending the money on myself would not be right.

This is an example of a general objection to rule utilitarianism, that it amounts to 'rule-fetishism'. The point of the rules is to bring about the greatest happiness. If I know that, e.g., lying in a particular situation will produce more happiness than telling the truth, it seems pointless to tell the truth, causing unhappiness. The whole point of the rule was to bring about happiness, so that there should be an exception to the rule in this case. But then *whenever* a particular action causes more happiness by breaking the rule than by following it, we should do that action. And then we are back with act utilitarianism, weighing up the consequences of each action in turn.

Rule utilitarians respond that this will break down our trust that people will follow moral rules. So following a rule, even when in the particular case it will cause less happiness than breaking the rule, is still justified, because if people kept breaking the rules that would cause less happiness in the long run.

Objections to utilitarianism generally

Utilitarianism weighs the unhappiness of one person against the happiness of another, whether this is in deciding which action to do or which rule to adopt. Philosophers object that it isn't concerned with people as individuals, but as 'receptacles' for happiness, which fails to show them proper respect. Furthermore, the *distribution* of happiness – who gets happy by how much – is irrelevant, which fails to respect justice.

Utilitarians may reply that not treating people as individuals will cause unhappiness – people want to be respected for themselves. So we should treat them as individuals. But this reply doesn't work, because the objection is about how utilitarianism *thinks* of people, not about how we treat them. In its commitment to 'adding up happiness', utilitarianism replaces a concern for individuals as individuals by a concern for happiness generally; and this is not right.

Kant argued that happiness (or satisfying people's preferences) is not always morally good. For example, the happiness child abusers get from hurting children is morally bad. The fact that the abusers are made happy by what they do doesn't make their action better *at all*, but worse. So there must be some other standard than happiness for what is morally good.

● **KEY POINTS**

- Mill is an act utilitarian, but argues that we should apply the greatest happiness principle only to an act when two common-sense rules conflict.

- Rule utilitarianism claims that an act is morally right if, and only if, it complies with rules which, if everybody follows them, lead to the greatest happiness.

- This theory avoids many objections to act utilitarianism. However, act utilitarians object that it amounts to 'rule fetishism'. If breaking a rule would create more happiness on that occasion, we should break it. Rule utilitarians respond that people need to trust that others will abide by the rules, so we shouldn't break it.

- We may also object that utilitarianism doesn't show respect to individuals as persons and isn't concerned with justice.

- Kant objects to all utilitarian theories on the grounds that happiness is not always morally good.

❓ QUIZ QUESTIONS

Briefly explain the difference between act and rule utilitarianism. (AQA, 2a, 2005, *6 marks*)

Outline and illustrate **two** ways in which rule utilitarianism improves on act utilitarianism.

❓ DISCUSSION QUESTIONS

Assess utilitarianism. (AQA, 2c, 2005, *24 marks*)

Deontological views: certain acts are right or wrong in themselves

Deontologists believe that morality is a matter of duty (the Greek *deon* means 'one must'). We have moral duties to do things which it is right to do and moral duties not to do things which it is wrong to do. Whether something is right or wrong doesn't depend on its consequences (cf. ACT UTILITARIANISM, p. 65). Rather, it is something about any particular action that makes it right or wrong *in itself*.

Deontologists give different answers to how we can discover moral duties. Intuitionists, such as W. D. Ross, argue that there are several irreducible and distinct duties, and we have to use our moral intuition to tell what these are (see INTUITIONISM, p. 102). For example, he lists keeping promises, not harming others, and duties of justice, among others. Ross argues that there is not just *one* thing that unites all duties and makes them duties. Other philosophers argue that our duty is to do what God commands, which we may discover through scripture or conscience. Still others argue that we need to reason about what is fundamentally good. Kant argues that our duties are determined by 'pure practical reason'.

Most deontological theories recognize two classes of duties. First, there are general duties we have towards anyone. These are mostly prohibitions, e.g. do not lie, do not murder. But some may be positive, e.g. help people in need. Second, there are duties we have because of the particular personal or social relationships we stand in towards other individuals. If you have made a promise, you have a duty to keep it. If you are a parent, you have a duty to provide for your children. And so on.

We each have duties regarding our *own* actions. I have a duty to keep *my* promises, but I don't have a duty to make sure promises are kept. Deontology claims that we should each be most concerned with complying with our duties, not attempting to bring about the most good. In fact, all deontologists agree that there are times when we *should not* maximize the good, because doing so would be to violate a duty. However, some deontologists, such as Ross, argue that there is a duty to maximize the good where possible. Nevertheless, this is just one duty among others, and that we should not maximize the good on some occasions when this conflicts with other duties. Most deontologists do not think we have a duty to maximize the good, although they argue that there is a duty to do *something* for people in need. As this illustrates, many deontologists think our duties are quite limited. While there are a number of things we *may not* do, we are otherwise free to act as we please.

Finally, deontologists may disagree on whether duties are absolute or not. A duty is absolute if it permits no exceptions. This causes problems in cases where it seems that two absolute duties conflict with each other. So many deontologists argue that if an act runs counter to a duty, this is a very strong reason against doing it, but the reason may be outweighed in certain circumstances. For instance, there is a duty not to lie, but it may be permissible to lie in order to save someone's life.

Conflicts of duties

An important objection to deontology complains of the lack of guidance about how to resolve an apparent conflict of duties. For theories which hold that duties are absolute, this is particularly problematical: nothing we can do will not be wrong. However, most deontologists hold that a *real* conflict of duties can never occur. If there appears to be a conflict, we have misunderstood what at least one duty requires of us. This means one of two things: either duties never conflict, which means that we have to formulate our duties with great care; or duties can 'give way' – Ross argues that our usual duties are not absolute, but '*prima facie* duties' – they are duties 'at first sight'. In cases of conflict, one will give way and no longer be a duty in that situation.

But *which* duty should give way? Deontological theories argue that general prohibitions are the most stringent, and take precedence in a conflict. So, e.g., you should not lie rather than help someone. But this can seem counter-intuitive. Surely we can lie in order to save a life. In any case, this guidance isn't enough. What if two general prohibitions conflict or two other duties do? Should I break a promise in order to help someone? Since we have no criteria for making these decisions, disagreements about what to do will be irresolvable.

Deontologists may reply that this lack of guidance is a *strength* of the theory. Choices in life *are* difficult and unclear, a moral theory should not pretend to provide all the answers. A moral life calls for insight and judgement, not knowledge of some philosophical theory. Finally, we are wrong to think that disagreements can be resolved only if we have clear criteria. Discussions about what is reasonable can resolve many disagreements.

We may object that this is an unsatisfactory answer for a *deontologist* to give (see VIRTUE THEORY, p. 87, for another discussion), because one of the two acts we are considering is *wrong in itself* while the other is not. If one act was good, but the other act better, the issue of not being able to tell which was which might not be so pressing.

Going further: rationality and consequences

Utilitarians object that deontology is irrational. If it is my duty not to murder, for instance, this must be because there is something bad or wrong about murder. But if murder is bad, surely we should try to ensure that there are as few murders as possible. If I *know* that unless I kill someone deliberately, many people will die, how can I justify *not* killing them by appealing to duty? Surely it is my duty not to kill only because death is bad. So I should prevent more deaths. To insist that *I* don't do anything 'wrong' seems a perverse obsession with 'keeping my hands clean'.

Utilitarianism understands all practical reasoning – reasoning about what to do – as *means–end* reasoning: it is rational to do whatever brings about a good end. Deontology rejects this view. First, it may claim that we do not have a duty to maximize what is good. The utilitarian thinks it is just *obvious* that if something is good, more of it is better, and we ought to do what is better. There is no further argument to be given. The deontologist disagrees. Second, deontology offers an *alternative* theory of practical reasoning which rejects the means–end reasoning of utilitarianism. We will see two such accounts in the next section.

Going further: actions and intentions

In judging whether an action is right or wrong, deontology emphasizes the agent's intention (see also THE MOTIVE OF DUTY, p. 82). This is because it understands actions to be determined by intentions. We may ask: 'What type of action is this? Is this the same action as that?' For example, a person may kill someone else. A conventional description of the action is 'a killing'. But not all 'killings' are the same type of action, morally speaking. If the person *intended* to kill someone, i.e. that is what they wanted to bring about, that is very different than if the killing was accidental or if the person was only intending to defend themselves against an attack.

Actions are the result of choices, and so should be understood in terms of choices. Choices are made for reasons, and with a purpose in mind. These considerations determine what the action performed actually is. So deontology argues that we do not know what type of action an action is unless we know the intention. We should judge whether an action is right or wrong by the agent's intention. This does not make moral judgement subjective. What matters is the *real* reason the person made the choice to act as they did. It may be difficult to know what the real reason is, but that is a different point.

 KEY POINTS

- Deontology claims that actions are right or wrong *in themselves*, not depending on their consequences. Deontology identifies different types of action, and so judges whether they are right or wrong, on the basis of the agent's intention.

- Different theories identify different bases for duties, including reason, God's will and the view that there is no one basis.

- We can have general duties, e.g. do not lie, and duties that depend on our specific relationships to others, e.g. keep your promises.

- Our duties are concerned with *our* actions, not with attempting to bring about the most good. It can be against our duty to do what maximizes the good.

- Philosophers disagree whether duties are absolute or *prima facie*.

- Two objections to deontological theories are that they don't provide guidance when duties conflict, and that it is irrational not to maximize what is good.

QUIZ QUESTIONS

Explain and illustrate how deontological ethics differs from rule utilitarianism. (AQA, 2b, 2004, *15 marks*)

Explain and illustrate **two** differences between deontology and act utilitarianism.

Outline and illustrate **one** objection to deontology.

Our awareness of what is right and our duty to act rightly is given by reason

Kant: the basics

Immanuel Kant argued that moral principles can be derived from practical reason alone. To understand his claim, we need to put some premisses in place.

First, Kant believed that, as rational animals, we don't just 'do things', we make choices. Whenever we make a choice, we act on a *maxim*. Maxims are Kant's version of intentions. They are our personal principles that guide our choices, e.g. 'to have as much fun as possible', 'to marry only someone I truly love'. All our choices have some maxim or other behind them, which explains our reasons for that particular choice.

Second, morality is a set of 'laws' – rules, principles – that are the same for everyone and that apply to everyone. If this is true, it must be *possible* that everyone could act morally (even if it is very unlikely that they will).

From this, Kant devises his *categorical imperative* for working out whether acting on a particular maxim is right or wrong. Suppose you want a gift to take to a party, but you can't afford it, so you steal it from the shop. Your maxim is something like: 'to steal something I want if I can't afford it'. This can only be the right thing to do if everyone could do it. The categorical imperative is: 'Act only on that maxim through which you can at the same time will that it should become a universal law'.

The two tests

There are two different ways in which we could fail to be able to will our maxim to become universal. The first, which Kant calls a 'contradiction in conception', is if the situation in which everyone acted on that maxim is somehow self-contradictory. If we could all just help ourselves to whatever we wanted, the idea of 'owning' things would disappear. But if I don't own something – like the things in my shop – you can't really 'steal' them from me. You can only steal something if it isn't yours. Stealing assumes that people own things, and people can only own things if they don't all go around helping themselves whenever they want. So it is logically impossible for everyone to steal things. And so stealing the gift is wrong.

The second way our maxim can fail the categorical imperative Kant calls a 'contradiction in will', and his example is helping others. It is logically possible to universalize the maxim 'not to help others in need'. The world would not be a pleasant place, but this is not what Kant focuses on. Kant does *not* claim that an action is wrong because we *wouldn't like* the consequences if everyone did it. His test is whether we *could choose* for our personal maxim to be a universal law. His test is about what it is possible to choose, not what we like to choose.

So, although it is logically possible, Kant argues that we cannot *will* that no one help anyone else. First, a will, by definition, wills its ends, its purposes. Second, to truly will the ends, one must will the necessary means. And so, third, a will that is incapable of bringing about its ends must – logically must – will the only alternative means, the help of others. The only way of avoiding this conclusion is to cease to will any ends at all. One cannot, therefore, will a situation in which no one helps anyone else, for it contradicts the very act of willing anything at all.

Perfect and imperfect duties

Kant calls duties established by the first test 'perfect' duties. Perfect duties are absolute in the sense that they do not allow any exceptions based on what we want. It is never right to murder, lie or steal. It is also possible to fulfil perfect duties just by *acting* in certain ways. For example, you might decide not to steal because you are afraid of being caught, rather than because you think it is right not to steal.

Duties established by the second test are 'imperfect' duties. Imperfect duties allow for judgement regarding when and how we fulfil them. While we have the duty to help other people, this duty doesn't specify how much or on what occasions we should help. It says only we must not never help. Kant also argues that you fulfil your imperfect duties only if your motive is right. If I give money to someone in order to impress a friend, I am not fulfilling my duty to help other people.

The categorical imperative is based on reason

An imperative is just a command. The command is categorical because we can't take it or leave it. It is not just morally wrong to disobey, Kant thought, it is also irrational. It must be possible for all rational animals to choose to behave rationally. So choosing to behave in a way that it is impossible for everyone to follow is irrational. So we must obey the categorical imperative because it is irrational not to. So it is our duty to act only on maxims that can be universalized. Reason both determines what our duties are and gives us the means to discover what our duties are.

But why should morality be about behaving rationally? Whatever else we think about morality, it is supposed to guide our actions. It can only do this if we can be motivated by morality. Kant argues that there are, ultimately, only two sources of motivation: happiness and reason.

Morality and happiness

Morality can't be based on happiness, Kant argues, for two reasons. First, what makes people happy differs from person to person. If morality was about happiness, then different people would be motivated to act in different ways. But morality is the same for everyone. A utilitarian would object that morality can be the same for everyone and be about happiness if morality is about creating the *greatest* happiness. Kant would respond that everyone else's happiness does not necessarily motivate me, only my own happiness does.

And, in fact, utilitarians usually appeal to reason here themselves, saying that caring about other people's happiness is *rational* or *reasonable*.

Second, happiness is not always morally good. If someone is made happy by hurting others, this is no reason to say that it is morally good to hurt others. In fact, their happiness is morally bad. So we evaluate happiness by morality. That means the standard of morality must be independent of happiness.

Morality and reason

Since morality can't be based on happiness, then it must be based on reason. This is confirmed by the characteristics that morality and rationality share. Morality is universal, the same for everyone; so is reason, says Kant. Morality and rationality are categorical; the demands to be rational and moral don't stop applying to you even if you don't care about them. Neither morality nor rationality depend on what we want. Finally, we intuitively think that morality applies to *all and only* rational beings, not just human beings. In Douglas Adams's *The Hitch-Hiker's Guide to the Galaxy*, Arthur Dent protests to the Vogons, aliens who are going to destroy the Earth, that what they are doing is immoral. Morality doesn't apply to beings that can't make rational choices, such as dogs and cats (pets misbehave, they don't act *morally wrongly*).

Objections to the categorical imperative

In addition to the objections posed to deontology generally (see pp. 72–3), Kant's theory faces the objection that the categorical imperative is a flawed test. First, couldn't any action be justified, as long as we phrase the maxim cleverly? In stealing the gift, I could claim that my maxim is 'to steal gifts from large shops and when there are seven letters in my name [Michael]'. Universalizing this maxim, only people with seven letters in their name can steal only gifts and only from large shops. The case would apply so rarely that there would be no general breakdown in the concept of private property. So it would be perfectly possible for this law to apply to everyone.

Kant's response is that his theory is concerned with my *actual* maxim, not some made-up one. It is not actually part of my choice that my name has seven letters, or perhaps even that it is a *gift* I steal (some people do, however, have 'principles' about stealing only from large shops). If I am honest with myself, I have to admit that it is a question of my taking what I want when I can't afford it. For Kant's test to work, we must be honest with ourselves about what our maxims are.

Second, Kant's test delivers some strange results. Say I am a hard-working shop-assistant, who hates the work. One happy Saturday I win the lottery, and I vow 'never to sell anything to anyone again, but only ever to buy'. This is perhaps eccentric, but it doesn't seem morally wrong. But it cannot be universalized. If no one ever sold things, how could anyone buy them? It is logically impossible, which makes it wrong according to Kant's test. So perhaps it is not always wrong to do things which requires other people to do something different.

Respecting humanity

Kant gave an alternative formulation of the categorical imperative, known as the 'formula of humanity': 'Act in such a way that you always treat humanity, whether in your own person or in the person of any other, never simply as a means, but always at the same time as an end'.

Kant does not say we cannot use people as a means, but that we can't use them *simply* as a means. We rely on other people in many ways as means to achieve our own ends, e.g. people serving me in a shop are a means to getting what I want to buy. What is important, says Kant, is that I also respect their humanity as an end in itself. By 'humanity', Kant means our practical rationality, our ability to rationally determine which ends to adopt and pursue. To treat someone's humanity simply as a means, and not also as an end, is to treat the person in a way that undermines his or her power of making a rational choice themselves. Coercing someone or lying to them, so not allowing them to make an *informed* choice, are examples.

The ability to make free, rational choices gives human beings dignity. It is also the ground of their absolute value. Everything else has value only because it is adopted by a being with humanity, Kant argues (see THE MOTIVE OF DUTY, p. 82).

In one sense, which limits what we may do, to treat humanity as an end is to *respect* it, which forms the basis of various perfect duties, including not coercing others, not lying and not stealing. In another, more positive sense, treating humanity as an end means adopting it as an end to be *pursued*. On this basis, we seek to encourage the ability to make rational and worthwhile choices in ourselves and others. This sense is the basis of various imperfect duties, including helping other people and developing one's mind.

KEY POINTS 1

- Kant argues that choices are made according to maxims, and that morality is a set of principles everyone can follow.

- He therefore concludes that it is morally right to 'Act only on that maxim through which you can at the same time will that it should become a universal law' (the categorical imperative). Acting on a maxim that does not pass this test is morally wrong.

- A maxim can fail the test in two ways: (1) it cannot be consistently universalized, because a situation in which everyone acted on it is impossible; (2) it cannot be willed in a universal form, because a situation in which it was universally followed undermines the operation of the will.

- Perfect duties are established by the first test, imperfect duties by the second.

- Kant argued that only happiness or reason can motivate us to act. Morality cannot be based on happiness, since what makes people happy differs and happiness is not always morally good. The categorical imperative is based on pure practical reason. Reason and morality are categorical, universal and independent of our desires.

- However, the categorical imperative delivers some counter-intuitive results.

- Kant reformulated the categorical imperative as the formula of humanity: 'Act in such a way that you always treat humanity, whether in your own person or in the person of any other, never simply as a means, but always at the same time as an end'. This requires us to respect and encourage the ability to make rational choices in ourselves and others.

Natural law

Natural law theory also claims that we discover what is right or wrong through reason, but it understands reason differently from Kant. Practical reason is not an abstract test of universalizability, but a matter of insight into what is fundamentally good or bad for us. The basis of natural law is what is intelligibly good, and the moral life is one that is lived according to what is good. Most natural law theorists argue that the ultimate explanation for natural laws is God, as the source of reason and moral value (see the next section). However, most also argue that we can know what is right and wrong without referring to God.

The connection with 'nature' is *not* anything to do with scientific laws of nature. Instead, natural law is 'natural' for two reasons: it is 'law' that is not the product of human convention; and following it will lead to human flourishing, so it is intimately connected to human nature. However, unlike VIRTUE THEORY (p. 84), natural law theory does not try to *derive* claims about what is good from a prior conception of human nature. We have direct rational insight into what is good; and this informs our idea of what human nature is.

Natural law provides the standards for rational choice. These standards are obligatory, 'laws', since it is unreasonable not to choose according to them. However, natural law theory disagrees with utilitarianism that the right response to what is good is to maximize it. Morality is about bringing what is good into one's choices and actions. It is not about bringing what is good into the world as a whole (except through one's good will). Morality provides standards for choices rather than consequences. Intentions are central because it can never be right to act against what is good.

Aquinas

The most famous natural law theorist is St Thomas Aquinas. He argues that the fundamental natural law is: 'Good is to be pursued, and bad avoided'. On its own, like Kant's categorical imperative, this tells us nothing about what to actually do. But it provides the framework for moral duties. It lays down that what is good is truly desirable, and what is bad is truly undesirable. Aquinas then argues that certain things are truly desirable, and that this is **self-evident** (see INTUITIONISM, p. 103). With experience of them, we understand that they are good. For example, as children, we ask questions and receive answers; we later realize that answers form part of a general possibility, viz. knowledge, and we realize that knowledge is not just a possibility, but a benefit, something good. So we understand that knowledge is to be pursued. Aquinas argues that life, marriage, living in friendship and harmony with others, and practical reasonableness are other basic goods.

In realizing these are goods, we realize they are good for everyone. So we see that we should pursue them in others' lives as much as our own. The basic moral principle, Aquinas says, is 'Love one's neighbour as oneself'. All moral duties can be derived from this principle.

Going further: rationality and consequences (again)

Utilitarianism argues that it is irrational not to maximize the good. Kant argues that it is irrational to act in a way that not everyone could act in. This is not means–end reasoning at all, but picks up on other formal features of reason (universal, categorical, independent of desires). However, some philosophers argue that Kant has wrongly taken the features of *theoretical* reason – reasoning about facts, science, logic and so on – as features of *practical* reason. We cannot set the ends of action in this way, as shown by the fact that the categorical imperative produces strange results.

Natural law theory agrees with utilitarianism that practical reasoning starts with what is good, and so Kant's formal approach won't succeed. However, it argues that the rational response to what is good is to choose in accordance with it, not to maximize it. To *intend* to do something bad, such as to lie or to kill, in order to bring about something good is not to order one's will in accordance with what is good.

However, we may object that concentrating *only* on one's will and ignoring the consequences of what one does, even with the best of intentions, cannot be right or reasonable, when those consequences could adversely affect many people.

KEY POINTS 2

● Natural law, which we know through rational insight, is about what is intelligibly good, and forms the foundation of morality. It is 'natural' because it precedes any human laws, and following it will lead to human flourishing, so it is connected to human nature. It is 'law' because it provides the standards for rational choice.

● Aquinas argues that the fundamental natural law is 'Good is to be pursued, and bad avoided'. We then have insight into what is good, e.g. knowledge, friendship and life.

● Because we see these are good for everyone, Aquinas argues that the basic moral principle is 'Love one's neighbour as oneself'.

● Kant and natural law theory present two different accounts of practical rationality, both of which reject the claim that it is always rational to maximize the good.

❓ QUIZ QUESTIONS

Briefly explain **two** features of natural law theory.

Outline Kant's argument for the categorical imperative.

Outline and illustrate **one** objection to Kant's categorical imperative.

❓ DISCUSSION QUESTIONS

Assess the claim that it is always irrational not to do what maximizes the good.

Assess deontology.

Our awareness of what is right and our duty to act rightly are given by divine command

One reason for believing that certain types of action are right or wrong in themselves is that God has commanded us to do or not to do them. There is an extensive discussion of the relationship between morality and God's will in MORALITY (Ch. 3, p. 187). Read that section before attempting to answer the questions below. What follows compares that section with the discussion of natural law above.

In order to discover what is right and wrong, we need to discover what God has commanded. There are different ways that we might do this, in particular divine revelation, conscience and reason. Most natural law theorists, including Aquinas, argue that we can know what is right and wrong through reason, although the ultimate explanation of moral value and duty lies in God. Although some argue that natural laws and the resulting moral duties are obligatory because they are divine commands, most argue that they are obligatory because they are reasonable. It is not because God commands us to be moral that we should be moral; we should be moral because it is irrational not to be. This rationality has its source in God, but in God's intellect, not God's will.

Some philosophers argue that reason is not a secure route to knowledge of right and wrong (see Ch. 3, FIDEISM, p. 170), and we should rely on conscience, as the voice of God, and revelation. Aquinas connects our knowledge of morality through reason to conscience and revelation. First, he understands conscience to *be* reason, working out what is good or evil in particular situations. Second, he argues that many of the truths we discover by reason are confirmed by revelation, while others are clarified. So revelation plays an important role in *developing* our knowledge of morality.

● ▬ **KEY POINTS** ▬

- We may discover what God commands through revelation, conscience or reason.

- Most natural law theorists claim that we can know right and wrong through reason, although God is the source and standard of what is rational.

- Aquinas argues that conscience is reason and that revelation can confirm, and clarify, what we discover through reason.

❓ QUIZ QUESTIONS

Briefly explain and illustrate **two** reasons for thinking that our moral duties are dependent on God's will.

Outline **two** objections to the claim that morality is dependent on God's will.

❓ DISCUSSION QUESTION

Assess the claim that God's commands are the source of our moral duties.

The motive of duty

At the heart of deontology is the idea of the 'good will', a will that intends and chooses what is right *because it is right*. For Kant, a good will is one that obeys the moral law (the categorical imperative) because it is morally right to do so. In contrast to natural law, Kant argues that nothing is fundamentally good except the good will; everything else can be good or bad depending on circumstances or how it is employed. For example, knowledge may be bad if it is knowledge of how to achieve evil ends and is used for evil ends.

To do what is morally right because it is morally right is to act from the *motive* of duty. 'Duty' is not just the word for what we ought to do, but also the word for a reason for doing what we ought to do. Much of the time we do things just because we want to; and most of these things it is also morally permissible to do. However, if we do not *care* whether what we do is right or wrong, we are motivated *only* by what we want. But if we wouldn't do it if it was wrong, then we are, at least in part, motivated by duty. The clearest case of being motivated by duty is when we do something we don't want to do, because we feel we ought to.

Kant compares two shop-keepers, who both give the correct change to their customers. The first is honest because he is scared of being caught if he tries to cheat his customers. The second is honest because he believes it is morally right to be honest. The first shop-keeper doesn't act from duty; the second shop-keeper does. Even if the first shop-keeper gives correct change because he wants people to like him, or even because he likes his customers, this still isn't acting from duty.

Kant argues that the only actions that deserve our praise, that are morally good ('worthy') as well as morally right, are actions done from the motive of duty.

Objection

Many philosophers object to this last claim, and to the idea that we should be so concerned with 'doing the right thing'. Surely, if I do something nice for you, like visit you in hospital, because I like you, that is also a morally good action. Much of the time we do good things because we feel warmly towards the people we benefit. Kant seems to say that we have to want to benefit people because it is our duty to so, not because we like them. Some philosophers have thought that putting duty above feelings in our motives is somehow inhuman.

Kant can respond that he is not trying to *stop* us from being motivated by our feelings. His point is that, when we are choosing what to do, how we feel should not be as important as what it is morally right to do. But when you do something for a friend, should you think 'I'll do this because he is my friend; and it is morally right to do so'? Perhaps Kant can reply that what is important is that you've thought about this friendship at some point to ensure that it doesn't violate any duties, and you'd be willing to give it up if it did require you to do something morally wrong.

Natural law theory doesn't face this objection in the same way. A good will aligns itself with what is good, and that includes friendship. If we do something out of friendship, this is morally good. We do not need an additional motive of duty to make the action morally good.

KEY POINTS

- Deontology emphasizes the importance of a good will, choosing what is right *because* it is right.

- To act on this basis is to act from the motive of duty.

- Kant argues that only actions done from duty are morally worthy. Philosophers object that acting from certain emotions and desires is also praiseworthy.

❓ QUIZ QUESTION

Briefly explain and illustrate the motive of duty.

❓ DISCUSSION QUESTION

Assess the claim that only acting from the motive of duty is morally praiseworthy.

Virtue theory: the focus on how we should live, the cultivation of virtues and flourishing

Virtue theory claims that 'How shall I be?' comes before 'What should I do?' An action is right, roughly, if it is an action that a virtuous person would do. A virtuous person is someone who has the *virtues*, morally good traits of character. A right action, then, will express morally good traits of character, and this is what makes it right. Telling the truth expresses honesty, standing up to a bully expresses courage and so on. Our main aim, therefore, should be to develop the virtues, because then we will know what it is right to do and we will want to do it.

Aristotle argued that there are two types of virtue: virtues of the intellect and virtues of character. The virtue of intellect most relevant to morality is practical wisdom, which enables us to know what is right and wrong in any given situation (see below). Character involves a person's dispositions that relate to what, in different circumstances, he would feel, how he thinks, how he reacts and the sorts of choices he makes and actions he performs. So someone is short-tempered if he is disposed to feel angry quickly and often; intemperate if he gets drunk often and excessively. Aristotle says that what reveals our character above all is what we find pleasant. A virtue of character is a character trait that disposes us to feel desires and emotions 'well', rather than 'badly'.

The 'cardinal' virtues

In *The Republic*, Plato argues that the soul has three 'parts': reason, 'spirit' and desire. The virtue of reason is wisdom, the virtue of spirit is courage, the virtue of desire is temperance, or self-control. If reason rules the soul with wisdom, so that spirit moves us to courageously do what is right, and we desire only what is right, then the soul as a whole is just. These four virtues – wisdom, courage, temperance and justice – became known as the 'cardinal' virtues ('cardinal' means most important). Later Christian thinkers, in particular Aquinas, developing a remark made by St Paul (I Corinthians 13.13), added the three 'theological' virtues of hope, faith and charity (or self-giving love), which are concerned with our relationship with God and with other people.

Human nature and being virtuous

Plato developed his theory in response to the question 'Why should we be just?' Is the only reason not to cheat people because we might get caught? Plato argues that justice is its own reward, and that to understand why we should be just we need to understand what justice is. A just person is someone with a just soul. When our souls are just, they are in the right state, every part as it is meant to be, 'healthy'. And if my soul is in a bad, unhealthy state, the person who suffers most is me. The desire for material wealth that leads me to, e.g., cheat someone is out of control. If my desires are out of control, I can feel *driven, forced* to do things, by the strength of those desires. If I brought them under control, I would not want to act unjustly. This state of the soul would be good for me; I will be calm and able to choose well.

Many virtue theorists argue that virtues are qualities of a person that help them to 'live well'. Aristotle argued that what it is to 'live well' is determined by human nature. His term for 'living well' – *eudaimonia* – has been translated as 'happiness'. But the idea is more like 'flourishing'. We have an idea of what it is for a plant or animal to 'flourish'; we can provide an analysis of its needs and when those needs are met in abundance. According to virtue theory, moral philosophy is interested in the 'good life' for human beings as the particular sorts of beings we are. What it is to live well is based on objective judgements about human nature.

If living well is our ultimate goal, the moral question is not what to do, but how to live. Living involves choosing and acting as a central part, but also involves the nature and quality of one's relationships with others and the state of one's 'soul'. For Plato, this means that each part of the human soul must perform its designated task well, and in particular, reason must be in charge. Aristotle agreed that reason is central to human nature. He also agreed that 'unruly' emotions and desires can stop reason working well. But he argued that we should train, rather than curb, our emotions, so that we automatically and 'naturally' react and want to act in the best way.

Human nature and relativism

Different cultures have thought that different traits counted as 'virtues'. For example, Aristotle thought that it was important to occasionally do good public works of magnificence and expense. The Victorians thought chastity was important. We don't subscribe to either of these ideas. So virtue ethics seems to endorse a type of relativism (see THE EXISTENCE OF MORAL RELATIVISM, p. 110) – what is right is right according to a particular culture.

If this is an objection, virtue theorists could reply in two ways. First, in different cultures, people will need different traits in order to lead a good life. All human beings live in some culture or other; and we need to be able to lead our lives in the culture we find ourselves in. To some degree, what traits we need to live a good life will vary from one culture to another. But, second, Aristotle argues that the list of the virtues is not a random collection of character traits; it is based on human nature. And this is universal – everyone needs courage, loyalty, temperance and so on, because life throws the same challenges at us all. So, first, the *essential* virtues won't be relative; and, second, on this basis, we may be able to criticize different cultures for having the 'wrong' list of virtues on the grounds that they don't really help people lead a good life.

Going further: is virtue good for you?

Aristotle and Plato argue that being virtuous is good for the virtuous person. But is this right? If we are each trying to achieve the best life for *ourselves*, will we do this by being morally good?

This challenge has two parts. First, do all virtues contribute to *my* flourishing? Couldn't some virtues, perhaps related to self-sacrifice, charity, commitment to a political cause, contribute to other people's flourishing, but at the cost of my own? Second, do all virtues have to contribute to my *flourishing*, or do some contribute to an admirable or meaningful life, but not a *good* life, let alone a morally good life, e.g. artistic creativity that causes the artist despair and suffering, or a single-minded commitment to knowledge?

Virtue theorists could respond that admirable or meaningful lives just are 'good' lives. Everything that is truly admirable or meaningful can be part of living 'in accordance with reason', so we can understand its relation to human nature as rational. And if my life is lived in accordance with good reasons, it is a good life.

However, this reply is unsatisfying. Doing what you see good reason to do and flourishing just don't seem to be the same idea, so it is a mistake to reduce flourishing to no more than 'living in accordance with reason'. Which raises the question 'Are virtues traits that help us flourish or traits that help us live our lives on the basis of good reasons?'

Knowing what is good

How do we know what is morally good? Plato and Aristotle make the formation of a good character (see below) a prerequisite to acquiring knowledge of what is good. What else is required?

Plato argued that if you are wise, then you know what is good and what is bad. Wisdom is knowledge of the 'Forms', including the Form of the Good, and you gain this knowledge through doing philosophy. However, the Forms are very abstract, and it is unclear from Plato's argument how having knowledge of something as abstract as the Forms can really help us in practical life. For further discussion of Plato's Forms and knowledge of what is good, see Ch. 4, THE THEORY OF FORMS (p. 194), PLATO'S ACCOUNT OF THE GOOD (p. 204), ETHICAL IMPLICATIONS OF THE THEORY OF THE FORMS (p. 206), and THE NATURAL QUALITIES OF THE PHILOSOPHER (p. 211).

Aristotle agrees with Plato that knowledge of what is good comes through reason, but his idea of reason is much less abstract. Because human beings are rational, for a human being to live well he or she must live 'in accordance with reason'. If we feel emotions and desires, and make choices, 'well', i.e. virtuously, we feel and choose 'at the right times, with reference to the right objects, towards the right people, with the right motive, and in the right way'. The virtue of intellect that helps us know what is 'right' in each case is *practical wisdom*.

The doctrine of the mean

In a situation in which you are being bullied, you could feel angry too much or too little, 'and in both cases not well'. There are lots of ways in which we can act and feel 'unreasonably'. Aristotle defends the 'doctrine of the mean', the idea that a virtuous response or action is 'intermediate'. Just as there is a right time, object, person, etc., at which to feel anger (or any emotion), some people can feel anger too often, about too many things and towards too many people, or they get too angry or get angry to scare others. Other people can feel anger not often enough regarding too few objects and people (perhaps they don't understand how people are taking advantage of them). Someone who gets angry 'too much' is short-tempered. We don't have a name for someone who gets angry too little. Someone who has the virtue relating to anger is good-tempered. The virtue is the 'intermediate' state between the two vices of 'too much' and 'too little'. Aristotle's doctrine of the mean does *not* claim that when you get angry, you should only ever be moderately angry. You should be as angry as the situation demands, which can be very angry.

Many virtues fit this model, Aristotle argues. Some, like good temper, work with feelings. Other virtues, like honesty, work with motives for actions. Telling the truth 'too much' is tactlessness. Telling it 'too little' is lying when you shouldn't. The virtue of honesty involves telling the truth at the right times, to the right people, etc.

Knowledge of the good life

This knowledge, of what is the right time, objects, people, motive and way for certain emotions or choices, is practical knowledge of how to live a good life. Moral knowledge involves some general knowledge, viz. 'What sorts of thing conduce to the good life in general?' But, above all, it is knowing how to live a good life here and now, in this particular situation.

To know what is right, I need to be able to understand my situation and how to act in it, yet situations always differ. And so, Aristotle argues, ethical understanding is not something that can be *taught*, for what can be taught is general, not particular. Rules and principles will rarely apply in any clear way to real situations. Instead, moral knowledge is only acquired through experience.

Objections

The doctrine of the mean isn't much help practically. First, 'too much' and 'too little' aren't quantities on a single scale. The list of 'right time, right object, right person, right motive, right way' shows that things are much more complicated than that. Second, to know whether a character trait or action is 'intermediate' is just to know that it is virtuous. How often should we get angry, and how angry should we get? There is no independent sense of 'intermediate' that can help us answer these questions. However, perhaps Aristotle didn't mean the doctrine of the mean to be of real guidance. He repeatedly emphasizes that the mean is where the person of practical wisdom judges it to be.

The real question is whether virtue theory can provide guidance about what to do. Many philosophers have objected that it doesn't. If I am not a virtuous person, telling me to do what a virtuous person would do doesn't help me know what to do.

But virtue theory doesn't *aim* to provide an exact method for making decisions. Practical wisdom is not a set of rules. That doesn't mean it provides no guidance at all. It suggests we think about situations in terms of the virtues. Rather than ask 'Could everyone do this?' (as Kant suggests) or 'What will bring about the best consequences?' (as utilitarianism suggests), we can ask a series of questions: 'Would this action be kind/courageous/loyal, etc.?' If we think of actions as expressions of virtue, this could be very helpful.

What about cases in which virtues seem to conflict? For example, can we show justice and mercy, or do we have to choose? Or, again, loyalty involves sticking up for your friends even when they are wrong, while courage can involve challenging them. In these cases, Aristotle falls back on practical wisdom – you need practical wisdom first, to understand what each virtue actually requires in general (isn't challenging your friend also a form a loyalty to them?), and if this doesn't resolve the conflict, to see what to do in this particular situation.

Acquiring virtue

Aristotle argues that character is related to habit – when we act *in character*, we do what we habitually do. Acquiring a good character is a matter of acquiring morally good habits. This is a matter of training, rather than (just) teaching. It is like learning to play an instrument. Knowing the mechanics of playing the piano won't help you be able to play it. You have to actually practice. Likewise, 'by doing the acts that we do in our transactions with other men we become just or unjust, and by doing the acts that we do in the presence of danger, and by being habituated to feel fear or confidence, we become brave or cowardly'. For a good character, we have to be brought up well, because we form our characters when we are young.

A good character isn't enough for knowledge of what is right and wrong. For that, we also need practical wisdom. Only when we are both virtuous and have practical wisdom can we really be said to act virtuously. A fully virtuous action is one that requires the agent to *know* what it is she is doing, to choose the act because it is in accordance with virtue and to make the choice from a firm and unchangeable character.

Objections

Must we first acquire virtue in order to know what is good? This means that knowledge of the good is not within everyone's reach. By contrast, many philosophers argue that everyone is sufficiently rational to understand what is right, or to know what is right or wrong through their conscience.

Furthermore, if acquiring virtue depends on how we are brought up, it is not our fault that we are not virtuous and that we don't know what is good. Making moral knowledge dependent on character, and character dependent on childhood, means that we cannot hold people properly morally responsible.

Virtue theorists can respond that this overstates the case. First, we may reject the claim that character depends *entirely* on childhood. People are responsible for their characters, because they can reform them to a certain degree; and they are responsible for their actions, because they have some control over how they express their characters. Second, knowledge of the good can come in degrees. If someone has had a completely depraved childhood, perhaps they really don't know what is good or bad. But most people will have been brought up sufficiently well that they have enough understanding of the good for us to hold them morally responsible.

Going further: is it virtuous to overcome temptation?

Nevertheless, whether you are virtuous depends not just on your will, but on the habits you learned as a child. And we all find it easiest to act according to our own character. Because a virtuous person has a virtuous character, he finds it easy to do the right thing. Aristotle argues that only when the right emotions, choices, actions come naturally are we properly virtuous. But we may object that someone who finds it difficult to do the right thing, but does it anyway because it is right, shows virtue. She shows a commitment to duty (see THE MOTIVE OF DUTY, p. 82).

If the person is showing courage, then Aristotle could agree that she is virtuous. Courage involves doing an action for some good end in the face of fear. Finding the action difficult is no objection to calling the person virtuous in this case.

But in other cases, Aristotle would call this person 'strong-willed', but not virtuous. After all, she still suffers from the temptation *not* to do the right thing. If I'm tempted not to help someone, but do so anyway, am I 'generous'? No, though I'm 'acting generously' (but it is *an act*). I'm still 'virtuous', we might think. But now 'virtuous' doesn't mean 'having all the virtues', which is what Aristotle means, but 'showing a commitment to morality' and acting on it. Aristotle argues that you are truly virtuous only if this commitment penetrates through your character as a whole, not just your will.

KEY POINTS

- Virtue theory claims that ethics should focus on how we should live and what traits of character (virtues) we should develop to help us live well, not just what we should do.

- Virtue theorists argue that virtues help us flourish. The basis of ethics, then, is human nature. Because we are rational animals, living well involves living in accordance with reason. Plato argued that reason is *in charge*. Christian writers emphasized traits of the soul in relationship with God and other people.

- Philosophers have objected that virtue theory leads to relativism, as different cultures have counted different traits as virtues. Virtue theorists reply that there is some universal human nature underlying the differences that provides a critical basis for assessing cultures.

● It seems that virtues do not always help *their possessor* to live a good life. They may, alternatively, support an admirable or meaningful life; or they may help *others* to lead good lives, but at a cost to the virtuous person.

● Plato and Aristotle argue that we know what is good through reason. Plato argues that a training in philosophy is needed, as the good is highly abstract. Aristotle argues that the knowledge is so practical that it can't be taught, but requires experience.

● Aristotle's doctrine of the mean claims that virtuous traits, choices and emotions commonly lie between two vices. However, this is little use in helping us discover what is virtuous, since the mean is not the 'middle' nor the 'average' nor the 'moderate'.

● Virtue theory can't provide a method for making morally good decisions, though thinking in terms of the virtues can be helpful. If the virtues conflict, only practical wisdom will help.

● To know what is good, Plato and Aristotle argue, you must first acquire virtues of character. This depends on being brought up well.

● We may object that this makes moral knowledge and the good life available only to some people, and outside their control. Whether this undermines moral responsibility depends on whether people have *enough* moral knowledge to judge what is good or bad.

● Aristotle argues that an action is virtuous only if it comes 'naturally' to the agent. But finding it difficult to do the right thing and doing it anyway also seems virtuous.

❓ QUIZ QUESTIONS

Outline Aristotle's doctrine of the mean.

Identify and briefly describe **two** virtues. (AQA, 2a, 2001, *6 marks*)

Explain and illustrate **one** criticism of virtue theory. (AQA, 2b, 2005, *15 marks*)

❓ DISCUSSION QUESTIONS

Assess whether it is useful to focus on virtue in order to explain why we should be moral. (AQA, 2c, 2001, *24 marks*)

Assess the view that morality is concerned with virtues, not just actions.

● II PRACTICAL ETHICS

Euthanasia: voluntary, involuntary and non-voluntary; active and passive

The *New Oxford Dictionary of English* defines 'euthanasia' as 'the painless killing of a patient suffering from an incurable and painful disease or in an irreversible coma'. 'Euthanasia' comes from two Greek words, *eu-*, a prefix meaning 'good' or 'well', and *thanatos*, meaning 'death'. Literally speaking, when someone undergoes euthanasia, their death is good. Normally, for death to be good, living would need to be worse than death. Incurable painful disease and irreversible coma are two ways in which living can be worse than dying. In these cases, we might say life is not worth living.

We can distinguish six forms of euthanasia:

Involuntary euthanasia is euthanasia when the patient does not want to die. Nonvoluntary euthanasia is euthanasia when the patient has not expressed his choice; for example, if he is too young to express choices, or he can't express choices now – e.g. because of being in a coma or mentally impaired through senile dementia – and did not express his choices earlier. Voluntary euthanasia is euthanasia when the patient wants to die and has expressed this choice.

Each of these three forms can be either active or passive: active euthanasia is when the patient is killed, for instance, by a lethal injection; passive euthanasia is when the patient is allowed to die, for instance, by withholding treatment for the disease that then kills them.

Passive euthanasia does not fit the dictionary definition above, because it involves letting the patient die rather than killing them. It also doesn't fit because it can sometimes be very painful and prolonged. Active euthanasia, by contrast, is almost always painless, since very high (fatal) doses of painkillers can be given with the injection.

 QUIZ QUESTION

Briefly distinguish between active and passive euthanasia. (AQA, 2a, 2002, *6 marks*)

When, if at all, is euthanasia justified?

Morality, legality and utilitarianism

One of the most common arguments against euthanasia is the possible abuse that could happen. Patients might feel pressured into agreeing to euthanasia by families who don't want to look after them or by doctors who want to use the hospital resources for other patients. Alternatively, patients who feel depressed might choose euthanasia, when with help they could become less depressed.

These are important points. But we should distinguish the question whether voluntary euthanasia can be *morally permissible* from the question whether it should be *legalized*. The question of whether euthanasia should be legal is not our question here.

An act utilitarian considers euthanasia on a case-by-case basis. However, we might consider that the argument from abuses is relevant if we adopt a rule utilitarian approach, as rule utilitarians seek those rules that will create the greatest happiness. If making a rule that allows voluntary euthanasia could make people unhappy, this is relevant.

However, the case from abuses describes what might happen when people *don't* follow the rule on voluntary euthanasia, i.e. when they act immorally. So it turns out not to be an argument against the *morality* of voluntary euthanasia after all.

Utilitarians will not think the differences between the various forms of euthanasia are morally important unless they involve different consequences. The only important question is whether euthanasia creates more happiness (or less suffering) than preventing it. Involuntary euthanasia is clearly different from voluntary euthanasia, since the person does not want to die – so is 'made unhappy' by his or her death (or at least by the prospect of death). It might still be right, if the person's life really will contain more unhappiness than happiness. But if a person wants to stay alive, it is very difficult to make this claim. People commonly agree that, because it is important for us to be able to make choices about things that matter to us, involuntary euthanasia will almost always turn out to be wrong. Voluntary euthanasia, however, will be right in those cases in which it maximizes happiness. The only question is whose happiness should be considered.

Deontology

Kant argued that people who commit suicide destroy their rationality in service to something else – pain. And our rationality is more valuable than anything else. So suicide and asking for euthanasia do not show respect for our own rationality; they do not treat it as an end in itself. But this doesn't deal with cases in which the reason why someone requests euthanasia is that they are about to lose their rational faculties (as in advanced Alzheimer's disease) or cases in which someone doesn't have any rational faculties (where children are born without a complete brain).

We may agree that rationality is what bestows *dignity* on human beings, and we must respect people's dignity. Therefore, a human being who may lose her dignity and her rationality through illness and pain may legitimately request euthanasia. We respect and protect her dignity by helping her die in circumstances of her own choosing. This is one of the most powerful arguments for voluntary euthanasia.

But deontologists don't argue that we should always respect someone's choice when what she wants is morally wrong; sometimes it is morally right to prevent her from doing what she wants. So voluntary euthanasia could still be wrong if asking to die is morally wrong.

Active v. passive euthanasia in deontology and virtue ethics

If voluntary euthanasia is ever morally permissible, is there a moral difference between active and passive euthanasia? An act utilitarian may argue that there is not. In both cases, the person dies. All that matters is that he doesn't suffer. However, other theories argue that there is a difference.

Not killing someone is related to the virtue and duties of *justice*. Justice requires that we *respect* people, their choices and rights. Not letting someone die is related to the virtue and duties of *charity*. Charity requires that we help other people's lives go well. For example, people all over the world are dying from hunger and disease. It is difficult to argue that because you did not give more to charity you have done something as bad as if you had actually *killed* them yourself.

However, there are some cases in which letting someone die is equivalent to killing him, e.g. when you have a duty to provide food or medicine to someone and you do not. A parent who didn't give her child food would be guilty of murder. In such a case, both justice and charity require the same thing, and so there is no practical difference between killing and letting someone die.

Is there a practical difference in the case of euthanasia? Normally, killing is forbidden by justice as it violates the person's choice; but in voluntary euthanasia, respecting the person's choice means killing him or her. But some deontologists argue that we have a duty not to kill human beings, even if the person who dies requests it. This is one interpretation of the idea of the *sanctity of life*, that we must respect someone's right to life even when she wants to die. These deontologists may allow passive euthanasia, but not active euthanasia.

Many doctors think that the idea of administering lethal injections goes against the idea and duties of practising medicine. However, in addition to the duty to protect the lives of their patients, doctors also have the duty to do what is best for their patients, including relieving pain. One way of trying to respect both duties at once is to allow the patient to die while doing everything possible to ensure their death is painless. In cases in which passive euthanasia is painful, giving large doses of painkillers is permissible, even if this actually causes them to die sooner. (So to *intend* to kill someone is always wrong; but the intention here is to relieve pain.)

But does the duty to protect life involve the duty to prolong life for as long as possible, even if the quality of life is very poor? If so, then active euthanasia is permitted if doctors must always do what is best for their patients, and death can be what is best. At this point, virtue theory may appeal to virtues such as mercy and compassion to permit euthanasia.

● **KEY POINTS**

- Act utilitarianism argues that there is no relevant difference between the different forms of euthanasia unless they lead to different amounts of happiness. Involuntary euthanasia is likely to cause much more unhappiness than voluntary euthanasia. However, there is little difference between active and passive voluntary euthanasia; in fact, passive euthanasia tends to cause more pain, so active euthanasia should be preferred.

- Rule utilitarianism takes into account whether a rule permitting voluntary euthanasia would lead to more happiness than one prohibiting it. Opponents argue that permitting euthanasia could be open to abuse. However, this is only an objection to legalizing euthanasia, not to its being morally permissible.

● Deontological views present arguments both for and against voluntary euthanasia. One argument against is that seeking euthanasia values pain more highly than rationality. But a response is that, when one is about to lose one's reason, euthanasia enables a dignified death.

● Both deontology and virtue ethics see a difference between active and passive voluntary euthanasia. Killing someone usually violates the duty and virtue of justice, while not letting someone die does not. We may therefore violate no duty in letting someone die.

● However, if the sanctity of life principle is mistaken, it may not be unjust to kill someone who requests it, so active voluntary euthanasia may also be permissible, and may also be more compassionate.

❓ QUIZ QUESTIONS

Outline **one** argument for the claim that there is a morally relevant difference between active and passive euthanasia.

Outline and illustrate **one** deontological argument against voluntary euthanasia.

Explain how, in any **one** situation, killing might be seen as a virtuous act. (AQA, 2b, 2001, *15 marks*)

❓ DISCUSSION QUESTIONS

Assess whether utilitarianism supports the view that voluntary euthanasia is morally permissible.

Assess deontological ethics with reference to any **one** of: euthanasia; **or** abortion; **or** animal rights. (AQA, 2c, 2004, *24 marks*)

Abortion

Abortion is the termination of a pregnancy. We usually use the term to refer to the deliberate termination of a pregnancy, but in medicine, a miscarriage is also called a 'spontaneous abortion'. Our concern is with deliberate abortion.

A woman becomes pregnant when a sperm fertilizes one of her eggs ('conception'). The fertilized egg is a 'zygote' until it implants in the wall of her uterus, five to seven days later. It is now called an 'embryo' until eight weeks old, when it is called a 'foetus'. However, I use the term 'foetus' for the developing organism at all stages from conception to birth.

What is the moral status of the foetus? How is demarcation between fertilized egg, foetus, infant and adult possible?

Deontology and rights

People who oppose abortion usually claim that the foetus has a right to life, because it is a human being and all human beings have a right to life. This is a deontological argument. But why should we think that all human beings have a right to life? Many people don't think that animals have a right to life, since they are happy to eat them; what is special about being human?

One thing that would make us special is that we have a soul, while animals do not. The traditional point at which we are said to acquire souls is conception. Two facts are worth noting. First, two-thirds of zygotes are spontaneously aborted, i.e. rejected naturally by the uterus. If each is made special by the presence of a soul, that seems a moral tragedy. Second, some types of contraception, such as the IUD (intra-uterine device) and certain types of contraceptive pill, work by changing the lining of the uterus so that fertilized eggs cannot implant in it. These methods of contraception do not stop eggs being fertilized. If abortion is wrong because a being with a soul is prevented from developing, then these types of contraception are equally wrong.

Drawing the line

Once we allow that abortion immediately after conception is permissible, we are faced with the difficulty of trying to find a point at which to draw the line. The foetus develops a little each day until it is born, and after that the child develops a little each day until it is an adult with reason and rights. So how is it possible to say 'Now the foetus does not have a right to life. Now it does'? At any point where we draw the line, the foetus is not very different just before this point and just after this point.

One way to solve this difficulty is to consider why human beings might have a right to life. The things that come to mind – such as reason, the use of language, the depth of our emotional experience, our self-awareness, our ability to distinguish right and wrong – are not things that a foetus yet has. But many other human beings, including those with severe mental disabilities and senile dementia, also don't have these characteristics. Yet we do not normally think it is permissible to kill them.

There is one important characteristic we do all share, and that a foetus acquires around 20–24 weeks, and that is *sentience*. Sentience is the primitive consciousness of perception, pleasure and pain. If the right to life depends on sentience, then a foetus has a right to life from around 20 weeks, but not before. However, if we choose this quality as the basis for a right to life, it means that many animals have a right to life as well (see ANIMAL RIGHTS, p. 98).

The argument from potential

If the foetus does not have the characteristics that give someone a right to life, we might argue that, unlike animals, it will have them if it is allowed to develop. It has a right to life now because it has the *potential* to become a person with a right to life in the future.

But we may object, first, that the sperm and the egg that combined to form the foetus also had the potential to become a person. If it is potential that matters, then contraception of any form would be as wrong as abortion. An obvious reply to this is that the sperm and egg don't form a natural *unit* for us to ascribe potential to. But why think that it is only the potential of natural units that matters?

Second, it is not normal to treat potential as though it was already realized. Someone who has only the potential to become a teacher is not yet a teacher, and should not be put in charge of lessons. Someone who has the potential to become a millionaire cannot spend the money yet.

● **KEY POINTS**

- Many arguments regarding abortion focus on the moral status of the foetus, in particular whether it has a right to life.

- Unless we give all human beings, including foetuses, a right to life, we have to say that we acquire it at some point. But when, and on the basis of what property? One suggestion is sentience.

- Some philosophers argue that foetuses have a right to life because they have the potential to become human adults. But we do not extend rights to something that is only potentially a future rights-holder.

❓ QUIZ QUESTION

Explain the moral importance of sentience.

❓ DISCUSSION QUESTION

Assess the claim that abortion is wrong because the foetus is a potential person.

On what grounds, if any, might abortion be permissible?

Deontology and rights continued

We have considered whether, if a foetus does not have a right to life, it may be morally permissible to abort it. Do any other considerations support this? Yes: we generally think that people have a right to do what they want with their bodies and what to do in their lives. The foetus is part of (or at least within) the woman's body; it cannot survive without her body. If she has a right to choose what to do with her body, and the foetus has no right to life, then she is not acting wrongly if she chooses to have an abortion. Second, having a child will make a very big difference to her life. We can argue that since she has the right to choose how to live, she has the right to choose not to have a child, especially if she is not responsible for becoming pregnant (e.g. cases of rape or failed contraception).

However, we may object that this argument does not apply once the foetus is able to survive outside the woman's body, a stage known as *viability*. After viability the foetus could be delivered, kept alive outside the woman's body, and put up for adoption. This could make it wrong to abort the foetus.

What if the foetus *does* have a right to life? This doesn't mean abortion is automatically and always wrong. Before viability, at least, the rights of the woman may outweigh the foetus's right to life.

Act utilitarianism

Act utilitarianism asks us to consider happiness in the two situations of abortion and giving birth. The possible consequences are so complex, it is difficult to say what might happen. However, we normally believe it is better to be alive than not alive. So the future life of the foetus weighs heavily in its favour, and certainly outweighs the inconvenience to the woman of carrying the pregnancy to term and then putting the baby up for adoption. But there is a question whether the *future* experience or preferences of the foetus *count now*, because before sentience it is not yet a being with the ability to experience pleasure and pain. Utilitarianism doesn't give us an obvious answer about future beings.

Virtue theory

Virtue theory takes a very different approach. The discussion so far seems to treat women as containers for a foetus rather than creators of a life out of their own bodies. The *meaning* of pregnancy and abortion are not explored.

Rosalind Hursthouse argues that to think of an abortion as though the foetus does not matter is callous and shows a lack of appreciation for the type of being a foetus is – that it is quite literally one's flesh and blood, developing from oneself. It shows the wrong attitude to human life, death and parenthood. But this doesn't automatically make all abortions wrong. If a woman has an abortion because she fears she cannot afford to feed the child or because she has a very demanding job and may neglect it, this is not a callous thought. However, the fact that she prioritizes her job above children may indicate that her priorities in life are wrong, that she hasn't understood the value of parenthood. But it depends on the particular case. It may be that the woman leads a very worthwhile, fulfilling life, and cannot fit motherhood into the other activities that make her life as good as it is. For virtue ethics, then, each abortion is an individual case, involving an individual woman in a unique set of circumstances. Each case must be judged by its own merits.

● **KEY POINTS**

- A woman's right to choose what to do with her body and her life supports the claim that she is not wrong to have an abortion, at least before viability. These same rights may even outweigh any right to life the foetus has.

- Act utilitarianism considers whether abortion would create more happiness than giving birth. However, it is unclear whether we should count the potential happiness of the foetus if it isn't sentient at the time of the abortion.

- Virtue theory emphasizes the meaning of birth and abortion in human life. It suggests that there may be virtuous motives for having an abortion, and whether a particular abortion is right or wrong will depend on these.

❓ QUIZ QUESTIONS

Outline and illustrate **one** deontological argument against abortion.

Explain how, in any **one** situation, killing might be seen as a virtuous act. (AQA, 2b, 2001, *15 marks*)

❓ DISCUSSION QUESTIONS

Assess whether utilitarianism supports the view that abortion is morally permissible.

Assess deontological ethics with reference to any **one** of: euthanasia; **or** abortion; **or** animal rights. (AQA, 2c, 2004, *24 marks*)

Animal rights: on what grounds, if any, should non-human animals be included in our moral thinking and with what consequences?

Utilitarianism

Peter Singer argues that the way we commonly treat animals – for food, clothing and medical experimentation – is not morally justifiable. We do not think that it is right to treat women worse than men just because they are women (this is sexism), nor to treat one race worse than another (this is racism). Likewise, it is wrong to treat animals differently just because they are not human. This is 'speciesism'.

There is a disanalogy here. With women and men, and different races, there is no difference in those important capacities – reason, the use of language, the depth of our emotional experience, our self-awareness, our ability to distinguish right and wrong – that make a being a person. But there is a difference between human beings and animals with all of these.

Singer argues that these differences are not relevant when it comes to the important capacity that human beings and animals share, viz. sentience. He quotes Bentham: 'The question is not, Can they *reason*? nor Can they *talk*? but, *Can they suffer*?' For a utilitarian, an act (or rule) is wrong if it produces more suffering than an alternative. Who is suffering is irrelevant. When it comes to suffering, animals should be treated as equal to people.

Does this mean that we should prohibit eating meat, wearing leather and animal experiments? Not necessarily. There is first the question of whether stopping these practices would reduce the amount of (animal) suffering in the world more than it would increase (human) suffering.

Second, the utilitarian position objects only to suffering, not to *killing*. This leads to the 'container' view of life: an animal's life is only valuable because of the happiness it contains. If you painlessly kill an animal and bring another animal into being (as is done when rearing animals), you haven't reduced the total amount of happiness in the world. Utilitarianism implies making sure that animals are happy when they are alive and slaughtering them painlessly. This would make eating meat much more expensive, because animals would have to be kept in much better conditions. Eating meat isn't always wrong, but it is wrong at the moment if animals are not treated as well as they could be.

But if killing animals is permissible on this theory, what about babies? We don't think that killing babies, using them for food or experiments, is morally permissible, yet babies are no different in their psychological capacities than many animals. Is it speciesist to think there is a real difference here?

Deontology

Deontologists argue that killing human beings is wrong because they have a right to life. Having rights is related to our rationality and choices – they protect the *space* which we need in order to make free, rational choices. Animals don't make choices the way we do, so they don't have rights.

But babies also aren't rational and are yet to make free choices and some people with severe mental disabilities never do. If they have a right to life, and do not have different psychological capacities from certain animals, then to deny those animals a right to life would be speciesist. With any property that only human beings have that justify a right to life, some human beings won't have it. For any psychological property that all human beings have, some animals also have that same property.

Tom Regan argues that to have a right to life, a creature needs only to be a 'subject of a life'. By this he means to have beliefs, desires, emotions, perception, memory, the ability to act (though not necessarily free choice) and a psychological identity over time. If a creature has these abilities, there is a way its life goes *for* it, and this matters *to* it. A right to life protects this. Although we can't know exactly which animals meet this criterion, we can be sure that almost all mammals (including humans) over the age of a year do so.

Because these animals have a right to life, Regan argues, we cannot kill them for any reason less important than saving life. Because we do not need to eat meat or wear leather to live, we should not use animals for these purposes. Regan also argues that an animal's right to life is equal to a human being's. We do not normally discriminate between 'more valuable' and 'less valuable' human lives, even though some people are capable of much greater things than others. So we should not discriminate between 'more valuable' human lives and 'less valuable' animal lives. This means we cannot justify medical experiments that involve killing animals by the human lives the experiment may help save.

Regan's view is very counter-intuitive. Our intuitive judgements that the lives of human beings are more valuable than those of animals, and that it is permissible to kill an animal when we *need* to, are very strong. But it is not usually permissible to violate a right just because one needs to. So, we might conclude, animals can't have the right to life, though perhaps they have the right not to be caused unnecessary suffering.

Virtue theory

But is the speciesism argument valid in the first place? Virtue ethics encourages us to think further about human nature and our place in the natural world. 'Speciesism' isn't the only case where we *naturally* privilege those closest to us. We also privilege our families and friends, and we are loyal to the places we grow up in and the companies we work for. None of this seems morally objectionable. Perhaps it is not *just* the capacities of the being that determine how we should treat it, but also our *relationship* to it. There is a moral importance to bonding, the creation of special ties with particular others. Our bond to other human beings is special because we share humanity.

The capacities of a being are still very important. To treat another being that is rational as though it is not rational is to show it disrespect. Not to recognize that it can suffer is to show a lack of compassion. To treat a living creature as a meat-growing machine or experimental object is likewise to display a relationship with it that resembles selfishness, because we reduce it from what it is in itself to something that exists only for our sake.

Does this mean that eating meat and animal experiments are wrong? Virtue ethics has left us without a clear answer, but with a sense of the difficulty of the question.

●

KEY POINTS

- Singer, a utilitarian, argues that the differences between animals and human beings do not justify how we treat animals. What matters is that animals can suffer; who is suffering is irrelevant, and to think otherwise is speciesism. However, babies have the same mental capacities as many animals; are we permitted to treat them the same way?

- Utilitarianism claims that whether eating meat or animal experimentation is wrong depends on whether it produces more suffering than alternatives. Killing an animal painlessly, if you bring another animal into existence, won't reduce happiness, so is permissible.

- Many deontologists argue that rights protect our rational choices; as animals don't make rational choices, they don't have rights. But this is also true of babies, so do they have no rights?

- Regan argues that any creature that is a 'subject of a life' has a right to life. The right to life is equal in all cases. However, our intuition that human lives are more valuable than animal lives is very strong.

● Virtue theory brings out the dependence of morality on relationship (not just capacities), and defends partiality. It also emphasizes the importance of respect and compassion in our treatment of animals.

❓ QUIZ QUESTIONS

Outline and illustrate **one** deontological argument against killing animals for food.

Explain how, in any **one** situation, killing might be seen as a virtuous act. (AQA, 2b, 2001, *15 marks*)

❓ DISCUSSION QUESTIONS

Assess whether utilitarianism supports the view that killing animals for food is morally permissible.

Assess deontological ethics with reference to any **one** of: euthanasia; **or** abortion; **or** animal rights. (AQA, 2c, 2003, *24 marks*)

Answering exam questions on practical ethics

Unlike other areas of philosophy, practical ethics touches on everyday life immediately. So it is easy to slip out of doing good philosophy into thinking in more 'everyday' ways. Doing well in exam questions on practical ethics involves thinking hard about the question in a philosophical way. Here are some tips to help:

1   While the facts are important, just talking about the facts is not philosophy. Nor is repeating what people generally say or feel about these cases. You are not doing social science, but discussing ultimate *justifications*.

2   Because whether an action is right or wrong may well depend on just what the facts are, and as philosophers, we may not know all the facts, philosophical arguments are often 'conditional'. It is not just acceptable, but good, to say: 'If it turns out like this, then this follows (the action is right/wrong).' Avoid lengthy discussions of how it turns out. For example, you might say: 'If a woman's life is harmed by having a child now, abortion is right'; don't discuss whether her life would actually be harmed, how it 'might happen' that she comes to love the child, and so on.

3   Avoid oversimplification wherever possible. Practical moral issues are very complex. In particular, if you are evaluating a theory by its success in practical cases, as in the question 'Assess deontology with reference to abortion', the complexity is crucial to being fair. In thinking about this, consider whether practical ethics *ought* to be easy or not. Can we expect clear rules and algorithmic decision procedures in life? Is the presence of grey areas really a failure in practical ethics? Virtue theory suggests not.

4   Likewise, try to avoid objections that just point out our ignorance. For example, 'Who knows what consequences follow from an abortion?' is not helpful. This move is simply a refusal to do philosophy. A consequentialist will quickly reply that we must simply

do our best to work out the consequences. The same with 'Who is to say what is right?' *You* as a philosopher are to say what is right, as you see it and to the best of your ability (this is not arrogance, but the contribution of a rational human being to a rational debate).

5   Make a distinction between morality and legality. Whether a practice should be legalized is a separate debate from whether it is morally acceptable. There are many legal practices that are not morally acceptable (betraying your friends), and there may well be illegal practices that are morally acceptable (euthanasia).

6   Separate metaethical issues from practical issues. So relativism and subjectivism should be kept out of discussions of practical ethics as far as possible. The premiss of practical ethics is that we are searching for the (or a) right thing to do. Challenging this premiss is unhelpful in this context.

● III META-ETHICS: COGNITIVISM

Meta-ethics is the study of ethical concepts, such as right and wrong, good and bad, and of sentences that use these concepts. Cognitivism is the view that we can have moral *knowledge*. One main cognitivist theory, moral realism, claims that good and bad are properties of situations and people, right and wrong are properties of actions. Just as people can be five feet tall or run fast, they can be morally good or bad. Just as actions can be done in ten minutes or done from greed, they can be right or wrong. These moral properties are a genuine part of the world.

Intuitionism: goodness and rightness are not understandable in terms of natural properties but are metaphysically real and intuited

G. E. Moore and W. D. Ross argued that we come to know about moral properties by *intuition*. As we discussed Ross's theory in DEONTOLOGICAL VIEWS (p. 72), we will concentrate on Moore here.

Moore and the naturalistic fallacy

In *Principia Ethica*, Moore argued against the claim that moral properties are natural properties. For example, a preference utilitarian might say that what is bad about murder *just is* the frustration of the victim's preferences. Goodness is maximizsing the satisfaction of people's preferences. And whether people's preferences are satisfied is a natural (psychological) fact.

Moore called the attempt to equate goodness with any natural property the *naturalistic fallacy*. Goodness, he claimed, is a simple and unanalysable property. It cannot be defined in terms of anything else. Colours are similar. Blue is a simple property, and no one can explain what blue is, you have to see it for yourself to understand what blue is. But unlike colours, goodness is a *non*-natural property. It is not part of the natural world, the world of science; but it is part of reality. (If we have souls, these aren't part of the natural world, but they are part of reality.)

Moore's main argument for believing that it is a **fallacy** – a mistake – to identify goodness with a natural property is the 'open-question argument'. If goodness just is happiness, then it wouldn't make sense to ask 'Is it good to make people happy?' This would be like asking 'Does what makes people happy make people happy?'. This second question isn't a real question (the answer has to be 'yes'), but 'Is it good to make people happy?' is a real question – the answer can logically be 'yes' or 'no'. And so goodness cannot be happiness, or any other property. 'Is x good?' is always a real question while 'Is x x?' is not. And so goodness cannot be any other property.

Going further: is the 'naturalistic fallacy' a real fallacy?

This argument doesn't work. Here is a similar argument. 'The property of being water cannot be any property in the world, such as the property of being H_2O. If it was then the question "Is water H_2O?" would not make sense – it would be like asking "Is H_2O H_2O?" So water is a simple, unanalysable property.' This is not right, as water *just is* H_2O.

The reason the argument doesn't work is that it confuses *concepts* and *properties*. Two different concepts – water and H_2O – can pick out the same property in the world. You knew about water before you knew it was H_2O – during this time, you had the concept of water, but not the concept of H_2O. So they are different concepts, but they both refer to the same thing. Likewise, the concept 'goodness' is a different concept from 'happiness', but perhaps they are exactly the same property in the world. We may doubt this for other reasons, but the point is that the open-question argument does not show that they are different.

'Intuition' and self-evident judgements

Nevertheless, perhaps Moore is right that goodness is a non-natural property. After all, for something to be good or right is quite different from its being heavy or 'over there' (see next section). If values are non-natural properties, how do we know about them? Moore's answer is 'intuition'. Basic judgements about what is good, e.g. pleasure, beauty, etc., are intuitions. They are **self-evident** judgements.

A self-evident judgement has no other evidence or proof but its own plausibility. This doesn't necessarily mean that everyone can immediately see that it is true. 'Self-evident' is not the same as 'obvious'. Our ability to make these judgements needs to develop first, and we need to consider the question very carefully.

The difficulty with 'self-evident' judgements is that people disagree about whether they are true or not. Moore thought it was self-evident that pleasure is good and that maximizing the good is right. Ross, on the other hand, thought it was self-evident that there are times when it is wrong to maximize pleasure. The problem is, because the judgements are supposed to be self-evident, we cannot give any further reasons for believing them.

But this doesn't mean we can reject the idea of self-evidentiality. Suppose we *could* give reasons for thinking that pleasure is good, e.g. because it forms part of a flourishing life for human beings. Is it self-evident that being part of a flourishing life makes something good? If not, we need to give a further reason for this judgement. And we can ask the same question of any further reason we give. And so on, forever. It seems that if judgements about what is good are not self-evident, then judgements about what counts as a reason for thinking something is good must be. (See Ch. 1, FOUNDATIONALISM, p. 28.)

Some philosophers suggest an alternative: judgements about what counts as a reason depend on a particular set of beliefs that are not being questioned at the moment. When we then question those beliefs, we can give reasons for believing any one belief or judgement at once, but must in turn assume others. This way no judgement is self-evident, because it can be supported by others. Why should we believe *any* of the judgements in the set? Because the set as a whole is coherent and makes sense of our experience. (See Ch. 1, COHERENTISM, p. 33.)

We discuss objections to intuitionism in ASSOCIATED PROBLEMS (p. 107).

Going further: updating intuitionism

Moore's idea of an 'intuition' seems quite mysterious, especially because Moore claims that moral properties are not natural properties. Our usual ways of knowing things are no good here. Some recent philosophers, inspired by VIRTUE THEORY (p. 84), have argued that it is our *emotions*, together with practical wisdom, that give us this kind of intuitive knowledge. For example, if I am courageous in sport, then I can feel pain or fear – which tells me something bad is happening or may happen – yet I continue to push myself anyway, because I also feel the importance and good of achievement. Virtuous feelings are actually kinds of cognition – cognitions of values.

● **KEY POINTS**

- Moore argued that the claim that moral properties are some type of natural property (e.g. good = greatest happiness) is a 'naturalistic fallacy'. If they were, then e.g. 'Is the greatest happiness good?' would be a meaningless question. But it isn't.

- However, Moore shows only that moral concepts are distinct from natural concepts. He doesn't show that moral concepts don't refer to a natural property.

- Moore concluded that moral properties are simple and unanalysable, and we know them through moral intuition, which makes self-evident judgements.

❓ QUIZ QUESTIONS

Explain and illustrate what a self-evident judgement is.

Outline Moore's 'naturalistic fallacy' argument.

Moral realism: moral claims correspond to, and describe, objective properties

Moral realism is perhaps the *common-sense* position on ethics for many people. Many people believe that things really are right or wrong; it is not our views that make them right or wrong. People are, of course, also aware of cultural differences in moral beliefs, a fact that can lead some to give up moral realism for relativism (see THE EXISTENCE OF MORAL RELATIVISM, p. 110). But tolerance of cultural differences tends to be quite limited. For example, very few people seem to think that because murder of members of other tribes or female circumcision is morally permitted in some societies, that makes murder or female circumcision right, even in those societies.

The moral realist believes that statements like 'Euthanasia is not wrong' are expressions of beliefs, which can be true or false. Whether such statements are true or false depends on the way that the world is, on what properties an action, person or situation actually has. They must 'fit the facts'.

Moral experience

Moral realists argue that our experience of morality suggests moral realism. First, we think we can make mistakes. Children frequently do, and have to be taught what is right and wrong. If there were no facts about moral right and wrong, it wouldn't be possible to make mistakes. Second, morality feels like a demand from *outside* us. We feel answerable to a standard of behaviour which is independent of what we want. Morality isn't determined by what we think about it. Third, many people believe in moral progress. But how is this possible, unless some views about morality are better than others? And how is *that* possible unless there are facts about morality?

Facts and values

But if there are facts about right and wrong, what sorts of facts are they? Moore's argument for the naturalistic fallacy tries to draw a distinction between natural facts and moral values. But Moore still believed there were 'facts' about these values, i.e. he believed that moral properties existed as part of reality, and that beliefs about moral properties could be true or false.

While Moore emphasized the distinctiveness of moral facts, most moral realists claim that there is a close relationship between natural facts and moral facts. VIRTUE THEORY (p. 84) provides one account of how this might work. It claims that whether an act is right depends on whether it is what a virtuous person would do. A virtuous person is someone who has the virtues, traits of character, that enable him or her to live a good life. What a good life is depends on human nature, and this is a matter of objective fact. So moral facts are closely related to human nature, our universal desires, our needs and our ability to reason. Moral facts exist in virtue of natural facts. However, virtue theorists disagree over whether moral facts themselves are natural facts (is what 'a good life' is a *natural* fact?) or whether Moore is right that moral facts are distinct.

The deeper puzzle is how a value (a moral 'fact') can be *any* type of fact. Values are related to evaluations. If no one valued anything, would there be any values? Facts are part of the world. The fact that dinosaurs roamed the Earth millions of years ago would be true whether anyone had found out about it or not. But it is more difficult to believe that values *exist* independently of us and our talk about values.

This contrast is unfair. There are lots of facts – for example, facts about being in love, or facts about music – that *depend* on human beings and their activities (there would be no love if no one loved anything). But they are still facts, because they are independent of our judgements, and made true by the way the world, in this case the human world, is. You can make mistakes about whether someone is in love or whether a piece of music is baroque or classical.

KEY POINTS

- Moral realism argues that moral judgements express beliefs and are made true or false by how the world is. Actions and people can have objective moral properties.

- Moral realism appeals to our experience of morality: we feel we can make mistakes, that moral demands are independent of us, that moral progress is possible.

- While intuitionism emphasizes the distinction between moral and natural facts, virtue theory illustrates one way in which moral facts might depend on non-moral facts, as what is virtuous depends on human nature. Moral facts could even be a form of natural fact.

❓ QUIZ QUESTIONS

Briefly explain the claim that there are moral facts.

Explain and illustrate the cognitivist view that we can know moral facts. (AQA, 1b, 2003, *15 marks*)

Associated problems: whether moral disputes can be resolved by appeals to fact; the is–ought gap and attempts to bridge it; the link between (external) moral values and action

Values still seem different from facts about love and music, and we can make three objections to moral realism, inspired by David Hume.

First, when two people disagree over a matter of fact, whether it is about the natural world (dinosaurs) or the human world (love), we normally know how we could prove the matter one way or the other. Facts are things that can be shown to be true. But if two people agree over all the natural facts about abortion, say, but still disagree about whether it is right, we cannot appeal to any more 'facts' in the same way. What we would call 'the facts' seem to be *all* agreed, but the dispute about values remains. Value judgements always go beyond the facts. And appealing to 'intuition' doesn't help, since we can't *investigate* the truth of intuitions!

Hume argues that the moral judgement, the 'intuition', doesn't pick out a fact, it expresses a feeling, which is why you can't reach moral agreement just by discussing the facts. Disagreeing about values seems to be quite different from disagreeing about facts. So values aren't facts.

One implication of this is that there are no moral experts, because there are no moral facts for anyone to know. Instead, moral judgements are expressions of our emotions (EMOTIVISM, p. 112), personal principles (PRESCRIPTIVISM, p. 115), or choices (see Ch. 7, RELATION OF CHOICE TO VALUE, p. 305).

A second objection, sometimes also known as the *is–ought gap*, plays on the distinction between (natural) facts and values that Moore noted with his open-question argument: no fact can logically entail a moral value. Whatever facts you get together to support your moral judgement, you cannot logically infer the judgement. Hume notes that there always seems to be a leap in moral reasoning. We describe the facts of the case, and then we suddenly say 'he ought not to have done that': 'this *ought* . . . expresses some new relation [of which it] seems altogether inconceivable, how this new relation can be a deduction from others, which are entirely different from it'.

The third objection can provide an explanation for this. Moral judgements guide our behaviour. If I think pleasure is good, I aim to bring about pleasure. If I think abortion is wrong, I will not commit or encourage others to commit abortion. Moral motivation seems puzzling if the moral realist is correct. A fact, in and of itself, doesn't lead to action. It seems that I need to *care* about the fact, and then the motivating force comes from the caring. If a fact could motivate me, just by itself, how strange would that be?

Hume argued that in order to act, we need beliefs, about how the world is and how to change it, and a desire, in order to be motivated to change it. For example, the fact that it is raining doesn't motivate me to pick up my umbrella unless I don't want to get wet. But surely, claims this objection, statements about right and wrong, good and bad, are motivating *in their own right*. But in that case, they are not like beliefs (about facts), they are like desires.

Moral facts are reasons

The objections are powerful against Moore intuitionism. But other forms of moral realism can respond by pointing to the connection between facts and values. We always appeal to the facts when we are trying to justify a moral judgement. If there were no connection, this would seem silly. But we can give *reasons* that support our moral claims, e.g. that eating meat is wrong because of the suffering it causes to animals. It is either true or false that the practice of eating meat causes suffering to animals. This may be hard to prove, but we know roughly *how* to prove it. So facts can be reasons that support moral beliefs.

The moral realist claims that this relation 'X is a reason to believe Y *is either true or false*. Moral realists claim there are facts about the reasons we give for our moral judgements. Like all facts, these facts about reasons are part of the way the world is. It can be difficult to establish whether a natural fact constitutes a reason for believing something is right or wrong, and how strong this reason is. But this is the case in all types of investigation into reality.

Going further: reasons as facts

Compare reasons for other types of belief. If radiometric decay indicates that dinosaur bones are 65 million years old, this is a reason to believe that dinosaurs lived on Earth 65 million years ago. It is not *proof*, perhaps, but it is a reason. (Reasons can come in different strengths – there can be good reasons, really good reasons and proof. Bad reasons are not actually reasons at all.) The result of the radiometric dating of dinosaur bones is a reason to think dinosaurs lived on Earth 65 million years ago, whether you think it is a reason or not. Facts about reasons are objective, just like facts about the natural world. But facts about reasons are another *type* of fact.

What type? Well, it is not a fact that science can discover. There is no scientific investigation into what reasons there are. But this doesn't mean it is not part of reality. Philosophers would say facts about reasons are **normative** facts. They are facts about justification and reasoning.

Answering the objections

Resolving disputes: we said that two people agree on all the 'facts' about abortion, but disagree on whether it is wrong. The realist's reply here is that it is true to say we can't resolve moral disputes by appealing to facts if you are only talking about *natural* facts. But there are other types of fact that people are disagreeing on, viz. facts about reasons. For example, is the fact that the foetus will become a human being a (strong) reason for thinking abortion is wrong? If we resolved the disagreement about both natural facts and what counts as a reason for what, people would agree on the moral judgement as well. One of them is making a mistake, because he or she is not seeing certain natural facts as reasons at all or, at least, not seeing them as strong reasons. (*If* some people are better than others at discovering what reasons there are, then there can be moral experts. But moral realism doesn't commit itself to this.)

The is–ought gap: there is a gap between natural facts and moral judgements, and unless we recognize facts about reasons, then the objection is *right* to say we can't get from one to the other. But whether a natural fact counts as a reason for believing a certain value judgement is itself a matter of objective fact. It is still true that natural facts don't logically *entail* value judgements, but then it is rare for reasons to entail the judgements they support.

Moral motivation: there are two possible responses here. The first is to claim that moral judgements are *not* motivating. There certainly seem to be people – and perhaps all of us at certain times, e.g. when we are depressed – for whom statements about morality are not motivating. They just don't care about morality. Moral judgements, then, are only motivating to people who care about morality. Since most of us do most of the time, it is easy to think that the judgements are motivating on their own.

The second response is to agree that moral judgements are motivating. And this would be a puzzle if they were judgements about natural facts. But they are not; they are judgements about what we have reason to do. And judgements about reasons are motivating on their own, because we are rational creatures.

But isn't the idea of values existing in the world like facts a very strange notion? Realists will deny that they claim anything strange at all. If Moore was right, then perhaps moral values are strange. But values can be understood in terms of facts about reasons. And we need these even to do science. Reasons aren't strange. For example, virtue theorists claim that certain facts about being human means that a certain way of living is the best, most flourishing life. We therefore have reason to develop our characters in ways that allow us to live like this and meet ours and other people's needs. More simply, utilitarians claim that pleasure gives us a reason to try to create it (it is good).

● **KEY POINTS**

- Moral realism can reply to many objections by arguing that moral facts are reasons. We need to accept that reasons are objective for any form of reasoning, e.g. science.

- Objection: values, and *oughts*, seem very different from facts. In particular, two people can agree on all the facts and disagree on the moral judgement. Reply: the two people are disagreeing whether and how the facts are reasons.

- Objection: the is–ought gap: moral judgements cannot be logically inferred from (natural) facts. Reply: this is true, but it doesn't mean that natural facts aren't reasons in support of a moral judgement; it just means the support isn't entailment.

- Objection: motivation: moral judgements guide and motivate us to act in particular ways. But facts are not motivating – I need to care about a fact. Moral judgements are therefore more like expressions of desire or emotion than of belief. Reply: *either* beliefs about reasons are motivating if we are rational; *or* moral judgements are expressions of belief, but aren't motivating, as we also have to care about morality.

❓ QUIZ QUESTIONS

Describe and illustrate **one** account of how moral language can guide or influence action. (AQA, 1b, 2001, *15 marks*)

Briefly explain **two** reasons for believing that there are no moral facts. (AQA, 1a, 2002, *6 marks*)

❓ DISCUSSION QUESTIONS

Assess the view that we can't get an 'ought' from an 'is'. (AQA, 1c, 2003, *24 marks*)

Assess the claim that intuitionism entails that we are unable to resolve moral disputes.

The existence of moral relativism

All relativism starts with disagreement; but disagreement isn't enough for relativism. If two people disagree, one could be wrong. It's the same with cultures. There are two ways of understanding ethical disagreements between cultures. We can either say that different cultures, with their different ethical practices, their different ethical concepts, their different ethical judgements, are all trying to get at the *truth* about ethics, just as scientists are trying to find out the truth about the world. Or we can say that ethical practices are simply part of a culture's *way of living*. The relativist will say the latter, claiming that two cultures that disagree over a moral practice or judgement are actually making claims that are each 'true for them'.

Relativism in ethics is more attractive to many people than relativism about scientific claims. To understand why, we should look at the nature of disagreement in science and ethics. In particular, how can we understand what would explain an *end* to disagreement in each case? With science, the best explanation is that the scientific theories we have agreed on represent how the world is – the world has *guided* our investigations, confirming or falsifying hypotheses through experiment, until we understood what the world is like. Science investigates the *one* physical world. Is this true in ethics?

The idea that two cultures which disagree are both trying to find *the truth* about ethics doesn't sit well with an understanding of the history of culture and how ethical practices develop. And since at least one culture is wrong, we also need to explain why that culture had 'got it wrong': why couldn't people in that culture see what was independently right and do that? This is a very awkward question.

Relativism, however, understands ethical practices as part of a culture; ethical practices have developed to help people find their way around a social world. But there are *many* social worlds, many cultures, and they have developed different ways of doing things. Relativism argues that there is not just one social world which can guide ethical practices towards agreement.

Relativism does not need to claim that *all* social practices are acceptable, that no individual and no practice can be condemned. People do wrong all the time, and relativism does not pretend otherwise. But it claims that to condemn an action or practice as wrongful, one must use resources from *within the culture* to which that practice or individual belongs. You can't judge a practice from outside a culture.

The realist's response

Realists have three responses. First, they can say that different ethical practices reflect the different particular conditions in which different cultures are situated, but not different ethical principles. For example, the Inuit used to abandon their old people on ice flows to die, while we try to keep them alive for as long as possible. But this doesn't mean killing old people is right for the Inuit and wrong for us. It is simply due to the harsh conditions of survival in which the Inuit lived. It would be right for us if we lived in their conditions, and wrong for them if they lived in ours.

Second, realists draw attention to just how many general ethical principles and virtues different cultures share. For example, most cultures have prohibitions on killing, lying and theft and encourage care of the weak.

Third, realists draw attention to moral progress. We have become more humane than in the past, and there is greater agreement about moral judgements than before. This is because we are discovering real moral truths.

● **KEY POINTS**

- Relativism argues that cultures disagree on moral judgements, and that this disagreement is not resolvable by appealing to how the world is. Morality is just part of a culture's way of living, its social world.

- To dispute this seems to involve saying that a culture has got ethics *wrong*, which raises the need to explain *why* they got it wrong. If moral values are objective, why weren't they able to discover the truth?

- However, cultures do change in response to moral criticism. But relativism can allow this: moral criticism from within a culture is possible.

- Realists can argue that different cultures have different moralities because they have different situations; that different cultures share many general ethical principles; and that there has been moral progress.

❓ QUIZ QUESTION

Outline and illustrate the challenge to moral realism from relativism.

❓ DISCUSSION QUESTION

Assess moral realism. (AQA, 1c, 2005, *24 marks*)

● IV META-ETHICS: NON-COGNITIVISM

Non-cognitivism maintains that there is no ethical knowledge, because ethical judgements are not statements which can be true or false. In this way, non-cognitivists draw a sharp distinction between facts and values.

Emotivism: moral judgements are expressive of emotions and preferences and are intended to affect the feelings of others

Ayer and the principle of verification

In the 1930s, a school of philosophy arose called logical positivism. The cornerstone of its beliefs was the principle of verification. This claims that a statement has meaning only if it is either **analytic** or empirically verifiable. An analytic statement is true (or false) just in virtue of the meanings of the words. For instance, 'A bachelor is an unmarried man' is analytically true, while 'A square has three sides' is analytically false. A statement is empirically verifiable if **empirical** evidence would go towards establishing that the statement is true or false. For example, if I say 'The moon is made of green cheese', we can check this by scientific investigation. If I say 'The universe has 600 trillion planets', we can't check this by scientific investigation in practice, but we can do so *in principle*. We know how to show whether it is true or false, so it is 'verifiable' even though we can't actually verify it.

The principle of verification entails that statements about right and wrong are *meaningless*. They are neither true nor false, because they do not actually state anything. If I say 'Murder is wrong', this is not analytic, nor can any empirical investigation show this. We can show that murder causes grief and pain, or that it is often done out of anger. But we cannot demonstrate, in the same way, that it is *wrong*. Moore, however, would agree that moral judgements are neither analytic nor empirically verifiable (see INTUITIONISM, p. 102). But he believed that they are nevertheless true or false, because they are about non-natural properties.

If ethical statements don't state truths, and are therefore literally meaningless, what do they do? A. J. Ayer argued that ethical judgements express feelings: 'If I say to someone, "You acted wrongly in stealing that money" . . . I am simply evincing my moral disapproval of it. It is as if I had said, "You stole that money", in a peculiar tone of horror'. Our 'intuitions', as Moore would describe them, are simply our feelings of approval or disapproval. Feelings are not cognitions of value, and value does not exist independently of our feelings.

The main difficulty with logical positivism is that according to the principle of verification, the principle of verification itself is meaningless. The claim 'A statement has meaning only if it is analytic or can be verified empirically' is not analytic and cannot be verified empirically. But if the principle of verification is meaningless, then what it claims cannot be true. So it does not give us any reason to believe that the claims of ethics are meaningless.

Stevenson's theory

Fortunately for Ayer, his theory of ethics, known as 'emotivism', does not depend on the principle of verification. Charles Stevenson did not use the principle of verification to claim that the only types of meaning are descriptive and analytic meaning. Stevenson argues that moral words have *emotive* meanings, which is a different type of meaning again. The sentence 'You stole that money' has a purely descriptive meaning, viz. that you took money that did not belong to you without permission from the owner. But it can be used with an emotive meaning ('You *stole* that money!'), a meaning that expresses disapproval. Many moral terms ('steal', 'honesty', 'respect') have both descriptive and emotive meanings. The central ones, though, 'right', 'wrong', 'good' and 'bad', have only emotive meanings.

Stevenson analyses emotive meaning by connecting meaning to *use*. The purpose of moral judgements is not to state facts. When we use the terms 'good' and 'right', we express our approval. The whole point of ethics is to influence how we behave. We use moral judgements to express our feelings and to influence the feelings and actions of other people. Words with emotive meaning do just that. If moral language is just descriptive of moral facts, as we saw in ASSOCIATED PROBLEMS (p. 107), it is difficult to see why we should care about moral facts. Emotivism, by contrast, connects caring, approving, disapproving with the very meaning of ethical words.

But, we can object, the key moral terms 'good', 'right', 'wrong' and 'bad' *aren't* particularly or necessarily emotive. They *may* arouse emotions in others or express ours, but this depends on context, as it does with 'steal' and 'honesty'. Yet if their meaning is emotive, then the connection should be stronger than that. So perhaps like 'steal' and 'honesty', 'good' and 'right' do have a descriptive meaning. If so, emotivism has mistaken the emotional *use* of moral terms for their meanings.

Going further: emotivism and moral disagreement

One of the most powerful objections to emotivism is that it seems to entail an unsatisfactory view of ethical discussion. If I say 'Abortion is wrong' and you say 'Abortion is right', I am just expressing my disapproval of it and you are expressing your approval. I'm just saying 'Boo! to abortion' and you're saying 'Hurrah! for abortion'. This is just like cheering for our own team – there is no *discussion*, no *reasoning*, going on at all. Even worse, emotivism claims that we are trying to influence other people's feelings and actions. But trying to influence people without reasoning is just a form of manipulation.

Ayer thought this objection partly false, partly true. It is false because emotivists claim that there is a lot more to ethical discussion – the facts. When arguing over animal rights, say, we are constantly drawing facts to each other's attention. I point out how much animals suffer in factory farms. You point out how much more sophisticated human beings are than animals. And so on. In fact, says Ayer, *all* the discussion is about the facts. If we both agree on the facts, but still disagree morally, there is no more discussion that can take place. And this is why the objection is true – but is not an objection. When all the facts are in, there is nothing left to discuss.

The disagreement that remains, Stevenson argues, is a disagreement in attitude. It is a practical disagreement – no one can live both by the attitude that 'Eating meat is wrong' and by the attitude that 'Eating meat is right'. These *can* be discussed, because people do not have feelings or make choices in isolation. The attitudes we adopt have implications for other attitudes and mental states. If I disapprove of an action, practically speaking, I must also have similar feelings about similar actions, or my attitudes will not provide consistent guidance about how to live. Moral disagreement, then, can be about the relations between different feelings that we have. For example, deciding whether abortion is right or wrong is complicated because there are many feelings involved – sympathy towards the mother, sympathy towards the foetus, feelings about human life, death and parenthood. It is difficult to work out how these feelings can all be acted on, and that is why people disagree.

But we may still object that a sense of people's *rationality* in weighing up which feelings or attitudes to give up, which to keep, is still missing. We have no sense of one set of attitudes being part of a 'better life' than any other.

Further objections to emotivism will be discussed as objections to non-cognitivism generally (see p. 118).

KEY POINTS

- Ayer argued that a statement has meaning only if it is either analytic or empirically verifiable. Moral statements are neither, so they are meaningless, neither true nor false. Instead, they express emotions, in particular, moral approval or disapproval.

- However, the principle of verification, according to itself, is not meaningful, because it is neither analytic nor empirically verifiable.

- Stevenson argued that, nevertheless, moral statements have only emotive meaning. They express emotions, and are intended to influence the emotions and actions of other people.

- But 'good' and 'right' aren't always emotive. We may object that Stevenson has confused use with meaning.

- Ayer argued that all moral discussion is disagreeing over the facts, while Stevenson argued that there is also disagreeement in attitude. As any attitude will have complex implications for other attitudes, these disagreements can be complex.

- We may object that emotivism doesn't allow for moral reasoning, for if moral judgements are attempts to influence others' feelings without appealing to reason, this is just manipulation.

❓ QUIZ QUESTIONS

Explain and illustrate emotivism's claim that moral language does not describe facts.

Explain and illustrate the emotivist view of moral language (AQA, 1b, 2001, *15 marks*)

Describe and illustrate **one** account of how moral language can guide or influence action. (AQA, 1b, 2001, *15 marks*)

❓ DISCUSSION QUESTION

Assess emotivism. (AQA, 1c, 2002, *24 marks*)

Prescriptivism: moral judgements express rational, and universalizable, commendations and guide actions

R. M. Hare argued that moral words are neither just descriptive nor *emotive* in meaning; they are descriptive and *prescriptive*. This difference, he claimed, allows a greater role for reason in moral discussion.

Prescriptive meaning

Prescriptive meaning works like commands, also known as imperatives. If I say 'Leave the room', I am telling you to do something. Hare argued that if I say 'Eating meat is wrong', I am saying 'Don't eat meat'. In claiming that moral judgements are like imperatives, Hare's theory is like Kant's (see OUR AWARENESS OF WHAT IS RIGHT AND OUR DUTY TO ACT RIGHTLY IS GIVEN BY REASON, p. 75).

We use the idea of 'right' and 'wrong' to command. We use the word 'good', says Hare, when we want to *commend* something to someone. There is a difference of emphasis between 'good action' and 'right action': 'good action' *commends* the action without necessarily *commanding* it – we are saying it should be praised, but not necessarily that you *have* to do it to be a good person. If we say an action is the 'right action', then we are commanding it – it is a guideline for behaviour that people should follow.

We can talk about good chocolate, good teachers and good people. In each case, we are saying the chocolate, teacher or person is praiseworthy in some way. In each case, there is a *set of standards* that we are implicitly relying on. Good chocolate is rich in the taste of cocoa. Good teachers can explain new ideas clearly and create enthusiasm in their students. A good person – well, a good person is someone who is the way we should try to be as people. VIRTUE THEORY (p. 84) would say a good person is someone who has the virtues.

When we use 'good' to mean 'morally good', we are appealing to a set of standards that apply to someone as a person. If we say that an action is a good action or a right action, we mean it is an action that complies with the standards for how someone should act to be a good person.

So the prescriptive meaning of good relates to the fact that it commends. What about its descriptive meaning? This comes from the set of standards that is being assumed. Its descriptive meaning picks up on the qualities that the something must have to be a good . . . (chocolate, teacher, person, whatever).

Prescription and the is–ought gap

Because 'good' is always used relative to a set of standards, it always has a descriptive meaning. And since we usually use 'good' to commend, we generally use it with prescriptive meaning as well. But we don't always. This can happen with any word that both commends and describes – we can use it just to describe and not commend or disapprove. Take moral words like 'steal' or 'honesty'. We often use the word 'honest' to commend someone. But I can say 'If you weren't so honest, we could have got away with that!' This is an expression of annoyance, not praise. Again, I can agree that a 'good person' is one who is honest, kind, just, etc. But I can still think that good people are not to be commended, because, as Woody Allen said, 'Good people sleep better than bad people, but bad people enjoy the waking hours more'.

Hare is making a point similar to that of the emotivists – that descriptive meaning and prescriptive meaning are logically distinct. And when we use words with a moral meaning, we use them with a prescriptive meaning. This means that nothing about being honest (i.e. telling the truth: descriptive meaning) can make me commend honesty (telling the truth is how to behave: prescriptive). More generally, nothing about the facts can entail a moral judgement. We are *free* in the prescriptions that we make.

Universalization

However, Hare argues that this freedom is rationally constrained. As we saw, prescriptions relate to a set of standards. Whenever we apply a standard, we are committed to making the same judgement of two things that match the standard in the same way. If I say this chocolate is good but that chocolate is not, I must think that there is some *relevant difference* between the two. Likewise, we can choose what standards we live by, but the standards apply universally. If I think that it is wrong for you to steal from me, because it infringes my rights of ownership, then I must think that it is wrong for me to steal from you, because it infringes your rights of ownership – unless I can say that there is some relevant difference between the two cases.

Prescriptivism and emotivism

Emotivists thought that the only role for reason in ethical discussion is establishing the facts. Hare has developed three more ways in which reason is part of ethical discourse.

First, there is a difference between commanding someone to do something and commending an action and trying to get him or her to act that way. We saw that emotivism is open to the objection that it makes ethical discussion a matter of manipulation. Hare's theory sees the *guiding* aspect of ethics as a matter of prescription, rather than a matter of influencing someone through emotion. This makes ethical discussion more straightforward and rational.

Second, we can argue about consistency and relevance. For example, Singer claims there is *no relevant difference* between the suffering of people and the suffering of animals (see ANIMAL RIGHTS, p. 98). If we are going to say that causing the suffering of people is wrong, we are committed to saying the suffering of animals is wrong – unless we can find a relevant difference. Moral disagreements can be about consistency in applying certain standards, and reason can help resolve this.

Third, we can infer prescriptions from other prescriptions. A famous argument against abortion says 'Taking an innocent human life is wrong. Abortion is the taking of an innocent human life. Therefore abortion is wrong'. This is a valid argument, even if we rephrase it as Hare would understand it: 'Do not take innocent human life. Abortion is the taking of an innocent human life. Therefore, do not commit abortion'. To disagree with the conclusion, we must disagree with at least one premiss. And so our prescriptions are logically related to one another. So we can use reason to discuss these relations.

● **KEY POINTS**

- Hare argues that moral words are not emotive in meaning, but prescriptive. Prescriptive language commands ('right') or commends ('good') certain objects, actions or traits, according to a set of standards.

- Moral language can be used purely descriptively, if the speaker doesn't agree with the standard. Description and prescription are logically distinct, which is why you cannot infer an 'ought' from an 'is'.

- Standards apply universally, so to be consistent, speakers must be willing to universalize their moral judgements. If not, they must point to a relevant difference between cases. This allows moral disagreement to be about relevant differences as well as the facts.

● Prescriptivism also enables us to infer one moral judgement from another, as prescriptions are logically related to each other.

QUIZ QUESTIONS

Identify **one** similarity and **one** difference between emotivism and prescriptivism. (AQA, 1a, 2003, *6 marks*)

Explain and illustrate the view that moral language is prescriptive. (AQA, 1b, 2002, *15 marks*)

Outline and illustrate **one** theory of how moral judgements influence how we act.

Briefly explain what prescriptivism involves. (AQA, 1a, 2005, *6 marks*)

Associated problems: is value given by the form rather than the content of judgements? Can anything be valued?

We have discussed the issue of moral reasoning in non-cognitivism. A further, and very important, difficulty non-cognitivism faces relates to the fact that it doesn't place limits on what we can approve or disapprove of. It identifies moral judgements with a particular *kind* of judgement – approval, disapproval, a commanded or commended principle – rather than a particular *content*. Now it seems right that moral judgements are special or different in some way. This is shown, for instance, in the close relation between making a moral judgement and being motivated to act on it. But is the special nature of moral judgements to be explained just in terms of their *form* (emotional expression or universal prescription), or are they special because of their *content*, i.e. what it is they are about? Isn't morality about sympathy, loyalty, courage, happiness and so on?

Because non-cognitivists understand moral judgements in terms of their form, not their content, they seem to allow that *anything* could be morally approved or disapproved of or chosen as a principle of action. Imagine someone believed in maximizing the number of florists in Kensington, and all their *moral* feelings and actions related to this: they are willing to do anything to pursue their goal (even murder), they try to stop florists closing down, they try to change the law to protect florists in Kensington, they feel no disapproval towards theft, lying, disloyalty, no approval of kindness or courage – unless they relate to florists in Kensington. Such a person would be classed as a psychopath!

Not just any set of expressions of approval or principles can count as 'morality'. The idea of morality is not so unrestricted. VIRTUE THEORY (p. 84) argues that morality is about what is good or bad for human beings generally, given our nature and the variety of problems life throws at us. Values are not so detached from facts that we can understand any system of principles or feelings as embodying a system of moral values. They must relate in some way to what is good for people (or more broadly, animals, the environment, God).

The objection is that we cannot value and call *morality* anything we choose to. Non-cognitivism claims, first, that a judgement is a value judgement if it has a particular form; and, second, that value judgements *create* values rather than *discover* them. Values are a reflection of our value judgements. But if values depend entirely on our will, it seems we could value anything we chose to. But this is difficult to make sense of. Outside certain limits, we would consider people mad rather than thinking that they just had a different set of values from ours. We have to presuppose certain ideas about moral values in order to understand feelings or choices as moral at all. It is not just a matter of the form of the judgement.

Non-cognitivists can agree that we can't value just anything, and it is precisely because human beings have certain needs, have a particular nature, that we do not value things that are not related to human (animal, etc.) welfare. And this is just a natural fact about human beings. *Valuing* is an activity of the will, but the will is guided by its nature. But there is no *logical* restriction on possible *moralities*, there is just a considerable *factual* one. We are all set up, by evolution perhaps, to value actions and people in particular, familiar sorts of ways. This is why we call only particular sets of feelings or principles 'moral'. The objection doesn't prove that there are facts about morality that our feelings or choices must answer to. It only shows that a common human nature underlies our feelings and choices. But it is still these feelings and choices that create morality.

The objection can be pressed in a different direction. If we don't distinguish morality by its content, how can the non-cognitivist draw a distinction between *moral* approval and disapproval and, say, *aesthetic* approval and disapproval? Given that 'approval' is the central concept in a non-cognitivist theory of morality, we really need an account of what makes approval moral or not moral.

KEY POINTS

- Non-cognitivism does not identify moral judgements by what they are about, but by their form (emotive or prescriptive). This seems to allow that the content of morality could be anything. But not any set of *approving* or *commending* judgements counts as moral.

- Non-cognitivists may respond that there is no logical restriction on what morality is about, but there is a factual, e.g. a psychological, one. Our moral judgements don't *answer* to these facts as some kind of moral standard, although they may be influenced by them.

- We may object that non-cognitivism is still unable to distinguish between varieties of emotional expression or commendation, e.g. aesthetic and moral.

❓ QUIZ QUESTIONS

Outline and illustrate how a non-cognitivist can accept that our moral judgements are guided by facts about human nature.

❓ DISCUSSION QUESTION

Assess the view that morality is based on our feelings and decisions, not facts.

The (supposed) normative implications of scepticism about moral truths: nihilism, tolerance, relativism

Another set of objections to non-cognitivism comes from its denial of moral truth.

Nihilism

The objection from nihilism is that non-cognitivism entails that there are no values, so anything goes. If morality is the product of my feelings and choices, then morality has no authority over me. I can do whatever I like, as long as I don't get caught. *Morality* becomes no more than a matter of taste.

Non-cognitivists argue that this is either an unfair simplification of their theories or a straightforward misunderstanding. The adoption of nihilism is itself a choice or expression of feeling, and one that moral people will disapprove of morally. The theory that moral values are a reflection of our feelings does not imply that we should stop having moral feelings. Nihilism is not *more correct*, but a cynical and immature view of life. We should disapprove of anyone who advocates that morality doesn't matter or is just a matter of taste.

Tolerance

If morality is a reflection of our choices or feelings, and my choices or feelings are different from yours, then who are you to tell me that my morality is wrong? Non-cognitivism implies tolerance, many people claim, because no one can correct anyone else. This can become an objection to the theory, since although tolerance can appear to be a virtue, it can also be a vice. Should we tolerate every view, including racism, sexism, female circumcision, etc.? Doesn't morality require that we *take a stand* against what is wrong?

The objection is based on a mistake, because non-cognitivism does not entail tolerance for two reasons. First, tolerance is itself a moral value. 'You ought to tolerate other people's values, because there are no moral values' is self-contradictory. We ought to be tolerant only if tolerance is a good or right thing to be. So, turning the tables, who are you to tell someone else to be tolerant? This is no different from saying that they ought not to eat meat or ought not to be racist. It is a moral claim. Non-cognitivism doesn't entail that we ought to be tolerant or that we ought not to be tolerant.

Second, if my morality is different from yours, then not only will I disagree with you about whether a particular action is right or wrong, I may also disapprove of people who disagree with me and try to persuade them to change their mind. This follows from Stevenson's observation that our attitudes don't exist on their own. Disapproving of abortion can lead to disapproving of people who approve of abortion. Tolerance is a moral attitude towards other people's attitudes, so it may conflict with other moral attitudes I have. I might feel that tolerance is a moral value, but this tolerance will have its limits. Very few people think that tolerance is a more important value than preventing a racist murder, say.

Relativism

For similar reasons, non-cognitivism does not imply relativism (see THE EXISTENCE OF MORAL RELATIVISM, p. 110). Non-cognitivists can argue that to claim that moral judgements can be right for you and wrong for me because we have different cultures is itself a moral claim. If I feel approval towards a particular action, I may disapprove of people who behave as if the action is wrong. How tolerant I am of other cultures depends entirely on whether I think such tolerance is a good thing.

But can I really justify interfering with how other people behave just because their actions don't accord with my feelings or choices? This seems very petty. But this isn't the reason I am interfering, claims the non-cognitivist. It is not because it offends me, but because they are being racist, or cruel, or cowardly or whatever. The difference between non-cognitivism and moral realism is this: for the non-cognitivist, that I think racist discrimination is a good reason to prevent an action is an expression of my moral feelings; for the realist, that this is a good reason to interfere is a fact about reasons. The realist claims to have the backing of reality.

KEY POINTS

- Nihilism argues that non-cognitivism reduces morality to an optional matter of taste. Non-cognitivists may reply that nihilism is itself a moral position, and one we should disapprove of.

- The objection from tolerance argues that non-cognitivism implies we should tolerate moral differences, but there are some things which are intolerable that we should condemn. Non-cognitivists reply that their theory does not necessarily entail tolerance (or intolerance), since this is not a matter of metaethics, but a matter of what moral judgements we should make.

- Non-cognitivism also does not entail relativism, if this is understood as a moral judgement about tolerating other cultures.

QUIZ QUESTIONS

Explain non-cognitivism's reply to the claim that if non-cognitivism is true, anything goes.

Outline the relationship between non-cognitivism and tolerance.

Can we speak of moral progress?

A final objection to non-cognitivism is that it does not allow for the idea of moral progress. If there is no moral reality, then our moral beliefs or feelings cannot become better or worse. Obviously, they have changed – people used to believe that slavery was morally acceptable and now they do not. But how can non-cognitivism say that this is *progress*? There are two responses non-cognitivists can give.

First, non-cognitivists can claim that there can be very real improvements in people's moral views if they become more rational. This can happen in several different ways. First, people may come to know certain facts that they didn't know before. In the case of slavery, people believed many things about slaves that were not true (one popular false belief was that they were stupid). Moral progress here means basing one's moral feelings or principles on the facts, not mistakes. Second, people can become more consistent, more willing to universalize their principles. Some utilitarians, such as Peter Singer, argue that if we were consistent in our feelings about preventing suffering, we would not eat meat. If he is right, then this would be moral progress. Third, people can become more coherent in their moral judgements. Many of us have moral feelings that come into conflict with each other, e.g. over abortion. Moral progress here would be a matter of working out the implications of our views, and changing what needs changing to make them coherent with each other.

Because people are ignorant, do not always think logically and have not resolved the conflicts between their different feelings, the non-cognitivist can say that there is plenty of room for moral progress. But moral progress just means becoming more rational in our moral thinking, not becoming more *correct* in our moral judgements.

The second response non-cognitivists can give is this: if I disapprove of the moral feelings or principles of societies in the past and approve of the moral feelings and principles of society in the present, then I will also say that we have made moral progress. Society has moved from moral principles that were bad (i.e. principles I disapprove of) to moral principles that are good (i.e. principles I approve of). That is what moral progress is.

This response means that moral progress is visible only from a particular moral point of view. If you disagree with me, you might claim that today's moral principles are much worse than those 200 years ago and so we have not made moral progress. But this is now just the familiar problem of moral disagreement or relativism, and we saw how the non-cognitivist answered these problems above. The problem of moral progress is just another example of these problems.

KEY POINTS

- We may object that if there is no moral truth, as non-cognitivism argues, we cannot talk of moral progress, because changes in moral beliefs are neither right nor wrong.

- Non-cognitivists reply that moral beliefs can improve by becoming more rational, i.e. changing in the light of previously unknown facts or becoming more consistent or coherent.

- From our perspective now, we can say only that the change from previous views to current views is morally good (i.e. we express our approval of it).

❓ QUIZ QUESTION

Explain the objection to non-cognitivism from moral progress.

❓ DISCUSSION QUESTIONS

Assess emotivism. (AQA, 1c, 2002, *24 marks*)

Assess the view that we can't get an 'ought' from an 'is'. (AQA, 1c, 2003, *24 marks*)

Assess the view that there are **no** moral facts.

3

philosophy of religion

UNIT 2

I THE MEANING AND JUSTIFICATION OF RELIGIOUS CONCEPTS

Conceptions of God: as personal, ideal mind, omnipresent, creator and sustainer of all possible universes, transcendent, perfectly good, omniscient and omnipotent

We usually understand 'God' to signify two, closely related, fundamental thoughts: God is the ultimate reality, the ground of everything that exists; and God is perfection. Augustine says that to think of God is to 'attempt to conceive something than which nothing more excellent or sublime exists'. Some philosophers claim that God is the most perfect being that *could* (not just does) exist.

The ideas of God as perfection and as ultimate reality are linked by the thought that perfection and reality are intimately connected – what is perfect is more real than what is not. (This idea is developed, for example, in Plato; see Ch. 4, THE THEORY OF FORMS, p. 194 and PLATO'S ACCOUNT OF THE GOOD, p. 204.) Perfection has also been thought to involve complete self-sufficiency, i.e. not to be dependent on anything; and not to lack anything. Again, this connects with being the ultimate reality: that which is not the ultimate reality will depend on that which is, and so not be perfect. And something that is not ultimate reality will lack ultimate reality, and so not be perfect.

Perfection also implies that God possesses no properties which are not essential to him. If the property is a perfection, then it isn't non-essential, because God necessarily has all perfections. But if the property is not a perfection, then God possesses an imperfect property. But then God isn't perfect. So God's properties are all perfections and all essential.

These two ideas of perfection and ultimate reality are taken to define what God is; a being that is not perfect and not the ultimate reality is just not God. They are at the heart of the more detailed conceptions of God and lie behind many of the ARGUMENTS FOR THE EXISTENCE OF GOD (p. 140).

A note on referring to God: I have adopted the traditional personal pronoun 'he' in referring to God. There are two reasons for this: first, the conception of God that is discussed in the syllabus is personal, so the impersonal 'it' sounds awkward. Second, English unfortunately has only two personal pronouns, 'he' and 'she', both gendered. If God exists, I don't believe that God is gendered in either way. My use of 'he' is purely to avoid the awkwardness of alternating 'he' and 'she' and of using 's/he'.

God as personal and ideal mind

Many philosophers have argued that being a person is a perfection. Properties that essentially characterize a person include intellect and will. The intellect is characterized by rationality and knowledge, the will by morality, freedom and the ability to act. To lack either intellect or will is to lack perfection.

However, if God were a person, he would be very unusual. As the most perfect possible being, God cannot become more perfect; nor can God become less perfect, as then he would not be the most perfect being possible, and so not God. So unlike other persons, God cannot change.

Intellect and will are properties of mind. If God is a person, he is so in virtue of being a mind. Persons usually also have bodies. But the most perfect being can't have a body, at least literally. Anything made of matter changes over time, but God can't change. And anything made of matter must have parts. God cannot have parts, because whatever has parts depends on them for its existence. So God can't be material. But God could be a mind, since a mind is often thought not to have parts. We talk of 'parts of the mind', but don't normally think of these parts being distinct from the mind, and being added together to make up the mind. Instead, we usually mean the different activities, functions or aspects of the mind (see Ch. 5, ARGUMENTS FOR DISTINGUISHING MIND AND BODY, p. 228).

Some philosophers argue that God can feel (have emotions). But if God can't change, then God cannot have emotions, or at least *reactive* emotions. For example, if God is made sad or angry by our sinfulness, then the way God is depends on us. But as perfect, God is completely self-sufficient, independent of everything else. If God can have emotions, then they must depend entirely on his will alone, and they never change, e.g. God's love towards us.

For these reasons, philosophers have said God is *personal* rather than a *person*, i.e. God has attributes essentially associated with being a person, but God is not a person because he does not change and does not have a body.

Being perfect, if God is a mind, then he is an ideal mind. He will have perfect intellect and perfect will. Perfect intellect involves perfect wisdom, perfect rationality and perfect knowledge. Perfect will involves perfect goodness and perfect power.

Omniscience

Perfect knowledge is usually taken to mean 'omniscience'. The most obvious definition of omniscience is 'knowing everything', but we need to remember that God is the most perfect *possible* being, and perhaps it is impossible to know *everything*. So, being omniscient, God knows all the truths that it is possible to know. For example, if human beings have free will, then perhaps it is not possible to know what they will do in the future. What we think it is possible for God to know will depend on other attributes of God, e.g. whether we think God exists outside time (so there is no 'future' for God).

Omniscience is not just a matter of *what* God knows, but also of *how* God knows. Aquinas argues that God knows everything that he knows 'directly' and 'immediately', rather than through inference or through understanding a system of representation (such as language or thinking in terms of **propositions**). Other philosophers disagree, and argue that if we say that God doesn't know all true propositions, then there is something that God doesn't know; so God does have propositional knowledge as well as direct and immediate knowledge.

Omnipotence

As perfect, God will have perfect power, or the most power possible. Power is the ability to do things. The most obvious definition of omnipotence is 'the power to do anything'. But does 'anything' include the logically impossible? For instance, could God make 2 + 2 = 5? Could God create a married bachelor? Some pious philosophers have wanted to say yes – logic is no limit on God's power. Unfortunately, there is simply no way we can meaningfully say this.

What is logically impossible is not anything at all. Any description of a logically impossible state of affairs or power is not a meaningful description, because it contains a contradiction. The *limits* of the logically possible are not *limitations*. So almost all philosophers have restricted omnipotence to 'the power to do anything that is logically possible'. Even if God can't do the logically impossible, there is still nothing that God can't do.

Perfect goodness

There are two ways of understanding perfect goodness. If goodness just is perfection, then saying God is perfectly good is just to say that God is perfectly perfect – or the most perfect possible being. This is a metaphysical sense of 'goodness'. As perfection has also been connected to what is real, then God is the ultimate reality. The other sense of 'goodness' is the moral sense. In this sense, 'God is perfectly good' means that God's will is always in accordance with moral values. The relation between God's will and morality is discussed in MORALITY (p. 187).

Plato and Augustine connect the two understandings of perfect goodness. What is perfect and real includes what is morally good; evil is a type of *lack*, a *falling short* of goodness.

Creator and sustainer

Being perfect, God is self-sufficient, dependent on nothing else for existence. By contrast, it is usually thought that *everything* else that exists is dependent on God. If something exists completely independently of God, then God is not the ultimate reality. So God is traditionally thought of as the creator of the universe. If there are any other universes, then God must be the creator of those universes as well. In fact, of any universe that could *possibly* exist, God would be the creator.

God's activity in creating is traditionally thought of as completely unconstrained in two ways:

1 God freely chose to create, by an act of will. Being self-sufficient, God had no need to create the universe. His creation is an act of generosity, an expression of God's perfect goodness.
2 God created out of nothing, *ex nihilo*. God was not constrained or impeded by matter or the laws of physics. God could choose the laws of physics, and so the nature of matter, to be anything he wanted.

Some philosophers, called 'deists', argued that once God created the universe, it could continue on its own. God just needed to set it running, like winding up a clock. But if God is timeless, then his creation of the universe doesn't, from his perspective, have a time, after which the universe continues its own way. Rather, the whole universe from start to finish is his act of creation – so God's act of creation is occurring at every moment in time. Second, if God merely created the universe at the outset, the only further actions God takes in the world would be miracles. This separation of the activity of God from the world flies in the face of the religious sense of being close to and dependent on God.

So God is traditionally thought of as not just creator but also sustainer of the universe. Although science may describe how one state of matter can become another state, through causal laws, it doesn't provide an account of how anything *stays in existence*. God keeps the universe in existence throughout time: without God's constant activity of keeping things in existence, the universe would simply cease to be. Because this activity is similar (or possibly the same as) God's *original* act of creation, it is known as 'continuous creation'. God continuously creates everything that is.

Omnipresence

God's continuous creation means that God's activity is everywhere. Omnipresence is the idea of 'being everywhere' at once. There is a puzzle as to how God could literally be *anywhere*, given that God is not a material object, and so not in space. Furthermore, because God does not have parts or have a size, it seems that God can't be 'spread' through the universe in the way that I am (my body is) spread over a certain area of space. Rather, omnipresence means that God is *wholly* present everywhere. God immediately and directly supports the existence of everything; and God knows everything that happens everywhere directly and immediately.

Transcendence

The idea of transcendence marks the way God is very different from creation. First, God is 'outside' or 'goes beyond' the universe. Since God is the ultimate reality, self-sufficient and the creator of the universe, clearly God is not reducible to the universe. Second, God is not spatial as the universe is, and many philosophers argue that God also transcends time in the sense that God is timeless (eternal), rather than existing forever in time (everlasting). Third, while God is personal, he has intellect and will in a way quite different from persons.

KEY POINTS

- Traditional conceptions of God stem from two, closely related, fundamental ideas: God is the most perfect possible being; and God is the ultimate reality.

- *Personal*: God has traits similar to those of a person, in particular intellect and will.

- *Ideal mind*: God has no body, and intellect and will are properties of a mind. Being perfect, God is an ideal mind.

- *Omniscience*: God knows everything it is possible to know. At least much of what God knows, he knows directly and immediately.

- *Omnipotence*: God has the power to do anything it is possible to do.

- *Perfect goodness*: God is the most perfect possible being, and because moral goodness is a perfection, God's will is in accordance with moral values.

- *Creator and sustainer*: God freely chose to create the universe, and did so out of nothing. God sustains the universe in existence throughout time.

- *Omnipresence*: God is wholly present at all places, supporting the existence of everything and knowing directly and immediately all that happens.

- *Transcendence*: God is more than the universe, being outside space and perhaps also outside time.

❓ QUIZ QUESTION

Identify and briefly describe **two** of God's properties. (AQA, 3a, 2001, *6 marks*)

Whether these attributes can be expressed and combined in an intelligible and coherent way

If God is the most perfect possible being, then each of the perfections attributed to God must be possible, and the combination of the perfections must also be possible. Both of these requirements lead to difficulties. For example, it is unclear what it means to say that 'God knows everything it is possible to know'. And the attributes can appear incompatible with each other. For example, can God will evil? Omnipotence suggests 'yes', perfect goodness suggests 'no'. In light of this, some philosophers say that God has the perfections he does to the greatest possible *degree* that is *compatible* with his having all perfections.

In this section, we will discuss a number of these issues, though there are others. One, however, we shall leave for later (see MORALITY, p. 187) is the puzzle of God's perfect goodness: does God conform his will to what is independently morally good, or is what is morally good whatever God wants it to be? We will also leave aside for now the further incompatibilities that arise when we take into account other claims. For example, we may be able to argue without contradiction that God is both perfectly good and omnipotent. But the existence of evil creates a new tension, called THE PROBLEM OF EVIL (p. 177): if evil exists, then being good, wouldn't God want to prevent it, and being omnipotent, wouldn't God be able to? So why does evil exist, unless God is either not perfectly good or not omnipotent?

Omniscience

What is it to know everything it is possible to know? If God exists in time, then does God know what will happen in the future? If not, e.g. because we have free will and so God does not know what we will do, then it seems that there is something God does not know. Furthermore, as the future unfolds, God would gain new knowledge. But as the most perfect possible being, God is unchanging. Doesn't his gaining knowledge mean his 'omniscience' increases? But if God gains knowledge, he wasn't previously omniscient.

We may reply that if God does not know the future, this may not be a *restriction* on or a *lack* in God's knowledge. If it is *impossible* to know the future, e.g. because of the existence of free will, God's not knowing the future is no failure; God still knows everything it is possible to know *at any given time*. And God's gaining knowledge as time passes is consistent with God being omniscient: God always knows everything it is possible to know. It is just that *what* it is possible to know changes over time.

If God exists outside time, the problem doesn't seem to arise. God never gains new knowledge, and God already knows what happens in the (our) future. Although this is a coherent view of omniscience, it appears to conflict with the idea that we have free will.

Going further: omniscience, transcendence and perfect goodness

Transcendence (of time) coheres well with omniscience, it seems, but it conflicts with God's perfect goodness in this way: free will is thought to be a good thing (it's an essential attribute of being a person), and, as perfectly good, God wants the best for us. But can we have free will if God already knows all of our decisions in advance?

Simply being able to *predict* what someone is going to do is not enough to undermine free will. For example, you can predict that a friend of yours will help this old lady across the street, because he is a kind person, is in a good mood and has just said that this is what he will do. But it is different if we could predict an action with total certainty, i.e. the prediction is not simply reliable, but *infallible*. Furthermore, knowing someone's character enables knowledge of the general shape of their choices and actions, but not every minute detail.

Both these points cause problems in the case of God's knowledge. If God knows now what I will be doing on 23 May 2022, this can't simply be because he knows my character well! For a start, God must know whether I will be alive then, and could only know that if the future is fixed in some way, e.g. by physical determinism. Second, God's (perfect) knowledge is surely infallible, not just reliable. For instance, much of God's knowledge is direct and immediate, not inferential. And if God is 'outside' time, then surely he knows all moments in time *in the same way*. Past, present and future are all the same to God. It is hard for us to understand how God can know the future in the same way as the past unless the future is fixed just as the past is. But if the future is fixed, do we have free will? But if we don't have free will, is this compatible with God being perfectly good?

Going further: knowing what God doesn't

If omniscience is knowing everything it is possible to know, then God should surely know everything that we do. However, some of what we know derives from *sense experience*, such as how red looks or how coffee tastes. God does not have sense organs, so could God know things like this?

We might argue that God does not know this, but that is no lack in knowledge, because only an *imperfect* being has this type of knowledge, since it relies on having a body. But we need to rephrase omniscience as 'knowing everything it is possible for a perfect being to know'.

Alternatively, we could argue that God does know these things. God knows everything that exists directly and immediately; how red looks and so on are real properties, and so God has direct knowledge of these properties, even though God doesn't have sense organs.

Omnipotence and the stone paradox

Can God create a stone that he is unable to lift? If he can, then he will not be able to lift the stone. But otherwise, he can't create such a stone. Either way, it seems, there is something God cannot do. But the paradox actually presupposes the possibility of something logically impossible. 'The power to create a stone that an omnipotent being can't lift' is logically incoherent, so it's not a possible power. If God lacks it, God lacks no possible power. Alternatively, we may allow that God could create such a stone, but in that case the stone is, *by definition*, impossible to lift (clearly it will not be the stone's *weight* that prevents its being lifted by God, so it must be some other essential attribute). If God lacks the power to lift a stone it is logically impossible to lift, there is still no power God lacks.

Going further: doing what God can't

Is omnipotence the power to do whatever it is logically possible to do? I can go jogging, which shows that to be a logically possible act, but God can't. So perhaps omnipotence is 'the power to do whatever it is possible for a perfect being (or the greatest possible being) to do'. One interpretation of this is *maximal power* – it is not possible for any being to have more power overall than an omnipotent being.

A different response says that God possesses every power it is logically possible to possess. We need to take care in how we should identify and individuate powers. The power to go jogging isn't a distinct power. It is a combination of free will and the power to move my body in accordance with that free will, but subject to laws of nature. But this is not a power God lacks. God has free will and God can move bodies, including my body, in accordance with his will. God can even move bodies without regard to the laws of nature. So there is no logically possible power I have that God lacks.

Omnipotence and perfect goodness

Can God commit evil? If God is perfectly good, then God cannot commit evil. But is this a lack of *power*? 'I could never do that', we sometimes say, faced with the option of something horrendous. This is not because we lack the power, but because we don't will it, or can't bring ourselves to will it. What does it mean for God not to be able to will something? If God is *morally incapable* of doing evil, is this a lack of power, or is God's will being different a logically impossible state of affairs? But then how is God's will free if it is *logically* impossible for it to be different? Three possible solutions:

1   There is a distinction between powers and acts of will. God has the power to commit evil, but simply chooses not to.
2   There is no distinct 'power to commit evil', because 'evil' doesn't name a distinct act. To commit evil, God would have to do something, e.g. hurt someone unjustifiably. God has all the powers to bring this about – there is no power he lacks to do whatever the evil act would be – but chooses not to act in that way.

3 There is no distinct 'power to commit evil', because evil is not a 'something', but an absence of good. Asking whether God can commit evil is like asking whether God can fail. Being *able* to fail is not a power: failing demonstrates the lack of power to succeed. There is no 'power to commit evil' as committing evil is the result of the lack of power to do good. As God does not lack the power to do good, God cannot commit evil.

Transcendence and the personal

One personal attribute is a free and rational will. We exercise our wills, make choices, in time. If God transcends time, how is God active *in* time? How can God bring things about, e.g. miracles, at a particular time? From God's timeless perspective, all times are *simultaneous*. Furthermore, God's will doesn't undergo changes but is constant, so there is no time at which God makes a choice. One suggestion is that God doesn't make choices in time, even though what he chooses to happen occurs in time. Or better, God's actions aren't in time; but what is *brought about* by his actions can be in time. If God cured a man of cancer in 2003, he was cured in 2003, but God didn't choose or act in 2003.

● **KEY POINTS**

- We face difficulties both in saying coherently what God's individual attributes are and in our attempts to combine them. Some important debates are:

  ● Is omniscience knowing everything it is possible to know? Or is it knowing everything it is possible for a perfect being to know?

  ● Is it possible for God's knowledge to increase over time?

  ● Is God's omniscience compatible with human free will, as a gift from a good God?

  ● Can God create a stone that he can't lift?

  ● Is omnipotence having the power to do everything it is possible to do? Or having the power to do everything it is possible for a perfect being to do? Or having as much power as it is possible to have?

  ● Can God commit evil?

  ● Can God act in time if God is outside time?

❓ QUIZ QUESTION

Explain **one** philosophical problem which arises when combining two or more of God's properties. (AQA, 3b, 2001, *15 marks*)

DISCUSSION QUESTIONS

Assess whether and how God can be both omnipotent and perfectly good.

Assess whether there is any coherent conception of omniscience.

The nature of religious language: what does religious language express and how are religious claims to be understood and/or confirmed?

There are many religious uses of language, e.g. in prayer and worship. However, philosophical discussions of religious language have tended to concentrate in particular on the questions: 'Are statements about God really used to make truth claims about a divine reality that is independent of us? How can we meaningfully ascribe attributes to God?'

Univocal language

Many people start from the assumption that talk about God is *univocal*. To use a word univocally is to use it with the same meaning in different contexts. A univocal word yields a contradiction (i.e. nonsense) when affirmed and denied of the same thing. Yet many theologians have wanted to say God is loving, but not in the way we are. We also say that God is love, not just God is loving. So when we ascribe the quality of love to God, we don't mean it in the same way as when we ascribe love to other people. We saw in CONCEPTIONS OF GOD (p. 125) that God's intellect and will, while resembling the intellect and will we have as persons, are nevertheless very different in many important ways. Or again, when we make things, we do so using our bodies. God doesn't have a body, so the way he makes things must be different.

The difficulty of thinking that religious language is univocal is doing justice to the transcendence of God while avoiding self-contradiction. God is so different from anything else we talk about that using our words in the usual way is problematic. The meaning of the term as applied to God involves negating features of its meaning as it applies to human beings, in particular our understanding of people's finitude v. God's infinite perfection. So the word is not being used in the same sense.

Via negativa

The opposite extreme is to argue that nothing can be *said* about God that really has any meaning. God is beyond all categorical language and thought, so the only way to talk about God is to *deny* statements about God. Pseudo-Dionysius said that God 'transcends all affirmation by being the perfect and unique Cause of all things'. This doesn't mean that experiences of God aren't real. They are incredibly real, but they are *ineffable*, literally indescribable.

The *via negativa* faces some fundamental challenges. In order to say why we can't say anything about God, many philosophers end up affirming something of God, which is supposedly impossible. Pseudo-Dionysius says that God is the 'perfect and unique Cause of all things'. This is a description of God. But if God transcends all affirmation, then we will not be able to say why by describing what God is like.

Second, if we can say nothing of God, then *no* description is right, e.g. God is not perfect nor imperfect. This is difficult to accept, and very much at odds with traditional CONCEPTIONS OF GOD (p. 124), which hold that God is perfection. According to the *via negativa*, this is no more true than saying God is imperfect.

Third, we can object that we therefore know nothing about God. However, we don't have to accept this conclusion. We have ineffable experiences of God; it's just that we cannot put that experience into words. We can't have any *propositional* knowledge of God, but that doesn't mean we can't have any *acquaintance* knowledge of God (on types of knowledge, see Ch. 1, BELIEVING-THAT AND KNOWING-THAT, p. 19). But the *via negativa* does entail that we can't know about God nor share our knowledge of God with other people.

Aquinas: meaning by analogy

Aquinas argues that we can talk about God, but the words we use can't be literally or univocally applied to God. We must first extend the meaning of the terms. Meaningful talk of God relies on analogy. For example, there is enough of an analogy between human intellect and God's intellect for us to understand something of what 'God is wise' means.

Analogy is not the same as metaphor. To say 'God is the Good Shepherd' is metaphorical; it is not even tempting to think it applies literally. To say 'God is good' needs a different kind of understanding: 'good' isn't metaphorical in the way that 'good shepherd' is. Aquinas says there are two ways in which analogies work.

Analogy of attribution

Analogy of attribution applies a word to something it doesn't literally describe by virtue of its connection with the thing it does literally describe. So organisms are healthy, but we can speak of healthy food, meaning food that helps keep us healthy. To say God is love, then, is to say that God is the cause or ground of all love.

But is the sentence 'God is the cause of all love' literally true or true only by analogy? If God is literally a cause, then at least some talk of God is univocal. If God is not literally, but analogically, a cause, then how should we understand the analogy? Is God analogically a cause (the cause of love) by being the cause or ground of all causation? But then is God analogically the cause of all causation? We haven't solved the problem. We've explained the idea of analogy by using analogy; which is no explanation at all. So we haven't yet really understood what it means to say 'God is love'.

Analogy of proportion

Analogy of proportion relates the meaning of a term to its context. A dog can be loyal and a person can be loyal, but loyalty for dogs and for people involves something different. To say that a human father loves his children and God loves his 'children' is to say that the human father loves in the way and sense appropriate to human fathers and God loves in the way and sense appropriate to God.

However, we don't have any independent conception of God, so we have no further idea about what the *appropriate* sense of 'love' is, applied to God. From 'person', 'human loyalty' and 'dog', I can understand 'dog loyalty'. But if I didn't know what a dog was, I couldn't! So if I don't already have some idea of God, I can't really understand God's love by analogy with human love.

One solution is to argue for a *partial* overlap (partial univocity of meaning) in applying terms to God and to human beings. For example, we noted that we create using our bodies, while God does not. But we can understand 'create' in a way that is neutral between creating with a body and without one, e.g. 'to bring about a state of affairs by an act of will'.

Going further: God's essence

However, Aquinas gives an argument against even partial univocity. First, in CONCEPTIONS OF GOD (p. 124), we noted that God possesses no properties that are not essential to him. All of God's properties are his essence. If God *is* goodness, for example, then 'God is good' is more like a definition, an **analytic** truth, than a description. To say 'bachelors are unmarried' isn't merely to attribute a property to bachelors, it defines what a bachelor is. All attributions of properties to God attribute essential properties. This is strongly disanalogous from our attributions of properties to people.

Second, Aquinas argues that God's properties aren't in fact *different* from each other, otherwise God's existence would depend on these different properties. Rather, each and all of God's properties just are God. God is *simple*, one unitary thing. There is no *real* difference between God's attributes; they are only different ways in which we think of God. God's knowledge and omnipotence and love are all *one and the same thing*, viz. God. This is again very different from how we talk about people.

Symbolic language

Paul Tillich argues that it is a mistake to ask whether our attributions of properties to God are true or false. In this, the *via negativa* was right; God transcends the concepts we have. But Tillich argues that we can talk of God symbolically. Our understanding of God takes the form of symbols, in four ways:

1   through words, e.g. Jesus as 'the Way, the Truth and the Life';
2   through images, e.g. God as 'light';
3   through events, e.g. the resurrection; and
4   through things, e.g. the cross.

Religious language tries to express these symbols and the understanding of God they embody.

Tillich argues that symbols 'participate' in the being of God: they point beyond themselves to a deeper reality. They are 'irreducible', i.e. their meaning cannot be fully expressed in literal language, and they can't be straightforwardly replaced by something else. Over time, as the human situation changes, different symbols become more powerful and other ones die; but this is not a matter of *choice*.

We can argue that the meanings of symbols don't follow any obvious rules. First, while we cannot give a literal statement of the meaning of a symbol, we are able to understand symbols even though we cannot say exactly what it is we understand. Second, although trying to spell out its meaning is useful, we will never do so fully. And third, we need to be sensitive to the fact that symbols point beyond themselves so that we don't mistakenly try to draw literal implications from them (e.g. God as father does not imply that God is male).

● **KEY POINTS (1)**

- 'Univocal' means a word has the same meaning (in different contexts). We can object that talk of God is not univocal, because God is very different from anything else, if God is transcendent and simple.

- The *via negativa* claims that no affirmation about God is true. We can only deny things about God. God is beyond all categories.

- Aquinas claims talk of God is analogical. For example, God is wise in being the cause and ground of all wisdom (analogy of attribution); and God has wisdom of a nature and in a way appropriate to God (analogy of proportion). But we don't know what is the appropriate way for God to have wisdom unless we already know about God; and we don't understand how God can be the cause of wisdom if 'God is the cause of wisdom' is only analogically true.

- Tillich argues that although God is beyond all categories, we may talk of God symbolically. Symbols are irreducible, and point beyond themselves to a deeper reality.

Religious language is meaningless

Not all philosophers have tried to show *how* religious language has meaning. Some have argued that it does not. A. J. Ayer argued that all meaningful statements are either **analytic** or **empirically** verifiable (can be shown by experience to be probably true/false). This is the 'principle of verification'.

The principle of verification can be understood as a development of Hume's theory of knowledge (see Ch. 1, EMPIRICISM, p. 12). Hume claimed all knowledge was either **a priori** knowledge of analytic truth or **a posteriori** knowledge of **synthetic** truth. The principle of verification extends this division to meaning. Any statement that is not analytic or cannot be shown to be true or false by experience is *meaningless*.

'God exists', and with it all other talk of God, is such a statement, claims Ayer. Despite the best attempts of THE ONTOLOGICAL ARGUMENT (p. 140), we cannot prove 'God exists' from a priori premises using deduction alone. So 'God exists' is not analytically true. Therefore, to be meaningful, 'God exists' must be empirically verifiable. Ayer argues that it is not. If a statement is an empirical hypothesis, it predicts that our experience will be different depending on whether it is true or false. But this isn't true of 'God exists'. It rules nothing empirical in and it rules nothing out. So it is meaningless.

Some philosophers argue that religious language attempts to capture something of religious experience, although it is 'inexpressible' in literal terms. Ayer responds that whatever religious experiences reveal, they cannot be said to reveal any facts. Facts are the content of statements that purport to be intelligible and can be expressed literally. If talk of God is non-empirical, it is *literally* unintelligible, hence meaningless.

Objections

We can object that many people do think that 'God exists' has empirical content. For example, THE TELEOLOGICAL ARGUMENT (p. 150) argues that the design of the universe is evidence for the existence of God. And, on the other hand, THE PROBLEM OF EVIL (p. 177) takes the existence and extent of suffering to be evidence against the existence of God.

John Hick argues that even if we can't verify the existence of God in this life, that doesn't mean religious language is meaningless. He develops the idea of 'eschatological verification', whereby experiences of God in the afterlife would establish the truth of the existence of God. In arguing that talk of God is meaningless, Ayer overlooked possible experiences of life after death.

These responses accept the verification principle. But the most common response has been to reject it, as it famously faces serious objections. First, what is the status of the principle itself? It does not appear to be analytically true; and it is difficult to know how it could be verified empirically (since it is a criterion of meaning, we cannot go around looking for sentences we already believe meaningful or meaningless and then seeing whether they accord with the principle). So if it were true, it would be meaningless – it cannot be both true and meaningless, so it's not true. If it's false, then it's false!

Second, the verification principle entails that universal statements, such as 'All swans are white' are meaningless – because although you could prove this false, no experience will prove it true (there might always be a swan out there somewhere which isn't white). One response to this is to broaden the verification principle, and claim that a sentence is meaningful if it is analytic or empirically verifiable, or empirically *falsifiable*. Anthony Flew argued that religious language is meaningless because, for a believer, nothing could prove that God *doesn't* exist.

Wittgenstein: expressivism

If talk of God is meaningful, we are returned to the question of what sort of meaning it has. If we think of talk of God as referring to a divine reality completely independent of ourselves, we face the questions of whether God exists, and if so, how we can know this and talk of God. There are, however, ways of understanding religious language that avoid both these challenges. Perhaps the most famous was developed by Ludwig Wittgenstein.

Wittgenstein argued that we cannot understand language without understanding the ways in which language is used, and how it interacts with how we live and what we do. Religious language must be understood as part of a religious life. Wittgenstein agreed with Ayer that 'God exists' is not an empirical statement. But rather than dismissing it as meaningless, he looked at how the statement is *used*, what it *expresses* for people who believe it. Of course, if it is not an empirical statement, then believing it is not an empirical belief. Wittgenstein claimed that it expressed a form of commitment.

Wittgenstein attempted to illuminate the nature of language by likening language to games. In particular:

1 Like games, language is an activity guided by rules – in games, rules govern what one can do, in language, rules govern meaning.
2 Meaning is learned from the rules governing the use of the word or sentence, like 'pieces' in a game are understood by how they can be used.

Meaning, then, is often a matter of how words are *used*. Wittgenstein lists as examples of language games asking, thanking, cursing, praying, greeting and so on.

Surface and depth grammar

Appreciating this requires a distinction between *surface grammar* and *depth grammar*: words or sentences in one context describing *objects* or an *event* may be similar on the surface to ones that in another context do nothing of the sort: e.g. 'the bus passes the bus stop', 'the peace of the Lord passes all understanding'. To understand a particular 'piece' of language, one must look at how the language is used, as meaning is not given by the form of words alone.

Wittgenstein argued that religious language has a depth grammar quite distinct from its surface grammar. 'God exists' is not a statement about a *thing*, an *object*, that exists as part of the world like natural objects do. It is not a claim about an entity at all: 'a religious belief could only be something like a passionate commitment to a system of reference. Hence, although it's a *belief*, it's really a way of living, or a way of assessing life. It's passionately seizing hold of *this* interpretation'.

This can be illustrated by talk of the Last Judgement. This is not an hypothesis about a possible future event; if it was, it would be utterly bizarre (what's the evidence? how is such a belief formed?). The Last Judgement is a 'picture', an understanding of life by which the believer is guided through life. Religious language expresses an emotional attitude and understanding of life, not a description of the way the world is. To understand religious language is to understand the place of certain statements in the life of the believer and the religious community. And the nature of religious faith and morality shows that these statements are not factual.

Objections

Philosophers have objected that Wittgenstein's argument rests on the idea that because religious beliefs express attitudes, they cannot be descriptive. But there is no reason to think that they cannot be *both*. Wittgenstein was right to connect language to behaviour, but, they say, he was wrong to think that religious language can have *no* factual content at all. After all, believers *do* think they are saying something factual when they say 'God exists'. It has this use.

We will discuss Wittgenstein's view of religious belief further in FIDEISM, p. 173.

● **KEY POINTS (2)**

- Ayer argues that the verification principle is the standard of meaningfulness. The principle claims that only statements that are analytically true or false, or can be empirically verified to be true or false, are meaningful. 'God exists' is neither, so is meaningless.

- But 'God exists' has been taken to be empirically meaningful, e.g. in the teleological argument and the problem of evil.

- Hick argues that experiences after death could prove the existence of God, so religious language is meaningful.

- The verification principle is self-defeating: it is neither analytically true nor empirically verifiable. Therefore, by its own standard, it is meaningless.

- Wittgenstein argues that religious language does not refer to an independently existing God, a thing that exists. Instead, its meaning lies in its use, and it is used to express a commitment to a particular way of living and to a framework for understanding and guiding life. But we may object that religious language can express all this *and* still refer to an independent divine reality.

❓ QUIZ QUESTIONS

Explain and illustrate **one** theory that claims religious language is meaningful.

Briefly explain the verification principle and Ayer's argument that religious language is meaningless.

Explain and illustrate **two** features of Wittgenstein's theory of religious language.

❓ DISCUSSION QUESTIONS

Assess the view that talk about God is unintelligible. (AQA, 3c, 2001, *24 marks*)

Assess whether religious language is meaningful. (AQA, 3c, 2003, *24 marks*)

Evaluate **one** of the following claims:

(a) Talk of God is analogical.

(b) Talk of God is symbolic.

● II ARGUMENTS FOR THE EXISTENCE OF GOD

The ontological argument: an a priori argument establishing God's necessary existence from analysis of conceptual truths

St Anselm and Descartes both famously presented an ontological argument for the existence of God. Their versions of the argument are slightly different, but they both argue that we can deduce the existence of God from the idea of God. Just from thinking about what God is, we can conclude that God must exist. Because it doesn't depend on experience in any way, the ontological argument is **a priori**.

Anselm

Anselm's argument relies on 'conceivability':

1   By definition, God is a being greater than which cannot be conceived.
2   I can conceive of such a being.
3   It is greater to exist than not to exist.
4   Therefore, God must exist.

In CONCEPTIONS OF GOD (p. 124), we saw that the idea of God as the most perfect possible being has a long history. And perfection has also been connected to reality: what is perfect is more real than what is not. Anselm's argument makes use of both these ideas.

Anselm received an immediate reply from a monk named Gaunilo: you could prove anything perfect must exist by this argument! I can conceive of the perfect island, greater than which cannot be conceived. And so such an island must exist, because it would be less great if it didn't. But this is ridiculous. So the ontological argument must be flawed. You can't infer the existence of something, Gaunilo argues, from the idea of its being perfect.

Anselm replied that the ontological argument works *only* for God, because the relation between God and greatness, or perfection, is unique. An island wouldn't cease to be what it is – an *island* – if it wasn't perfect; of course, it wouldn't then be a perfect island. But islands aren't perfect by definition: perfection is something an island can have or not have.

It is an *accidental* not an *essential* property of islands. An essential property is one that something must have to be the thing that it is.

By contrast, God, argues Anselm, *must* be the greatest conceivable being – God *wouldn't be God* if there was some being even greater than God. Being the greatest conceivable being is an essential property of God. But, to be the greatest conceivable being God *must* exist.

Notice that this conclusion is more than 'God does exist'; it claims God *must* exist – God's existence is **necessary**. That isn't true of you or me or islands – we can exist or not, we come into existence and cease to exist. Our existence is **contingent**. The ontological argument works only for God, says Anselm, because only God's existence could be necessary.

Descartes

Descartes's version of the argument relies on perfection alone, not conceivability:

> It is certain that I . . . find the idea of a God in my consciousness, that is the idea of a being supremely perfect: and I know with . . . clearness and distinctness that an [actual and] eternal existence pertains to his nature . . . existence can no more be separated from the essence of God, than the idea of a mountain from that of a valley . . . it is not less impossible to conceive a God, that is, a being supremely perfect, to whom existence is wanting, or who is devoid of a certain perfection, than to conceive a mountain without a valley . . . (*Meditation* V).

Descartes's argument is this:

1 I have the idea of God.
2 God is a supremely perfect being.
3 Existence is a perfection. Therefore
4 God must exist.

Everyone agrees the problem lies with (3). What is a 'perfection'? It's a property that it is better to have than not have. So is existence this kind of property? Descartes and Anselm are supposing that it is – that something that *has* existence is greater than something that doesn't.

Descartes is aware of the objection that there is a gap between the idea of God existing and God's actually existing. So he objects to himself that,

> just as it does not follow that there is any mountain in the world merely because I conceive a mountain with a valley, so likewise, though I conceive God as existing, it does not seem to follow on that account that God exists . . . .

But, he replies,

the cases are not analogous . . . it does not follow that there is any mountain or valley in existence, but simply that the mountain or valley, whether they do or do not exist, are inseparable from each other; whereas, on the other hand, because I cannot conceive God unless as existing, it follows that existence is inseparable from him, and therefore that he really exists: not that this is brought about by my thought, or that it imposes any necessity on things, but, on the contrary, the necessity which lies in the thing itself, that is, the necessity of the existence of God, determines me to think in this way: for it is not in my power to conceive a God without existence . . . .

We can clearly understand that there is a conceptual connection between the concept of God and God's existence, and this entails that God must exist.

Objections

Gassendi objects that existence is *not* part of the idea of God as a supremely perfect being. Can't I form the idea of a God who does not exist? Descartes replies by claiming, with Aquinas, that divine perfections all entail each other (see THE NATURE OF RELIGIOUS LANGUAGE, p. 135). Because our minds are finite, we normally think of the divine perfections – omnipotence, omniscience, necessary existence, etc. – separately and 'hence may not immediately notice the necessity of their being joined together'. But if we reflect carefully, we shall discover that we cannot conceive any one of the other attributes while excluding necessary existence from it. For example, in order for God to be omnipotent, God must not depend on anything else, and so must not depend on anything else to exist.

Ironically, Aquinas *doesn't* think existence is a perfection. He objects – and Johannes Caterus put the point to Descartes – that this doesn't demonstrate that God really exists. It shows only that the *concept* of existence is inseparable from the *concept* of God. Descartes's argument is only convincing for the claim that *if* God exists, God exists necessarily. Descartes responds that *necessary* existence does entail actual existence.

Immanuel Kant, however, responds that this doesn't work. The problem with the ontological argument is that it wrongly assumes that existence is a *property*. But things don't *have* existence in the same way that they *have* other properties. Consider whether 'God exists' is an **analytic** or a **synthetic** judgement. According to Descartes, it must be analytic: his argument is that 'God does not exist' is a contradiction in terms, for the concept 'God' contains the idea of existence (necessary existence belongs to God's essence). But, Kant claims, existence does not add anything to, or define, a concept itself; to say something exists is to say that some object corresponds to the concept.

When we list the essential properties of something, we describe our concept of that thing. For instance, a dog is a mammal. But now if I tell you that the dog asleep in the corner is a mammal and it exists, I seem to have said two very different sorts of things. To say that it exists is only to say that there is something real that corresponds to the concept 'dog'. It is not to say anything *about* the dog *as* a dog.

Existence, Kant argues, is not part of any concept, even in the case of God. So it is not true to say that 'God exists' must be true.

> ### Going further: necessary existence
>
> If existence isn't a property that something *has*, then it can't be a property that God has necessarily! However, it is plausible to think that *if* God exists, God exists necessarily. God cannot be a contingent being. If God's existence were not necessary, God would depend on something else that could cause God to come into or go out of existence.
>
> There is a difference between saying 'Necessarily, God exists' and 'God exists necessarily'. The first means that it must be true that God exists. The *necessity* applies to the claim: 'God exists' is necessarily true. The second means that the *type* of existence God has (if God exists at all) is 'necessary', i.e. not contingent, without dependence on anything else. The ontological argument confuses the two. Because God's existence is necessary (second meaning), it wrongly infers that necessarily, God exists (first meaning).

● **KEY POINTS**

- The ontological argument is a priori; it works from an analysis of concepts, not from any fact of experience.

- The ontological argument takes for granted the idea that God is perfect, the greatest conceivable being.

- The conclusion of the ontological argument is that God necessarily exists. Everything else only exists contingently.

- Kant's objection claims that the argument is wrong to think that existence is a property of something. To say something exists is to say only that something corresponds to a concept we have; it is not to say anything further about that concept. So existence can't be an 'essential property'.

❓ QUIZ QUESTION

Explain and illustrate **one** objection to the ontological argument.

❓ DISCUSSION QUESTION

Assess the ontological argument for the existence of God. (AQA, 4c, 2004, *24 marks*)

The cosmological argument: an argument from the fact of the universe to God as the explanation of its occurrence

The question at the heart of the cosmological argument is 'Why does anything exist? Why something rather than nothing?' The argument is that unless God exists, this question is unanswerable. Unlike THE ONTOLOGICAL ARGUMENT (p. 140), the cosmological argument is **a posteriori**; it relies on the fact that something, the universe, exists, and we can only know this through experience.

There are different forms of the argument. Two central ones are the *Kalam* argument and the argument from contingent existence. They are usually presented as **deductive** arguments; an **inductive** variation is given by Richard Swinburne.

The *Kalam* argument

The *Kalam* argument observes that

1 of anything that begins to exist, you can ask what caused it. For example, what caused me (my birth)? In a sense, my parents. But then, we can repeat the question: 'What caused my parents?' And so on. We can go back to the beginning of the universe, and then ask: 'What caused the universe?' If
2 the universe began to exist, then
3 it must have a cause of its existence. Something can't come out of nothing.
4 What we need is something that causes things to exist, but the existence of which isn't caused itself.
5 Only God could be such a thing.

In support of this conclusion, we can argue that science can't provide us with the right sort of answer. Science must assume the existence of something in order to provide explanations. Of any scientific answer to (1) – e.g. the Big Bang – we can still ask: 'Well, what caused *that*?' So the answer can't be scientific.

There are three key issues that need to be addressed to defend the argument. First, is the causal principle, that everything that begins to exist has a cause, correct? Second, does the universe have a beginning? Third, must the explanation be God? We will leave this third question to the very end of this section.

The causal principle

Must every event have a cause? David Hume famously argued that we cannot know this. It is not an **analytic** truth (by contrast, 'Every effect has a cause' *is* an analytic truth; but is every event an effect?). 'Something cannot come out of nothing' is also not analytic. Hume argued that we can know only analytic truths **a priori**; therefore, we can establish the above claims only through experience. And although our experience is that everything so far has a cause, can this principle be applied to the beginning of the universe?

First, the beginnings of universes are not something we have any experience of. Second, the beginning of the universe is not an event like events that happen within the universe. It doesn't take place in space or time, since both come into existence with the universe. Even if everything within the universe has a cause, that doesn't mean that the universe as a whole does. We cannot apply principles we have developed for events *within* the universe to the universe as a whole. Bertrand Russell famously put it: 'the universe is just there, and that's all'.

Does the universe have a beginning?

Rather than challenge the causal principle, we can ask why we cannot reject the idea that the universe has a beginning at all. Because time came into existence with the universe, the universe didn't 'happen' *at a time*; so, in a sense, it *has no beginning*. We can reply that, even if this is true, science suggests the universe has a finite past (it is about 13 billion years old). We may then argue that whatever has a finite past must have a cause of its existence. In the case of the universe, that cause can't exist *in* time if time didn't exist before the universe. But that doesn't mean there was no cause, only that the cause must exist outside time – which God does, according to many theists.

Alternatively, even if *this* universe has a beginning, perhaps it was caused by a previous (or another) universe, and so on, infinitely. In other words, rather than infer that God exists, we may think there is just an infinite regress of causes. Something has always existed.

It is, however, difficult to imagine what infinity is; it is not, for instance, simply a 'very long time'. It is very different from a 'very long time' – it means, quite literally, that there was no beginning, ever. Because the universe exists, this response claims that an *actual* infinity – something that is in fact infinite – exists. This is quite different from talking about the *idea* of infinity. The idea of infinity makes sense; but does it make sense to think that something infinite exists?

For example, the universe gets older as time passes. But this couldn't happen if the universe was infinitely old, because you cannot add any number to infinity and get a bigger number: $\infty + 1 = \infty$. So if the universe is infinitely old, it is not getting any older as time passes! Or again, to have reached the present, an infinite amount of time would need to have passed. But it is not possible for an *infinite* amount of time to have passed, since infinity is not an *amount*. So if the universe was infinitely old, it could never have reached the present.

Given that science tells us that the (this) universe has a beginning, this discussion of something *always* existing means that we must think of preceding universes. But given that the beginning of this universe was also the beginning of time as we know it, we may wonder what sense to make of talking about anything existing *before* this universe. We should not talk about an infinity of time, therefore, but an infinite series of causes (some operating outside the time of this universe).

But the puzzles arise for an infinite series of causes, too. Each new cause doesn't add one more cause to the series, since $\infty + 1 = \infty$. And we would never have reached the point in the series at which we are now if it were an infinite series.

We noted that the question at the heart of the cosmological argument is: 'Why something rather than nothing?' If we have an infinite series of causes, although each cause can be explained in terms of the previous cause, we may wonder what explains the *whole series*. If we say something exists because something has always existed, we still haven't answered the question why anything exists at all. This takes us to the next form of cosmological argument.

The argument from contingent existence

This version of the cosmological argument, defended by Frederick Copleston in a radio debate with Bertrand Russell, emphasizes the need to *explain* what exists:

1 Things in the universe exist **contingently**: they might not have existed or they might stop existing.
2 Something that exists contingently has (and needs) an explanation of why it exists; after all, it is not inevitable.
3 This explanation may be provided by the existence of some other contingent being (as in the example of me and my parents). But then we must explain these other contingent beings.
4 To repeat this *ad infinitum* is no explanation of why anything exists at all.
5 So what explains why contingent beings exist at all can only be a non-contingent being. A non-contingent being is one that cannot not exist, i.e. it exists **necessarily**, it doesn't need some *further* explanation for why it exists.
6 This necessary being is God.

Objections

Russell objected to what the argument claims is needed for a satisfactory explanation – (2) and (4). Perhaps of any particular thing in the universe, we need an explanation of why it exists, which science can give us. But it is a mistake to think that we can apply this idea to the universe itself. A form of explanation developed for the *parts* of the universe needn't apply to the universe as a *whole*.

However, we can reply that the universe is itself a contingent being – if every part of the universe ceased to exist, so would the universe. So as a contingent being, the universe is like its parts. What is wrong with the principle that all contingent beings require an explanation of their existence?

A second objection is that although, as philosophers and scientists, we should *look for* explanations of contingent beings, we cannot know that in fact every contingent being *has* such an explanation. Without this, the argument fails as a deduction. However, this objection can be avoided if we give up the idea that the cosmological argument is deductive, and claim that it is an inference to the best explanation instead (see below).

A third objection attacks the conclusion. It is not God but matter/energy (in some form) that is a necessary being. A fundamental law of physics is the conservation of energy: the total amount of matter/energy in the universe remains constant, it cannot be increased or decreased. If a version of this law applied even at the beginning and end of universes, then matter/energy is a necessary being. However, we have no reason to believe that this law *does* apply at the beginning (and possibly the end) of the universe. The Big Bang theory suggests that matter/energy was created, along with time and space, i.e. the universe came into existence – so it is contingent.

Going further: necessary being again

The argument claims that a necessary being exists. However, Kant objected that the idea of a necessary being is the idea of a being that has existence as one of its properties. But existence is never a property, so the idea makes no sense, and the argument is flawed (see THE ONTOLOGICAL ARGUMENT, p. 142).

Kant was right that 'Necessarily, God exists' cannot be true. It is not a logical contradiction to deny the existence of anything, even God. However, 'If God exists, God exists necessarily' allows this. It does not claim that God's existence is *logically* necessary, but that *if* God exists, God's existence is not contingent, without dependence on anything else.

This doesn't solve the problem. If God's existence is not contingent, then the explanation of God's existence, if God exists, rests in God himself. God's *essence* provides the explanation for God's existence. If this were not true, then God's existence would need to be explained by something else. So for God's existence to be necessary, his existence must be inseparable from his essence. But that treats (necessary) existence as a property of God, which is what Kant argued cannot be right.

Swinburne: an inductive argument

Both deductive versions of the cosmological argument face serious objections. Swinburne claims that the cosmological argument is better understood as an inference to the *best explanation*. God's existence isn't logically proven, but it is probable, given the premises. Considered on its own, the claim 'God exists' is very improbable, says Swinburne. But in the light of the cosmological argument it becomes more probable, because God's existence is the best explanation of why the universe exists.

Swinburne thinks that THE TELEOLOGICAL ARGUMENT (p. 150) and THE ARGUMENT FROM RELIGIOUS EXPERIENCE (p. 155) work the same way. When we put all these arguments together, he claims, it becomes more probable that God exists than that God doesn't. Whenever God is used to explain anything, e.g. MIRACLES (p. 182), we may ask whether the existence of God is the best explanation, i.e. whether the existence of God genuinely helps us understand something, rather than making us more puzzled, and no other explanation will do as well.

A conclusion is only probable if its premises are also plausible. Although it is not an analytic truth that everything that begins to exist has a cause, it is extremely probable – our experience supports it. And the theory of the Big Bang and the problems with infinite existence make it more plausible that the universe (or matter/energy) has not existed without beginning, but came into existence. So, Swinburne argues, it is probable that God exists and caused the beginning of the universe.

So we now need to consider whether God is the *best* explanation.

Personal explanation

Swinburne argues that science can't offer *any* satisfactory explanation, because science can't provide us with the right sort of answer to 'What caused the universe?' Science must assume physical laws and the existence of something in order to provide explanations. If we explain this universe in terms of another universe, we then have to explain the existence of that universe. And science can't explain scientific laws – where they come from or why they are the way they are, because all scientific explanations presuppose laws. Scientific laws are *brute* – they have no explanation unless we can find some other kind of explanation of them.

We use another type of explanation all the time, viz. *personal explanation*. We explain the products of human activity – this book, these sentences – in terms of a person. I'm writing things I *intend* to write. This sort of explanation explains an object or an event in terms of a person and their purposes. The hypothesis that God exists and intended to create the universe (including its laws) provides a personal explanation for the existence of the universe.

Why God?

But does any cosmological argument support the existence of God, as we normally think of God? For example, it doesn't show that there is only one cause of the universe; nor does it show that that cause is perfect, omniscient, omnipotent or cares about people. The cosmological argument only needs 'God' to be able to create the universe. It doesn't say anything else about God.

Swinburne's response is to accept this. The argument doesn't *prove* that the cause of the universe is the traditional theistic conception of God. However, he argues, God as we usually think of him remains the *best* explanation.

Going further: best explanation

Swinburne says an explanation is good 'when the explanatory hypothesis [in this case, the existence of God and his intention to create the universe] is simple and leads us with some probability to expect the data which we would not otherwise expect'. 'Simplicity' means not invoking more different kinds of things than you need to; and not giving them more properties, or more complex properties than they need for the explanation to work.

Simplicity requires that we shouldn't suppose that two possible causes exist when only one will do. Supposing there to be more than one cause of the universe is a worse explanation, because it is not as simple. It is also simpler to suppose that the cause of the universe is itself uncaused, or we have a problem of regress. It is also simpler to suppose that God has infinite power and intelligence, or we would have to explain why God had just the amount of power and intelligence he has (enough to create the universe, but no more), i.e. what limits God's power and intelligence?

(Swinburne adds infinite goodness to the properties of God, but we can question this – why does God need to be *good* in order to create the universe? This objection becomes more pressing when we consider THE PROBLEM OF EVIL, p. 177.)

But is this enough to show that 'God' is a simple explanation? Personal explanations explain something in terms of a mind that intended that thing. But a mind is very complicated, much more difficult to explain! The mind that intends to create something must be able to think of the thing it intends to create – so in a certain sense, it must be as complicated as that thing, in this case, the universe. It seems that now we have to ask 'What explains God?', and this seems to be an even more puzzling question than 'What explains scientific laws?'.

Swinburne responds that science will introduce an entity – like sub-atomic particles – in order to explain something, even though those entities need explaining themselves, and scientists don't yet know how to explain them. So we can still say that God is a good explanation for scientific laws even if we can't explain God.

But if we will always have *something* we can't explain, why invoke God? Why not just say we can't explain scientific laws? Because scientific laws leave fewer things unexplained, and we should explain as much as we can. This is a principle of science and philosophy. If you give up on this, you give up on pursuing these forms of thought.

We will discuss a further objection with THE TELEOLOGICAL ARGUMENT (p. 150).

● **KEY POINTS**

- The cosmological argument tries to answer the question 'Why does something exist rather than nothing?' The arguments from cause and contingent existence try to *deduce* that God exists; Swinburne argues that God's existence is the *best explanation*.

- The *Kalam* argument claims that everything that begins to exist has a cause, and that the universe began to exist. The only way to avoid an infinite regression of causes is to say something exists that did not begin to exist, viz. God.

- Hume objects that we can't know that everything that begins to exist has a cause. Russell objects that we can't apply this principle to the universe itself. Other philosophers argue that an infinite regression of causes is possible, so we can't infer that God exists.

- The argument from contingent existence claims that the existence of anything that exists contingently has an explanation, and that an infinite regress of explanations is not an explanation of why anything exists at all. So we can deduce that some non-contingent being exists, viz. God.

- We can object, with Russell, that there is no explanation of the universe as a whole; and that we cannot know that every contingent being actually *has* an explanation for its existence. Another objection suggests that matter/energy exists non-contingently, so we can't infer that God exists. Kant objected that the conclusion of the argument, that something exists necessarily, makes no sense because it treats existence as a property.

- Swinburne claims that although the cosmological argument fails as a deductive proof of God's existence, the best explanation for the existence of the universe is the existence of God. However, showing that it is the best explanation is difficult.

❓ QUIZ QUESTIONS

Explain and illustrate **two** differences between personal and scientific explanation.

Outline **one** form of the cosmological argument.

Outline **one** criticism of the cosmological argument.

❓ DISCUSSION QUESTION

Assess whether the existence of the universe is good evidence for the existence of God.

The teleological argument: an argument from order and design to God as the explanation of order and design

Cosmological arguments start from the fact that the universe exists contingently and infer the existence of a *creator*. Teleological arguments start from the observation of order and design in nature and infer the existence of a *designer*, a mind that can order things for a purpose.

The argument from analogy

In his *Dialogues on Natural Religion*, Hume expresses the argument from design like this:

> The curious adapting of means to ends, through all nature, resembles exactly, though it much exceeds, the productions of human contrivance; of human design,

thought, wisdom, and intelligence. Since, therefore, the effects resemble each other, we are led to infer, by all the rules of analogy, that the causes also resemble; and that the Author of Nature is somewhat similar to the mind of man, though possessed of much larger faculties, proportioned to the grandeur of the work which he has executed.

This argument explicitly uses analogy: nature is *like* human inventions in the way it displays purpose (the adaptation of means to ends, e.g. the arrangement of the parts of the eye to enable sight, of the heart to pump blood), so it must have a similar cause to human inventions, viz. a mind that intended to create such design.

Hume argues against the analogy:

1   The analogy is weak: human artefacts, e.g. watches, are not very like natural things, e.g. watches aren't alive and don't reproduce. Nature, or the universe as a whole, is even less like a watch. Because the effects aren't very like, we can't infer similar causes.
2   The basis for inference is very weak. We can't generalize from such a small part of the universe to the creation of the whole: 'why select so minute, so weak, so bounded a principle as the reason and design of animals is found to be upon this planet' from which to infer the cause of the universe?
3   There are other possible explanations we cannot rule out; in particular if there are a finite number of particles, then over an infinite time they will appear in every possible order and position. With alternative possible causes of a similar effect, we can't infer from the similarity of the effects that the causes are similar.

Hume also argues that, even if the analogy worked, we couldn't infer that the designer is God:

1   If we take the analogy seriously, we could infer that, just like human beings, the designer of the universe needed to be trained up. In fact, the many examples of poor design, e.g. *natural evil* (see THE PROBLEM OF EVIL, p. 177), would suggest that the universe is the work of an apprentice who made mistakes. Alternatively, if we think that natural evils are equally evidence of design, rather than mistakes, we have to hold the designer morally responsible for them.
2   If like effects are evidence of like causes, we should also say that the cause is proportionate to the effect. Since the universe isn't infinite, we shouldn't infer that God is infinite. We also can't infer that the designer of the universe also created the universe.

Finally, Hume argues that, having inferred the existence of a designer, we now need to explain him. But we can't: the cause is as mysterious as the effect, so we haven't really explained anything.

These objections can be debated. For example, it is not necessarily objectionable to infer from the part of the universe of which we have experience to the whole: Einstein did exactly that in creating his theory of relativity. Or again, the fact that we can't explain the designer isn't necessarily an objection: science often supposes a cause which itself needs explaining if doing so helps us understand the effect. However, philosophers have usually responded by changing the argument so that it doesn't rely on analogy.

Paley's variant

It is often thought that William Paley argues from analogy; but in fact, his argument works slightly differently. Paley argues that if I found a stone lying in a field, and wondered how it came to be there, I might rightly think that, for all I knew, it had always been there. However, if I found a watch lying on the ground, I wouldn't feel the same answer was satisfactory, because on inspecting the watch, I would find its parts to have been put together for a purpose. And so I would infer it had a designer. Paley spends a considerable time exploring this inference, and whether it is valid *in the case of the watch*. For example, would it undermine the inference if the watch sometimes went wrong, or if I'd never seen a watch being made? Paley is trying to identify exactly what it is about a watch that allows us to infer a designer. After all, in the case of a watch, this does seem a good inference. Paley then argues that we can make exactly the *same* argument in the case of natural things that exhibit an organization of parts for a purpose.

Paley is relying on the idea that the sorts of properties he takes as evidence of design – in the cases of the watch and of nature – cannot be produced by *natural means*, and so must be the result of a mind. In the case of the watch, this seems right – a watch *isn't* the kind of thing nature produces. However, natural things are precisely the sort of thing that nature *does* produce.

There is no question that natural things have *design-like* properties. The difficulty is that unlike watches, natural things don't show evidence of being *manufactured artefacts*. In this different context, their design-like properties aren't so clearly good evidence for actually having been designed. Although we are making the same inference from design-like properties to a designer, the argument doesn't have the same force in the case of natural things, since we don't know that nature can't produce such properties. Although Paley's argument is not explicitly an argument from analogy, an important difference between artefacts and natural things still undermines his argument.

Darwin and developments

Paley seems right when he says that, on finding a watch in a field, we would want an explanation of how it got there; and we may agree that the appearance of design in nature similarly requires *some* explanation. What explanations, then, are on offer and which is the *best* one?

Darwin's theory of evolution by natural selection provides an excellent account of how the appearance of design could come about without genuine design. Millions of alterations randomly take place. Most disappear without a trace. But something that *coincidentally* helps an organism to survive and reproduce, to function well, slowly spreads, and more and more organisms end up with it. What appears to be designed is actually just evidence of good *functioning*. So organisms appear to be designed when they are in fact the product of coincidence.

Darwinism is sometimes thought to eliminate the question of design in nature. But we can now ask 'What explains evolution?' Perhaps design is *built in* to natural processes. In fact, many philosophers *before* Darwin argued that the apparent design of nature is evidence that God designed nature in the moment of creation and could then let it unfold. God set up nature so that life evolves by natural selection. Darwin himself accepted this view.

The 'fine-tuning' argument

Swinburne argues that his version of THE COSMOLOGICAL ARGUMENT (p. 147), that God is the best explanation of the existence of the universe, is strengthened by a similar version of the teleological argument, viz. that God is the best explanation of the order and purpose that we find. In particular, the conditions for *life* to come into existence are so precise that they require explanation. That the particular scientific laws that apply in the universe and the 'initial conditions' are exactly how they need to be for us to come into existence seems a staggering coincidence. He says that

> the matter–energy at the time of the Big Bang when the universe began . . . had just the quantity, density, and initial velocity as to lead in the course of time to the evolution of organisms. . . . Only a certain sort of critical arrangement of matter and certain kinds of laws of nature will give rise to organisms. And recent scientific work on the fine-tuning of the universe has shown that the initial matter and the laws of nature had to have very, very special features indeed if organisms were to evolve.

Just for stars to be able to form, the initial strength of the explosion in the Big Bang had to be precise to one part in 10^{60} – it couldn't vary by more than 0.000000000000000000000000000000000000000000000000000000000001 *per cent*. That's as precise as hitting a 1-inch target at the other side of the observable universe! And that's just for stars to form. For life to form on planets is *even more* improbable, because so many more laws are involved.

What's the best explanation for this? Swinburne again appeals to the need for personal explanation. Science can't explain scientific laws – in this case, the ones that allow evolution of intelligent life to occur. But if God created the world and intended for life to evolve, then we would expect precisely the laws there are. Instead of being a massive coincidence, they become inevitable. God's existence is the best explanation *both* for the existence of the universe *and* its nature.

We discussed some objections to Swinburne's argument in THE COSMOLOGICAL ARGUMENT (p. 148); we will look at one further one here.

Does the universe need explaining?

Do we need an explanation of why the universe appears designed? Some things that appear to be coincidence are in fact inevitable, e.g. winning the lottery: it is very unlikely that you will win, but it is inevitable that *someone* will win. For whoever wins, that *he* or *she* won is a huge coincidence; but we don't need any special explanation of it (such as 'Someone intended them to win, and rigged the lottery').

Suppose, then, that instead of just this universe there are or have been millions of universes. Each had different scientific laws, and in most cases the laws didn't allow the universe to continue to exist – as soon as it began, it ended. Others existed, but there was no life. It was inevitable, we might think, that given all the possible variations in scientific laws, a universe such as ours would exist, and therefore so would life. It doesn't need any special explanation – it had to happen.

But why *ours*? Well, it had to be ours because we wouldn't be here if it wasn't! Given that life *does* exist in it, *this* universe has to have the right scientific laws for life to exist. If it didn't, life wouldn't exist in it. There is nothing special about this universe, except that it has the right laws; just like there is nothing special about the ticket that wins the lottery.

But for this response, we have to assume the existence of *huge* numbers of other universes, which are completely inaccessible to us, and for which we have (virtually) no other evidence. The existence of God by contrast, Swinburne argues, is also supported by THE ARGUMENT FROM RELIGIOUS EXPERIENCE (p. 155). So the existence of just one universe, designed by God, is a simpler and better explanation.

However, as with all **inductive** arguments, we should not reach this conclusion without also looking at the evidence against the existence of God (see THE PROBLEM OF EVIL, p. 177).

KEY POINTS

- Teleological arguments are inductive, **a posteriori**, arguments from the apparent order, purpose or design of natural things to the existence of a divine designer.

- One form uses analogy: artefacts created by humans exhibit purpose and order, and so do natural things. From purpose and order in artefacts, we infer that artefacts are designed. As natural things are similar in exhibiting design, we may infer that a similar cause, an intelligent mind, explains their design.

- Hume objected that the analogy is weak – natural things aren't very like human artefacts – and that we cannot infer similar causes from similar effects, because there are many other possible causes of the apparent design in natural things.

- Hume also objected that we can't infer that the designer is God. If similar effects have similar causes, then the designer is imperfect and finite, because natural things appear to be imperfect and finite.

- Paley tries to identify precisely what it is in human artefacts that supports the conclusion that they were designed. He then claims that these same properties exist in natural things, so the inference is equally valid.

- However, even if design-like properties exist in natural things, the inference to a designer is not supported, because natural objects are not like artefacts. Darwin's theory of evolution explains how nature can produce design-like properties.

- The modern teleological argument asks *why* nature is capable of producing apparently designed things, i.e. what explains the laws of nature that enable this. As the chance of these laws occurring randomly is incredibly low, Swinburne argues that the best explanation is that God intended the evolution of apparently designed things.

- However, chance could be a good explanation (or, rather, no explanation is required): if there are or have been huge numbers of universes, the chance that *one* would have laws that enabled apparent design is much higher. However, this requires that many such other universes do or have existed, a claim for which we have little independent evidence.

❓ QUIZ QUESTIONS

Explain and illustrate the use of analogy in the teleological argument.

Outline and illustrate **one** criticism of the teleological argument for the existence of God. (AQA, 4b, 2004, *15 marks*)

❓ DISCUSSION QUESTION

Assess whether the apparent existence of design in the universe supports the claim that God exists.

The argument from religious experience: an argument from the widespread occurrence of religious experiences, supposedly with a common phenomenological core, to the existence of God

The argument

Many people have experiences they identify as *religious*. Experiences that are part of a religious life include the ups and downs of faith, doubt, sacrifice and achievement. We are interested in those experiences which seem to the person as though he or she is directly aware of God or God's action.

Some philosophers have argued that these experiences are importantly similar to perception, an immediate awareness of something other than oneself. We usually treat perceptual experiences as **veridical**, unless we have good reason to doubt them. Furthermore, the fact that other people have similar perceptual experiences supports the claim that perceptual experiences show the world accurately. Some philosophers have argued that religious experiences are also similar to each other, despite occurring to very different people in very different circumstances. The best explanation of these experiences, and their common nature, is that they are veridical, i.e. they are experiences of something divine. Therefore, God exists.

There are three important questions to discuss. First, what is the similarity between religious experiences, and how do their characteristics support the existence of God? Second, what philosophical problems are there for thinking that these experiences can give us knowledge of God? Third, is there an alternative explanation for the experiences?

James: What is religious experience?

In *The Varieties of Religious Experience*, William James argues that, for all the apparent differences between religions and religious experiences, it is possible to detect a 'common core' to all (genuine) religious experiences.

1 Religious experiences are *experiential*, like perception. They are quite different from *thinking* about God or trying to *imagine* God's nature.
2 However, they aren't connected to any particular mode of sense perception (sight, hearing, etc.). Sometimes they can be, e.g. the person may feel God is speaking to them; but the 'inner words' are not normally everything about the experience. They are part of an awareness that transcends sense perceptions, that doesn't have sensory content.
3 The person feels *immediately* aware of God, and so connected to him.
4 This awareness tends to block out everything else temporarily, perhaps even to the degree that the distinction between the person and what he or she is aware of disappears ('mystical union').

The heart of religious experience, James claims, is a immediate sense of the reality of the 'unseen'. By this, he means to contrast what we are aware of in a religious experience with the usual 'visible world'. Our awareness of the 'unseen' may be inarticulable, beyond even an ability to think in any usual terms about it. Conceptualization, an attempt to describe it, to say *what* was experienced, comes later.

Experience and consequence

If we are to take such experiences seriously, as something more than momentary insanity, we must connect them up to the rest of our lives, thinks James. Religious experiences are connected to having a religious attitude to life; those experiences that have no impact on how someone understands life are dubitable, and may not be genuine. James says that a religious attitude is 'solemn, serious and tender', and has five main characteristics. We should understand religious experiences in relation to them:

1 The visible world is part of a spiritual universe which gives it meaning.
2 A harmonious relation with that spiritual universe is our true purpose in life.
3 This harmony enables spiritual energy to flow into and affect the visible world.

James understands these first three beliefs to be the most immediate implications of religious experience (the third belief is perhaps better rephrased as: 'Our harmony with the spiritual universe allows spiritual energy to flow through us'). All religion, he argues, points to the feeling that there is something wrong with us as we stand, and that this is corrected by becoming in touch with a higher power. Realizing this is connected to an awareness of being in touch with something 'more' in religious experience. He then adds two further traits:

4   Religious experience produces a new zest which adds itself like a gift to life.
5   Such experiences bestow an assurance of safety, a feeling of peace and, in relation to others, a preponderance of loving emotions.

All of this, notes James, is very interesting psychologically, but we don't yet know what the truth of such experiences is, i.e. whether they are experiences of God. In being aware of something *more*, is this *more* just our own 'higher selves' or something objectively real? James remarks that there is *more* to us than we consciously realize – a claim with which anyone who believes in a spiritual dimension to human beings will agree. This already makes it literally true that in religious experience we are in touch with something external to ourselves as we usually experience ourselves. But in addition, religious experience has real effects upon us.

In both these ways, religious experiences are of something real, which is transformative in a positive way. James is happy to call this reality, considered abstractly, 'God', and so religious experiences give us knowledge. Furthermore, 'God is real since he produces real effects'.

James claims that if we try to say more about God than this, then we speculate. But we might argue that we can know something about God by the *type* of effects he produces – a zest for life, the predominance of love, the sense that there is something wrong with us without God. We may also argue that God is not only the spiritual side of people. For example, how could human beings have a spiritual side if there is no divine being? Philosophers may argue that although it remains an hypothesis, the existence of God is the *best explanation* of the experiences James describes.

Philosophical issues

We noted that religious experiences are similar to perceptions and that we usually assume perceptual experiences are veridical unless we have reasons to think otherwise. We can conclude that we should assume religious experiences to be experiences of something divine unless we have reasons to think otherwise. However, philosophers have argued that religious experiences are not really like perceptions, so the principle doesn't apply; and that, even if they were, we do have reasons to doubt that they are veridical.

Religious experience is not like perception

First, sense experience is universal among people, and is continuously present to us when we are awake. It provides very rich detail and information ('A picture is worth a thousand words'). By contrast, only some people have religious experiences, and only rarely. They find it very difficult to say anything that is very informative. So we shouldn't assume that religious experiences are veridical.

The fact that only a small number of people have religious experiences doesn't show those experiences to be non-veridical: only a small number of people can recognize an eighteenth-century piece of furniture, but that doesn't mean they aren't right or reliable. We can't tell the truth of something from its frequency. Furthermore, while the experience doesn't give *much* information, that doesn't mean it doesn't give *any*.

However, the objection is that because religious experiences are rare, we shouldn't *assume* that they are veridical until we have reason to doubt them. Surely part of the reason we trust perception *is* because it is so widespread, common and informative.

Another reason we trust perception is that we have intersubjective agreement; if you and I start seeing things very differently, we wouldn't be so sure. And if I'm not sure about what I see, I can check with you. This isn't true of religious experience, which is more private.

In response, we may appeal to James's five characteristics of a religious attitude. If a religious experience has no transformative consequences, we may doubt that it was veridical; if it does transform the person, then we have reason to think it was. Second, we can argue that religious experiences are more like experiences of what we *feel* than what we perceive. And I don't check how I'm feeling by seeing how you feel, nor do you have direct access to what I feel. Rather, we judge how people feel by the impact of their feelings on their lives (in the first instance, on their behaviour, facial expressions and so on). James suggests that we can make similar claims about religious experience.

Reasons to doubt that religious experiences are of God

By and large, people from different cultures have used similar ways of understanding the world, in terms of objects with colour, size, solidity and so on. By contrast, religious experience has produced very different ideas of what the 'divine reality' might be, from the Christian idea of God explored in CONCEPTIONS OF GOD (p. 124) to Buddhist ideas of 'nothingness'.

James would respond that we shouldn't think that religious experience can give us a whole theological system. At most, we can argue to the reality of something spiritual, and perhaps reach tentative conclusions about what that reality is like. We may also argue that people can experience the same thing while disagreeing about what it is they have experienced (think of witnesses in court). So disagreements between religions don't show that religious experiences aren't veridical, only that they can tell us very little about the nature of the divine.

However, we may still wonder whether the existence of God is the *best* explanation of religious experiences, or whether some other explanation is as good. For example, we might argue that people who have a religious experience are simply imposing certain religious ideas or expectations on to an emotional experience which is not awareness of the divine at all. One response to this points out that there are many cases of conversion as a result of religious experience, in which the person wasn't expecting anything religious to occur.

Freud: a psychological explanation

In *The Future of an Illusion*, Sigmund Freud presents a different explanation of what might be happening in religious experiences. He argues that they could be hallucinations, like dreams, caused by a very deep unconscious wish that human beings have. This wish goes back in history to the emergence of the human race, and in each individual to his or her earliest infancy. The wish is for consolation and reassurance.

In the face of the uncontrollable forces of nature, we feel vulnerable, afraid and frustrated that there is so little we can do. We want to rob life of its terrors. Likewise, when we are infants, we are completely helpless and dependent and need protection. Both motives come together in the thought that there is a God, a protector, a means by which we can control nature (for early religions) or feel safe in the face of danger and uncertainty. Our relationship to God takes on the intimacy and intensity of our relationship to our parents (Freud thought that the father gives protection and security, so we think of God as more of a father than a mother).

Religious beliefs are 'fulfilments of the oldest, strongest and most urgent wishes of mankind. The secret of their strength lies in the strength of those wishes.' Isn't it remarkable, he says, that religion describes the universe 'exactly as we are bound to wish it to be'? A belief that is based on a wish, rather than on evidence, Freud calls an 'illusion'. It isn't necessarily false; it's just that it isn't based on seeking the truth.

Just as religious beliefs are based on wishes, so religious experiences are as well. Freud argues that dreams are caused by deep desires we are unaware of, and he argues that religious experiences are similarly caused. They are hallucinations that happen when we are awake, caused by the wish for security and meaning, for things to 'be OK'.

Freud's theory seems to account for many of the characteristics James noted about religious experiences. If they are hallucinations, then we can expect them to be experiences, rather than thoughts, in which the person seems to be aware of something directly. Given the nature of the wish, we can expect them to involve intense feelings; and because the wish is abstract, they won't be particularly related to any mode of perception. They will feel like there is something beyond or outside oneself that can offer security, upon which one can depend.

Objections

James argues that Freud's theory doesn't undermine the possibility that religious experiences are experiences of God.

1   We can't evaluate the truth of an experience just by its origin. We should look at its effects, its place in our lives. We must evaluate it by other things we feel are important and by what we know to be true. Religious experiences produce real effects, which are positive.

2   We can agree that religious experiences come to us in the first instance from the unconscious. But it is entirely possible that the unconscious is a *conduit* of spiritual reality. Almost everyone who believes in a spiritual dimension to human beings thinks that this goes beyond what we are aware of.

3   *Even if* religious experiences are caused by a wish for security and meaning, if God does exist and we do need him, then our wish for contact with God would be realistic – if we are made by God, then a relationship with God would be one of our deepest desires. The wish Freud identifies may not be the result *only* of the experiences he describes.

Freud would agree with much of this. Knowing why an artist paints may be no help at all in saying whether her painting is beautiful; knowing why a scientist dedicates his life to research won't tell us if what he discovers is true. Freud argues only that religious experience, in itself, gives us *no reason* to think it is an experience of God. It is perfectly possible for religious experience to have an entirely psychological cause, and seem exactly as it does now. Until we have some *independent* reason to think that God exists, then we cannot use religious experience to support the claim that God exists.

●   **KEY POINTS**

- The argument from religious experience claims that in (genuine) religious experiences people are directly aware of God. This claim is supported by two considerations: religious experiences exhibit great similarity in certain core aspects; and they are similar to perceptual experiences, which we usually trust unless we have reason to doubt them.

- James argues that religious experiences are a sense of the reality of the unseen. They are:

  - experiential;

  - not usually connected to any specific mode of perception;

  - a felt immediate awareness of God; and

  - often block out everything else from the person's mind.

- He argues that we should evaluate religious experiences in relation to the life and attitudes of the person more generally. Three beliefs and two characteristics mark a religious attitude:

  - the visible world is part of a spiritual universe which gives it meaning;

  - a harmonious relation with that spiritual universe is our true purpose in life;

  - this harmony enables spiritual energy to flow into and affect the visible world;

  - a new zest which adds itself like a gift to life; and

- an assurance of safety, a feeling of peace and, in relation to others, a preponderance of loving emotions.

● He claims that religious experiences are of something *more*, in the first instance, the spiritual dimension to human beings that can transform us. Arguing for a God who exists over and above this is to put forward an hypothesis.

● Philosophers have objected that religious experience is not like perception: it is much rarer, has little detail and we can't check our experiences for intersubjective agreement. However, this doesn't show that religious experience is not veridical, though we may argue that we shouldn't automatically trust it.

● Religions make different claims about God, but this doesn't show that religious experience isn't experience of God. People can experience the same thing, but interpret it differently.

● Freud argues that religious experiences are hallucinations caused by a very deep wish for security and meaning in an uncertain world. Because of this, we cannot tell if they also contain some truth. We cannot therefore use them to argue for the existence of God.

❓ QUIZ QUESTIONS

Outline and illustrate **two** characteristics of a religious experience. (AQA, 4b, 2003, *15 marks*)

Outline and illustrate **two** criticisms of the argument from religious experience. (AQA, 4b, 2002, *15 marks*)

❓ DISCUSSION QUESTION

Assess the claim that religious experiences are experiences of God.

● III FAITH, REASON AND BELIEF

In ARGUMENTS FOR THE EXISTENCE OF GOD (p. 140), we looked at attempts to show that it is rational to believe in God because we have good reason to think that 'God exists' is a true statement. The arguments tried to deduce the existence of God from the idea of God, or the existence or the nature of the universe. Or they tried to show that the existence of God was the best explanation for the universe or for religious experience.

These arguments try to base belief in God's existence on some ground that seems more secure or certain. In IS RELIGIOUS BELIEF 'BASIC'? (p. 165), we will look at arguments that suggest this to be a mistake. But first, we will look at a very different argument for the claim that believing in God is rational.

Is it rational to believe in God? Pascal's Wager

Pascal's Wager doesn't claim that we have good evidence for God's existence, so it isn't *theoretically* or *cognitively* rational to believe in God. Rather, it argues, we have good *practical* reason to believe in God, because we stand to benefit greatly from such a belief. It is an attempt to justify belief in God quite independently of any attempt to prove God's existence. Here is Pascal's argument, though the format and numbering is mine:

1 'God is, or He is not.' But to which side shall we incline? Reason can decide nothing here . . . Since you must choose, let us see which interests you least.
2 You have two things to lose, the true and the good; and two things to stake, your reason and your will, your knowledge and your happiness; and your nature has two things to shun, error and misery.
3 Your reason is no more shocked in choosing one rather than the other, since you must of necessity choose. . . .
4 But your happiness? Let us weigh the gain and the loss in wagering that God is. . . .
5 If you gain, you gain all; if you lose, you lose nothing. . . .

That is very fine. Yes, I must wager; but I may perhaps wager too much.

6 Since there is an equal risk of gain and of loss, if you had only to gain two lives, instead of one, you might still wager. But if there were three lives to gain . . . you would be imprudent, when you are forced to play, not to chance your life to gain three at a game where there is an equal risk of loss and gain.
7 But there is an eternity of life and happiness . . . there is here an infinity of an infinitely happy life to gain, a chance of gain against a finite number of chances of loss, and what you stake is finite. . . .
8 Wherever the infinite is and there is not an infinity of chances of loss against that of gain . . . you must give all. . . .

Pascal says (1) we cannot use reason to prove that God exists or that God does not exist. But we must believe one or the other. In this sort of case, it is perfectly acceptable to decide your belief on practical grounds. The pros and cons can be summarized in a decision matrix (a table of the benefits and losses of each possible decision):

	God exists	*God does not exist*
Wager for God	Infinite gain	Finite loss
Wager against God	Finite or infinite loss	Finite gain

The potential gain of wagering for God and being right is infinite. As long as there is *some* chance that God exists, i.e. the probability that God exists is not zero, this outweighs any finite gain that may come from wagering against God and any finite loss that may come from being wrong. It is irrational, therefore, not to wager for God. For now, we will treat 'wager for God' to include 'believe in God'; but we'll return to this point in the last objection to Pascal's argument.

Going further: two inconsistencies

Pascal first says (2) that what is at stake is 'the true and the good'. We want to avoid error and believe what is true; but we also want to secure our happiness. He then claims (5) that if we believe in God, but God does not exist, we lose nothing.

This seems wrong on two counts: first, we have believed a falsehood, so we have 'lost' truth. However, by (3) – that reason is indifferent to which way we wager – this might be counted as no personal loss; we have not violated or undermined our rational capacities. But the second loss could be to our happiness: belief in God is usually thought to carry certain burdens of piety and morality. Pascal doesn't provide any argument to suggest that we will be as happy believing in God as not believing in God. But it turns out that it doesn't matter if belief in God carries a loss, because it will be finite. Against the infinite possible gain, this carries no force.

The second inconsistency relates to the probability of God's existence. For the argument to work, Pascal must suppose the probability is not zero. Absolutely no chance of an infinite gain is no incentive! But he says (6) there is an equal chance of loss and gain. This is unwarranted – by his earlier assertion (1) that 'reason can decide nothing here', we cannot know that the probability of God's existence is 0.5. Worse, (1) also questions whether we can *know* that the probability of God's existence is not zero.

But Pascal's assertion in (1) could be taken as an assertion that we cannot know that God does *not* exist. We cannot establish what the objective probability of God's existence is; *subjectively*, then, the probability of God's existence cannot be zero. We must assign some positive probability to God's existence; this much reason can decide, even if it cannot establish what that probability should be.

But why shouldn't we refuse to assign any figure of probability to God's existence? If we do this, then the wager does not work. As Pascal notes in (7) there must be *a chance* of gain; if we cannot say whether there is such a chance or not, there is no decision we are rationally obliged to make.

Analysis of the argument

The main argument comes in 6–8. In (6), Pascal explains the rationality of gambling. (He measures utility in terms of 'lives', perhaps intending to capture the contrast between this one life and eternal (infinite) life.) If there is an equal chance of winning or losing, it is rational to bet 1 to gain 3. If we are betting money, then:

	Win £3	Lose	Expected utility
Bet £1	3	–1	(0.5×3) + (0.5×–1) = 0.5
Don't bet	0	0	0

Since 0.5 > 0, it is rational to bet if the chances are 50:50 and the gain is 3 times the stake.

In wagering for God, Pascal cannot claim that the chances are 50:50. We don't know what the chance is of God's existing. However, (7) the gain is infinite, while the stake remains finite. So no matter how small the chance of God's existence, ∞ × any finite chance = ∞. Therefore (8) infinite gain is the choice to wager for.

Objections

Philosophers have raised four types of objection to the argument. First, the decision matrix is wrong: if there are more options than Pascal allows for or the weightings are different, the argument doesn't work:

(a) The utility of eternal life can't be infinite, either because infinite utility makes no sense or because infinite utility couldn't be appreciated by finite beings like us. Whether we should wager for God depends on how large the potential gain is × the probability of God's existence. Since we don't know either, we aren't rationally compelled to wager for God.

(b) Why think that God bestows infinite utility on all and only those who wager for him? Perhaps all are saved. Or perhaps only the predestined are. Or perhaps God bestows different utilities on different people, depending on other factors.

(c) Which God should we believe in? If Pascal's wager works, doesn't it work for any god? So should we believe in Roman, Greek and Hindu gods as well? But we can't be rationally required to hold inconsistent beliefs.

A second objection is that rationality does not require us to maximize expected utility. Beliefs are a matter of *theoretical* rationality, while maximizing utility is a criterion of *practical* rationality – if it is a criterion of rationality at all. Pascal could argue that whatever the criterion of theoretical rationality (e.g. proportioning belief to the evidence – see Is RELIGIOUS BELIEF 'BASIC'?, p. 165), it doesn't apply here (by (1)). But that is no reason to assume that the criterion of practical rationality takes over, rather than suppose there is no belief it is rational to adopt.

Third, we might argue that it is immoral to wager for God. To form beliefs by wagering, rather than by evidence, is to corrupt oneself (Pascal is wrong to think that we do not corrupt reason). Or, again, if God condemned all those who do not wager for him, including honest non-believers, God is immoral. Or the entire matter of 'wagering' is simply unworthy of such a grave issue as belief in God.

Finally, we can object that Pascal's wager wrongly assumes belief in God to be a matter of will. But although it seems that the wager begins this way, Pascal goes on to argue that to wager for God is to take steps to cultivate a belief in God, which includes acting as if one believes. This one can do at will. We might reasonably think that God would reward such sincere striving just as if it were a case of believing.

● KEY POINTS

- Pascal argues that because reason cannot prove the existence or non-existence of God, we should decide what to believe by the possible benefits of our beliefs.

- If we believe in God and are right, the possible benefits are infinite. If we are wrong, we have lost little (only a finite amount). If we don't believe in God and are right, we have gained little (a finite amount). If we are wrong, we could lose a great deal. Whatever the chances of God's existence, we should believe in God, because a very small chance of an infinite gain still outweighs a very large chance of a finite gain.

- Objections: the decision matrix is set up wrongly, e.g. we don't know that believing in God, and God exists, will produce an infinite gain. We don't know which God to believe in.

- We aren't rationally required to hold beliefs that maximize potential benefit.

- It is immoral to form beliefs about God in this way.

- We cannot influence what we believe by what we want directly. To this, Pascal can say that his wager doesn't argue that it is rational to believe in God, but that it is rational to cultivate such a belief.

? QUIZ QUESTIONS

Briefly outline Pascal's Wager. (AQA, 3a, 2002, *6 marks*)

Outline and illustrate **two** objections to Pascal's Wager.

? DISCUSSION QUESTION

Assess whether Pascal's Wager proves that it is rational to believe in God.

Is religious belief 'basic'? For example, is it properly adopted without justification, e.g. through religious experience as noninferential cognition analogous to sense?

In ARGUMENTS FOR THE EXISTENCE OF GOD (p. 140), we looked at ways to argue for belief in the existence of God from other beliefs. These arguments provide evidence for the truth of their conclusion. Pascal (see IS IT RATIONAL TO BELIEVE IN GOD?, p. 162) suggests that reason cannot make the judgement on whether this evidence is good enough or not. But there is an alternative to both these approaches to believing in God, viz. that the belief in

God is *not inferred* from any other beliefs. Rather, it is 'basic', believed without support either from other things we know independently or from a process of reasoning.

Religious belief can be compared to beliefs based on sense perception. We do not *reason to* such beliefs, we form them immediately in the presence of sense perception. If I see a brown tree, I believe 'The tree is brown'. I don't, even subconsciously, *infer* this belief: I don't think 'I seem to see a brown tree'. What I seem to see is often accurate. Therefore, I believe 'The tree is brown'. Instead, my belief that the tree is brown is justified 'noninferentially' (on noninferential justification, see Ch. 1, FOUNDATIONALISM, p. 28).

Philosophers who argue that religious belief is basic *do not* claim that it is *without justification*. They claim that the justification for religious belief is not based on *evidence*. One interpretation of FIDEISM (see p. 170) is that religious beliefs may be adopted without justification, but the claim that religious beliefs are basic is not a form of fideism, as we will see.

Plantinga's argument against evidentialism

The view that all beliefs should be proportionate to the evidence is known as 'evidentialism': we should only believe things we have evidence for, and we should only believe them with the certainty that the evidence allows for. It is irrational to believe anything on insufficient evidence. For instance, we should not believe that something exists rather than that it doesn't unless we have good evidence for its existence. So we should not believe that God exists unless we have good evidence that God exists.

Rather than argue whether we have good evidence that God exists, the philosopher Alvin Plantinga asks why we should accept evidentialism. Not *all* beliefs can be based on evidence, because then every belief would rest on other beliefs. So some beliefs, says Plantinga, must be acceptable without evidence. A belief is 'basic' if it is not accepted on the basis of other beliefs. Many philosophers have argued that two sorts of beliefs rightly fall into this category: **self-evident** beliefs and beliefs that are based on 'what is evident to the senses'. So, Plantinga argues, evidentialism leads to FOUNDATIONALISM (Ch. 1, p. 28).

According to foundationalism, a belief is justified if and only if it is either *properly* basic or it is accepted on the basis of evidence, which eventually comes to rest on properly basic beliefs. Any belief that is neither properly basic nor based on evidence is not rationally justified. This means that a belief in God could be justified without resting on evidence, viz. if it is properly basic. However, since the existence of God is neither self-evident nor evident to the senses, belief in God isn't properly basic.

Plantinga argues that this form of foundationalism cannot be right, because it is self-contradictory. How do we know that 'Only what is self-evident and what is evident to the senses is properly basic'? This claim is not itself self-evident nor evident to the senses, so it is not properly basic. But then what is the evidence for it? No foundationalist has argued that foundationalism can be deduced or inferred from properly basic beliefs! (We saw a similar objection when discussing FOUNDATIONALISM in Ch. 1 (p. 31).) So on what grounds can we argue that belief in God is not properly basic?

Objections

We will look at Plantinga's positive argument that belief in God is properly basic in the next subsection. We first consider two objections to his argument so far.

Evidence

Plantinga equates *evidence* with *inferential* justification. A belief is supported by evidence, according to him, only if it is supported by other beliefs. While it is not unusual for philosophers to say that evidence is always propositional and distinct from the belief it supports, should we accept this? After all, the two types of properly basic belief foundationalists talk about are what is self-*evident* and what is *evident* to the senses. The evidence in each of these cases is something about the belief itself or about the circumstances in which it is formed (e.g. believing 'The tree is brown' when looking at a brown tree). The evidence is not other beliefs, but that doesn't mean there is *no evidence* for these beliefs. The evidence for believing the tree is brown is your experience, that you see a brown tree. To call this 'evidence' doesn't have to mean that we *infer* the belief from the experience. It just means that when perceptual experience is your evidence, the belief is noninferentially justified.

This is the *intuitive* way of understanding the claim 'It is irrational to believe anything without sufficient evidence'. This claim does not entail that your beliefs must always be inferred from evidence, but that they must be supported by evidence. Plantinga is only right to argue that properly basic beliefs may be accepted *without evidence* if we narrow the idea of evidence to inferential justification.

Foundationalism

In fact, Plantinga never directly attacks evidentialism directly. He argues that evidentialism goes hand-in-hand with foundationalism, and foundationalism is self-defeating because we cannot infer the theory of foundationalism from what it identifies as properly basic beliefs. But this is no objection to evidentialism. It shows only that the foundationalist interpretation of it is misguided. (Plantinga's objection could be an objection to evidentialism only if evidentialism *entails* foundationalism, so that anyone who accepts evidentialism *must* accept foundationalism of the sort Plantinga describes. But we have no reason to believe this.)

These objections claim that Plantinga is wrong to claim that religious belief, if it is properly basic, may be accepted and held *without evidence*. However, we have not discussed whether religious belief *is* properly basic.

Is religious belief properly basic?

Plantinga points out that many theologians, particularly in the tradition of reformed theology (theology that came out of the Reformation), argue that religious belief is not usually accepted or held on the basis of arguments, and that this is entirely appropriate. Some argue that arguments for the existence of God don't work; but even if they did, religious faith in God is not dependent on them. The existence of God is simply *apparent* to the believer. In this, it is like belief in the external world. We don't believe in the existence of the external world because we have good arguments for it; we take it for granted, it is simply given to us in experience.

If the ground of belief in God is not argument, then what is it? John Calvin argues that God implanted a direct awareness of himself in every mind. We lose touch with this awareness only through sin. Other theologians argue that we see God in his creation. This claim must be distinguished from THE TELEOLOGICAL ARGUMENT (p. 150). We don't *infer* God's existence from nature; we *see* God in nature. Others argue that we have a direct awareness of God in religious experience (see THE ARGUMENT FROM RELIGIOUS EXPERIENCE, p. 155). Again, this is distinct from saying that we infer God's existence from religious experience. We don't *infer* that the tree is brown from what we see; we simply see a brown tree. Likewise, we don't infer God's existence from religious experiences, these theologians argue; we simply experience God.

On any of these views, religious belief is basic.

Going further: what is properly basic?

But can religious belief be *properly* basic? Obviously, Plantinga and other reformed epistemologists reject the claim that only self-evident beliefs and beliefs based on what is evident to the senses can be properly basic. Beliefs based on experiences of God can be properly basic, too, they argue. And why not?

How do we know what is properly basic? The notion that only self-evident beliefs and beliefs based on what is evident to the senses can be properly basic is itself not basic; nor can we infer it from what it claims is basic. The only way we can decide what is properly basic is to see what examples we are willing to agree on as *obviously* properly basic, and go from there.

Plantinga suggests that noninferential beliefs are *properly* basic if they are caused by the circumstances in which they are formed (e.g. the experience) and are a product of 'proper functioning'. My belief that 'The tree is brown' when I'm looking at it is caused by my looking at the tree, and is a product of my senses and cognition working properly.

Is the belief that God exists *caused by* the circumstances reformed theologians appeal to or are people's beliefs in the existence of God caused by something else entirely, e.g. upbringing? Second, is forming this belief an example of *proper* functioning? Is it part of the proper functioning of the human mind to see God in nature? Are religious experiences an example of proper functioning (Freud would argue not – see THE ARGUMENT FROM RELIGIOUS EXPERIENCE, p. 159)?

Going further: religious belief, argument and fideism

Properly basic beliefs based on what is evident to the senses can still be defeated. For example, if I know that I'm in a museum of optical illusions, I won't believe what I see. Perceptual experience gives us **prima facie** justification: we treat perceptual experiences as veridical *unless we have reason to doubt them* (see THE ARGUMENT FROM RELIGIOUS EXPERIENCE, p. 155).

Plantinga argues that the same is true for religious belief. Even if it is properly basic, that does not mean that it is immune to arguments. Experiences that support it provide only prima facie (noninferential) justification. Arguments against the existence of God are still relevant, and may defeat our belief in the existence of God. To claim that religious belief is properly basic is not to claim that it is properly *dogmatic*.

Second, if religious belief is properly basic, this doesn't mean that it is held on faith rather than reason (cf. FIDEISM, p. 170), depending on what we think 'reason' covers. Most philosophers think that perception is rational; it is certainly part of normal cognition. We don't believe in the existence of the external world on *faith*; that would be to misuse the word 'faith'. Plantinga argues that the sorts of experiences that support belief in God are likewise part of reason. If he is right, then religious faith is based on reason and trying to draw a contrast between the two is mistaken.

● **KEY POINTS**

- Some philosophers argue that religious beliefs are 'basic', not inferred from other beliefs we have. Traditional examples of basic beliefs include self-evident beliefs and those based on what is evident to the senses. Reformed theologians argue that the existence of God is apparent to the believer both in nature and in religious experience.

- A 'basic' belief is not one without justification. However, Plantinga argues that it is justified without evidence.

- He argues that evidentialism, the view that it is irrational to believe anything on insufficient evidence, is mistaken. He claims that evidentialism is related to foundationalism, and that foundationalism is self-defeating. The claim that only self-evident belief and beliefs based on what is evident to the senses can be basic is not itself basic; nor has anyone shown it can be inferred from basic beliefs.

- Philosophers have objected that evidentialism does not *depend* on foundationalism; and that Plantinga wrongly restricts 'evidence' to inferential justification. Experience is evidence for beliefs formed noninferentially on the basis of experience. On this broader understanding of 'evidence', evidentialism has not been refuted.

● There is no agreed criterion for what is properly basic. Plantinga argues that beliefs that are caused by the circumstances in which they formed and as a product of proper functioning are properly basic. Whether belief in God is properly basic depends on whether forming this belief in certain circumstances, e.g. religious experience, is caused by those circumstances and is an example of proper functioning.

❓ QUIZ QUESTIONS

Explain and illustrate the idea of a basic belief.

Outline Plantinga's argument against evidentialism.

❓ DISCUSSION QUESTION

Assess the claim that religious belief is properly basic.

Fideism: faith as opposed to reason and involving commitment, trust, 'a leap in the dark' is necessary in order to attain a greater good

The two ideas of fideism described in the syllabus – that faith is opposed to reason and that faith involves trust or commitment – are quite different. All fideism involves the second claim, but not all involves the first.

Some Christian fideists stressed the inferiority of reason to faith when forming beliefs about religious truths. They argued that sin has damaged our ability to reason. For example, what we think to be *reasonable* or *rational* to believe might be a reflection of our pride, or self-centredness. If we rely on reason, we won't discover the truth about God and ourselves. Faith provides the necessary corrective. On this strong form of fideism, it is *only* faith that should be relied on in coming to religious beliefs; we can simply ignore what reason has to say, and if faith flies in the face of reason, so much the worse for reason.

The Catholic Church has repeatedly rejected this position and, as recently as 1998, Pope John Paul II argued that rational knowledge and philosophical discourse are important for 'the very possibility of belief in God'. A number of philosophers have argued that faith involves 'going beyond' what reason can conclude without arguing that faith necessarily opposes reason, or that there is anything wrong with reason. For example, Pascal argues that because theoretical reason cannot decide the issue of God's existence, we do not go against reason in believing in God. In fact, practical reason supports this belief (see Is IT RATIONAL TO BELIEVE IN GOD?, p. 162).

James

W. K. Clifford argues that it is 'wrong always, everywhere, and for everyone, to believe anything on insufficient evidence'. Belief, he argued, must be earned through patient investigation, not by stifling doubts. No real belief is insignificant, and this will be especially true for religious beliefs. A belief inclines us to believe other similar things, while it weakens beliefs that are contrary to it. Forming beliefs on insufficient evidence makes us credulous, it weakens our cognitive powers and it makes other people less concerned about telling us lies. Religious faith, if it amounts to belief without sufficient evidence, is therefore always wrong.

William James argues that Clifford is wrong; it can sometimes be right, and in fact, reasonable, to believe something without sufficient evidence for its truth, viz. when we face a 'genuine option' that cannot be decided on the basis of evidence. A 'genuine option' involves three conditions:

1   The alternatives for what to believe, e.g. 'God exists' and 'God does not exist', are *live* – the person feels they really could believe either. Some people may not feel this way, in which case one or other alternative is *dead*.
2   The alternatives exclude each other (not more than one of them can be true) and there are no other alternatives – the choice between them is *forced*.
3   The alternatives are *momentous* rather than trivial, e.g. this is your only opportunity to get it right or the stakes are high.

If these three conditions apply, and we cannot decide on the basis of evidence, then it is not unreasonable for us to incline towards one belief or another on other grounds.

In belief, we have *two* goals – to avoid error, as Clifford argues; but also to *secure the truth*. Although avoiding error is important in science, in other areas of life, we often need to form beliefs with some risk of error. For example, in forming a friendship with someone, you need to trust them, which will involve the belief that they are trustworthy before you really have good evidence of this. And it is reasonable to do this, given that we want to form the friendship. It is not always wrong, then, for our wills to influence our beliefs.

In the case of genuine options, if our intellect can't decide, then our emotions and will *must*. To not form a belief, e.g. for fear of getting it wrong, is itself a decision made on the basis of an emotion. But given what is at stake in a genuine option, getting it wrong might be less bad than losing out on truth: 'worse things than being duped may happen to a man in this world'. Clifford opposes reason and emotion in forming beliefs, arguing that we must only form beliefs on the basis of reason. But his argument is itself supported by emotion and moral values. Emotions come into what we believe, or don't, whichever way we argue.

Religious faith, for many, involves a genuine option. The *religious hypothesis* is that the best things are eternal, and we are better off now if we believe. James says it clearly presents an option that is forced and momentous; if it is live for the individual as well, then it is reasonable for them to believe.

James's argument faces similar objections to Pascal's (see Is IT RATIONAL TO BELIEVE IN GOD?, p. 164). While religious faith clearly deals with things that are important, it is not obvious that the choice between having religious faith and not is either forced or momentous. There are many religions, so the question arises as to *which* religious faith to adopt. And some of these faiths, e.g. Buddhism, do not say that God exists. So the options are not forced. Second, is religious faith necessary for the good and eternal things James mentions? If believing in God is not necessary for God to reward one with eternal life, then the choice is not momentous.

Unlike Pascal, James is *not* arguing that faith is *more* rational than agnosticism or atheism. He is arguing only that it is not less rational. He is arguing that there is a place for faith that reason can respect. Reason can recognize its limitations, and can recognize that faith may rightly act when reason is limited. Having faith on the basis of the will does not fly in the face of reason; it simply goes where reason cannot.

Kierkegaard

Kierkegaard argues that we are wrong to think of religious beliefs in the same way as other beliefs. Religion is not a type of philosophical system, and we shouldn't weigh up religious beliefs in a philosophical way. Instead, faith is characterized by passionate commitment; beliefs formed *objectively* are not, and they may have no impact on one's life. To believe that God exists, but to treat this as just another fact, about which we feel nothing, is not to have faith. Faith isn't (just) a matter of what, but of *how*, we believe. The commitment that characterizes faith requires a decision, a 'leap'; it is not something that can be established intellectually. This leap actually *requires* objective uncertainty: 'If I am able to apprehend God objectively, I do not have faith; but because I cannot do this, I must have faith. If I want to keep myself in faith, I must continually see to it that I hold fast the objective uncertainty.'

Some philosophers argue that reason can't determine whether God exists because God wants us to have this type of committed, passionate relationship with him. If we felt we knew the answers, something would be lost. Kierkegaard emphasizes the importance of this: objective certainty will not have the same impact on one's life as faith in the face of uncertainty.

But without reason to guide us, why should we 'leap' in the direction of religious *belief*? Philosophers disagree on what Kierkegaard thought about the place of reason in religious belief. On the one hand, he describes faith as 'incomprehensible', on the other, he says that reason – if it recognizes its limitations – can help us understand the commitment we make in faith. But then *can* we just believe whatever we choose to? Is the leap of faith possible?

Kierkegaard remarks that we 'cannot believe nonsense against the understanding, which one might fear, because the understanding will penetratingly perceive that it is nonsense and hinder [us] in believing it'. Neither James nor Kierkegaard think belief is completely under the control of the will, but that we can form beliefs without relying on reason in certain circumstances. For Kierkegaard, religious faith in its trust and commitment is incomprehensible in that it lies outside the limits that reason can reach for itself. But, like James, he thinks reason can recognize that it has limits, and that faith might *legitimately* lie outside these limits. To achieve it, we must leap. By contrast, if faith were just nonsense, reason would inhibit our ability to leap.

Wittgenstein

Wittgenstein was greatly influenced by Kierkegaard in his understanding of religious belief. Wittgenstein sought to understand religious language by relating it to religious activity (see THE NATURE OF RELIGIOUS LANGUAGE, p. 138), and does the same with faith.

The idea of language games emphasizes the foundation of language in activity. Wittgenstein says that a language game is the speaking part of a 'form of life'. A form of life is far broader than any specific language game, it is the foundation out of which language games grow, the collection of cultural practices which embed language games. The very foundation is biology, and Wittgenstein often emphasizes how our natural reactions form the basis for language games. But the biology is always taken up in a particular culture, and what is 'natural' is often only natural within a particular way of living as a human being. *Human nature* involves both biology and culture.

As part of forms of life, language games do not need any justification. They are rooted in natural human reactions and activities. If, then, religious faith and language are a particular language game, part of a human form of life, its claims need no justification. We need only to understand what is distinctive about it in order to understand what it claims and implies.

In THE NATURE OF RELIGIOUS LANGUAGE (p. 138), we saw that Wittgenstein argued that religious language and belief are not empirical. As such, religious faith neither needs *nor can be given* support by arguing from questions of evidence. *No* language game can be criticized by standards of rationality that are external to that game. As religious claims are not empirical hypotheses, they are not susceptible to 'proof' by evidence and rational argument. Faith, then, is not founded on reason. It is a distinctive and natural part of being human.

Objections and replies: Phillips

Philosophers have objected that Wittgenstein's theory cuts religious beliefs off from other aspects of human life. But religion can't be isolated from other cultural and linguistic practices that criticize it. Religion is not a whole form of life, for it is always situated in and among many other human practices. D. Z. Phillips, defending Wittgenstein, agrees. The objection confuses the autonomy of language games (the rules that determine the meaning and legitimacy of claims within the game) with total isolation. Language games are part of a form of human life: 'Religion has something to say about aspects of human existence which are quite intelligible without reference to religion: birth, death, joy, misery, despair, hope, fortune and misfortune. The connection between these and religion is not contingent'.

But the question is really whether religion is a distinctive language game, with its own rules. If asking, cursing, praying, greeting and so on are examples of language games, we do all these things in religious and in secular contexts. However, Wittgenstein identifies many linguistic practices at different levels of generality as games; he even identifies language itself as a language game. Second, whether something counts as the 'same game' itself depends on the context. So *asking* is a game; but asking your boss for a rise and asking God for prosperity could well count as different games. The context guides how we are to understand the *game*. Religious language, though it contains the many different games of praise and worship, prayer, miracles and so on, can be understood as forming a game governed by particular rules.

Another objection is that this means we can't criticize religious beliefs. But, Phillips argues, given the connection between religious beliefs and the rest of life, if faith makes no sense in the light of such experiences we will rightly reject it. And religious beliefs may be criticized from within religion. Not anything can be believed, not anything can be lived. But this does not mean that such connections to life *justify* or refute religious beliefs. Religion cannot be criticized on the ground that it is *not true* or highly *improbable*; for this presupposes that it makes factual claims, and it does not.

Wittgenstein and Phillips claim that religious language is not empirical *at all*. For example, Phillips argues that if someone thinks that prayer is a means to obtaining something, he has misunderstood the nature of religion, and his belief has become superstition. Likewise, if someone believes that 'God' is the name of an entity in the world or that God is logically prior to religion, this is a 'monstrous illusion' (the phrase comes from Kierkegaard); religious language is not a deviant form of scientific hypothesizing.

But, philosophers object, this flies in the face of how many believers *do* think of God and their faith. Wittgenstein's account of faith looks like a *reinterpretation* of it. In defending faith against criticism from *external* standards, his theory makes a claim about what religious language means which seems equally external to (and critical of) faith. It also makes what you *believe* much less important, as faith is about how we live. Yet many believers who act in similar ways and hold similar values also argue that there is something distinctive and important about the different beliefs they hold.

A summary

James and Kierkegaard, like Pascal, argue that reason is limited, that there are certain questions it cannot answer. So it can be perfectly reasonable for faith to go beyond reason. Kierkegaard and Wittgenstein argue that faith is not the right sort of thing to be held to the standards of philosophical or empirical reasoning.

None of them is rejecting reason *itself*, but they reject the view that reason is capable of deciding on all matters of truth, and the view that all beliefs should be formed just on the basis of available evidence. If faith is opposed to reason, for them it is opposed only to particular *ideas* of reason. Faith is not opposed to reason in being *unreasonable*, they argue. Faith goes beyond reason, and reason is not applicable to questions of faith; but this does not need to be understood as an opposition.

Early Christian fideists were more critical. They argued that reason is flawed rather than simply limited, and so cannot be relied upon to deliver truth in religious matters. But even this view can be interpreted as claiming that faith is in tension only with a particular form of reason that is damaged by sin. If reason is able to recognize that it is damaged, then even here there doesn't need to be a tension, as reason will see the reasonableness of giving way to faith.

An objection

Fideism faces the following potential objection: if faith goes beyond reason, then it must accept that we do not have *any reason* to believe in God. The arguments of James and Kierkegaard show only that faith is not unreasonable. They don't show that we *should* leap in a particular way. Wittgenstein would reject the question of whether we have *reason* to believe in God as mistaken.

But many believers think that they do have *some* reason to believe in God, appealing to some argument that says God is the best explanation, e.g. THE COSMOLOGICAL ARGUMENT (p. 144), THE ARGUMENT FROM RELIGIOUS EXPERIENCE (p. 155), or an argument from MIRACLES (p. 182). But they are willing to accept that the evidence for God's existence is not very strong, so they say it is a matter of faith.

This seems inconsistent: it accepts that belief in God *is* a matter of evidence and argument, but that we don't need to justify our conclusion by the balance of evidence. If we are getting into the question of evidence, shouldn't we be consistent and come to the belief that the evidence supports the best? We should believe in God only if the evidence suggests that it is *more* likely that God exists than that he doesn't, i.e. if belief in God is supported by reason.

But there are other possibilities:

1 that belief in God is precisely as reasonable as not believing in God (the evidence is exactly balanced);
2 that we cannot tell what the balance of evidence is;
3 that, for some reason, our belief needs to be more certain than the evidence (either way) allows, so we should consider not just the evidence, but other issues as well.

Fideists have not tended to argue for (1), but some of their arguments support (2) and (3). So one interpretation of fideism is that, while reason cannot settle the question of belief in God, this does not mean we have no reason at all for such belief. (Of course, other fideists may simply accept that because faith does go beyond reason, it is true that we have no reason to believe in God.)

KEY POINTS

- Fideism has included two distinct ideas: that faith is opposed to reason; and that faith involves trust or commitment. The two ideas are distinct, and only the idea of commitment has been adopted by all fideists.

- The claim that faith is opposed to reason has been defended by philosophers who think that reason is damaged by sin. Other philosophers argue that faith is opposed only to particular conceptions of reason, e.g. that reason can determine all matters of truth or that all beliefs must be proportionate to the evidence.

- James argues that it is reasonable to decide what to believe when faced with a genuine option, i.e. a forced and momentous choice between claims that are live and not settled by intellectual enquiry. Only in these circumstances *can* the will create belief. Belief does not seek only to avoid error, but also to secure the truth.

- James faces the objection that religious faith may not be a genuine option, because it is not forced or momentous.

- Kierkegaard argues that faith is distinct from *objective* belief in involving a passionate commitment. Faith requires a 'leap' in the face of uncertainty. Faith is incomprehensible to reason, but it is not rejected by reason. If it were, we would not be able to believe by making a decision.

- Both James and Kierkegaard argue that faith is not unreasonable. But we need independent considerations to suggest that we *should* believe in God.

- Wittgenstein argues that religious faith is part of a distinctive language game (or form of life – philosophers disagree on interpretation). Language games have their own standards of meaning and justification. Religious faith is not empirical, so that it is wrong to assess it by empirical or philosophical reasoning.

- Philosophers have objected that this cuts religious faith off from the rest of life too severely. Phillips replies that faith still needs to 'make sense' of our experiences. But this doesn't mean that our experiences *justify* or *refute* religious beliefs.

- However, many believers think that their faith is partly empirical, while Wittgenstein's account claims that it is not. If it is empirical, then it should be held to answer to the usual standards for empirical belief.

❓ QUIZ QUESTIONS

Briefly explain the view that faith is opposed to reason. (AQA, 3a, 2003, *6 marks*)

Outline and illustrate what James means by a 'genuine option'.

Outline **two** reasons for thinking that faith goes beyond reason.

❓ DISCUSSION QUESTIONS

Assess the role of faith in supporting religious belief. (AQA, 3c, 2002, *24 marks*)

Assess the claim that religious faith legitimately does not answer to reason.

● IV THE IMPLICATIONS OF GOD'S EXISTENCE

The problem of evil: how is God's omnipotence and goodness to be reconciled with the existence of evil?

In CONCEPTIONS OF GOD (p. 124), we saw that God is traditionally understood to be perfectly good, omnipotent and omniscient. The existence of evil causes problems for this definition. If God is good, then he has the desire to eliminate evil. If God is omnipotent, then God is able to eliminate evil. If God is omniscient, then God knows that evil exists and knows how to eliminate it. But if God wants to eliminate evil and can eliminate evil, then why does evil exist? We can conclude that since evil exists, God – at least an omnipotent, good God – does not exist.

Understanding the argument

To understand the argument, we need to be clear on what 'evil' means in this context. We usually use it to mean morally wrong actions or motives, 'moral evil'. But in this context, 'evil' also covers 'natural evil', i.e. suffering which is caused by non-moral means – by earthquakes, illness, the predation of animals on each other and so on. This will prove very important when we look at responses to the problem of evil.

The second thing we need to clarify is how the argument is supposed to work. One version, called the 'logical problem of evil', claims that the mere existence of evil is logically incompatible with the existence of an omnipotent, good God. It understands the argument **deductively**.

For the existence of evil to be logically incompatible with the existence of God, we have to suppose that, being good, God has the desire to eliminate *all* evil. But this isn't true if some evil is *necessary for a greater good*. For example, unless we felt pain, we could never learn endurance; or, again, what would love be like without sadness when we lose someone we love? But, as Shakespeare put it: ''tis better to have loved and lost, than never to have loved at all.' So some evil is actually necessary to make the world as good a place as it is. A variation of this argument is that we could not *appreciate* what is good, and so would not desire it as we do, unless we experienced evil to contrast it with. So, being good, God does not desire to eliminate all evil.

However, it does seem that God would desire to eliminate all *unnecessary* evil. The 'evidential problem of evil' claims that the amount and distribution of evil that exists is incompatible with the existence of an omnipotent, good God. It understands the argument **inductively**: the way evil actually exists is good evidence for thinking that God does not exist. Evil is not evenly spread over lives, and beings who are innocent can suffer dreadfully. For example, children can die of terrible diseases or they can be brutally treated. Animals can suffer in natural disasters such as drought. This seems exactly the kind of thing an omnipotent, good God would want to eradicate. Even if evil is necessary for certain goods, is *so much* evil necessary? It is this version of the problem that we discuss here.

A *theodicy* is an argument which tries to justify evil, making evil compatible with the existence of an omnipotent, good God. Theodicies work only if they can show that this is, in a sense, the *best* of all possible worlds, that any less evil would lead to some important good being lost.

The appeal to ignorance

The evidential problem of evil appeals to an intuition, that there is *no good reason* that *could* justify the amount and distribution of evil in the world. However, a theist may simply reply that we don't know this. It may be that all evil serves some higher purpose, but we simply don't, and perhaps can't, know what that purpose is or how evil serves it.

But, do we have any good reason to think that all evil *does* serve such a purpose? Or, a better reply, we can argue thus:

1 There is no good *that we know of* that could justify the evil that we see. Any higher good we can think of could be obtained without God *having* to allow the evil that exists.
2 *Whatever* higher good evil is supposed to be necessary for, if it's anything we can think of already then it won't justify evil.
3 Therefore, evil can be justified only by a higher good that we are simply not familiar with.
4 It is *probable* that we know most goods.
5 So it is *probable* that there is no such higher good.

When reasoning about what is *probable*, we don't usually allow the appeal to ignorance. And we are always inferring from what we know to what we don't know. For example, we constantly form beliefs about the future: the sun will rise tomorrow, chairs won't suddenly sprout wings and so on. Inferring from 'Nothing we know of will justify evil' to 'Nothing will justify evil' is just the same. The appeal to ignorance is like an appeal to radical SCEPTICISM (Ch. 1, p. 38).

The appeal to ignorance needs a *good reason* for thinking that *there is* some higher good that we don't know about. However, an appeal to, for example, a revelation from God that everything is for the best won't really count. If it is unlikely that God exists, it is unlikely that the revelation is genuine. But we don't know whether it is unlikely that God exists until we have solved the problem of evil.

The free-will defence

One theodicy argues that evil is the result of our free will. God gave us free will, as something that is very good. It is better to have a universe with free will than without. But God cannot make people with free will act in certain ways. Being morally imperfect, however, we do not always use our free will for good, but sometimes bring about evil. Given how good free will is, it is still better that we have free will and sometimes use it to bring about evil than that we don't have free will at all.

This argument presupposes a very strong notion of free will, which philosophers debate. But, more obviously, it deals only with moral evil, evil that *we bring about*, through our choices. It doesn't account for natural evil at all. Augustine has a variation of the theory that tries to deal with this objection.

Going further: how good is free will?

Even if free will is a great good, that doesn't mean we should never interfere with it. If we see someone about to commit murder and do nothing about it, it is no defence to appeal to how wonderful it is that the murderer has free will. The existence and goodness of free will is compatible with interfering with it. So why doesn't God prevent evil actions?

We can reply that God would have to interfere *very often* to prevent all the evil we cause, and this would undermine our sense of free will. But perhaps that depends on how God interferes. Couldn't God arrange it that we would be *tempted* to harm one another, and believe that we were capable of doing so, but when it actually came to acting on such motives a strong sense of conscience prevented us? Even if God cannot control what a man with free will chooses, he might be able to control what he does.

Second, God could have given us free will without giving us the power to commit terrible evil. Is free will, as it is now, such a good thing that its existence outweighs all the evil in the world? Wouldn't a limited kind of free will have been better? Richard Swinburne replies that the value of free will depends on what one can do with it. A world in which we couldn't harm each other would also be one in which we would have very little responsibility for each other's well-being. It would be a 'toy world'.

But this doesn't follow. We could still have a world in which we could choose to greatly benefit each other or not. Or, again, we could harm each other in more minor ways, but because of a strong conscience feel terrible about it, so be less inclined to commit harm.

Augustine's argument

Augustine argues that all natural evil is a result of moral evil. He claims that the choice of Adam and Eve to disobey God led to the 'Fall'. The Fall was a *metaphysical* change, altering nature, human beings and the relationship between them: there is enmity between human beings and animals; giving birth causes pain; we must work hard to survive (Genesis 3:15–19). Nature and human nature are *out of sorts*. So all evil, natural evil as well as moral evil, was caused by human free choice.

A first objection is that the Fall was not an actual event in human history. If it didn't happen, and if, for instance, animals were suffering long before human beings even existed, then free will can't be the cause of natural evil. Many Christians now understand the Fall as an important myth about the relationship between human beings, nature and God. But this means that we cannot claim the Fall is *literally responsible* for all natural evil.

A second objection is that, if it were true, it seems *grossly unfair*. Why should animals and children suffer as a result of a choice made by two people a very long time ago? It is not just to punish children for what their parents do; if your dad steals something, it isn't right that *you* get sent to prison! So how could a good God make the evil chosen by two people lead to such terrible consequences for so many other people? Surely it didn't *have* to be this way, and a good God wouldn't allow it.

The laws of nature defence

A different theodicy tackles natural evil directly. For free will to exist, for us to do anything at all, things need to happen in a regular way (chairs don't sprout wings, water does quench thirst, etc.). If events are going to happen in a regular way, then the world needs to be governed by natural laws. However, these laws will give rise to natural evil. Natural evil is justified, then, because the alternative is a much worse world in which nothing takes place in a regular way.

But for this to justify evil, we must suppose that no *alternative set* of natural laws could lead to less natural evil. But this seems hard to believe. Is it *impossible* that there are no droughts? Is it *impossible* that animals all eat plants rather than each other? Is it *impossible* that cancer didn't exist? Surely not. Surely there could be natural laws that meant these things never happened; and a good God would choose those laws that didn't lead to natural evil.

The 'vale of soul-making' argument

A third theodicy argues that evil is necessary for us to become good people. Evil is necessary for moral and spiritual growth; and a world with moral and spiritual growth is better than a world without. Virtues are impossible unless there is evil (natural and moral) to respond to and correct. For example, we can't be courageous unless there is *real* danger, we can't be benevolent unless people have needs and so on. Through struggles and suffering, we mature and develop spiritually. This argument was put forward by Irenaeus and was recently defended by John Hick.

A first objection asks why God couldn't *create* us virtuous. Why do we need to *become* good? Hick replies that someone who has become good through confronting and dealing with evil 'is good in a richer and more valuable sense' than someone who is simply created good. In a phrase, no pain, no (real) gain.

A second, much stronger, objection notes that all evil is justified by this argument only if all evil leads to spiritual growth. But this doesn't seem plausible at all. Many people suffer terribly in a way that breaks their spirit, e.g. children who never recover from being abused; others suffer at the end of their lives when there is little time to develop further; people who need to grow spiritually don't suffer much at all; others who are already leading good and mature lives suffer a great deal; people die prematurely, before they have a chance of spiritual growth.

We may respond that the death and suffering of others which don't help *them* may nevertheless help *us*. But it is difficult to argue that this is true in *every case* of suffering. Swinburne argues that if evil was predictable, being matched exactly to the need for growth, then two important virtues in particular couldn't flourish: faith and hope. These require a considerable amount of unpredictability – if the pattern of evil looked rational, we wouldn't need them.

However, neither of these answers deals with why there is *so much* evil; can't goodness grow against more minor evils?

A final objection is that this theodicy deals only with the suffering of beings who can grow spiritually. It doesn't deal at all with the suffering of animals.

Going further: a good God?

The evidential problem of evil argues that the existence of God is *less probable* than the non-existence of God. However, these aren't the only options: given the mixture of good and evil in the world, the most probable divine being is one that is either partly good and partly evil or indifferent to good and evil. It is only a wholly good divine being that is so improbable given evil.

Questions of what is probable depend on what you take as your evidence. Swinburne accepts that the problem of evil makes the existence of God less probable, but the COSMOLOGICAL and TELEOLOGICAL ARGUMENTS (see p. 144 and p. 150) make the existence of God more probable. He argues that the balance of probability ends up favouring God's existence.

However, the cosmological and teleological arguments don't provide any evidence for a *good* God. But it is *this* claim that the problem of evil attacks. Even if we have reason to believe that God exists, the problem of evil argues that we don't have reason to believe that God is good.

KEY POINTS

- If God is good, then he has the desire to eliminate evil. If God is omnipotent, then God is able to eliminate evil. So if an omnipotent, good God exists, why does evil exist?

- 'Evil' means moral and natural evil. Moral evil is that caused by beings with free will. Natural evil is suffering caused by natural processes, e.g. drought and predation.

- The logical argument: the existence of evil is incompatible with the existence of an omnipotent, good God. This is implausible, since some evil must exist for certain goods to be possible.

- The evidential argument: the amount and distribution of evil is incompatible with the existence of an omnipotent, good God.

- The free-will theodicy argues that evil is the result of our choices, and that it is justified by free will, which is good. But this is not a justification for not interfering with free will or limiting it so that we cannot cause great harm to others. And it doesn't cover natural evil.

- Augustine argues that natural evil is a result of the free choice of Adam and Eve. But this is implausible if the Fall is a myth. And, if it were literally true, it is very unjust, so that a good God would not allow it.

- Irenaeus argues that evil is necessary for moral and spiritual growth. But this doesn't justify all evil if only *some* evil leads to these goods; and we may ask whether so much evil is necessary for them. It also doesn't deal with animal suffering.

❓ QUIZ QUESTIONS

Briefly explain and illustrate the evidential problem of evil.

Outline and illustrate **one** response to the problem of evil.

❓ DISCUSSION QUESTIONS

Assess whether any theodicy successfully answers the problem of moral evil.

Assess whether the amount and extent of natural evil are compatible with the existence of a good and omnipotent God.

Miracles: what would constitute a miracle and what conclusions should be drawn from the occurrence of miraculous events? How, and why, does God intervene in the universe?

There are different ways to define what a miracle is. Three important definitions are:

1 an event that has religious significance;
2 an event caused by God; and
3 an event that violates (or is otherwise not in accordance with) the laws of nature, caused by God.

The appeal of the first definition is that people do talk of events as miracles even when an event isn't outside the laws of nature. However, it allows an element of subjectivity, or interpretation, on whether an event has 'religious significance' or not. An event can qualify as a miracle for one person and not another, even when both are theists.

The second definition rules out subjective interpretation, as miracles are only those events that are *in fact* caused by God. But it says that *every* act of God is a miracle, e.g. God's continuous creation in sustaining the existence of the universe (see CONCEPTIONS OF GOD, p. 127) or all genuine religious experience.

The third definition has been most common among philosophers. Aquinas says a miracle is 'beyond the order commonly observed in nature', while Hume talks of it as a 'transgression' or 'violation' of a law of nature. We shall follow the syllabus in focusing on this account. The first issue to discuss is what the best formulation of the definition is.

Miracles and the laws of nature

It can seem merely technical, but it is actually very important to say exactly what a miracle is. If we say a miracle is a *violation* of the laws of nature, we risk defining miracles out of existence. Here's how: following Hume, a statement is a law of nature only if it is true, general (or universal) and **contingent**. (It must be general to be a law, and it must be contingent to be a law of *nature* rather than a law of logic – 'All bachelors are unmarried' is true and general, but not a law of nature!) However, the occurrence of a natural event that violates the law makes the statement either not true or not general. But if it is not true or not general, it is not a law. Any statement that is a law of nature cannot be violated while remaining a law. Therefore, by definition, there can be no violations of a law of nature; if a miracle is a violation of a law of nature, then a miracle is a contradiction in terms.

But this is wrong. Miracles are not *logically* impossible. Assume that miracles are caused by God. How are they related to the laws of nature?

1   A miracle is a violation of *known* laws of nature. *Objection*: if the miracle occurs, then it would be wrong to call what we *believe to be* laws of nature laws. Instead, we should say:
2   A miracle is a violation of *what we believe* the laws of nature to be. *Objection*: this means that whether an event is a miracle depends on what we believe. Suppose God causes an event, which is in accordance with the *real* laws of nature: if we know these laws, it isn't a miracle, but if we don't know these laws, it is. This isn't right. It also implies that miracles are not exceptions to the real laws of nature.
3   A miracle is an event that is *outside* or *not in accordance with* the laws of nature. This definition preserves both the idea that miracles are somehow *at odds* with the laws of nature and the idea that they are still laws.

One argument for (3) is this: the laws of nature apply only to *natural* events. If an event is caused by God, it is not a natural event. So the event doesn't *violate* the laws of nature, it just falls outside them. (You aren't *breaking* the US law on speeding if you drive faster than 55mph on a motorway in the UK.) Because it is outside the laws of nature, a miracle is *physically* impossible. But that doesn't mean it is logically impossible.

Going further: non-repeatable exceptions

Richard Swinburne defends a fourth definition. He argues that the *generality* of a 'law of nature' is not absolute; the law describes what happens in terms of regularity and predictability. A miracle, therefore, is *not* logically incompatible with a law of nature as a counter-instance to it. So if an event *violates* a law of nature, we should not conclude that the law is not genuine unless we think that the counter-instance could or would *recur* under similar conditions. To formulate or revise laws of nature, science needs to be able to test and repeat events. If we think the miracle is 'a one-off', then we shouldn't revise the law – it remains a good and accurate predictive tool.

So Swinburne argues, we shouldn't say (3) miracles aren't natural events, because then they aren't genuine exceptions to the laws of nature. They are natural events because they happen to natural objects within the natural universe. So we should say miracles are genuine, non-repeatable exceptions to the laws of nature.

However, some philosophers reject Swinburne's notion of 'laws'. They argue that the laws of nature are not *just* descriptions of what normally happens, but define the limits of what is physically *possible*. On Swinburne's account, miracles aren't physically impossible, strictly speaking; they just fall outside the usual and regular pattern of events.

A second objection to Swinburne's analysis is that while *we* may not be able to repeat the miracle, we might think that if God acted in the same way again, then the miracle would happen again. For example, could the many cures of diseases count as repeatable events from the perspective of God's activity? If so, then miracles aren't non-repeatable events. It's just that *we* can't repeat them.

Hume's argument against miracles

Hume appears to adopt definition (1): 'A miracle is a violation of the laws of nature', caused by God. However, we have seen that if this definition is true miracles are a contradiction in terms. But Hume doesn't argue this. He argues instead that we never have a good reason to believe that miracles occur. So Hume's argument must actually work with some other definition, but we don't need to worry about which one until we look at responses to his argument.

Hume claims that 'as a firm and unalterable experience has established these laws [of nature], the proof against a miracle, from the very nature of the fact, is as entire as any argument from experience can possibly be imagined'. In other words, a miracle goes against our very regular and extensive experience of how the world works. Therefore, on the basis of experience, the probability that a miracle has occurred must always be less than the probability that it hasn't. Because it is rational to believe what is most probable, we never have a good reason to believe that a miracle has occurred.

In fact, Hume considers only the evidence for miracles from *testimony*, rather than from (apparently) experiencing a miracle oneself. He argues that to rationally believe the testimony, it must be less probable that the testimony is false than that the miracle occurred. He argues that it is more probable that the testimony is false:

1 There is no miracle attested to by people of good sense, education, integrity and reputation (he lists these as the attributes of people we can trust not to be easily fooled), where the miracle is witnessed by many such people.
2 Human nature enjoys surprise and wonder, which gives us a tendency to believe unusual things when the belief isn't warranted.
3 Tales of miracles abound among ignorant peoples, and diminish in civilization.
4 Every religion proclaims miracles, but not all religions can be true; assuming that tales of miracles are intended to support doctrinal claims, the force of each claim to miracles destroys the force of the others, and it is rational not to believe any claim.

Going further: miracles and unexpected events

We can understand the importance of these arguments if we compare miracles to unexpected events. After all, these *also* go against our experience, so do we ever have good reason to believe some unexpected event has occurred? Yes, says Hume, on two conditions: first, that there is widespread, consistent agreement that the event occurred; and second, that there are 'analogies' of the event in our experience. Our experience leads us to expect the unexpected, *within limits*. These may vary from person to person; Hume presents the case of an Indian who, never having lived anywhere cold enough, refused to believe that water turned into ice. Hume thought he was right to do so until more evidence appeared. If we hear of someone coming back from the dead, we would be in a similar situation, and should not believe it.

If the evidence mounts up, we should then not believe that a *miracle* has occurred; we should try to find what the natural cause of the event is. The only rational response is scientific discovery, not religious belief.

Objections

Suppose we investigate an event and are unable to find any natural causes that would explain it. Can't we reasonably conclude a miracle had occurred? Swinburne's definition of miracles as non-repeatable exceptions supports this: if we are able to discover the natural causes, we would conclude that the event was repeatable. Of course, this presupposes that we have good evidence for considering the event to have really occurred in the first place. There must be no other plausible explanation for the event, e.g. in terms of human psychology. Hume argues that there will be.

According to Hume, we have only two choices: reject the claim that the event happened or look for a natural cause of it. His argument is supposed to be based on experience.

But does experience support his claim? Is there *no* experience that could support a belief in a non-natural cause?

This question leads to the heart of the debate. Hume would claim that no *experience* is evidence for a non-natural explanation, because we never experience a non-natural *cause*. To suppose that God caused some event will always be speculative, for we have no experience of God. So even if we don't find a natural cause, we can conclude only that *we don't know* what the cause is, not that the cause is God. Furthermore, if we have good enough reason to believe the event actually happened, we must think it is sufficiently analogous to our experience. But then we can conclude that it is sufficiently analogous to have a natural cause, like the other events we have experienced.

Hume's rejection of miracles depends entirely on what we have experienced and how he thinks we should argue from experience. On Hume's account, if I personally witness someone, undoubtedly killed before my eyes, get up, wounds healing, and walk off, I *still* shouldn't think there is a non-natural cause of this because nothing in my previous experience is sufficiently analogous. This demonstrates that Hume's constraints on reasoning from experience are faulty. If we have experienced a number of apparent miracles personally, it may not be irrational to believe in a non-natural cause.

This conclusion doesn't justify many people believing in miracles. It also doesn't mean that miracles have ever occurred.

A theological objection to miracles

If miracles are somehow *outside* the laws of nature, caused by God, then God acts very selectively, and this considerably sharpens THE PROBLEM OF EVIL (p. 177). If God cured your son of cancer, why did he not cure mine? If he gave you a premonition not to board the doomed plane, why did he not share that information with the rest of the passengers, who then died? Many theologians argue that God's activity in the world is not selective in this way, so miracles in this sense don't occur.

● **KEY POINTS**

- The most common philosophical definition of miracles is that of events caused by God and not in accordance with the laws of nature.

- Some philosophers claim that a miracle is a *violation* of the laws of nature. But a law is true and general, so, if an event is a violation of it, the law is not a genuine law. Therefore, no event can be a genuine violation of a law of nature. However, it is possible that an event violates what we *believe* the laws the nature to be, and thereby proves we are mistaken.

- Swinburne argues that miracles are genuine violations of, non-repeatable exceptions to, laws of nature. He argues that laws are only regularities, and if the event is non-repeatable, the law remains a true description of natural regularities.

● Another definition claims that the laws of nature apply only to natural events, while events that are caused by God are not natural events. Miracles, then, are not in accordance with the laws of nature (they are not physically possible), but they are not violations of the laws of nature.

● Hume argues that we never have good reason to believe, on the basis of testimony, that a miracle occurred. Experience always provides overwhelming evidence that the miracle didn't occur, so it is more probable that the testimony is false. If the testimony is very well supported and the event has 'analogies' with our experience, then we should believe an unexpected event has occurred and look for its natural cause. To believe that there is a non-natural cause of the event is never supported by experience, since we never have experience of non-natural causes.

● We can object to Hume's rejection of miracles that it is possible to experience an event so completely at odds with previous experience that it is rational to suppose there can be no natural cause for it.

● If God does cause miracles, it seems that God's activity in the world is selective and the problem of evil becomes yet more problematic.

❓ QUIZ QUESTIONS

Briefly explain the meaning of the word 'miracle'. (AQA, 4a, 2004, *6 marks*)

Explain and illustrate **one** argument against the occurence of miracles.

❓ DISCUSSION QUESTION

Assess the claim that we can never be justified in believing that miracles occur.

Morality: could God's will be the sole ground of our moral duties?

In WHETHER THESE ATTRIBUTES CAN BE EXPRESSED AND COMBINED IN AN INTELLIGIBLE AND COHERENT WAY (p. 129), we noted a puzzle about God's goodness: Does God conform his will to what is morally good, which is independent of what God wants, or is what is morally good whatever God wants it to be? Is morality whatever God wills or commands or something independent of God's will?

You do not have to believe in God to consider this an important question. Some philosophers argue that morality depends on God's will: it is the only way to make sense of morality. They then argue that because God doesn't exist, neither do moral duties.

There are different strengths of the claim that morality depends on God's will. The strongest version claims that all of morality – what is morally good, what is virtuous and moral duties – depend on what God wills. A weaker version claims that only our moral duties depend on God's will. We will start with the stronger version, and then see if the weaker version solves objections to the stronger version.

Finally, we should note that, if God exists, how we should act probably depends on God's will, given the nature of God. However, this doesn't solve the question of how God's will and morality are related to each other. Our question is whether moral values, virtues and duties are *conceptually* or *metaphysically* dependent on God's will. Is God's will the metaphysical source of morality? Is to talk of morality to talk of what God wills?

Morality and God

In arguing that morality depends on God's will, we might note that moral concepts and theological concepts have been linked historically. So we can't explain morality properly without reference to God.

Second, we can argue that morality must depend on God's will, given the nature of God. For instance, if God is perfectly good, but morality is independent of God, then God cannot will anything (only what is good). This would mean that God is not omnipotent. Since God is omnipotent, morality is not a restriction on God's will, but is dependent on it. (See WHETHER THESE ATTRIBUTES CAN BE EXPRESSED AND COMBINED IN AN INTELLIGIBLE AND COHERENT WAY, p. 131, for other solutions.) Or, again, if God exists and is good, then everything that is morally valuable must relate back to God as the ultimate reality. What is moral must depend on God.

Third, we can argue that the various properties of morality don't make sense unless God exists; hence morality depends on God:

1 *Normativity*: moral judgements are **normative**, they tell us what we *ought* to do. But what does it mean to say we 'ought' to do something? Why ought we? One answer is that God wills it. We can then ask why we ought to obey God, but that can be answered by referring to the nature of God as the ultimate reality.
2 *Impartiality*: morality is impartial, not favouring anyone, but treating everyone as equals. But people aren't impartial, so where does the requirement to be impartial come from? We may say it is God's impartial love for us.
3 *Obligation* and *authority*: the idea of a moral law implies a law giver, while ideas of obligation, duty, etc., suggest a relationship between persons in which some demand is made. Who do we owe moral duties to? Any attempt to explain moral obligation naturalistically, e.g. in terms of society, fails to account for the authority of morality. An explanation of moral obligation in terms of God secures both authority and the personal nature of morality.
4 *Absolute value*: if being good was the only thing that entitled people to be treated well, we could treat many people badly. People are only finitely good, so not of unconditional worth. Yet people have certain *rights* independently of how good they are. The respect we owe people as persons doesn't depend on their goodness. It must therefore relate to something of absolute worth; and God's valuing of persons would explain this.
5 *Respect for morality*: it doesn't make sense to revere morality itself. It isn't respect for people either, since morality transcends people. But we rightly think the personal is more important than the impersonal. Our respect for morality would make sense if morality has a personal source greater than human persons.

None of this is an argument for God's *existence*. It is an argument that morality depends in some way upon God's will. If the argument is right, but God doesn't exist, then moral values, virtues and duties don't either.

Going further: does good = what God wills?

One interpretation of 'What is morally good depends on God's will' is that 'morally good' *means* 'what God wills'. However, this entails that people who don't believe in God don't understand or can't use the words 'morally good' meaningfully, which is very counter-intuitive.

It is also open to a famous objection by G. E. Moore, who argued that it is a **fallacy** to identify goodness with any other property (see Ch. 2, INTUITIONISM, p. 102). Though Moore focused on natural properties, we can extend his point to 'what God wills'. If goodness just is what God wills, then it wouldn't make sense to ask 'Is it good to do what God wills?' because this would be like asking 'Is doing what God wills doing what God wills?' This isn't a real question (the answer has to be 'yes'), but 'Is it good to do what God wills?' is a real question – the answer can logically be 'yes' or 'no'. So goodness cannot be the same as what God wills. Goodness cannot be any other property; it is just goodness.

This argument does show that 'good' can't *mean* 'what God wills'. But it doesn't show that good can't *be the same thing* as what God wills. Here is a similar argument: 'The property of being water cannot be the property of being H_2O. If it was, then the question "Is water H_2O?" would not make sense – it would be like asking "Is H_2O H_2O?" So being water cannot be the same as any other property.' This is not right, as water *just is* H_2O.

Moore's argument doesn't work because it confuses *concepts* and *properties*. Two different concepts – water and H_2O – can pick out the same property in the world. (You learned about water long before you knew it was H_2O – during this time, you had the concept of water, but not the concept of H_2O. So they are different concepts, but they both refer to the same thing.) Likewise, the concept 'goodness' is a different concept from 'what God wills', but perhaps they are exactly the same property in the world. They are just *different ways of thinking of the same thing*.

This argument entails that *moral ideas and language* are autonomous – they aren't dependent on ideas about God – but that moral values, virtues and duties could be dependent on what God wills.

The *Euthyphro* dilemma

In his dialogue *Euthyphro*, Plato considered the question 'What is piety?': is piety doing whatever the gods want or do the gods want what is pious? Plato argued that both answers seem unsatisfactory, creating a dilemma. Our version substitutes 'morally good' (or 'morally right') for 'pious'.

If we say that morality exists independently of God's will, then we must answer all the points above that suggest they are linked. In particular, we must explain why morality is not a *constraint* on God, and how God can still be understood as the ultimate reality.

On the other hand, saying that what is moral goodness is whatever God wills faces two powerful objections.

Is 'God is good' a tautology?

If good is whatever God wills, then 'God is good' doesn't say anything substantial about God. *Whatever* God wills is by definition good. This empties the claim 'God is good' of meaning. Here are four responses:

1   'God is good' means 'God is good to us', i.e. God loves us and wants what is best for us. And what is best for us can be understood in a way that is not dependent on whatever God wills. But if this is so, what is best for us does not depend on what God wills, which leads to (2).
2   Not *all* of morality depends on God's will, only our moral duties. We discuss this below.
3   'God is good' should be understood *metaphysically*, not morally. In CONCEPTIONS OF GOD (p. 124), we noted this other meaning of 'good', and the connection between perfection and reality. But then what is the connection between the metaphysical sense of 'good' and the moral sense of 'good'? Does God's being perfect entail that God is *morally* good? If so, then 'God is (morally) good' still has no meaning. But if not, then is morality independent of metaphysical perfection?
4   'God is good' is not an **analytic** truth, because 'God' and 'morally good' are different concepts. However, goodness is the same property as what God wills. This is what 'God is good' states; it is similar to 'Water is H_2O'. It is informative, because it provides an account of what 'good' refers to, viz. God's will.

  This doesn't mean that God is only *accidentally* good, or that morality is independent of God. Once we know that water is H_2O, we also know that anything that isn't H_2O *can't be* water. Water is necessarily H_2O. Likewise, what is good *can't be* anything other than what God wills, because it is the same thing as what God wills. So it is dependent on what God wills.

Morality is arbitrary

Another objection to saying that what is goodness is whatever God wills is that it makes morality arbitrary. There is no answer to why God wills what he wills. God doesn't will what he wills because there is some moral reason or value he is responding to. God *invents* morality. But if God has no reasons to will what he does, this means that there is no rational structure to morality. Furthermore, it entails that it would be right to slaughter innocent children if God willed it. This doesn't seem right!

There must be some standard we are implicitly relying on to say that what God wills is, in fact, morally good. So we might argue that it is right to do what God wills only if what God wills is good. But how can we tell whether this is true unless we have some independent standard of goodness? But then morality is independent of God.

We may reply that although God's will does not respond to anything independent of it, it is not arbitrary. For example, we can appeal to God's other attributes, such as love. But then aren't we judging God's will to be the standard of love? So morality is still independent of God. No – the claim is not that the basis of morality is love, but that it is *God's* love.

There is, however, still no further basis to morality than God's (loving) will. But is this a problem? Suppose morality didn't depend on God's will, but on some set of *ultimate* moral values or judgements, such as 'Unnecessary suffering is bad' or 'Rationality should always be treated as an end in itself'. Are these any less arbitrary than God's will, especially if we claim that God is ultimate reality? It seems not.

Still, how can we judge whether God's will is good without an *independent* standard of goodness? We may argue that this is a question of how we *know* what is good, not what goodness turns out to *be*. We can judge that water is H_2O only if we have some independent idea of what water is. But that doesn't mean water is not H_2O. Likewise, to judge that what is good is what God wills, we need, *at least initially*, an independent conception both of what is good and of what God wills. Which is fine, since we do form these ideas in distinct ways. Furthermore, once we think that water is H_2O, we will say that whatever is H_2O is water. So once we come to believe that what is good is what God wills, we may use what we believe God's will to be to start judging what is good. God's will, we may argue, is our best source of knowledge about what is, in fact, good.

Only our moral duties depend on God's will

Some philosophers argue that not *all* of morality depends on God's will, only our moral duties, which are what God commands us to do. This theory has several strengths:

1 God's commands are not arbitrary because God is perfectly virtuous, i.e. God's will *complies* with but doesn't define what is morally good. What is morally good or virtuous gives God reasons to command what he does.
2 'God is good' is informative.
3 The nature of morality is explained. Moral duties are impersonal, absolute, authoritative, deserve respect and rely on a personal relationship in which demands are made. All this can be explained by saying that moral duties are commanded by God.

However, the theory allows that moral goodness and virtue do not depend on God, and this leads to problems. First, there is something that is ultimately real that does not depend on God. Second, as God is perfectly good, what God wills is dependent on something independent of God, which seems to be a constraint on what God can will (but see WHETHER THESE ATTRIBUTES CAN BE EXPRESSED AND COMBINED IN AN INTELLIGIBLE AND

COHERENT WAY, p. 131, for responses). Third, if what God commands is based on what is morally good, then do we need to refer to God's commands to say what our moral duties are? Why not say that our moral duties are given directly by what is morally good, i.e. the *reasons* for God's commands, not God's commands themselves?

KEY POINTS

- Is morality dependent on what God wills, not just in the sense that we should do what God wills, but in the sense that what is morally good or right depends *conceptually* or *metaphysically* on God's will?

- Arguments that morality is dependent on God's will invoke God's nature (as omnipotent or the ultimate reality) and the nature of morality. Philosophers have argued that we cannot explain how morality is normative, impartial, obligatory, authoritative, absolute and deserving of respect unless the source of morality is God's will.

- The claim that 'morally good' *means* 'what God wills' entails that anyone who disagrees doesn't understand the words 'morally good'. It also entails that the question 'Is it good to do what God wills?' is not an open question. So we should claim that 'morally good' and 'what God wills' are different concepts.

- But they could be the same thing (property), and we are just thinking of that thing in two different ways.

- We can object that if good is whatever God wills, 'God is good' doesn't say anything substantial about God. Replies to this include the claim that 'good' means 'good to us'; that 'good' means 'metaphysically good'; and that 'God is good' is informative even though goodness is the same property as what God wills, since they are separate concepts.

- A second objection is that if good is whatever God wills, morality is arbitrary. God has *no reasons* to will what he does; and if God willed something we think is evil, it would actually be good. So the standard of morality must be independent of God's will for us to judge whether God is good.

- However, morality must depend on some ultimate set of values, which will be no less *arbitrary* than God's will. And while it is true that we need an independent way of knowing what is good to judge that God's will is good, this doesn't mean that goodness is in fact independent of God's will.

❓ QUIZ QUESTIONS

Briefly explain and illustrate **two** reasons for thinking that morality is dependent on God's will.

Outline **two** objections to the claim that morality is dependent on God's will.

❓ DISCUSSION QUESTIONS

Assess the claim that if morality is dependent on God, the statement 'God is good' is meaningless.

Assess the claim that God's will is the source of our moral duties.

4

• Plato's
The Republic

(Book V, 474c–Book VII, 521b)

Quotations and page references are from the AQA recommended edition of Lee's translation (Penguin Classics, ISBN 0-140-44914-0).

The theory of Forms; metaphysical implications

From sense experience to the Forms

In Book V (476f.) of *The Republic*, Plato argues that all objects we experience through our senses are particular things. We don't ever sense anything *abstract*, but always some individual thing or other. For example, we only ever see this particular beautiful thing or that particular beautiful thing, but we never see Beauty. But, obviously, more than one thing can be beautiful. Beauty is a property that more than one thing can have. So, Plato claims, if many different things can be beautiful, then there is something they share in common, viz. beauty. So there must be something which is Beauty, even though we never experience Beauty itself through our senses. This idea of a universal, a property that more than one thing can have, is a first approximation to the idea of a Form. The Form of Beauty manifests itself in all the different things, in all the different ways, we call 'beautiful'.

But why should we agree that just because many different things can be beautiful, there is some *thing* which is Beauty? Because, Plato goes on to argue, Forms exist independently of particular things. All particular beautiful things could be destroyed, yet that won't destroy Beauty itself. So Beauty must be a separate thing, existing in its own right. So, he concludes, particular things 'share' or 'participate' in the Forms, but these exist independently.

Plato gives another argument for this claim, relating to the nature of knowledge, which we return to in the next section.

Metaphysics of the Forms

In arguing that Forms exist independently of the particular things that 'participate in' them, Plato constructed an original and controversial metaphysics (one that Aristotle, for example, rejected). Plato discusses several essential properties of the Forms:

1 *Self-predication*: the Form of Beauty is itself beautiful. But this is different from the way in which all other beautiful things are beautiful. Every other beautiful thing is beautiful because it 'participates in' the Form of Beauty; but the Form simply *is* beautiful. It is what it is in virtue of itself. This also provides an explanation of why things that participate in Beauty are beautiful: participating in Beauty makes a particular thing beautiful because the Form is itself beautiful. Beauty is *transmitted* to particular things that participate in it.

2 *Independence from particulars*: it follows from (1) that each Form is its own essence. Because this is what a Form *is*, we can understand *why* it is that Forms (can) exist independently of whether any particular object participates in them. Because it is its own essence, it is what it is regardless of whether particulars participate in it; it is not essential to its existence that it is exemplified in particulars. A Form, therefore, also does not exist in time or space (either at a particular space/time or as distributed across all particulars exemplifying it).

3 *Perfection*: a Form is the perfect example of itself. Nothing can be more beautiful than the Form of Beauty, and there is no way in which the Form is not beautiful. This is sometimes suggested as an important difference between 'participating in' and 'being' Beauty: all particular things only approximate to the property of Beauty, which is only perfectly possessed by the Form.

4 *Permanence*: Forms do not change. The Form of Beauty cannot become not beautiful, nor can it have ever been not beautiful. If it changed, then to judge by the new Form of Beauty, the previous Form would not have been perfectly beautiful; by the previous Form, any change would be a change away from being beautiful. As this is impossible, Forms do not change.

5 *Simplicity*: Plato says repeatedly the Forms are 'one'. Each Form has just the one property of which it is the Form: the Form of Beauty is only beautiful (and the only thing which is only beautiful). However, Plato also suggests that each Form is good, and that the Form of the Good is the Form of Forms (see PLATO'S ACCOUNT OF THE GOOD, p. 204). Furthermore, Plato attempts to give full accounts of each Form that explains what it is. For example, in *The Republic*, Plato argues that justice is doing one's own job (433a). This equates justice to a particular set of properties, so it is not simple or just 'one'.

In contrast to Forms, particulars are complex, changeable and imperfect. These important differences suggest that the way Forms and particulars *exist* is different, and that the existence of the Forms is superior: they *are* in a way that particulars are not. Forms exist independently, but particulars exist only through participating in the Forms. Plato speaks of 'two worlds', the world of Forms and that of particulars. But if they are so different, how can particulars 'share' or 'participate' in the Forms *at all?*

One suggestion is that the properties particulars have are *copies* of the Forms. The beauty of this rose is a copy of the Form of Beauty. While particulars are material (made of matter), they can possess properties that are copies of the Forms. Unlike the Forms, a particular can lose its properties (e.g. its beauty) and even cease to exist as that particular (a rose can become ash). A particular is what it is in virtue of the properties it has (e.g. a rose, beautiful, etc.). But its properties are how it participates in the Forms. So a particular only exists by participating in the Forms.

● **KEY POINTS**

- Plato argues that many particular objects can have the same property, e.g. beauty. These properties can exist independently of the particular objects, as shown by the fact that if we destroy all beautiful things, we haven't destroyed beauty.

- We don't detect these abstract properties through sense experience.

- These properties are Forms. Forms are self-predicating, exist independently of particular things (and therefore outside space and time); they are perfect, permanent and (perhaps) simple.

- The existence of Forms is of a different and superior kind to the existence of particulars. Particulars exist by participating in the Forms. One understanding of this is that particulars possess (for a time) copies of the Forms.

❓ QUIZ QUESTION

Briefly explain and illustrate **three** properties of the Forms.

Knowledge, belief and ignorance – reasons for making these distinctions

Knowledge and the Forms

Plato's second argument for separating the Forms from the particular things we experience via the senses relates to the nature of knowledge. Particular things will always both be X – have some property, e.g. beauty or largeness – and not X, either at different times, or to different observers, or in different contexts. And so 'isn't it the case, then, that any member of a plurality no more *is* whatever it is said to be than it *is not* whatever it is said to be?' (479b)

Plato argues that because particular things are what they are (beautiful, large, etc.) only *relatively* and *transiently*, there cannot be *knowledge* of them. Knowledge needs more permanence and certainty. He argues that we cannot know what is not true; knowledge is about truth, about what *is*. So if something both is and is not X, then we cannot *know* that it is X.

In contrast to particular beautiful things, the Form of Beauty is beautiful under all conditions, to all observers, at all times. The Form of Beauty is pure beauty; it alone is not both beautiful and not beautiful. It is therefore possible for us to acquire knowledge of the Forms. (As noted above, we can't *experience* Forms through our senses. We have this knowledge through reason.) Because we can have knowledge of the Forms, but not knowledge of particular objects of sense experience, the Forms must be separate from particular things.

Distinguishing knowledge (*epistémé*) and opinion (*doxa*)

Plato's argument relies on making a distinction between knowledge (*epistémé*) and *doxa*, translated as 'belief' or 'opinion'. Just before giving the argument above, he argues that knowledge and opinion are different 'faculties' for two reasons (477a–478e):

(a) Knowledge is infallible – you cannot know what is false. Opinion, however, can be mistaken. So opinion cannot be knowledge.

(b) Knowledge is only of what is real. We cannot have knowledge of what is not real or does not exist. Knowledge is *about* what is real. By contrast, ignorance relates to what is not real, what does not exist, i.e. *nothing*. If you are completely ignorant of something, you don't think of it at all; if you don't understand it, you can't form an opinion about its reality. If there is something between what is real and what is not real (which Plato argues there are, viz. particular things, which are both X and not-X), then there must be something between knowledge and ignorance. We know from (a) that opinion is not knowledge; but opinion is obviously not ignorance either, because opinions are always *about* something or other. And opinion does seem to be between complete ignorance and knowledge.

According to (a), knowledge and opinion must have different powers. According to (b), knowledge and opinion must have different objects (what is real v. what is between what is real and what is not real). Therefore that about which we have opinions cannot be the same thing as that about which we have knowledge. Plato argues that opinion relates to the world of the senses, knowledge to the world of the Forms. So Forms must exist separately from particular things.

- Plato argues that particular things are always both X and not X, depending on context, observer, time and so on. So it cannot be said to *be* X rather than not X. By contrast, the Form of X is always X.

- Knowledge is of what *is*. So if something is both X and not X, we cannot have knowledge of it. But we can have knowledge of the Forms.

- Knowledge is different from opinion for two reasons. Knowledge is infallible, opinion is fallible. Knowledge is of what is real, ignorance is of what is not real, while opinion is of what is between what is real and what is not real.

- Forms are real, and so are objects of knowledge, but particular things, being both X and not X, are between what is real and what is not real, and so are objects of opinion.

❓ QUIZ QUESTIONS

Describe **three** features of knowledge which, for Plato, distinguish it from opinion. (AQA, 1b, 2003, *10 marks*)

Outline Plato's argument that the Forms are more real than the objects of sense experience.

The similes of the Cave and the Divided Line

Plato's arguments mean that acquiring knowledge involves turning away from the world of the senses, which can only ever produce opinion, towards the Forms and the world of the intellect. He uses metaphors and analogies to help us understand his theory.

The Divided Line

We may divide the world into the realm of the 'sensible' – what we detect through our senses – and the realm of the 'intelligible' – what we discover using the intellect (see THE SIMILE OF THE SUN, p. 204). Opinion relates to the former, knowledge to the latter. As we saw above, our epistemic states can be divided into two, and aligned with what is real. We can think of these states as lying on a line (see Plato's *The Republic*, p. 236 for a diagram), knowledge as one half, opinion as the other. Plato goes on to divide each half of the line again, making four divisions in total.

Opinion is divided into belief (*pistis*) and illusion or imagination (*eikasia*). Illusion, the lowest form of epistemic state, is characterized in Plato's discussion by shadows and reflections. These things, and our thoughts about them, are very changeable and unclear. But Plato means more than just physical shadows and reflections. He also means the sorts of second-hand, uninformed views that people hold, not finding out for themselves about the world, but just believing what they are told, e.g. in the newspapers; and in the last book of *The Republic*, Plato implies that art and poetry fall under 'illusion' as well.

One step up, our common-sense views on the physical world, and on other matters such as morality, fall under 'belief'. In the *Timaeus*, Plato also includes the natural sciences under belief, since they deal with the changeable, physical world. Unlike 'illusion', belief is informed by a direct study of the world, and it is more stable and a little clearer. But it still takes the world as it appears for reality, so it isn't yet knowledge.

Knowledge also has two divisions, *dianoia*, which we can translate (in this context) as 'reasoning', and *noésis*, which we can translate as 'intelligence' or 'full understanding'. Both relate to the Forms, but *dianoia* relies on assumptions and imagination (images from the realm of the sensible) while *noésis* does not. A good example of *dianoia* is geometry. In studying triangles, e.g. in proving that the three internal angles add up to 180°, students of geometry don't study the actual imperfect triangles they draw; they create proofs using the idea (the Form) of a triangle. They

> make use of and argue about visible figures, though they are not really thinking about them, but about the originals which they resemble; it is *not* about the square or diagonal which they have drawn that they are arguing, but about the square itself or diagonal itself . . . The actual figures they draw or model . . . – these they treat as images only, the real objects of their investigation being invisible except to the eye of reason (510d).

And that is why *dianoia* relates to the realm of the intelligible, not the sensible. But this type of knowledge works with unproven hypotheses, e.g. about different types of angle (obtuse, acute, right), and it uses images from the realm of the sensible to help its investigation.

Noésis is a *purer*, more perfect knowledge of the Forms, which doesn't use images and which treats the assumptions of mathematical reasoning *as assumptions*. We acquire this knowledge of the Forms, of the very first principles 'of everything' (511b), using *nous*. By engaging in dialectic – philosophical argument – we finally reach a vision or insight of the Forms directly, without relying on sensory images or assumptions. By seeking first principles, *nous* does away with the need for the 'hypotheses' that it takes for granted when using *dianoia* (*nous* can be said to include *dianoia*, but goes beyond it). When the first principle has been reached, *nous* can reason through the consequences to generate further knowledge, *noésis*, 'moving solely through Forms to Forms' (511c). When we know the Forms in this way, we understand what the objects of mathematical study, and all other Forms, truly are. This type of knowledge has the greatest clarity, and its objects (the Forms understood directly) have the greatest truth.

Plato has not yet told us exactly *how* we can gain direct knowledge of the Forms. We return to this question below.

The Cave

The Divided Line informed us of the different *types* of epistemic state we can have, and what they relate to. The simile of the Cave gives us a story about *moving* up the line, from illusion to intelligence, and the consequences of doing that.

In the cave, prisoners are chained to face a wall. Behind and above the prisoners, people carry objects along a road. Beyond the road, there is a fire. The fire casts shadows of the people on to the wall in front of the prisoners; so images are all the prisoners see. If a prisoner is freed, and forced to turn around, he will see the people on the road and then the fire. If he is then 'dragged' outside the cave – and he must be dragged, or drag himself, because the process will be painful as he won't be used to the light – he will experience reality as it is, not as it seems in the cave.

The simile of the Cave	
The cave	The world of the senses
Prisoners	People who believe 'second-hand'
Images on the wall	Illusion (*eikasia*)
The fire	The (physical) sun; more generally, what enables us to have sense experience
Seeing the fire and the people on the road	Belief (*pistis*)
Outside the cave	The intelligible world – reality
The prisoner dragged outside the cave	The philosopher
Objects outside the cave	The Forms
Looking at reflections of objects outside the cave	Reasoning (*dianoia*)
Looking at objects outside the cave	Intelligence (*noésis*)
The sun	The Form of the Good

Going further: the difficult ascent

Plato emphasizes that moving from being a prisoner to eventually being able to look directly at the sun itself will be a difficult and painful process. This fact also explains why philosophers, having achieved knowledge of the Forms, will not want to be rulers; and why people (the prisoners) would not welcome philosophers or recognize that what they say is true. Philosophers, having finally got used to sunlight, will not want to go back into the cave, and will (at least at first) find it very difficult to see properly in the darkness. Meanwhile, people who can see *only* the images cast on the wall by the fire will believe that those images are reality, and dismiss claims about a 'world outside the cave' as madness. Since the philosopher has difficulty seeing, they will also argue that 'the visit to the upper world had ruined his sight, and that the ascent was not even worth attempting' (517a) (see also THE STATUS OF PHILOSOPHERS p. 215).

The simile of the cave is about gaining knowledge. But it is also the beginning of Plato's focused argument that only philosophers should rule. Plato uses the analogy to argue that for society to be a just society the rulers must be educated as philosophers, so that they acquire knowledge of the Good, but then they must be forced 'back down' into the cave, to rule. This is discussed further in ETHICAL IMPLICATIONS OF THE THEORY OF THE FORMS, p. 206.

KEY POINTS

- The Divided Line divides into opinion, relating to the world of the senses, and knowledge, relating to the intelligible world.

- Opinion divides into 'illusion' (including second-hand views) and 'belief' (direct study of the physical world). Knowledge divides into 'reasoning', which uses assumptions and physical images to assist it, and 'intelligence', which is direct insight into the Forms.

- The simile of the cave (see table above) provides an analogical account of how we can gain knowledge and why it is difficult.

❓ QUIZ QUESTIONS

Outline the place of the divided line in Plato's argument about how we gain knowledge.

Outline the simile of the cave, and explain why Plato argues that philosophers will not be welcomed by people generally.

Epistemological implications of the theory of the Forms

How can we acquire knowledge of the Forms?

The people in Plato's republic who eventually acquire knowledge of the Forms are those guardians who become philosophers (see ETHICAL IMPLICATIONS OF THE THEORY OF THE FORMS, p. 208). The guardians are trained in arithmetic, geometry and astronomy to bring them to *dianoia*. But to achieve *noésis*, the guardians must be additionally trained in dialectic, or philosophical argument.

Using the simile of the cave, Plato argues that to gain knowledge of the Forms, a person must be *re-oriented*, away from being concerned and caught up in the world of the senses: 'the mind as a whole must be turned away from the world of change until its eye can bear to look straight at reality, and at the brightest of all realities which is what we call the good' (518c). The final step in the philosophers' education is not so much about imparting knowledge but turning the mind towards the Forms. However, the question still remains *how* dialectic leads to an understanding of the Forms.

In fact, Plato doesn't say. One theory is that, as shown in *The Republic* and other Platonic dialogues, dialectic establishes both the existence and the nature of the Forms. Another relates to the fact that the Forms are 'one-over-many'. A Form is unitary and simple, but many particular things can participate in it. There is only one Form of Beauty, but many things can be beautiful. Mathematics helps us understand the idea of 'one-over-many', and helps us understand how the 'one' is the real essence that the many share in. For example, mathematics establishes the necessary properties that all triangles must have in common. And all existing triangles are triangles because they share the essential properties of the Form of the Triangle. Dialectic helps us understand this more generally, or abstractly, because it searches for a unifying account of each and every thing. Dialectic asks 'what is justice?' or 'what is courage?', and so we think about the abstract ideas, the Forms, of Justice and Courage. (For more on the importance of unity-over-difference, see PLATO'S ACCOUNT OF THE GOOD, p. 205.)

Assessing Plato's theory of knowledge

Knowledge and reality

Many philosophers reject Plato's claim that knowledge must match something *real* in the sense that Plato means, viz. things that don't change and perfectly exemplify some property. Plato might be right that knowledge cannot change (*it* can't go from truth to falsehood), but that doesn't mean the *object* of knowledge can't change. For example, I can know (it seems) that a particular object of sense experience – this book – has a particular property, e.g. it is a certain size, even though its size can change – if you burn it, for instance. What I know is that the book is this size *now* (at a specific moment in time), and this truth won't change even if the size of the book changes. Plato seems to have confused a property about knowledge with a property about the object of knowledge.

From this, we can see that even if knowledge and opinion are different faculties because knowledge is infallible and opinion is not, that doesn't mean that they have different objects. There is no need for the object (particular thing, Form) to match the epistemic state (opinion, knowledge). We can make the distinction in some other way, e.g. knowledge is always *true* and *justified*, whereas opinion can be false and unjustified (see Ch. 1, BELIEVING-THAT AND KNOWING-THAT, p. 19).

Knowledge and certainty

Plato controversially sets the standard for knowledge very high, which has perhaps inspired sceptics ever since. Because knowledge by definition cannot be false, it seems he believes that knowledge must involve certainty. If we cannot be certain, we cannot know. Plato argues that we can have certainty about the Forms, and so know them, because they are unchanging; but we cannot be certain of, or have knowledge of, particular objects of sense experience. However, for an argument criticizing the link between knowledge and certainty, see Ch. 1, BELIEVING-THAT AND KNOWING-THAT (p. 21).

Going further: Plato's rationalism

Plato's conclusion is that only *nous* delivers knowledge of reality. However, we have seen that his account of how *nous* works, how we finally achieve *noésis*, is not clear. After all, unlike in the case of sense experience being caused by physical objects, Plato didn't claim that the Forms *cause* our knowledge of them. So what is the means by which *nous* knows the Forms?

Hume argues, indirectly, that there is no such thing as *nous*. There are only two sorts of knowledge: what reason can demonstrate (**a priori** knowledge), and what we confirm through the senses (a **posteriori** knowledge) (see Ch. 1, EMPIRICISM, p. 12). But, Hume argues, reason can demonstrate only **analytic** truths. It can't provide *insight*, i.e. it cannot prove **synthetic** truths. It is not surprising that Plato cannot give us a clear account of how *nous* works if there is no such thing!

Plato's best form of defence is probably attack. He could argue that unless we allow that there is such a thing as rational insight, we will fall into scepticism (see Ch. 1, THE LIMITATIONS OF EMPIRICISM, p. 17). For example, the first knowledge of the Forms we have is through mathematical reasoning. If he can argue successfully that this knowledge is based on reason, but isn't analytic, then his theory is supported – even if he can't then give us an account of *how* we have knowledge of the Forms. In other words, Plato can argue that we need rational insight to account for mathematical knowledge. If the argument from mathematical knowledge doesn't work, Plato could try the same argument in some other area of knowledge, e.g. moral knowledge (on moral insight, see Ch. 2, INTUITIONISM, p. 102).

● **KEY POINTS**

- To acquire full knowledge of the Forms, we must be trained in philosophical argument. This is not about imparting information, but 'turning the mind' towards the Forms.

- Mathematics may help us acquire this knowledge, as it helps us understand the idea of 'one-over-many' and that the one abstract thing is the essence of the many particular things. Dialectic develops this knowledge by searching for a unifying account for each thing.

- Philosophers have objected that Plato's claim that the objects of knowledge must be *certain* or unchanging for knowledge to be possible is based on a confusion. Opinion and knowledge can be about the same objects, although knowledge cannot be false, while opinion can. We may also object that Plato is wrong to think knowledge requires certainty.

- Plato's theory of *nous* remains unclear. However, if reason is incapable of insight, if it is limited to establishing analytic truths, then we may fall into scepticism.

❓ QUIZ QUESTION

Briefly describe Plato's conception of the relation between knowledge and the Forms. (AQA, 1b, 2002, *10 marks*)

❓ DISCUSSION QUESTION

Assess Plato's claim that we can only have **knowledge** of the Forms.

Plato's account of the Good, the Form of the Good and its relation to other Forms; the simile of the Sun

The simile of the Sun and the Form of the Good

Plato introduces the simile of the Sun after arguing (503–4) that philosophers must be prepared to undertake the difficult task of study he describes. Their studies will not be complete until they achieve the highest form of knowledge, knowledge of the Form of the Good. It is from the Good that 'things that are just and so on derive their usefulness and value . . . . Is there any point in having all other forms of knowledge without that of the good, and so lacking knowledge about what is good and valuable?' (505a–b) And so Adeimantus and Glaucon ask Socrates what the Good is, and he responds with this simile.

The simile of the Sun	
The visible world	The intelligible world (the Forms)
The Sun	The Form of the Good
The eye	The mind (reason)
Sight	Intelligence
To see	To know
Light	Truth
Growth	The being (reality) of the Forms

Unless there is light, our eyes cannot see, even though they have the power of sight, and objects that we can see exist and have colour and shape. It is only in the presence of light, which comes from the Sun, that we can see. The Sun also causes growth, and Plato says it is a cause of sight. This last claim is difficult to understand; Plato thinks of sight as a power that the eye gets from the sun (the eye is 'sunlike', he says), as though eyes actually make what they see *visible* in a way similar to how the sun makes things visible. However, the sun is not sight and it is not light; it is different from them, and because it is their cause, it is 'higher' than them.

The Form of the Good plays the same role in the intelligible world. We cannot come to know anything without the Form of the Good. Just as the sun is the source of light and the source of sight – together necessary to see anything – the Form of the Good 'gives the objects of knowledge [the Forms] their truth and the knower's mind the power of knowing' (508a). Both intelligence and truth have their source in the Form of the Good. And, just as the sun is the cause of growth, the Form of the Good is the source of the very being of knowable objects: 'The good therefore may be said to be the source not only of the intelligibility of the objects of knowledge, but also of their being and reality' (509b). And as we noted above, Plato says that everything derives its value from the Good (505b). Finally, just as the sun is not light nor sight nor growth, the Form of the Good is not intelligence nor truth nor the reality of the Forms, but 'beyond it, and superior to it in dignity and power' (509b).

The Form of the Good

It is obvious from these remarks that the Good is not just one Form among others. But what *is* the Form of the Good? Socrates states that he cannot say (506e), and offers the simile of the sun instead. We know that the Good is *not* intelligence, truth, knowledge or the reality of the Forms; and we know that it is the source of all these. Plato doesn't say any more, and we do not even know *how* the Good is the source for all of this. But we can speculate somewhat to fill out an account of what the Good is.

The Good is sometimes said to be the Form of the Forms. But we have listed at least five characteristics of all Forms (see THE THEORY OF FORMS, p. 194), and *goodness* will not be all of these. The obvious characteristic of the Forms that is related to goodness is perfection; Forms are purely and perfectly their own essence. By contrast, particular things fail to be completely their essence (hence their existence is inferior to the type of existence enjoyed by the Forms).

Going further: The Form of the Good and harmony

But this doesn't solve the puzzle. If the Good is *just* each thing exhibiting its own essence, the Good would seem to be different in each case, since it is dependent on what a thing *is*. However, in accordance with the rest of his theory of the Forms, Plato assumes that the Good is the same thing in every case. One suggestion is that if the Good is *coherence* or *harmony* or *unity-over-difference*, this would make sense of a great deal of Plato's theory of the Forms, and so it is worth taking seriously:

1 Mathematics leads to knowledge of the Good as it is through mathematics that we understand the account of the one over the many.
2 The Good is superior to other Forms, not just another Form alongside others, since it is the unity or coherence of other Forms.

3 It is the Form of Forms, and other Forms owe their being to it, since they are good in being unities (of that which participates in them) and in being part of a unifying and coherent order.
4 Unity and harmony play a very important role in the ethics and politics of *The Republic* – both the good state and the good soul are said to be harmonious.

This interpretation is also supported by a passage from the *Phaedo*, where Plato says 'that the truly good . . . binds and holds everything together' (99c).

How does this relate to the idea that the Good is each thing exhibiting its own essence? Plato argues repeatedly in *The Republic* that when each person plays his or her role in society, harmony is achieved. More generally, then, it seems he believes that when each thing exhibits its essence, harmony – the Good – is achieved.

However, Plato clearly thinks of the Good as not just a *property* that the Forms have, but a force from which reality emanates. If the Good is unity and harmony, it is also the first principle of everything, the standard by which everything is what it is, that has an existence and power all of its own.

KEY POINTS

● Plato has Socrates state that he cannot say what the Form of the Good is. He offers the simile of the sun (see table above) to explain that the Good is the source of truth, intelligence, knowledge and the being of the Forms. As the cause of all this, it has an existence superior to that of the Forms 'in dignity and power'.

● If the Form of the Good is something like harmony or unity-over-difference, we can explain many aspects of Plato's theory, including one central idea of *The Republic*, that when each person in society or each part of the soul plays its proper role, exhibits its essence, the result is a good, harmonious society or a good, harmonious soul.

❓ QUIZ QUESTION

Outline Plato's account of the Form of the Good.

Ethical implications of the theory of the Forms; the relation of the Good to Knowledge – ethical implications

Plato is clearly a COGNITIVIST (Ch. 2, p. 102) about ethics. We can have moral knowledge, knowledge of the Good. However, knowledge and the Good are more closely related to this.

First, there is a close relation between reality (which is what knowledge is of) and goodness. The Forms are perfect and more real, whereas particular objects are imperfect and derive their existence from the Forms. But the Forms in turn derive their being from the Form of the Good, which is the first principle of everything.

So, second, knowledge of what *is* is related to knowledge of what is *good*. To know what something is is to understand its essence. Exemplifying its essence is what it is for that thing to be good. So if we understand something's essence, we understand what it is for it to be good (of its kind). This is a clear example of the way in which the Form of the Good is the source of knowledge.

Third, in the case of understanding how a good state is organized, we need to understand the role that each person in the state needs to play. A good citizen is someone who plays their role in the good state. So we need knowledge of the Good in order to know how to organize a state (this argument is discussed in the next section).

Fourth, the Good and all the Forms do not change, which is why they can be known. Since the Good does not change, the good person and the good state will also not change. There is one absolute standard for being good, and the purpose of politics is to bring about the good state. Once this is achieved, the purpose of politics is just to maintain that state, not to allow it to keep changing. Likewise, the perfectly good person does not change.

'Turning the soul around'

In other works, Plato famously argues that virtue is knowledge: if you know what the good thing is, you will be good. We will discuss his claim that knowing the Form of the Good will make you good in more detail in the next section. In this section, we will look at how coming to know what is good involves becoming virtuous.

During his discussion of the simile of the cave, Plato says that the prisoner, when freed, must be turned around to face the fire and then the outside world. So, he infers,

> our argument indicates that the capacity for knowledge is innate in each man's mind, and that the organ by which he learns is like an eye which cannot be turned from darkness to light unless the whole body is turned; in the same way the mind as a whole must be turned away from the world of change until its eye can bear to look straight at reality, and at the brightest of all realities which is what we call the good . . . . (518c)

The philosopher, Plato argues, will not be concerned with or distracted by things of this world, but only with the Forms, and above all, with the Form of the Good. His *whole* mind must be turned around. He has to be this focused in order to acquire knowledge of the Good. But then, having achieved knowledge of the Good, what motivations could a philosopher have for not *being good* himself? The usual temptations won't be there, because as a philosopher he is just not interested in money, fame and so on. He is interested only in the Good. So to know the Good is to be good.

However, the philosophical temperament necessary to acquire knowledge of the Forms is very rare (503b–d). So Plato's theory of the Forms, and the Form of the Good, mean that most people will never achieve knowledge of what is good. This, of course, can be challenged. For example, Kant, while agreeing that ethical understanding depends on rationality, argues that everyone is sufficiently rational to understand the good (see Ch. 2, OUR AWARENESS OF WHAT IS RIGHT AND OUR DUTY TO ACT RIGHTLY IS GIVEN BY REASON, p. 75). Christians would argue similarly that everyone has a conscience. To agree with this universal knowledge of the good, if we do not reject Plato's theory of the Forms altogether, we must reject his stringencies on what is required to acquire knowledge of them and produce a different story about the development or nature of reason.

Plato's ethics in practice: the perfect state

Plato's argument in *The Republic* as a whole is to develop an account of what the perfect state would be like. How would it be organized? In the next section, we will see that Plato argues that in the perfect state, philosophers must be rulers. How does he get to this point?

The perfect state has, by definition, all the virtues. Plato accepts the idea that the four main virtues are wisdom, courage, temperance or moderation (being self-controlled about pleasure) and justice. If he can describe a state that has all these, he will have described the perfect state.

The state has its origins in the fact that human beings are not individually self-sufficient, so we naturally group together. First, Plato assumes that we are also naturally disposed to different types of task, we each perform well in different areas of life. This needs to be respected in a successful city, so we need a division of labour. Second, to defend itself against attack, or to launch attacks in order to become more prosperous, the city will need professional soldiers, 'guardians'. By the division of labour, these will be separate people from the farmers and traders. Good soldiers need to be both fierce in battle and gentle towards their fellow citizens. Third, the city's leaders, who should be selected from the guardians, will obviously need intelligence, and they will need to know what is good for the state as a whole. So they will be educated as philosophers, so that they come to have knowledge of the Good.

Plato then argues that this state is perfect. *Wisdom* lies with the rulers – their knowledge benefits the whole city; *courage* lies with the guardians; *temperance*, involving traits of restraint and self-control, Plato understands as the acceptance of the social order – all parts of society are in agreement about who should rule (432a). *Justice* must, by elimination, be the remaining organizing principle of the city (427e); and this is the assumption that got us started – that everyone does his or her own job, making their own distinctive contribution to the good of the whole, functioning as they should, and not interfering with the functions of the others (433a). So a perfectly good society is one in which everyone fulfils their task, which creates harmony.

In this account, philosophers again turn out to be fully virtuous. They have wisdom, courage (because they were first trained as guardians), temperance and justice, as they accept their role as rulers and preserve the just organization of society.

KEY POINTS

- Knowledge and the Good are closely related. What is real (which is the object of knowledge) also has more goodness than what is not real. To know what something is is to know its essence, which is also to know what it is for it to be good. We need to know what is Good in order to organize a good state. And what is Good, like knowledge, does not change.

- To come to have knowledge, the whole soul must be 'turned around', away from the world of the senses. The philosopher will become interested only in the Good, and so will not be tempted not to be good.

- The perfect state has all four virtues, *wisdom*, *courage*, *temperance* and *justice*. Wisdom lies with the philosopher–rulers, courage with the guardians, temperance with all citizens, accepting the social order, and justice with everyone doing their proper task. Philosophers also have all four virtues as individuals.

QUIZ QUESTIONS

Outline Plato's organization of the perfect state, and why he claims it is perfect.

Briefly describe Plato's conception of the relation between knowledge and the Good.

The natural qualities of the philosopher, his love of truth, his fitness to rule

Plato's discussion of knowledge – how and why it is different from belief, his theory of the Forms, his similes of the Sun, the Cave and the Divided Line – is part of a discussion about the education of selected guardians to become the rulers in his perfect city. Just before these discussions, Plato says that the only way the republic can come about is if philosophers become rulers or rulers become philosophers (473d). And after discussing the simile of the cave, he says that 'a necessary consequence of what we have said [is] that society will never be properly governed . . . by the uneducated, who have no knowledge of the truth' (518c).

The ultimate purpose of a philosophical education, in the perfect republic, is to gain knowledge of the Form of the Good. Until this has been achieved, the education is not complete. The rest of knowledge has little point, especially if you are a ruler, unless you know what is useful, valuable and good.

The argument and challenge in outline

Pappas (Plato's *The Republic*, p. 111) identifies Plato's central argument for philosopher–rulers as follows:

1　The good city is possible if and only if virtuous and expert rule by its leaders is possible (484d).
2　Virtuous and expert rule is possible if and only if the rulers are philosophers.

As (1) is relatively uncontentious, the rest of the argument offers support to (2):

3　Philosophers, as lovers (*philo-*) of wisdom (*sophia*), love every kind of learning (475c).
4　No one else loves every kind of learning (475c–480a).
5　The love of every kind of learning produces knowledge of ethical matters.
6　The love of every kind of learning produces virtue (485d).
7　Therefore, the love of every kind of learning makes one a virtuous and expert ruler.
8　Therefore, since only philosophers love every kind of learning, only philosophers can be virtuous and expert rulers.

Each of premisses (3)–(6) needs further defence, and this is the challenge Plato faces in making his case for the philosopher–ruler.

The philosopher's love of truth

When Plato has Socrates first introduce the idea that the rulers of the republic should be philosophers, Socrates does so with hesitation and in recognition that the view is somewhat ridiculous. But in fact, it was not so unheard of as might be thought; there were a number of city–states in which men of learning were the rulers. More to the point, however, is Glaucon's warning (473e) that Socrates would be punished for the proposal. Not long before, Athens, under the rule of Socrates's associates, had lost a war with Sparta, and very anti-democratic reprisals had followed which Athenians still resented. Plato therefore takes pains to distinguish the true philosopher from people who would pretend to be philosophers and have a false confidence in their wisdom.

A philosopher, by definition, loves wisdom. Plato conceives this as a form of real love; and as love, must involve the whole of the object – so philosophers love all learning. Glaucon suggests that many people love new experiences, and seek out new sights and sounds. But that isn't enough to be a philosopher. People who love sights and sounds don't have a genuine passion for truth and knowledge. They rest content with discovering and experiencing the many particulars; they don't search for the reality behind the appearances.

Plato then begins his discussion of the difference between particulars and the Forms (see THE THEORY OF FORMS, p. 194, and KNOWLEDGE, BELIEF AND IGNORANCE, p. 196), to explain his claim that experience of particulars is not knowledge, but opinion, and to think otherwise is to mistake appearances for reality. Only someone who has a passion for knowledge, who will not rest with experiences of particular things, can be called a philosopher. Only philosophers, he argues, can see the distinction between opinion and knowledge, because only they keep searching to attain true knowledge – of the Forms. Lovers of sights and sounds have only opinions, not knowledge (480a); whereas philosophers see that what others think of as 'knowledge' is just opinion, what others think of as 'reality' is just appearance.

This completes Plato's arguments for (3) and (4).

The other qualities of philosophers

Plato does not pretend that philosophy is easy. It is, in fact, very difficult, and the 'true philosopher', someone who loves all learning, is very rare. This is in part because we 'can't expect anyone to have much love for anything which he does with pain and difficulty and little success' (486c). So there are certain traits that philosophers need to have *naturally*, to equip them with the ability and temperament to love learning. A philosopher needs an ability to learn, a good memory, a sense of proportion, a breadth of vision and a quick mind.

Knowledge of the Good and virtue

Good rulers need to be expert and virtuous. Do philosophers have the right kind of expertise? Plato argues that the height of their knowledge, 'the greatest study' (503e), is knowledge of the Form of the Good. *It is this knowledge of the Good that is needed for good rule*; without it, a ruler does not know what is useful or valuable (505a), so he cannot think coherently about the plan for good human life. This defends premisse (5) and links – if only in an abstract way – philosophers' knowledge and the justification of their rule. They are *experts* on the Good, so they know what makes human life go well.

But are they also virtuous? Plato's defence of (6) is straightforward. The love of wisdom is a passion that subdues one's other passions: 'if a man's desires set strongly in one direction, they are correspondingly less strong in other directions' (485d). A person who desires knowledge will take pleasure in the things of the mind, so physical pleasures won't be tempting. He will be self-controlled, not greedy about money, broad-minded and generous, and not fear death, and so be courageous (see also the discussion in ETHICAL IMPLICATIONS OF THE THEORY OF THE FORMS, p. 207). Anyone who doesn't show these traits, Plato suggests, can be dismissed as not a true philosopher.

So philosophers are virtuous because of their *love* of wisdom. Does their knowledge of the Good, when they achieve it, also help? Plato argues that it does, because you cannot stop someone 'assimilating himself to anything with which he enjoys dealing. . . . So the philosopher whose dealings are with the divine order himself acquires the characteristics of order and divinity so far as a man may' (500d). So a philosopher who knows the Form of the Good will make himself good, i.e. virtuous.

So philosophers are both experts (they have the knowledge necessary to rule) and virtuous (7). Only philosophers have both the necessary knowledge and virtue; so only philosophers should rule (8).

KEY POINTS (1)

- Plato argues that only philosophers have the expertise and virtue needed to be good rulers.

- Only philosophers love learning, and will enquire deeply enough into reality to acquire knowledge of the Forms. Their expertise in ruling comes from their knowledge of the Form of the Good; without it, a ruler does not know what is good or useful.

- Because of their love of learning, philosophers are not susceptible to many vices, but are self-controlled, just, broad-minded, generous and courageous. Furthermore, because of their knowledge of the Good, they will become like the Good.

Assessing Plato's argument

Knowledge of the Good

Is Plato right when he argues that philosophers have the knowledge necessary to rule? His argument is that they have knowledge of the Form of the Good, and knowledge of what is good is necessary to rule. But is knowledge of the Form of the Good knowledge that helps with the *practical* matter of politics? Plato never provides an account connecting the highly abstract, theoretical knowledge of the Form of the Good to practical knowledge of the affairs of state, knowledge of how a good life for people should be organized. When Plato talks about the Form of the Good, it is as the source of all knowledge, truth and reality. How is *this* helpful in knowing how to make good, practical decisions?

Plato is not unaware of the gap between the knowledge philosophers gain and the practical world. It emerges in the simile of the Cave; when the philosopher returns to the cave, he is initially blinded, unable to make things out. But Plato suggests this will only last a while, and argues that his knowledge will be useful in the cave. But he never argues *how*, except to say that knowledge never loses its power (519a).

It is not easy to invent a defence on Plato's behalf, because it is difficult to understand how knowing the Form of the Good could help with practical decisions. However, we suggested earlier that the Form of the Good might be related to harmony, and both the good (virtuous) soul and the virtuous state were in harmony. Perhaps Plato means to suggest that knowledge of the Good enables the philosopher to recognize this harmony in the soul and the state. But first, that still doesn't imply that the philosopher knows how to *achieve* this harmony, which is what is needed for good decisions. And second, we still don't have an account of how very abstract knowledge of harmony could help one recognize it in real life.

Virtue

Plato argues that the philosopher will become virtuous simply by studying the Forms. But this is very vague, and Plato never says how this can occur. Why should knowledge of the Good on its own create the *motive* to be good oneself or to bring about goodness in society?

Plato is highly sensitive to the possibility that the guardians would become corrupt. He remarks that a philosophical nature is particularly prone to corruption (491d, 495a), that philosophical examination of moral principles is dangerous for young people, as they are not yet stable enough to cope with uncertainty (539d), that the rulers must be highly vigilant and weed out any guardian being trained to rule who shows signs of corruption.

Does this suggest that studying philosophy is not particularly effective at encouraging virtue? Plato could respond that in people who become corrupt the passion for wisdom is not sufficiently strong to reign in their other passions. But this begs the question: does the acquisition of philosophical knowledge help this self-restraint?

Going further: producing virtue

In Plato's perfect state, there is a lot of *selection* in creating philosopher–rulers. In his description of this selection process, Plato suggests that those guardians who *don't* show the character traits listed above can be judged not to be philosophers. The guardians who are selected to be educated as philosophers must not only show a natural ability for doing philosophy, but must also have stable, reliable characters (503c).

However, Plato's argument that love of wisdom produces virtue cannot only appeal to those cases that confirm the claim. Common sense and experience would suggest that philosophers are just as lacking in virtue as anyone else. Plato's argument, that love of wisdom suppresses physical pleasures, the desire for money and fear of death lacks empirical backing. His own argument that philosophers are particularly prone to corruption seems to assert that love of wisdom is not enough. In a democratic society, the naturally gifted philosopher will be influenced by popular praise and blame and become corrupt (see THE STATUS OF PHILOSOPHERS, p. 216). So a love of wisdom only produces virtue in a society that supports and encourages a love of wisdom. Becoming virtuous depends on being trained and encouraged to be virtuous, not just on philosophy.

A particular claim of Plato suggests that, even in the perfect republic, philosophers are not completely virtuous. At the end of his discussion of the cave, he remarks that 'a necessary consequence of what we have said [is] that society will never be properly governed . . . by those who are allowed to spend all their lives in purely intellectual pursuits . . . the intellectuals will take no practical action of their own accord' (518c). Plato says philosophers would prefer to spend their time engaged in philosophy. However, they will rule because the law compels them to, and it is for the greater good of the city. Compelling them to rule is not an injustice, since justice relates to the harmony of the whole.

If true philosophers are virtuous, why won't they be *motivated* to rule, i.e. to fulfil their role in society, which is what justice consists in? Doesn't virtue involve being motivated by the demands of justice, not just submitting to them? Yet perfectly virtuous philosophers lack this motivation independently of the requirements of law.

Going further: knowing justice and acting justly

What is the source of virtue in philosopher–rulers? Perhaps it is not different from that in anyone else. In Plato's account of the education of the rulers, there is much discussion of how to best form the characters of the guardians to make them virtuous. We could argue that justice is a character trait, and so the motive to be just – if not the knowledge of what justice is – is created through this early education. This childhood training creates the right balance between the parts of the soul, so that, when the person comes to know what justice is, his spirit and desires are ready to obey his reason. All the guardians, the ones who don't become philosophers as well as the ones who do, are motivated to act justly, i.e. to do their particular task in the city. There is no need, then, for a separate account of why philosophers would be motivated to be just.

However, if being motivated to be just is not the result of knowing what is just, Plato can still argue that knowing what is just is still necessary for the virtue of justice. To be just, one must also know what justice is. And to know what justice is, Plato has argued, involves knowing the Form of Justice. So philosophy is relevant for knowing what justice is. This isn't the same as being motivated to act justly, so philosophy doesn't produce virtue in the sense of motivating someone to be just. But Plato can argue that it is only philosopher–rulers who have *both* qualities, the motivation from their training as guardians and knowledge from their training as philosophers. So he can still argue that it is only philosopher–rulers who should rule the republic.

Going further: the nature of justice

Plato argues that justice consists in each person doing his or her own, specialist thing (433–434a). But there is an obvious tension with suggesting that philosophers should rule, viz. that this involves one person being both philosopher and ruler, thereby doing *two* things. If philosophy and ruling two separate tasks, according to Plato's principle of justice, they should be done by different people.

Plato must argue that these two things *necessarily* go together, and we have seen his argument that philosophy is necessary for knowledge of the Good, and knowledge of the Good is necessary for expert and virtuous rule.

However, we have questioned whether Plato succeeds in connecting the very abstract knowledge of the Good to political expertise. Furthermore, the education that philosophers receive must be sufficient to become good rulers; but we have also questioned whether there are really *two* types of education necessary, one to make them virtuous and practical (their education as guardians) and another to make them philosophers. This again suggests that ruling and doing philosophy are separate tasks. Finally, the fact that philosophers are reluctant to rule and would prefer to do philosophy also suggests philosophy and ruling are two distinct tasks.

- Plato claims that knowledge of the Form of the Good is necessary for expert rule, but he has not shown how it helps with the practical matter of politics. One possible response is that knowledge of the Good (as harmony) helps the philosopher recognize harmony in the state and the soul. But this is unclear, and it isn't yet knowledge of how to bring about that harmony.

- Likewise, Plato never says how it is that knowledge of the Good will make a philosopher virtuous. In fact, he seems concerned that philosophers may even be particularly prone to corruption. And even when fully educated, philosophers will not be motivated to rule, even though it is just.

- We may argue that the motivations required in a virtuous person may, instead, be produced by upbringing, so that all that is required for virtue is knowledge. Because philosophy is required for this knowledge, philosophy is required for (full) virtue.

- Plato faces the objection that doing philosophy and ruling are two separate tasks, and so according to his principle of justice, should be done by separate people.

❓ QUIZ QUESTIONS

Briefly explain and illustrate **two** differences between true philosophers and the lovers of sights and sounds.

Briefly explain and illustrate **three** qualities of the true philosopher.

Outline Plato's argument for the claim that only philosophers have the expertise necessary to be good rulers.

❓ DISCUSSION QUESTIONS

Critically discuss the simile of the cave in relation to the role of the philosopher–ruler. (AQA, 1c, 2003, *25 marks*)

Assess Plato's argument that philosophers should be rulers.

Critically discuss Plato's claim that true philosophers will be virtuous.

The status of philosophers; the simile of the Ship

Plato is very aware that his suggestion that philosophers become rulers will not be taken seriously by most people. Adeimantus objects that most people who study philosophy too much are 'very odd birds, not to say thoroughly vicious', and that even the best of them become completely useless to society (487d). Plato responds to the charge of uselessness by the simile of the ship, and then tackles the issue of corruption in philosophers.

The simile of the Ship

The simile of the ship (488a–489a) is intended to describe politics in a democracy. Politicians each seek to gain power, and they admire those able to help them do so. They do not know, and are not concerned with, what is good for the state – which is what politics *should* be about. They even argue that such knowledge is impossible. A philosopher, who spends time acquiring this knowledge, will be little help with how to influence other politicians. Unless his expertise is recognized, he will appear to be completely useless. But this is not because there is anything wrong with philosophers, but because politicians fail to *make use* of them. If philosophers seem useless, this is the fault of politicians, not philosophers.

The simile of the Ship	
The ship	The state (under a democracy)
The captain	The current ruler
The crew	Politicians
The art of navigation	The art of politics (what is good for a state)
The true navigator	The philosopher

Are philosophers vicious?

What about Adeimantus's objection that philosophers are vicious (not virtuous)? Plato's response is again to blame the *situation*, and not a training in philosophy. Plato argues that the natural qualities of the philosopher, in the wrong situation, become a source of corruption. Someone who is gifted will be sought after by other people, who will try to influence him. He will be 'swamped by the flood of popular praise and blame, and carried away with the stream till he finds himself agreeing with popular ideas of what is admirable or disgraceful' (492c). His training in philosophy, to seek the truth, will not be strong enough to withstand the constant pressure to do what people want. In fact, rather than sticking with philosophy, being gifted, he will become a leader (494b) and, winning popular praise, will become full of pride.

So, Plato argues, people with the ability to become true philosophers are corrupted by bad society, and end up agreeing with popular opinion. They may abandon philosophy to become politicians, and the corruption of their character will go further. In this situation, who actually practises philosophy? 'Second-rate interlopers', says Plato, people who are not naturally gifted nor love truth, who will be corrupt because they do not have the natural character to be virtuous.

If there are any true philosophers left in such a political state, they will be very few, and only remain true philosophers through some sort of miracle. And seeing the situation, 'they will live quietly and keep to themselves' (496d).

● **KEY POINTS**

- The simile of the ship describes, by analogy, the nature of politics in a democracy.

- It explains why philosophers will look as though they are useless and not virtuous. They look useless because no one recognizes the knowledge they have. They seem not virtuous because most truly talented philosophers will be corrupted by society, while most of those who continue to do philosophy lack the talent and the love of truth, so they lack the natural character to be virtuous. Any remaining true philosophers will live quietly and not be noticed.

❓ QUIZ QUESTION

Outline how Plato uses the simile of the ship to criticize democracy.

Critique of (Athenian) democracy: simile of the Beast

Plato's simile of the Ship (above) not only provides an account of the status of philosophers. It also accuses democracy of being a form of government which is disordered and harmful: the crew turn the voyage into a 'drunken pleasure-cruise'. Democracy is rule by ignorance, because politicians have no knowledge of what is good for the state as a whole; and rule by ignorance will be bad for everyone. Later in *The Republic*, Plato also argues that democracy is based on freedom of a particular kind – the freedom to do what you want. But if you don't know what is good for you, then this kind of freedom is actually harmful (555b–558c). Politicians who just do what they want harm the whole state.

The simile of the Beast

Plato illustrates both these points, about ignorance and the difference between what we like and what is good for us, in his simile of the beast. He compares people in a democracy to a powerful beast, and rulers in a democracy to the animal's tamer. The rulers govern by giving people what they want, and pretend that this is a science, something to be taught and studied by politicians. But it completely misses the question of what is *good*. The tamer (politicians) 'would not really know which of the creature's tastes and desires was admirable or shameful, good or bad, right or wrong; he would simply use the terms on the basis of its reactions, calling what pleased it good, what annoyed it bad' (494b–c).

The simile of the Beast	
The large and powerful animal	The people
The animal's tamer	Politicians in a democracy
Knowledge of the animal's moods and desires	Political 'science' as democrats think of it

Plato's argument against democracy

In his two similes, and his arguments about why philosophers should be rulers, Plato makes a number of assumptions about the nature of politics.

First, he assumes that politics should be an attempt to bring about the common good. For example, a ship has a purpose for its journey. This purpose, and so what is good for the ship, is independent of the desires of the crew. Again, what an animal wants does not tell us whether what it wants is good. Likewise, what is good for the state as a whole is not determined by what people want.

Second, Plato thinks there can be knowledge about what this common good is and how to bring it about – the true navigator must study the art of navigation. Likewise, rulers need to have knowledge of the Good in order to rule well.

If Plato is right, why think that democracy is going to be good rule? People are so often incompetent and irrational. In general elections, the way people vote is swayed by all sorts of irrational or personal desires and prejudices; thinking hard about what might be good for everyone is very rare, despite the fact that there is information available. How many people even bother to read party manifestos, let alone research the possible impact of different policies? Politicians – rulers – need many skills, knowledge and insightful judgement; they need to understand economics, psychology and motivation; they need intelligence, an enormous capacity for work, a good memory, attention to detail and excellent people skills. (Many of these skills Plato has argued are the natural talents of the true philosopher.) We won't get the best politicians by letting incompetent and irrational people to vote. We'll get people who are willing to give the people what they want. But people don't *know* much about what is good for society as a whole. And people *care* most – perhaps only – about getting the things *they* want for *themselves*. So if politicians give people what they want, they won't be governing by what is best for the state.

Plato argues that only philosophy gives us true and proper knowledge of what is good. It is philosophers, then, who ought to rule. Legitimacy is determined by what is good and just, and not by consent. Since people don't know what is good for them, consent can only tell us what they want, not what is good. Choice, freedom, consent in the absence of knowing what is truly good is not valuable. What is valuable is to choose what is good. And to choose what is good, we first need to know what the true good is. Philosopher–rulers will organize society so that it is truly good.

Assessing Plato's argument

Winston Churchill said: 'Democracy is the worst form of Government except all those other forms that have been tried from time to time'. So even if there is some truth in what Plato says, he might not be right to reject democracy. It is worth noting that Plato argues in favour of democracy in his more practical political work, *The Statesman*. There he says that democracy is resistant to the tyranny that could come about if rulers become corrupt.

Are philosopher–rulers a good idea?

In THE NATURAL QUALITIES OF THE PHILOSOPHER (p. 212), we discussed two objections to the assumptions Plato makes in criticizing democracy. First, does studying philosophy provide you with the other qualities, especially virtue, that a good ruler needs? Given that even Plato is worried that philosophers will be corrupted, avoiding tyranny is a good reason to adopt democracy. Second, does knowledge of the Form of the Good really give you the practical knowledge you need to make good political decisions? Even if democracy is, as Plato claims, rule by ignorance, this is not a powerful criticism unless it is possible for there to be rule by knowledge.

Knowledge of the Good

We may take this point further, and question whether there is such a thing as knowledge of the Good. In saying that there is, Plato argues for moral COGNITIVISM (Ch. 2, p. 102). But there are many philosophical arguments in favour of NON-COGNITIVISM (Ch. 2, p. 112). If non-cognitivism is true, there is no knowledge of what is good. But then democracy is not rule by ignorance: ignorance requires there to be some knowledge that the person doesn't have; but if there is no knowledge of what is good, no one can be said to be ignorant of it.

What is the Good?

Plato's criticism of democracy is that it gives people what they want, but not what is good. But according to UTILITARIANISM (Ch. 2, p. 65), what is good is what makes people happy, either pleasure (hedonistic utilitarianism) or what people want (preference utilitarianism). So knowledge of what is good for society *just is* knowledge of what people want. A utilitarian would argue that, in Plato's simile of the beast, politicians are right to think that their study of what pleases the people is a study of what is good for society. If there isn't a distinction between what is good and what pleases people, Plato's arguments against democracy don't work.

There are two responses to this objection. First, it is only as strong as the claim that utilitarianism is right, and there are many objections to utilitarianism (see Ch. 2, ACT UTILITARIANISM, p. 66 and RULE UTILITARIANISM, p. 70). Second, even if it is true that what is good is what makes people happy, this doesn't mean we should give people what *they think they want*. People often *don't know* what makes them happy, and they tend to care more about *short-term* happiness. If people get it wrong about what will make them happy in the long term, we shouldn't ask them about what is good for society. Democracy will still not produce a good society. We need rulers who know about true, long-term happiness – this is the knowledge of the Good that is necessary.

Going further: is politics only about the common good?

Even if Plato is right about there being a distinction between what is good and what people want, we can argue that there are *other values* that (only) a democracy embodies, values that would be lost in Plato's ideal republic. In other words, there are some good things a democracy has that other types of society do not.

First, we may object to Plato saying that the only freedom in a democracy is getting what you want. There is also the freedom of *self-rule*. While Plato might be right that it is valuable to choose what is good, John Stuart Mill argues that it is valuable simply to be able to live as you choose. Autonomy is essential, he argues, to human well-being, and a life in which someone else makes all the decisions for you is not a good life. In politics, this means that the people should have a say in the decisions about how to live. Being told how to live by those who know best – even if they do know best! – is not as good as being able to make the decisions oneself. Democracy is collective autonomy.

Second, Mill also argues that having this responsibility will make for better citizens, people whose rational and moral senses are developed. Plato is interested in a just society, one in which everyone respects the law and fulfils their own role. But he doesn't say how the people should be educated so that they are happy to do this; he only talks about the education of the guardians. Mill argues that democracy is the best way to create citizens who understand and care about what is right.

Third, Mill argues that democracy expresses a sense of collective identity, of 'being in it together'. This is good in itself. Human beings are social animals, as Plato recognizes. It is part of a good human life to be able to identify with the society in which one lives, it is bad if one feels alienated. Again, Plato implies that everyone will feel part of the just society, happy to play their role. Mill argues that this is much more likely if everyone has a say in how society is run. Otherwise, they won't feel that they, as individuals, are expressing themselves. Plato isn't concerned with self-expression, only with what is good. We can argue that identifying with society through self-expression is a good thing, and only a democracy can have it.

● **KEY POINTS**

- The simile of the beast illustrates Plato's claims that politicians in a democracy are ignorant of what is good, confusing it with what people want.

- Plato assumes that politics is just about realizing the common good, and that there can be knowledge of what is good. He has argued that philosophers have this knowledge. All three assumptions can be challenged.

● Using his two similes, Plato argues that people in a democracy do not vote on the basis of what they think is good for society, and even if they did, they rarely have this knowledge. So they elect politicians who will give them what they want, not what is good for society. Plato's assumption that what is good is different from what people want is challenged by utilitarianism.

● John Stuart Mill argues that democracy realizes many values that non-democratic states do not, including collective autonomy or self-rule, citizens who understand and care about what is right and a sense of collective identity.

❷ QUIZ QUESTIONS

Describe the simile of the beast and **one** of its possible purposes.

Explain and illustrate Plato's argument against democracy.

Outline **two** objections to Plato's rejection of democracy.

❷ DISCUSSION QUESTIONS

Critically discuss Plato's objection to democracy.

Critically discuss the simile of the large and powerful animal as an argument against democracy. (AQA, 1c, 2002, *25 marks*)

5

Descartes's *Meditations*

UNIT 3

(I, II, III, V and VI)

Quotations and page references are from the AQA recommended edition of Sutcliffe's translation (Penguin Classics, ISBN 0-140-44206-5).

Sceptical doubt and its use in the quest for certainty (*Meditation* I)

Descartes begins *Meditation* I by declaring that he has known for a long time that in order to establish anything 'firm and constant in the sciences' (95), he would have to start from the very foundations of all knowledge. He does not need to reject as *false* everything he thinks he knows, but he needs to 'avoid believing things that are not entirely certain and indubitable' (95). Descartes is adopting **scepticism**. He is aiming only to doubt, not to reject, his beliefs.

So Descartes begins by understanding knowledge in terms of certainty. To establish certainty, he tests his beliefs by doubt. Doubt, then, is the opposite of certainty. If we can doubt a belief, then it is not certain, and so it is not knowledge.

Descartes's understanding of knowledge, certainty and the need for doubt have been strongly criticized. Many philosophers have argued that Descartes sets the standard for knowledge too high. It seems that Descartes thinks that knowledge must be *indubitable*: we must be *unable* to doubt it. If that is true, then the belief must be, in some way, infallible (see Ch. 1, BELIEVING-THAT AND KNOWING-THAT, p. 19). However, this seems to be true only at the beginning of the *Meditations*. By *Meditation* III, Descartes argues that he can know whatever is 'clear and distinct'. This is neither indubitable nor infallible, because we can make mistakes, but what is clear and distinct is certain *if we are careful*.

But philosophers have also criticized Descartes's idea of certainty. It appears to be psychological: he is after beliefs that *he* is certain of. And this is not the same thing as a belief *being certain*. After all, we can make mistakes, and think something is certain (we can be certain of it) when it is not certain. But, Descartes responds, this is where the method of doubt comes in. Because we have the habit of jumping to conclusions, only the prudent can distinguish what is genuinely certain from that which merely seems so.

Certainty, as Descartes understands it, is not a feeling; it involves a type of rational insight. He later argues that only claims that are 'clear and distinct' can be certain (see DESCARTES'S RATIONALISM, p. 242), and these properties are established by what is immediately apparent to the mind. In *Meditation* III, he says that the 'things which I see clearly cannot be other than as I conceive them' (115). So certainty is tested by reason; things *cannot* be otherwise. Descartes thinks that certainty will establish truth, because what cannot be otherwise must be true. To show that something is certain in this way is to prove that it must be true, so it is true.

We will see arguments below which suggest that Descartes doesn't achieve this standard for many ideas, and so his method of doubting everything leaves us with scepticism, rather than finding the foundations of knowledge.

It is important to notice that Descartes doubts his beliefs only in order to find what is certain. Because certainty is the opposite of doubt, finding out what he can and can't doubt will establish what he can be certain of. Descartes's doubt, as we will see, is very *methodical*. He could, he says, consider each of his beliefs in turn; but this would take forever. So instead he considers whether the principles on which his beliefs are grounded, principles like 'Believe what you perceive', are certain or not. Descartes's doubt is *universal* – he attacks his beliefs all at once by attacking their foundations; and it is *hyperbolic*, extreme to the point of being ridiculous, e.g. the possibility of an evil demon whose whole aim is to deceive me. But this is how it needs to be. One false or uncertain first principle can lead us completely astray, so he must attack these. And it is not easy, he remarks, to really withhold assent from beliefs we have held since we were children. We can't doubt just by an act of will – that's why he gives arguments, and hyperbolic doubt helps make the point and support the arguments.

For further discussion of doubt, see Ch. 1, THE DIFFERENCE BETWEEN ORDINARY DOUBT AND PHILOSOPHICAL DOUBT, p. 38.

KEY POINTS

● Descartes adopts scepticism, bringing his beliefs into doubt, but not rejecting them as false. He does this in order to find out what in the end (we can know) is true.

- He understands doubt as the opposite of certainty. What we can know needs to be certain if we are careful. We can be certain of what is clear and distinct.

- His doubt is methodical, universal and hyperbolic.

 # QUIZ QUESTIONS

Briefly explain the relation between certainty and knowledge, according to Descartes.

Outline the nature and purpose of Descartes's doubt.

The waves of doubt – applications of the method; the possibility of total deception (*Meditation* I)

Arguments from perception

Descartes begins his method of doubt by considering that he has, in the past, been deceived by his senses – things have looked a way that they are not. Things in the distance look small; sticks half-submerged in water look bent; and so on. But, Descartes remarks, such examples from unusual perceptual conditions give us no reason to doubt all perceptions, such as that you are looking at a piece of paper with writing on it. More generally, we might say that perceptual illusions are *special cases* (and ones we can frequently explain). Otherwise we wouldn't be able to talk about them as illusions. So they don't undermine perception generally.

However, a stronger scepticism can arise from thinking about perception: perception only ever informs us what the world looks like *to us*. How do we know anything about what it is *really* like? Descartes's argument from perceptual illusions notes a difference between appearance and reality. Maybe this distinction applies to all *appearances*, all perceptions, and the world is nothing like how it appears. Descartes suggests this possibility, but for different reasons, with his argument from dreaming.

An argument from dreaming

Descartes extends his doubt by appealing to dreaming: he is 'a man, and consequently . . . in the habit of sleeping' (96). Sometimes when we dream, we represent to ourselves all sorts of crazy things. But sometimes we dream the most mundane things. Yet 'there are no conclusive signs by means of which one can distinguish clearly between being awake and being asleep' (97). So how can we know that what we experience we perceive rather than dream?

This argument attacks all sense-perception, even the most mundane and the most certain. You cannot know that you see a piece of paper because you cannot know that you are not dreaming of seeing a piece of paper.

Some philosophers have responded to Descartes by claiming that there are, in fact, certain indications by which we can distinguish perception from dreaming, such as the far greater coherence of perception. But Descartes could respond: we could be dreaming a perfect replica of reality. Do we really *know* that all dreams have less coherence than perception? We cannot know that what is apparently perception is not really a particularly coherent dream.

Other philosophers argue that this response makes no sense. The concept of a dream *depends* on a concept of reality that it contrasts with. If everything were a dream, we wouldn't be able to have the concepts of dreaming and reality. So it literally doesn't make sense to suppose that everything is a dream. While the objection makes a good point about our concepts of dreaming and reality, it isn't conclusive. First, we might argue that even in a dream we can dream that we wake up, but we are still asleep. Perhaps the development of our concepts of 'dream' and 'reality' are analogous: they refer to a difference within our experience, but this doesn't mean that the *whole* of our experience is disconnected from reality in the way that we think dreams are. It is not obvious that this supposition makes no sense. Second, and perhaps more importantly, the objection *misunderstands* scepticism. Descartes does not *need* to say 'Perhaps everything *is* a dream'; he needs to argue only that we *cannot know* when we are dreaming and when we are awake. This would allow us to develop concepts of dreaming and reality on the basis of our different experiences; but the correct application of those concepts isn't secure.

However, Descartes presents a different argument. At the very end of the *Meditations*, Descartes agrees that we can distinguish between dreaming and waking experience, by the greater coherence of perception (168). But this answer, he claims, was not available to him at the beginning of the *Meditations* because of the possibility of the evil demon.

Before introducing that possibility, Descartes presses the argument from dreaming further. It may *seem* that 'whether I am awake or sleeping, two and three added together always make five' (98). But people do make mistakes about matters they believe they know certainly. And so even truths of logic and of mathematics come under attack. Descartes says, 'it is possible . . . that I should be deceived every time I add two and three' (98). Are not just his perceptual experiences, but also his thoughts, open to doubt?

The demon

In order to take his scepticism to heart, Descartes introduces the suggestion that God does not exist and that all our experiences are produced in us by an evil demon who wants to deceive us. The possibility of the demon means that it is possible that, even if I could tell the difference between being awake and dreaming, my experiences when I am awake are no more real than when I am dreaming. All beliefs about the external world and events in time are thrown into doubt, as it is based on my experience, which the evil demon controls. And all knowledge, such as mathematics, which I believed I had on the basis of thought alone is undercut because the demon can control my thoughts, too.

Global scepticism

Descartes has reached a point of global scepticism (see THE EXTENT OF SCEPTICISM Ch. 1, p. 42). If he has no mental *agency*, no control over his mind at all, over what he experiences or what he thinks, then the very idea of knowing anything seems to be undermined.

In *Meditation* II, however, Descartes reconsiders this idea, and argues that, even if the evil demon exists, there is one thing he can be sure of. And in *Meditation* VI, Descartes goes on to resolve the issues that had led him into doubt in the first place. To do this, he needs to establish, in reverse order, that there could be no evil demon deceiving him; that he is not dreaming, and that a material world, including his body, really does exist; and that he can trust his senses. The answer to all these doubts, it turns out, is that God exists and is not a deceiver (see THE ROLE OF GOD IN DESCARTES'S SYSTEM, p. 250).

For further discussion of scepticism and how to resolve it, see Ch. 1, SCEPTICISM CONCERNING KNOWLEDGE AND BELIEF (p. 43).

● **KEY POINTS**

- Descartes's method of doubt is used in an attempt to undermine his beliefs systematically.

- His argument from perception throws doubt on believing everything our senses tell us.

- His argument from dreaming throws doubt on all sense perception, and on truths of logic and mathematics. Some philosophers have objected that it does not work because we can tell the difference between dreaming and being awake. Others argue that the idea that we are always dreaming makes no sense, because the concept of dreaming logically requires a concept of reality to contrast it with.

- Descartes's argument from the evil demon makes the previous doubts more vivid and throws doubt on all beliefs, because the demon is able to control his experiences and his thoughts.

❓ QUIZ QUESTIONS

Explain and illustrate **two** differences between the argument from dreaming and the argument from perception.

Outline Descartes's argument that even mathematics can be doubted.

❓ DISCUSSION QUESTIONS

Critically assess Descartes's method of doubt.

Assess Descartes's argument from dreaming.

Absolute certainty of the *cogito* and its implications (*Meditation* II)

Descartes argues that there is one thing he can be completely sure of, even if the evil demon exists: that he thinks, and from this, that he exists. He cannot doubt that he thinks, because doubting is a kind of thinking. If the demon were to make him doubt that he is thinking, that would only show that he is. Equally, he cannot doubt that he exists: if he were to doubt that he exists, that would prove he does exist – as something that thinks. The *cogito*, 'I think', is Descartes's first certainty, the first stepping-stone to knowledge.

In this argument, Descartes lays the foundations for his **rationalism**. When he reflects on why he is certain of the *cogito*, he says: 'In this first knowledge, there is nothing except a clear and distinct perception of what I affirm' (113). He goes on to argue for the general principle that, *at the time he considers it*, a thought which is clear and distinct he must believe to be true, he cannot doubt it. (See DESCARTES'S RATIONALISM, p. 243.)

The status of the *cogito* as the first certainty, and how he has arrived at it, also lays the foundations for Descartes's dualism, which we will look at in the next section.

Going further: do 'I' exist?

What does it mean to say 'I exist' or 'I think'? We will see below that Descartes claims that 'I' am a thinking *thing*, a substance. Many philosophers have thought that he means to show that I am the *same* thing from one moment in time to the next. The same 'I' persists from one thought to another. But how can Descartes be certain of this? Philosophers have objected that, with the hypothesis of the evil demon, Descartes cannot know that there is anything that persists in time which is a unity. There is *only a succession of thoughts*. When this objection was presented to him, Descartes's response, in an appendix to the *Meditations* called 'Objections and Replies', is to say that thoughts logically require a thinker. This claim, he thinks, is clear and distinct, so that we can be certain of it.

That depends on what he means by a 'thinker'. If he means a subject that persists over time, then this is not obvious. It doesn't seem to be contradictory to deny it. Perhaps the evil demon is simply creating a series of false thoughts, among which is the thought that a thinker, a substance, an 'I', exists. How could Descartes know otherwise?

But by 'thinker', Descartes may mean only a *momentary* subject of a thought: there can't be a thought unless something thinks it. Descartes is not arguing here that this thinker persists in time. But then there is a question whether this is enough for Descartes's later arguments. If I exist not over time, but only at a moment, it is difficult to see how I could ever know more than the thoughts 'I exist' and 'I think'. As soon as Descartes says that to be a thinker is to doubt, will, imagine and so on (see THE ESSENTIAL NATURES OF MIND AND BODY, p. 235), he assumes that we can say these activities belong to the *same* subject, that he (the same thinker) does all this. But that means he is taking it for granted that thinkers persist over time. But we have argued that Descartes can't know this.

KEY POINTS

- 'I think', the *cogito*, is Descartes's first certainty.

- He cannot doubt that he thinks because doubting is a kind of thinking.

- His argument for the *cogito* inspires his rationalism and his theory of clear and distinct ideas.

- His argument rests on the claim that thoughts logically require a thinker.

? QUIZ QUESTION

Outline Descartes's argument for the *cogito*.

? DISCUSSION QUESTION

Assess whether Descartes succeeds in establishing his first certainty. (AQA, 2c, 2005, *25 marks*)

Arguments for distinguishing mind and body (*Meditations* II and VI)

Mind

Having argued that he knows he thinks, Descartes then asks what kind of thing he is. Discussions of identity seek to establish the essential properties of something, what makes it the thing that it is. The question 'What am I?' can be answered by considering the question of what it is for me to exist. Descartes is trying to identify his essence, those properties which, if he lost them, would mean he was no longer what he is.

He remarks that he can continue to doubt whether he has a body; after all, he believes he has a body only as a result of his perceptual experiences, and so the demon could be deceiving him about this. But he cannot doubt that he has a mind, i.e. that he thinks. So he knows that he exists even though he doesn't know whether or not he has a body. From this Descartes concludes that it is possible for him to exist without a body. He is essentially a mind, not a body. He would not necessarily cease to be himself if he ceased to have a body, but he would necessarily cease to be himself if he didn't have a mind.

What about sensing, though? Surely sense perception requires a body, and I cannot doubt that I *have* sensory experiences, whether or not they are veridical. But, Descartes notes, I have sensory experiences in my dreams as well, when I am not in fact seeing or hearing at all. So all I can be certain of is the experience, not that the experience is caused by sensing. Understood like this, independent of their cause, these experiences are nothing other than a form of thinking (107), and so don't depend on having a body.

Body

Descartes's argument so far is that minds can exist without bodies. However, on its own, it doesn't establish dualism. For this, we need to know that bodies exist and that their nature is quite different from that of the mind. Descartes argues in *Meditation* II that the nature of body is different from that of the mind (see THE ESSENTIAL NATURES OF MIND AND BODY, p. 235). He doesn't present arguments for the existence of bodies until *Meditation* VI (see THE PROOF OF MATERIAL THINGS, p. 240), when he also argues explicitly for substance dualism, the claim that there are two distinct types of thing which can exist independently of each other.

In *Meditation* VI, Descartes repeats his argument that he exists as a thinking thing. He then claims: 'I have a distinct idea of the body in so far as it is only an extended thing but which does not think' (156). And so mind and body are distinct things, because they have different properties. Descartes develops this further when he argues that, unlike the body, the mind does not have any parts and cannot be divided. He argues: 'when I consider my mind, that is to say myself insofar as I am only a thinking thing, I can distinguish no parts' (164). It is with the *whole* mind that one thinks, wills, doubts and so on. These are just different ways of thinking, not parts of the mind. By contrast, the body does have parts. You can literally lose part of your body, e.g. a hand. So mind and body are entirely distinct types of thing. Since he has also argued that both exist, he concludes that substance dualism is true.

In the seventeenth century, the issue of the relationship between mind and body was much discussed, and the view that man is part angel, part beast was advocated by so many philosophers and theologians that it was deemed almost an orthodoxy. But unlike many of his contemporaries, Descartes defended dualism not (in the first instance) on the basis of theology, but by these arguments from epistemology and metaphysics.

Objections to Descartes's argument

Most philosophers believe Descartes's argument that the mind can exist without the body, as it is given above, doesn't work. Just because Descartes can *think* of his mind existing without his body, this doesn't mean that his mind *really can* exist without his body. Or, again, just because he knows he exists, but doesn't know if his body exists, this doesn't mean he can exist without his body. Perhaps there is some metaphysical connection between his mind and body that would make this impossible that Descartes doesn't know about. If materialism – the claim that everything that exists depends on something material in order to exist – is correct, then I cannot exist as a mind without also existing as a body. Descartes has used a test of what he knows and doesn't know as a test of what is possible. But the test is flawed, and so he hasn't shown that minds can exist independently of bodies.

Second, when discussing the *cogito*, we noticed a problem with Descartes's assumption that for there to be thoughts, there must be a mind which has these thoughts, if we suppose that a mind is something that persists over time, which is the same 'I' for all the different thoughts it thinks. Descartes has not shown that such a thing exists for more than a moment. So he has not shown that he is '*a* thing that thinks', i.e. that the same thing thinks in many different ways, rather than a sequence of such things.

To illustrate this further, consider that Descartes allows that 'it might perhaps happen, if I ceased to think, that I would at the same time cease to be or to exist' (105). In dreamless sleep, we certainly cease to think (at least consciously). If Descartes wishes to establish that he is the same person from one day to the next, he will again need the idea of the mind as a substance that persists even through those times when there is no thought. For example, when he comes to say he can distinguish dreaming from waking, he is presupposing that he – the same mind – has experienced both. But that means he must persist between dreaming and waking, and during some of that time he will have no thoughts at all. However, Descartes can reply that at this point he knows that God exists, and God guarantees that Descartes's clear and distinct memories are true. And memory logically requires being the same person from one moment to the next.

What about Descartes's argument that the mind doesn't have parts? It does seem right to say that we will, think, imagine with the whole of our minds, not with a literal part. However, cases of mental illness, e.g. multiple personality syndrome, might be used to suggest that the mind can be divided. In such cases, it seems that some aspects of the person's mind are unable to communicate with other aspects. Freudian ideas of consciousness and the unconscious suggest something similar: people may desire one thing consciously and the opposite thing unconsciously. While this doesn't make the mind *spatially* divisible, it makes sense of talking about 'parts' of the mind. However, Descartes could respond that the *way* in which the mind is divisible is entirely different from the way in which the body is. So his argument that mind and body are different because they have different properties is still viable.

Arguments about dualism

Quite independently of these arguments, we may ask whether Descartes's dualism is a good philosophical theory. It is most often rejected because it cannot give an adequate account of mental causation. The mind and the body have very different natures: the mind is essentially thinking, the body is essentially extended, i.e. it exists in and takes up space. The mind is not extended, it does not have parts. So how is it that something mental, which is not in space and has no physical force, can affect something physical, which is in space and is moved by physical forces? Descartes admitted that this was a problem he never solved.

Substance dualism famously faces a number of other objections as well. Here are two. First, substance dualism seems to make me, a person with both mind and body, essentially *two* things, connected together. This doesn't do justice to our experience of being just *one* thing, which we might call an 'embodied mind'. It *splits* our experience, which fundamentally seems unified. Descartes agreed that our experience was of the unity of mind and body, and we discuss this further in the next section.

Second, Descartes's claim is that the mind is not dependent on the body. That is why he can say the mind is a separate substance (substances, by definition, are not dependent on anything else to exist). But modern work on the brain suggests that the mind is very dependent on the brain in order to function and, in the end, to exist at all. Most importantly for Descartes's claim that the mind's essential property is thinking, damage to certain parts of the brain can make someone unable to think. So alterations in the body can affect the essential property of the mind; thus the mind does not have even its essential property independently of the body. Since this property of thinking defines the mind, we can say that our minds are not independent of our bodies.

Going further: minds without substance dualism

We can preserve Descartes's insight that we are essentially mental, and that what is mental is not the same as what is physical, without having to say that we exist as mental *substances*. There can be thoughts without a mental substance if thoughts are had by a material substance. The dependence of the mind on the brain suggests this to be plausible. So perhaps I am just my thoughts, or I am the continuity and connections between my thoughts, but my thoughts are *had* by my body. The properties that make me *me* are mental properties (memories, desires, beliefs, etc.) that my body has. There is no 'me' and no 'mind' apart from these mental properties.

An objection from Locke suggests this is the right way to answer the question 'What am I?' He argued that even if substance dualism were true, personal identity is comprised by psychological continuity, not by the continued existence of a mental substance. If all my thoughts, desires, beliefs, emotions, memories, etc. were swapped with those of another thinking thing, 'I' would go with my thoughts, etc., rather than remain the same thinking thing, but now with a quite different set of mental properties.

KEY POINTS

- Descartes asks 'What am I?', a question about his essence – those properties which, if he lost them, would mean he would be no longer what he is.

- He argues that he is a mind, but does not know if he has a body. This means, he thinks, that having a body is not essential to being what he is, a mind, and so minds can exist without bodies.

- Philosophers object that Descartes's conclusion doesn't follow: what he knows is not a good test of what is *really* possible.

- If I am my mind, independent of my body, and the mind only exists when it is thinking, I cease to exist in a dreamless sleep. Descartes can reply that once he has proved the existence of God, he can know that he is the same mind from moment to moment, and overnight, because he has clear and distinct memories.

● Descartes argues that bodies exist, and that minds and bodies have different properties, so that they aren't the same kinds of things. Minds are indivisible; bodies have parts. Considerations from mental illness and psychoanalysis suggest that minds might be divisible, but in a very different way from bodies.

● Three objections to substance dualism are:

   ● Because it claims mind and body to be so different, it cannot account for mental causation.

   ● Because it claims mind and body to be different substances, it cannot account for our experience of being a unified 'embodied mind'.

   ● The mind is dependent on the brain in order to function. So it is not an independent substance.

❓ QUIZ QUESTIONS

Outline Descartes's argument for the claim that his mind can exist independently of his body.

Explain and illustrate the relation between sensory experience and having a body, according to Descartes.

Outline and illustrate Descartes's argument that mind and body are different because the mind is indivisible.

❓ DISCUSSION QUESTIONS

Critically discuss Descartes's attempt to show that his mind is independent of his body. (AQA, 2c, 2001, *25 marks*)

Critically discuss Descartes's reasons for claiming that mind and body are different. (AQA, 2c, 2004, *25 marks*)

Assess Descartes's substance dualism.

The relation of mind and body; independence and the intermingling thesis (*Meditation* VI)

In *Meditation* VI, Descartes repeats his argument that the mind can exist without the body; so how is it related to the body? He says 'nature . . . teaches me by these feelings of pain, hunger, thirst, etc., that I am not only lodged in my body, like a pilot in his ship, but, besides, that I am joined to it very closely and indeed so compounded and intermingled with my body, that I form, as it were, a single whole with it' (159). Because 'one single whole' doesn't sound like 'two substances', this claim and its implications for Descartes's dualism are puzzling.

The argument from bodily sensations and emotions

Reflecting on perception, sensation and feeling, we notice that we perceive that we have bodies, and that our bodies – this particular material object that we have a close and unique relationship with – can be affected in many beneficial and harmful ways. This is brought to our attention through our bodily appetites, like hunger and thirst, through emotions, such as anger, sadness, love, and through sensations, like pain, pleasure, colours, sound and so on. All these experiences have their origins in the body.

This doesn't mean that mind and body aren't distinct; Descartes says that we can still conceive of ourselves existing complete without imagination or feeling. Nevertheless, our experiences of our bodies through bodily sensations and emotions show that the connection between the mind and body is very close: 'these feelings of hunger, thirst, pain, etc., are nothing other than certain confused ways of thinking, which arise from and depend on the union and, as it were, the mingling of the mind and the body' (159). ('Confused' here is not being opposed to 'clear and distinct', but means 'as a result of the fusion of the mind and body'.) Descartes argues that if mind and body were not intermingled, then when my body is hurt 'I would not on that account feel pain, I who am only a thinking thing, but I should perceive the wound by my understanding alone' (159). I wouldn't *feel pain*, I would merely observe damage.

Furthermore, this union of mind and body is a union between the mind and the *whole* body. We feel pain in the various parts of our body. The soul does have a privileged connection to the brain (a point of causal connection in the pineal gland), but the soul does not feel all pains to be in the brain! So Descartes argues that it is joined to all parts of the body, although it 'exercises its functions' at the pineal gland 'more particularly than elsewhere'. This is really just a physiological observation.

The point of 'union'

Descartes himself found it difficult to understand how it is that the mind and the body are distinct substances, yet form a 'union':

> It does not seem to me that the human mind is capable of forming a very distinct conception both of the distinction between the soul and the body and of their union; for to do this it is necessary to conceive of them as a single thing and, at the same time, to conceive of them as two things; and the two conceptions are mutually opposed. (Letter to Princess Elizabeth, 28 June 1643)

However, he spells out what he takes to be the *point* of the theory. The 'union' theory enables us to understand the nature and meaning of sensations and emotions: they inform us of what is beneficial and harmful. In the production and experience of these, mind and body are working together to secure the good of the *whole*. Our emotions, if well directed, remarks Descartes, allow us 'to taste the greatest sweetness in this life' (*Passions of the Soul*, article 212). If we abandon the idea of union, then the significance of bodily sensations and emotions, working for the good of the whole, is lost.

Going further: the metaphysics of union

It is hard to know what to infer metaphysically – about the mind and body as substances – from Descartes's appeal to what it is like to be a mind–body unity, experiencing bodily sensations and emotions. Descartes offers a suggestion as puzzling as it is illuminating in the same letter to Elizabeth: that the idea of the union between mind and body is a 'third primitive notion' – it is basic and unanalysable. Union is not *essential* to either mind or body, since either can exist without the other; but it is not accidental: 'since the body has all the dispositions necessary to receive the soul, and without which it is not strictly a human body, it could not come about without a miracle, that a soul should not be joined to it' (letter to Regius, December 1641). The comment that, unless united to a soul, a body is not a *human body* suggests (but not conclusively) that the 'human body', body and soul together, can be considered as a unity, a thing, a *substance*, in its own right, a substance created from the union of body and soul. However, philosophers don't agree on whether or not this is the implication we should draw from his union theory.

To the question, 'What am I?', Descartes's first answer is 'a thing that thinks' (105), and he repeats in *Meditation* VI that we can imagine ourselves existing 'whole' without feeling or imagination. But we might want to question this. Is it any less true to say 'I am a human being, a union of mind and body, an *embodied* mind' than to say 'I am a mind'? The mind takes on the body's experiences as its own, i.e. we refer our sensations, emotions, etc., to our *selves*. We *own* these states just as much as we *own* our thoughts. Our experience is of one thing. So we experience ourselves as persons – embodied minds – not just minds. Descartes accepts all this, but his argument that minds can exist without bodies leads him to say that to lose the experiences that depend on the body would not be to lose our identities.

● **KEY POINTS**

- ● Descartes claims that we (our minds) are intermingled with our bodies, forming a whole. We are not 'lodged' in our bodies like a pilot in a ship.

- ● His reason for this claim is our experience of perceptions, bodily sensations and emotions. These are not purely intellectual states, but direct experiences of our bodies, in particular what is harmful or beneficial for us as a whole.

- This doesn't mean mind and body aren't distinct: we can exist as ourselves (minds) without sensory perception, imagination or feeling.

- However, Descartes also suggests that perhaps the union of mind and body creates something new, that can't be analysed into mind + body.

QUIZ QUESTIONS

Briefly explain why, according to Descartes, we have the experience of being 'united' with our bodies.

Explain Descartes's example of the pilot and the ship and its relation to the intermingling thesis. (AQA, 2b, 2005, *10 marks*)

Outline Descartes's argument for the claim that feeling and imagination are not essential to him.

DISCUSSION QUESTION

Assess the claim that Descartes's argument for intermingling undermines his arguments for dualism.

The essential natures of mind and body, the wax example and its purposes (*Meditations* II, V)

The nature of mind

In *Meditation* II, after his argument that he is a thinking thing, Descartes lists the types of activity that a 'thinking thing' engages in, providing us with a more detailed description of the nature of the mind: 'a thing that doubts, perceives, affirms, denies, wills, does not will, that imagines also, and which feels' (107) (Descartes adds love and hate in *Meditation* III).

As we saw in ARGUMENTS FOR DISTINGUISHING MIND AND BODY (p. 208), perception should not be understood as perception of external objects yet – since Descartes cannot know they exist at this stage of doubt. So he puts forward a type of **sense-data** theory (see Ch. 1, REPRESENTATIVE REALISM, p. 49) – what is immediately available to the mind is perceptual experience, irrespective of whatever lies *beyond* that experience in the external world: 'it is very certain that it seems to me that I see light, hear a noise and feel heat; and this is properly what in me is called perceiving, and this, taken in this precise sense, is nothing other than thinking' (107).

Further knowledge of the mind comes from realizing that every thought we have about material objects illustrates something about the mind. In Descartes's famous example of the wax, he talks a little about the nature of body, but he is also exploring what we can know about the body, and how this knowledge can show us more about the nature of mind.

The wax example

Descartes's discussion goes like this:

1   When I melt a piece of wax, it loses all of its original sensory qualities (the particular taste, smell, feel and shape it has); yet I believe it is the same wax. So what I think of as the wax is not its sensory qualities.
2   So when I think of the wax, I am thinking of something that is extended, i.e. takes up space, and changeable, i.e. its sensory and spatial properties can change.
3   I also think that the possible changes it can go through outstrip what I can imagine; I can't imagine all the changes I know the wax can undergo. So it's not through my imagination that I have my conception of the wax. Rather, and somewhat surprisingly, I 'perceive' (comprehend) the wax through my understanding.
4   The wax I think of this way and the wax I detect through my senses is the same wax.
5   Although we say we 'see' the wax (through vision), in fact we judge (through understanding) that it is present from what we see.

The argument is about *our knowledge* of material objects, rather than the real nature or existence of material objects. The title of the meditation is 'Of the nature of the human mind; and that it is easier to know than the body'. Descartes's claims about the nature of body actually come in *Meditation* V, and his proof that they exist in *Meditation* VI (see THE PROOF OF MATERIAL THINGS, p. 240).

Descartes's question is not 'What is the wax?', but 'What is our idea of the wax?' So in (1), Descartes is not attempting to assert the identity conditions of the piece of wax; he is noticing that our conception of 'the wax' doesn't appear to depend on its particular sensory qualities. So what is our conception? That the wax is something that endures through such changes (it is changeable), but also that it is extended (takes up space). If this is our conception of the wax, then it is not a conception derived from our senses or imagination, but an intellectual conception of it, and as such, is given by our understanding. We will discuss this further in THE ROLE OF THE IMAGINATION (p. 239).

So, Descartes argues that, at first, our idea of the wax is of something defined by its sensory properties. But this is muddled. When we realize that we comprehend the wax through understanding, as something extended and changeable, our comprehension of the wax has become clear and distinct. To find out what can be known, Descartes pursues his method of forming a clear and distinct idea of the object of knowledge. The best idea we can form of material objects is that they are extended and changeable. We also realize that talk of 'seeing the wax' is misleading. We judge or infer the presence of material objects from our sensory experiences.

Descartes puts these conclusions to use in two ways:

1   *The nature of body*: In *Meditation* V, Descartes does ask the question 'What is the nature of material bodies?' Although Descartes has shown what our *idea* of material objects is in the wax argument, we may have got an entirely wrong-headed conception of

them, for we don't know that our clear and distinct conception of them corresponds to anything real or even possible. But in *Meditation* V, he claims that whatever we can conceive clearly and distinctly, we can know to be true (see DESCARTES'S RATIONALISM, p. 243). He has argued, in the wax example, that we can clearly and distinctly conceive of material objects as extended and changeable, but not as having particularly sensory properties. He therefore concludes that material objects, if they exist, are essentially extended and changeable.

2 *More on the nature of mind*: Descartes argues that the example of the wax helps us understand the mind in three ways. First, every thought about the wax confirms the existence of the mind. Second, thinking about how we know the wax helps to separate the different faculties of sensory perceptual experience, imagination and the understanding. So we gain a clearer and more distinct idea of what happens in the mind, we understand the different 'modes of thought' (113). Finally, because we comprehend the wax through understanding, rather than by sensory perception, although it seemed that bodies were known better than the mind, in fact they are not. Nothing could seem more obvious and certain than the beliefs we have about what we experience through our senses. But it turns out that we use the understanding to comprehend bodies. We use the understanding to comprehend our minds as well, but this is much clearer and easier than in the case of comprehending bodies. So we know the mind better than we know the body.

On the basis of introspection alone, Descartes feels able to confirm the different modes of consciousness that the mind is capable of. He doesn't consider the possibility that I am mistaken about my mode of thought – I can't mistakenly think that I'm imagining when I'm conceiving, can't think I'm doubting when I'm willing and so on, at least when what I am thinking about is immediately available to consciousness.

Modes of thought should not be thought of as *parts* of the mind. We saw in ARGUMENTS ABOUT DUALISM (p. 230) that Descartes argues that, unlike the body, the mind does not have parts.

Going further: Hume on extension

As an empiricist, Hume challenges Descartes's argument that our knowledge of material objects as extended comes from understanding, not the senses. He argues that our only chance of forming an idea of extension is *by abstraction* from particular sensory experiences. We have no conception of extension that is neither visible, and therefore derived from sight, nor tangible, and therefore derived from touch.

Descartes explicitly rejects this claim. In the wax example, he argues that his conception of the wax as extended is not given by the imagination, because he can understand that the possibilities of extension outstrip his imagination. The idea of extension outstrips what the senses can provide. But his claim that our concept of extension therefore derives from the understanding instead does not mean extension is neither visible nor tangible: the wax conceived by the understanding is the *same* wax that is perceived through the senses. However, it is certainly debatable whether Hume is right that our concept of extension is derived from the senses, formed through abstraction.

Going further: The different natures of mind and body

Descartes's insight into how minds and bodies are different still poses questions for philosophers today. Thoughts, in all of Descartes's varieties, are always *about*, or refer to, something. For example, if I believe Paris is the capital of France, my belief is about Paris. Every desire is a desire for something, e.g. chocolate. Every decision is a decision to do something. The 'something' in each case is *represented* in the thought, and this representation is essential to the thought. But the states of material things, such as chairs or trees, are never *about* anything, they never represent something (unless we use them in this way). Material states, such as an arrangement of certain molecules, just exist without reference to anything else. The states of your brain are just chemical states, like the states of a chair. How could they ever be *about* anything? So how could beliefs, desires, and so on be states of your brain?

Consciousness poses a similar problem. Visual perceptions look a certain way, you experience colour and shape; emotions feel a certain way, as do bodily sensations. There's nothing in what we know about the chemistry of the brain that would indicate that these properties exist.

● **KEY POINTS**

- Descartes argues that the nature of the mind is thinking, i.e. doubting, perceiving, affirming and denying, willing, imagining and feeling. These are different 'modes of consciousness'.

- In the wax example, Descartes discusses what our idea of material objects is. It is not until *Meditation* V that he claims our idea is true.

- Our idea of a material object, e.g. the wax, cannot be the ideas of its sensory properties, because these can change while we think the object is the same object. Our idea of a material object is therefore of something extended and changeable.

- This is an idea that comes not from the imagination but from the understanding, because we understand that the object can go through more changes than we can imagine.

- We know the mind better than we know the body. We use the understanding in both cases, but the mind is easier to know and our ideas of it are clearer.

❓ QUIZ QUESTIONS

Outline and illustrate Descartes's claim that we have different 'modes of consciousness'.

Explain what the essential properties of material bodies are, according to the wax argument.

Outline Descartes's argument that the mind is better known than the body.

❓ DISCUSSION QUESTIONS

Critically discuss Descartes's wax example.

Critically discuss Descartes's reasons for claiming that mind and body are different. (AQA, 2c, 2004, *25 marks*)

The role of the imagination (*Meditation* II)

By 'imagining', Descartes means creating images before one's 'mind's eye' (or if you imagine a sound, your 'mind's ear' and so on). Because imagination uses images derived from the senses, Descartes considers imagination along with sense perception as a possible objection to his argument that the mind can exist without the body. But, as we saw in ARGUMENTS FOR DISTINGUISHING MIND AND BODY (p. 228), he concludes that just having these images is a form of thought, and doesn't depend on the body. In *Meditation* VI, he goes further and says that he can conceive of himself as existing without imagination or sense-perception. These modes of consciousness, which he later argues result from the fusion of mind and body, are not essential to who he is.

In both the example of the wax and at the beginning of *Meditation* VI, he distinguishes imagination from the intellect. First, as we've said, imagination works with images that are derived from sensing. The wax example is meant to show that the intellect does not work in the same way – I *understand* the wax can have indefinitely many shapes, but I cannot run through all these shapes in my imagination. So my understanding of the wax, my idea of what the wax is, isn't derived from my imagination. And I can have ideas of very complex objects, like a chiliagon – a mathematical figure with 1,000 sides – without being able to form images of them. Second, this also brings to our attention that imagining requires effort (try imagining a figure with just 20 sides, let alone 1,000!). Finally, we have seen that while the intellect is essential to what I am, imagination is not. He adds in *Meditation* VI that we may say that when I turn my attention to my intellect, my mind turns towards itself; when I think about my imagination, my mind turns towards my body.

QUIZ QUESTION

Describe how Descartes distinguishes intellect from the imagination. (AQA, 2b, 2001, *10 marks*)

The proof of material things (*Meditation* VI)

Having thrown doubt on the existence of an external material world in *Meditation* I, Descartes must work to once again secure our knowledge of it. The argument spans the whole of the *Meditations*, and takes in discussions of the understanding and the senses, the existence of God, the doctrine of clear and distinct ideas and human nature.

Knowing that the external world exists

We saw above that Descartes's wax example doesn't show that material objects really are extended. But in *Meditation* V, Descartes asserts the principle that we can know that what we can clearly and distinctly conceive is true. So material objects really are extended, if they exist at all. In *Meditation* VI, Descartes claims that they do exist, and he seeks to establish that we can and do have knowledge of the material world, including of course, our own bodies.

He first considers whether we can know that bodies exist from our imagination. Unlike operations of the intellect, imagination uses images that it has apparently derived from the senses or created for itself, and it requires effort. Both of these features could be explained if we have bodies. So we *probably* have bodies, but this is hardly a proof.

He turns, then, to consider perception. We have experiences which appear, very forcefully, to be experiences of a world external to our minds, whether they are experiences of our own body or of other bodies. These experiences produce ideas without our 'contribution', i.e. they are involuntary. Among our perceptual experiences are sensations and feelings. We notice that we perceive we have bodies, and that our bodies can be affected in many beneficial and harmful ways, which we experience through our bodily appetites, feelings and emotions. Our faculties of feeling and sensation would seem to be dependent on our having bodies.

But, again, this is not a proof, so Descartes considers the matter from another angle. These experiences are involuntary, and if they were caused by our own minds, they would be voluntary. Because we know our own minds, we would know if they were voluntary. So they are not caused by ourselves. They must therefore have some cause which is sufficient to cause them (on this principle, see THE TRADEMARK ARGUMENT, p. 245). The options are: a real external world or God. If the cause was God, this would mean that God was a deceiver because he would have created us with a very strong tendency to believe something false. But we know that God is not a deceiver (see THE ROLE OF GOD IN DESCARTES'S SYSTEM, p. 251). So there must really be an external world.

Going further: knowing about the external world

So what can we know about the external world, having demonstrated that it exists? Descartes argues that God has set us up to learn from nature (see THE ROLE OF GOD IN DESCARTES' SYSTEM, p. 251). Nature teaches us through sensation that we have bodies, and through perception that there are other bodies. This can't *simply* be the abstract truth that a material world exists. It must be the stronger claim that, in many of our experiences, we are actually confronted with material objects. Our senses, then, will not be set up so that, with careful employment and the search for clarity and distinctness, they would systematically lead to error. This doesn't mean that any particular belief based on our senses is certain – we can still make mistakes. But unless perceptual experience was generally reliable, when we do what we can to avoid error, it would be difficult for Descartes to defend that we can trust what we learn from nature.

This does not, however, mean that that world is just as perception represents it. First, Descartes does not claim that the external world is as we commonly think it is. His argument has established that the material world exists and is an extended world. But the wax argument established that extension and changeability are *all* that is of the essence of the material world. Descartes's representative realist theory of perception argues that all other properties, of colour, smell, heat and so on, aren't actually properties of material objects at all, at least not considered on their own. Rather, 'all I have reason to believe is that there is something in [the external body] which excites in me these feelings' (161). We shouldn't think that the 'something' is itself colour, smell and so on. The external world is a world of geometry, as material objects have only spatial properties (e.g. size, shape, motion).

It is on the basis of its spatial properties that we judge, as in the wax example, that some material object is in fact present. But we must accept that our particular perceptions of the world are often confused. God's assurance doesn't mean we are always able to avoid error: 'because the necessities of action often oblige us to make a decision before we have had the leisure to examine things carefully, it must be admitted that the life of man is very often subject to error in particular cases' (168–9). Furthermore, even with caution and recourse to clear and distinct ideas, we can still make mistakes since our nature is fallible. Poor conditions of perception, such as bad light, confused thinking, prejudice and other factors mean that we can make mistakes; this does not make God a deceiver, because these are mistakes we must take responsibility for.

● **KEY POINTS**

- In *Meditation* II, Descartes argues that we have a clear and distinct idea of material objects as extended. In *Meditation* V, he argues that clear and distinct ideas are true. In *Meditation* VI, he argues that material objects actually exist.

- Imagination uses images deriving from the senses and requires effort. These are reasons to think that bodies exist, but not a proof.

- We have sensory experiences of bodies, as well, which are involuntary. But this is also not enough to show that bodies exist.

- We have forceful experiences of our bodies and other material objects. We do not cause these experiences, because they are involuntary. If God caused them, he would be a deceiver, since we are strongly inclined to believe material objects exist. Therefore, material objects must be the cause of our experiences of them. Therefore, they exist.

- The material world has, in itself, only properties of extension (shape, size, location, motion), which can change. It does not have many of the properties, such as colour and smell, that we tend to think it has.

- So we can know about the material world, but we must remember to stick to clear and distinct ideas to avoid error.

❓ QUIZ QUESTIONS

Outline Descartes's argument for the claim that material things exist.

Explain and briefly illustrate what nature teaches us, according to Descartes.

Outline and illustrate Descartes's claim that many of our particular perceptions are mistaken.

❓ DISCUSSION QUESTION

Assess Descartes's proof of the existence of material things.

Descartes's rationalism – the role of clear and distinct ideas

One way to understand the significance of Descartes's rationalism is to ask '*How* do we know what we know about the material world?' Much of this knowledge, as Descartes's argument has presented it, has not been derived from the senses. Rationalism enters into Descartes's argument in (at least) five places:

(a)   in the invocation of God, since proving the existence of God depends on reason alone (see THE TRADEMARK ARGUMENT, p. 245, and THE ONTOLOGICAL ARGUMENT, p. 248);

(b) **innate ideas**: both of Descartes's proofs of the existence of God start from his claim that we 'discover' the idea of God already in our minds;

(c) in his assertion that our experiences must have a cause, which for Descartes is a matter of logic (Hume rejects this claim as unsubstantiated – unless we already know that our experiences are *effects*, we can't know they have causes by logic alone);

(d) in his claim that our comprehension of material objects as extended doesn't derive from the senses, but from the understanding; and

(e) (a weaker claim) even regarding particular objects, the understanding must make a judgement, albeit based on sense perception, about what the truth of the matter is.

Clear and distinct ideas (*Meditation* III)

To be clear, an idea must be 'open and present to the attending mind'; to be distinct, it must be not only clear, but precise and separated from other ideas, so that it 'plainly contains in itself nothing other than what is clear' (*Principles* I.45). We saw that the *cogito* is the first clear and distinct idea. When Descartes reflects on why he is certain of it, he says: 'In this first knowledge, there is nothing except a clear and distinct perception of what I affirm' (113). He goes on to argue that *at the time we consider it*, a thought which is clear and distinct we must believe to be true, we cannot doubt it.

At this point, Descartes has argued only that we can know a clear and distinct idea to be true at the time we hold it in mind. However, he goes on, we cannot think of that one thing all the time so as to keep perceiving it clearly. When our attention is turned away from it, we can no longer be certain of it, even though we remember that we were certain of it. This is because we can go wrong, we can *think* we clearly and distinctly perceived some idea when we did not. In order to be certain that what we once thought was clear and distinct really is certain, we need to know that we are not being deceived by an evil demon. Descartes sets out to show that we can know this, because we can know that God exists, and would not allow an evil demon to deceive us, nor would God deceive us. (See THE ROLE OF GOD IN DESCARTES'S SYSTEM, p. 250.)

The Cartesian circle

In trying to prove the existence of God, Descartes will, of course, have to rely on what he can clearly and distinctly perceive, because this is the only way he can know anything. But Descartes also needs to prove that God exists for us to know what we clearly and distinctly perceived. This leads to a famous objection: that he uses the existence of God to establish his doctrine of clear and distinct ideas, and that he uses his doctrine of clear and distinct ideas to establish the existence of God. It seems that he says:

1 I am certain that God exists only because *I am certain of whatever I clearly and distinctly perceive*; and yet

2 *I am certain of whatever I clearly and distinctly perceive* only because I am certain that God exists.

But Descartes, in his replies to objections, rejects this reading. I can be certain of what I clearly and distinctly perceive without knowing that God exists, but *only at the time* that I perceive it. God's existence adds a *general* certainty that what I clearly and distinctly perceive is true: 'When I said that we can know nothing for certain until we are aware that God exists, I expressly declared that I was speaking of knowledge of those conclusions that can be recalled when we are no longer attending to the arguments by which we deduced them'.

In other words, there are two interpretations of the phrase in italics, and one interpretation is used in (1) and the second in (2). According to the first interpretation, while I am clearly and distinctly perceiving some *particular proposition*, then I am certain of that proposition. But because of the possibility of the evil demon, I lose this certainty as soon as I turn my attention away from it, as I may be deceived that I did perceive it clearly and distinctly. So I don't yet know that proposition is true unless I'm actually attending to it.

In his proofs of the existence of God, Descartes uses our clear and distinct understanding of the idea of God, held in our minds throughout the proof. Having proved God's existence, he can now claim (the second interpretation, in (2) above) that he is certain that *whatever* he has clearly and distinctly perceived, he can be certain of. And he is certain of this *general principle*, linking clearness and distinctness to truth, because God exists and is no deceiver.

The difficulty facing Descartes is whether he is entitled to claim that he can be certain of what he clearly and distinctly perceives, even at the time he perceives it, while it is still possible that he is being deceived by a demon. His response is that it is simply our nature to assent to such clear and distinct thoughts – we cannot but believe them, because 'things which I see clearly cannot be other than as I conceive them' (115).

KEY POINTS

- Descartes's rationalism appears throughout the argument of the *Meditations*:
  - The idea of God is innate.
  - The proof of God's existence depends on reason alone.
  - That experiences must have a cause is taken as a truth of logic.
  - We know through our understanding, not our senses, that physical objects are extended.
  - All empirical knowledge requires the understanding to make a judgement about the truth.
- Clear and distinct ideas are the foundation of knowledge. A clear idea is 'open and present to the attending mind'; a distinct idea is precise, separated from other ideas.

- We can know that an idea which is clear and distinct is true while we consider it. We can know that all ideas that are clear and distinct are true only once God's existence is proven.

❓ QUIZ QUESTIONS

Explain what Descartes means by a clear and distinct idea.

Explain Descartes's claim that God's existence is necessary for him to be certain of clear and distinct ideas in general.

Outline and illustrate **three** ways in which Descartes is a rationalist.

❓ DISCUSSION QUESTION

Assess Descartes's principle that we can know that whatever can be clearly and distinctly perceived is true.

The Trademark argument (*Meditation* III)

In the 'Trademark argument', Descartes tries to prove that God exists just from the fact that we have an idea of God. This idea is like the 'trademark' our creator has stamped on our minds.

Descartes says that every idea must have a cause, and argues that ideas can have any of three sources: they can be 'adventitious' (caused by something external to the mind), fictitious (caused by the mind) or innate. **Innate ideas** are not ones we think from birth, but ones that the mind has certain capacities to use and which can't be explained by our experience. But what is the cause of innate ideas?

We cannot in general be certain which of the three types of cause an idea has. However, Descartes argues that a cause must have at least as much *reality* as its effect. The philosopher Bernard Williams gives a common-sense example: if we discover a picture of a sophisticated machine, we automatically think that the machine must be the product of an advanced society or a highly fertile imagination, even though it's just a picture. If we actually found the machine, working as it should, this would be even more impressive – the machine has *more reality* as a working machine than as a drawing.

Going further: degrees of reality

The idea of 'degrees of reality' is foreign to us, but was a standard part of medieval metaphysics. A 'substance' is defined as something that can exist independently. An 'accident' is a property of a substance. And a 'mode' is a particular determination of a property. Thus, e.g., with a red book, the substance is a book, the accident is 'colour', and 'red' is the mode. A substance has more reality than an accident, because a property cannot exist without a substance, and so is dependent on it. A mode has less reality than an accident. Furthermore, a substance that is in some way dependent on another substance has less reality than it, e.g. an incomplete substance such as a hand has less reality than a whole human body.

Different types of thought are modes of the property 'thought', itself an accident of 'minds', which are thinking substances. Particular ideas are instances of these modes. As *ideas*, they all have the same degree of reality (the same 'formal' reality). But the *objects* of the ideas, what the idea is about, have varying degrees of reality. I can have ideas about a material thing (a substance) or about the colour red (a mode). Whatever my idea is about, the idea is still an idea, and so an instance of a mode. But because they are about different things, ideas have different *objective* realities. The objective reality of an idea is not the same as the formal reality the object would have if it actually existed; but it is correlated with it.

Descartes claims that the cause of an idea must have as much reality as the *object of the idea*, what that idea is about.

As thinking substances, we have considerable reality, and hence many ideas could be the products of our minds. But the idea of God is different, Descartes argues. The object of the idea of God is God, which has the greatest degree of reality, more reality than minds do, for the idea of God is the idea of a substance that depends on nothing else to exist. Our minds could not, therefore, have created it. This is a puzzling claim – the idea of God is still simply an idea, which is a mode, whereas I am a substance. But the special features of the idea of God, viz. the idea of something perfect and infinite, Descartes argues, place the reality of its cause far in excess of me, for I am imperfect and finite (this is clear, because I am in a state of doubt). Indeed, the only possible cause is God, because only God has enough reality to create the idea of God. So God must exist.

A variation

Descartes also presents a variation of the argument, which claims not just that God caused the idea of God, but God caused me. I, who have this idea of God, can't exist unless God does, because if I created myself, I could give myself every perfection. This is because to create substance requires more power than creating properties – hence causing myself (a substance) involves more power than creating perfections (which would be properties). But I can't give myself every perfection, so I could not have caused myself. Again, if I created myself, I could also have given myself the idea of God, but, as was argued above, I can't do this either.

Of course, we might think, I was created by my parents. But if *only* my parents were involved in explaining my creation, then they must have sufficient power to cause the idea of God in my mind. But they have no more power than I do. We could continue back to their parents, and so on. Descartes allows that there could be an infinite series of creatures, each causing the other. But, he objects, this won't be able to cause the idea of God. So since I have the idea of God, God created me.

Objections

One objection Descartes responds to immediately. As imperfect and finite, I could be the cause of an idea of something that is '*not finite*' and '*not imperfect*'. Could I not come up with the idea of God by simply thinking away all limitations? But this *negative* conception of infinity and perfection is not the idea of God, Descartes claims, which requires a *positive* conception of these properties – not the absence of limits, but something for which there could be no limits.

Because of this insistence that our ideas of the infinity and perfection of God are not negative ideas, Descartes is claiming that we have a very powerful – clear and distinct – idea of God, and not some hazy notion of something indefinitely great. But this requirement conflicts with Descartes's *own claim* that as finite minds we cannot form a *clear* idea of God's infinity. So he wants to say the idea of God is not clear, but it is clearly and distinctly positive rather than negative. This sounds like a contradiction, since an idea is not distinct unless it is clearly separated from other ideas, and it contains nothing other than what is clear. Yet Descartes must insist that the idea of God is positive; if we do have only a negative idea of God, because we are finite, then it becomes possible that we are the cause of that idea.

Second, the argument relies on the notion of 'degrees of reality', and the claim that a cause must have more reality than its effect. This is all outmoded. Indeed, we owe its rejection to Descartes's development of the mechanical view of nature.

Third, Descartes supposes that every idea must have a cause. Hume argued that we don't know this. It is not an **analytic** truth; so it is logically possible that some ideas have no causes. If the idea of God has no cause, Descartes's argument collapses.

● ⬤ **KEY POINTS**

- Descartes claims that all ideas have a cause. There are three types of idea: innate, adventitious and fictitious.

- All causes must have at least as much reality as do their effects. The cause of an idea must have as much reality as what the idea represents.

- Descartes argues that the idea of God is innate, and could have been caused only by God, because only God is a sufficient cause of the idea of God. The objective reality of the idea of God is greater than any finite substance.

- Likewise, because I have the idea of God, God must have caused (created) me.

QUIZ QUESTIONS

Outline Descartes's Trademark argument for the existence of God. (AQA, 2b, 2004, *10 marks*)

Outline and illustrate the three types of idea Descartes says there are.

Explain Descartes's argument that our idea of God is positive, not negative.

Outline Descartes's argument that he has been created by God.

DISCUSSION QUESTION

Assess Descartes's Trademark argument.

The ontological argument (*Meditation* V)

> It is certain that I . . . find the idea of God in me, that is to say, the idea of a supremely perfect being. . . . And I know no less clearly and distinctly that an actual and eternal existence belongs to his nature . . . existence can no more be separated from the essence of God . . . than the idea of a mountain can be separated from the idea of a valley; so that there is no less contradiction in conceiving a God, that is to say, a supremely perfect being, who lacks some particular perfection, than in conceiving a mountain without a valley. (144–5)

Descartes's argument is very simple. There are two ways we may phrase it:

(a)   The idea of God contains the idea of existence.
(b)   Therefore God must exist (the conclusion is not just that God does exist, but that God cannot not exist, i.e. God's existence is necessary).

Or, with a little more unpacking,

(a)   God is a supremely perfect being.
(b)   Existence is a perfection.
(c)   Therefore, God must exist.

The quotation makes clear that the argument is grounded on two central claims of Descartes's philosophy – the theory of innate ideas and the doctrine of clear and distinct ideas. The first theory supports the first premiss, the definition of God as supremely perfect. This just is the idea of God we find that we have. The second theory supports the validity of the argument. Descartes claims that it is clear and distinct that the idea of existence cannot be excluded from the idea of God, a supremely perfect being.

Descartes is aware that we might misunderstand him as claiming that 'thinking makes it so'. He objects to himself: 'just as it does not follow that merely because I conceive a mountain with a valley, there is any mountain in the world, so similarly, although I conceive God as having existence, it does not follow from that, that there is a God who actually exists' (145). But, he argues, the examples of a mountain and God are not analogous. The disanalogy is that the idea of existence is *part of the idea* of God: 'I cannot conceive God without existence' (145). It is not that my thought brings about God's existence (all my thinking can bring about is ideas!); rather the fact that God's existence is necessary makes me think of God in this way, viz. as existing. How things are determines what I am able to think, rather than vice versa.

This again rests on the doctrine of clear and distinct ideas. Descartes has argued that whatever one clearly and distinctly perceives is true. That we can clearly and distinctly perceive that existence is part of the idea of God, i.e. that there is a conceptual connection between the concept of God and God's existence entails that God must exist. Without this additional premiss, Descartes admits elsewhere, the gap between thought and reality is not bridged.

Objections and replies

We may doubt, with the philosopher Gassendi, whether Descartes is *right* to claim that existence is part of the idea of God as the supremely perfect being. Can't I form the idea of a God who does not exist?

Descartes replies by drawing our attention to the claim that the CONCEPTIONS OF GOD (Ch. 3, p. 124) all entail each other. Because our minds are finite, we normally think of the divine perfections – omnipotence, omniscience, necessary existence, etc. – separately and so we might not see immediately that they entail each other. But if we attend carefully to whether existence belongs to the supremely perfect being, and what sort of existence it is, we shall discover that we cannot conceive any one of the other attributes while excluding necessary existence from it. For example, in order for God to be omnipotent, God must not depend on anything else, and so must not depend on anything else to exist.

This may be a convincing argument for the claim that *if* God exists, God exists necessarily. But Descartes's argument is still open to the objection, made famous by Aquinas and cited by Johannes Caterus in response to Descartes, that this doesn't demonstrate that God actually exists. It shows only that the *concept* of existence is inseparable from the *concept* of God.

Descartes responds that this overlooks two things: first, his claim that clear and distinct ideas are true; and, second, that necessary existence as part of the concept of God entails actual existence. However, this sounds like Descartes is begging the question, for Caterus's objection is precisely that the connection in the concept does not prove a connection in reality.

Immanuel Kant, however, is sometimes thought to have presented a deadly objection. The whole argument makes the mistake of supposing falsely that existence is a property. Consider whether 'God exists' is an **analytic** or a **synthetic** judgement. According to Descartes, it must be analytic: the argument is that 'God does not exist' is a contradiction in terms, for the concept 'God' contains the idea of existence (necessary existence belongs to God's essence). But, Kant claims, existence does not add anything to a concept; to say something exists is to say that some object corresponds to the concept. To think of something (to entertain the concept of it) and to think of something existing is not to think of anything different. The concept itself is not altered; and so existence is not part of any concept. So, at best, it can be only the link between the concept of God and the *idea* of existence, and not existence itself, which the ontological argument establishes.

● **KEY POINTS**

- Descartes argues that the idea that God exists is part of the idea of God. Existence is a perfection, and the idea of God is the idea of a being that has all perfections.

- Descartes's argument rests on his theory of innate ideas (this is the idea of God we find in ourselves) and his doctrine of clear and distinct ideas. If the idea of God having existence wasn't clear and distinct, we couldn't know that God really exists.

- Kant argued that existence is not a property, i.e. it cannot form part of any concept. To say that something exists is not to describe the concept of that thing, but to say that something in the world corresponds to that concept.

❓ QUIZ QUESTIONS

Explain the disanalogy Descartes identifies between thinking of a mountain and thinking of God.

Briefly explain what Descartes means by 'God'.

❓ DISCUSSION QUESTION

Assess Descartes's ontological argument for the existence of God.

The role of God in Descartes's system (*Meditations* III, V, VI)

The *Meditations* begin with, and take as their theme, the search for truth and what we can know. And so in *Meditation* VI, Descartes seeks to resolve the issues that led him into doubt about what was true in the first place. To do this, he needs to establish, in reverse order, that there could be no evil demon deceiving him; that he is not dreaming, and a material world, including his body, really does exist; and that he can trust his senses.

God is not a deceiver

The answer to all these doubts is that God is not a deceiver. Descartes's claim to know this rests on his idea of God. First, he used the idea of God to prove that God exists in both the trademark and ontological arguments. Second, in those proofs we saw that it was an essential part of the idea of God that God is perfect. God, therefore, would not deceive us, as this would be an imperfection.

What does Descartes mean by this? It is important to note that Descartes explicitly denies that his invocation of God means we must be infallible. Rather, Descartes's claim is that God 'has permitted no falsity in my opinion which he has not also given me some faculty capable of correcting' (158). The method of doubt, and the central importance of clear and distinct ideas, is the best we can do in correcting our tendency to have false beliefs. By God's not being a deceiver, then, we are assured only that once we have done all we can to avoid error, and are judging on the basis of clear and distinct ideas, then we will not go wrong.

Going further: the connection to nature

Because God is not a deceiver, we can attain the truth. Descartes links this to the idea of nature in two ways. First, 'there is no doubt that everything nature teaches me contains some truth. For by nature, considered in general, I now mean nothing other than God himself, or the order and disposition that God has established in created things' (158–9). So, again if we are careful, we can learn truth from nature, because God has created nature.

We might object that God's purposes are inscrutable, so we don't know if he has set up nature in such a way that we come to know the truth. We cannot know whether God might have arranged it so that we believe in an external world when there wasn't one.

Although Descartes allows that we cannot know God's purposes, he argues that the objection fails. And this is the second link to nature, this time human nature. Given that we would have no way of correcting our error, such a mistake would constitute a frustration of our essential nature as rational minds. We cannot help but assent to what we clearly and distinctly understand. And it is difficult to reconcile ourselves to the idea that God would create beings and then thwart the exercise of their very essence. We don't need to know what God's purposes are in order to judge that this would amount to God being a deceiver.

How this solves scepticism

So how does the existence of God help solve Descartes's scepticism? First, because God exists and is not a deceiver, God would not allow us to be deceived by some demon. This would just be God being a deceiver by proxy.

What about the problem of dreaming? Descartes's answer is that we *can* tell the difference between dreaming and being awake, because 'our memory can never connect our dreams with one another and with the general course of our lives, as it is in the habit of connecting the things which happen to us when we are awake' (168). When we perceive, rather than dream, we know the object of perception and can connect the experience with others that we have. Again, as long as we judge only by clear and distinct ideas, God would not allow us to be deceived in this.

Finally, we saw, in THE PROOF OF MATERIAL THINGS (p. 240), that God is essential to establishing the existence of my body and material objects in general. But can we trust our senses to deliver the truth about material objects? Descartes recommends caution here. These judgements – about what properties material objects have and about particular perceptions – 'are very obscure and confused' (158). We can and do make mistakes about what we are perceiving. But, again, we can know that God has given us the means to correct mistakes and avoid error. If, therefore, we take care and assent only to clear and distinct ideas, 'I may conclude with assurance that I have within me the means of knowing these things with certainty' (158).

KEY POINTS

- Descartes argues that we know that God is not a deceiver, because we know that God is perfect.

- This does not mean that God guarantees every belief we have. It means that we have the means to correct any mistakes we make. If we only believe what we can clearly and distinctly perceive to be true, we will not go wrong.

- Because God is not a deceiver, and God is omnipotent, God would not let an evil demon deceive us.

- We can now also tell dreaming from being awake by the way our memory connects up our waking experiences.

- Because God is not a deceiver, a material world is the cause of our experiences of material objects. However, individual perceptual judgements may still be wrong, unless we stick to clear and distinct ideas.

❓ QUIZ QUESTIONS

Explain Descartes's claim that 'God is not a deceiver'.

Describe **three** ways in which we rely on God for knowledge.

Outline Descartes's argument that we can learn truth from nature.

❓ DISCUSSION QUESTION

Assess Descartes's argument that the existence of God solves the doubts he developed in *Meditation* I.

6

Marx and Engels's *The German Ideology*

UNIT 3   Jean-Marc Pascal

(Part 1, selections from Parts 2 and 3, *Theses on Feuerbach*)

Quotations and page references are from the AQA recommended edition (Lawrence & Wishart, ISBN 0-85315-217-9)

The critique of the Young Hegelians; philosophical accusations made against them

The Young Hegelians

German intellectual life was, for several generations, under the spell of Hegel's philosophy and its theory of the 'Idea' as the manifestation of triumphant Reason. Hegel considered that the 'history of the world is none other than the progress of the consciousness of freedom'. This total reliance on the power of reason led Hegel to proclaim a 'glorious mental dawn' for humanity as thought ought to govern reality and not the other way around. The task of philosophy is, for Hegel, 'to comprehend its time in thought', and the only method for understanding all natural phenomena and human events consists in identifying the *dialectical* process by which everything moves from thesis to antithesis before culminating in a synthesis of the two previous stages. All life processes, be they intellectual or physical, are eventually resolved in the 'Absolute Idea'.

THE DIALECTICAL PROCESS OF HISTORICAL MATERIALISM
IN *THE GERMAN IDEOLOGY*

Towards a Truly Human Society

Common ownership of the means of production: capacity to enjoy all this all-sided production of the whole earth

Autonomous ' self-activity': all-round development of individuals

Communist society
Classless, stateless; universal solidarity

Communist revolution
Revolution is the driving force of history
Proletarians acting 'all at once' and simultaneously
Abolition of the state and private property
End to the division of labour

Communist consciousness
Leads to the necessity of revolution

Alienated labour made unbearable

Capitalism in crisis
Intensified competition leads to worsening crises
Doomed to collapse due to inner contradictions

Living conditions deteriorating

Total hegemony of the bourgeoisie
Economic, political and ideological domination

Rise of capitalism
Nineteenth century: extensive industrialization; big industry and free competition
Seventeenth–eighteenth centuries: world-market and colonial expansionism
Late Middle Ages: manufacturing industry; rise of enterprising town merchants

Feudalism
Landed nobility v. serf labour force
Country v. town; guilds

Ancient world
Communal property of city states along with private property (slaves)

Tribal societies
Natural division of labour; communal, tribal slaves

Production of the means to satisfy basic needs
Men must be in a position to live in order to 'make history'

'Life is not determined by consciousness, but consciousness by life'

In his later work, Hegel claimed: 'History is the unfolding of God's nature'. However, his apparent support for the rigid bureaucratic Prussian monarchy and the pro-establishment Prussian Church was felt to be at odds with his implicit support for the political emancipation of mankind. So Hegel's disciples split into a group of conservatives and a more liberal group of Young Hegelians, eager for political change. Reacting against a climate of conservative politics, a group of Young Hegelians, composed of Ludwig Feuerbach, David Strauss and Bruno Bauer set themselves the task of debunking Hegel's philosophy of religion. Strauss reduced the life of Jesus to a messianic myth, and Bauer argued that the Gospels were 'human fantasies arising from man's emotional needs'. Feuerbach set out to investigate the essence of Christianity in an effort to free mankind from the pernicious influence of the Hegelian doctrine as well as the Christian dogma (see THE CRITIQUE OF ESSENTIALIST NOTIONS OF HUMAN NATURE, p. 260).

Religious concepts had become the benchmark by which all other concepts were judged, and German philosophy had fallen under the spell of 'dogmas and beliefs in dogma' (41) to the point of explaining everything in terms of religious or theological concepts. Philosophy was losing its way under such an unnatural dominance, since no philosopher can claim to deduce concrete knowledge of nature from a sublimated religious consciousness. In this respect, Hegel had severed man from his very roots by putting mind and spirit over the primeval experience of the senses. For Feuerbach, it was man who was the foundation of all philosophy and it was his relation with nature which needed to be urgently re-established.

Marx and Engels's critique

When Marx and Engels started their collaboration on *The German Ideology*, or, in full, *Critique of the German Ideology in the Guise of its Representatives, Feuerbach, Bruno Bauer and Stirner and German Socialism in the Guise of its Prophets*, their initial purpose was 'to settle accounts with [their] previous philosophical conscience'. The resolve was carried out in the form of a criticism of post-Hegelian philosophy. What was meant to strike a topical and polemical chord among its readers ended up as a 650-page unpublished manuscript, 'abandoned to the gnawing criticism of the mice' for nearly ninety years. Yet, Marx commented, 'we have achieved our main purpose – self-clarification'. Although far more vitriolic pages were originally dedicated to the critique of Max Stirner, the best critical arguments were directed against Feuerbach's *The Essence of Christianity*, and it was these that the editors of *The German Ideology* preserved.

For Hegel, self-consciousness is the immediate intuition of the ego by itself. It is an act of self-reflection in which consciousness is both subject (looking in its own mirror) and object (reflected image). Once that act of self-reflection has taken place, Hegel considers consciousness capable of bridging the gap between itself (subject) and any other image of the external world, *present in itself* (object). In this respect, consciousness of the world never resorts to primary sensory experience since all it has to do is to consult its all-encompassing reflective consciousness (sometimes called 'Reason' or 'Spirit' by Hegel). Man, therefore, defines himself in total opposition to the world to the point that an *idea*, such as the idea of God, seems to have no other source but man's consciousness itself.

Feuerbach was the first philosopher to react against such an extreme philosophical position, claiming that he was 'nothing but a *natural philosopher in the domain of the mind*', a 'materialist', eager to base his analysis of 'the essence of religion' on 'historical proofs'. Feuerbach's rejection of Hegel's Absolute Idealism was, in the first instance, welcomed by Marx and Engels who could not but approve his positioning of man at the centre of philosophy and his appeal to the senses as the only way to liberate mankind from its subjugation to religious superstition. However, as the *Theses on Feuerbach* made very clear, Feuerbach was no revolutionary thinker; he was, at best, a reforming democrat who believed in a gradual process of political emancipation. The rest of the Young Hegelians did not fare any better in the judgement of Marx and Engels, who accused them of being 'the staunchest conservatives, in spite of their allegedly "world-shattering" statements' (41).

The focus of Marx and Engels's criticism lies in the systematic debunking of an Hegelian philosophy turned by the Young Hegelians and so-called 'true socialists' into a frozen, reactionary ideology. The Young Hegelians continued to use Hegel's concept of 'self-consciousness' (see THE CRITIQUE OF ESSENTIALIST NOTIONS OF HUMAN NATURE, p. 260), and Marx and Engels set out to ridicule their opponents for believing that the essential task of philosophy was to liberate men from their mistaken ideas on religion (41). For much too long, they argued, the problems of mankind have been attributed to ideas instead of focusing on the real and practical contradictions at hand: 'In direct contrast to German philosophy which descends from heaven to earth [an allusion to Hegel's Absolute], here we ascend from earth to heaven' (47).

KEY POINTS

- Marx and Engels claimed that, despite their radical claims, the Young Hegelians failed to bring a new philosophy to light. In particular,

  - they continued to use the same ideological category of 'self-consciousness' as had Hegel, thus relapsing into conservative Idealism;

  - their critical analysis of religion was limited and ignored the material reality of social conditions.

The methodology of historical materialism

Developing a new methodology

The importance of *The German Ideology* lies in the development of a new method of understanding social and historical phenomena, away from the philosophical speculations of their predecessors. Marx and Engels are concerned primarily with the formulation of a materialist conception of history, based on the direct, empirical observation of man's reality in his everyday social and historical dimensions (47).

This new method of understanding man in his relations to himself (consciousness), to others (labour) and to the natural and human world around him is made possible only by rejecting, once and for all, all previous Idealist claims and by adopting a strictly materialist approach. It is time for 'positive science' to account for the 'real knowledge' of man's 'practical activity' (48).

The best introduction to the methodology of historical materialism, as well as further detailed criticisms of the Young Hegelians, is to be found in Marx's *Theses on Feuerbach*, which encapsulates the key steps to be taken in order to clear the way for a new philosophy of history. Marx felt so frustrated by the prevailing resigned attitude of his fellow philosophers that, in the spring of 1845, he jotted down the eleven sections which became the blueprint of historical materialism. Engels who found and published the *Theses*, in 1888, wrote that they were 'invaluable as the first document in which is deposited the brilliant germ of the new [communist] outlook'. The 11 theses highlight the unbridgeable gap between Marx's revolutionary aspirations and Feuerbach's conservative views, which Marx believed were equally shared by other Young Hegelian theorists.

Marx's *Theses on Feuerbach* (121–3)

Thesis I: Feuerbach holds a materialist conception of man's 'sensuous activity' (activity of the senses) which proves very similar to Hegel's contemplative or theoretical conception. On the one hand, Feuerbach craves a new critical theory, capable of furthering the emancipation of the alienated individual, but the 'alienation', which he describes at length, is purely intellectual and totally estranged from the social reality of real men and women (see THE RELATION OF THE DIVISION OF LABOUR TO ALIENATION, p. 270). For Marx, man's 'sensuous activity' is 'revolutionary' and 'practical–critical', an aspect totally neglected by Feuerbach. By 'practical–critical', Marx implies that, far from being incompatible, practice and theory must be applied together in order to achieve a radical ('revolutionary') transformation of the world.

Thesis II: What used to be pursued by philosophers such as Feuerbach as 'objective truth' must give way to thinking in practice, that is to say, applying one's critical rational faculty to real, concrete situations. The time for scholastic speculation is over (see THE CONCEPT OF 'PRAXIS', p. 262).

Thesis III: The third thesis insists on the urgency with which man is to be put in charge of his circumstances. Such a radical transformation of society cannot be accomplished by an appeal to (Hegelian) passive contemplation, but requires a revolutionary process of self-changing ('revolutionary practice'). In his new relations with both the natural and social environments, man will develop a new personal and social identity. Nature is, for Hegel, and for his followers, some idealized entity, 'a thing given direct from all eternity, remaining ever the same'. By contrast, Marx and Engels describe the sensuous world around man as 'an historical product', constantly evolving from one generation to the next (62).

Thesis IV: Feuerbach sees in religion the source of man's self-alienation but he fails to see that the secular, everyday aspect of religion must be analysed and destroyed, not only in words, but 'in practice', i.e. in reality (see THE CONCEPT OF IDEOLOGY, p. 272).

Thesis V: Marx reiterates the central argument of the first thesis, viz. that Feuerbach has failed to grasp the *practical* nature of human activity and his sensualism has not been used as an efficient critical weapon, but has been lost in contemplation.

Thesis VI: In order to resolve the problem of man's self-alienation, Feuerbach resorts to a spurious concept of 'human essence'. First, he wrongly sees man as 'abstract – *isolated* – human individual', instead of recognizing man as a real social human being. Second, his concept of 'essence' remains a blurred, unexplored generalization (see THE CRITIQUE OF ESSENTIALIST NOTIONS OF HUMAN NATURE, p. 260).

Thesis VII: 'Religious sentiment' cannot be taken out of its social context since it is produced by social circumstances. In the same way, the abstract individual analysed by Feuerbach is a real person, who 'belongs to a particular form of society'.

Thesis VIII: 'All social life is essentially practical', i.e. it is not concerned with transcendent, spiritual mysteries, but is engaged with the immediate demands of everyday-life activities. The only way to understand and resolve the problems of society is through action ('human practice') allied with critical theory ('the comprehension of this practice').

Thesis IX: The highest achievement of 'contemplative materialism', as opposed to Marx and Engels's 'historical materialism', is their futile contemplation of 'single individuals' (instead of Marxist social classes) and 'civil society' (instead of laying the groundwork for a new classless society).

Thesis X: For Feuerbach, humanity is nothing more than 'civil society', meaning the domain or sphere of particular individual interests. Marx's new materialism will take into account all the members of 'human society, or social humanity'. Notice that Marx does not introduce the notion of *class*, here.

Thesis XI: Until now, the meaning of human reality has been confined to the pure speculations and unproven interpretations of various philosophers, all disengaged from real human activity. Marx calls for a break away from centuries of empty mind games, as it is time for the world, as the totality of all its social actors, to be changed in a radical way through an historical revolutionary process: 'The philosophers have only *interpreted* the world, in various ways; the point is to change it'. As implied in Thesis VIII, Marx is neither proclaiming nor wishing for the end of philosophy as such, but for the demise of a purely abstract kind of philosophy offering no practical method of interpretation of social reality.

● **KEY POINTS**

- There is an urgent need for a new method of historical interpretation as philosophers (including Feuerbach) have failed to understand the 'practical' aspect of reality, focusing instead on abstract theory. It is, therefore, imperative to abandon scholastic speculation and start to 'think in practice'.

- Feuerbach is a typical representative of 'contemplative philosophers' estranged from social reality and still attached to an 'abstract' conception of man.

- The world cannot be changed by ideas but through action.

- The 'old' materialism must give way to a new 'historical' materialism.

❓ QUIZ QUESTIONS

Outline Marx and Engels's critique of the Young Hegelians. (AQA, 3b, 2005, *10 marks*)

Describe what is meant by 'practical–critical' activity.

❓ DISCUSSION QUESTIONS

Critically assess the importance given to religion by the Young Hegelians.

Critically discuss Marx and Engels's claim that a new method of historical interpretation is needed.

The critique of essentialist notions of human nature

Religion and human nature in Feuerbach

For Hegel, all forms of human knowledge converged towards the Absolute Idea, as the supreme manifestation of the divine mind. Feuerbach opposed Hegel's view, affirming that consciousness is not a reflection of God, but represents a collective mind, or 'species consciousness', only reflecting the qualities and attributes of human nature. In other words, man does not need God to constitute his identity as all the qualities that he may ascribe to the divine are already present *within* him. Feuerbach agrees with Hegel that consciousness of God is self-consciousness but, for him, knowledge of God is *self-knowledge* since 'to think is to be God'. There is, therefore, no transcendent or metaphysical conception of God, as human nature is the exclusive source of religion: 'how could the divine activity work on me as its object, nay, work *in me*, if it were essentially different from me?' When man contemplates God, he is contemplating only a purer and higher image of himself: 'the essence of man is man's supreme being'.

Because God is a projection of man's consciousness, this illusion must be dispelled if mankind is to emancipate itself from religious self-alienation. For Feuerbach 'there is no other essence which man can think, dream of, imagine, feel, believe in, wish for, love and adore as the *absolute*, than the essence of human nature itself'. The practical consequence of man's re-appropriation of his essence is the duty of mankind to redirect the qualities formerly ascribed to God to human experience: 'in religion man . . . sacrifices his relation to man to his relation to God. . . . If human nature is the highest nature to man, then practically also the highest and first law must be the love of man to man'. Feuerbach sees himself as a materialist who wants to free human nature from its *unnatural* dependence upon religion and point the way towards a new humanity, based on brotherly love.

Despite their early enthusiasm for Feuerbach, Marx and Engels rejected his altruistic humanism along with Stirner's anarchic individualism. Neither could fully grasp their fundamental discovery, namely that human consciousness is ultimately shaped and determined by *external* circumstances (61). The Marxist conception of human essence is not to be found in some abstract conception of 'Man' or sublimated notion of 'Nature', but in a revolution that will resolve all social tensions and economic contradictions. The dynamic essence of man will finally be reflected in the harmonization of both his 'practical' and 'critical' sides. Estranged from his natural milieu by centuries of alienated labour, communist humanity will renew its relation with its materialist roots. Man is a being constantly participating in the transformation of nature through historical praxis (see next section).

KEY POINTS

- For Feuerbach, the essence of man must be reclaimed from religion.

- Marx and Engels reject both Feuerbach's altruistic humanism and Stirner's anarchic individualism, in the name of historical materialism.

- There is no set communist notion of human nature as man develops his essence through historical praxis.

❓ QUIZ QUESTION

Briefly describe Marx and Engels's account of human nature. (AQA, 3b, 2001, *10 marks*)

❓ DISCUSSION QUESTION

Assess Marx and Engels's criticisms of Feuerbach's conception of human nature.

What Marx and Engels mean by 'materialism'; the concept of 'praxis'

By mapping out the evolution of social practices throughout history, Marx and Engels were no longer traditional philosophers, speculating on the progress of mankind, but revolutionary thinkers, looking for clear patterns of alienation and domination throughout the ages. Neither of them had in mind to give the world a new totalizing or all-embracing system of thought, like Hegel. Their ambition was to develop a practical method of socio-historical interpretation and their first fundamental discovery was that the products of human consciousness have their origins in material social conditions: 'Life is not determined by consciousness, but consciousness by life' (47).

Praxis

Praxis, the Greek word for 'action', was opposed to *theoria*, the term used by Aristotle to describe the divine activity of 'contemplation'. For Marx, praxis is, originally, man's purposeful action or activity, aimed at changing his environment (nature) for reasons of subsistence (survival). It is also associated with the concept of labour, as the physical strength necessary to produce any purposeful action and take it to its full completion.

Praxis, or conscious, voluntary action, is therefore closely associated with 'materialism' inasmuch as 'by producing their means of subsistence men are directly producing their actual material life' (42). Marx and Engels remark that the very necessity of physical survival, especially in Germany, had been relegated to some obscure 'prehistoric era', without any attempt to trace the origins of primitive human needs. Yet, the first priority of man is his own survival and he is, out of necessity, destined to toil in order to satisfy his most basic physiological needs. Marx and Engels have to remind their fellow Germans of 'the first premiss of human existence and, therefore, of all history . . . namely, that men must be in a position to live in order to be able to "make history"' (48). Human action or labour lies at the heart of man's historical development.

The development of history

For Marx and Engels, the development of history is totally determined by the forces of material production, i.e. whatever is needed to survive. The most distinctive aspects of 'the primary historical relationships' can be distinguished as follows:

1 Unlike animals, men are endowed with consciousness and are able to 'produce their means of subsistence' (42), thus satisfying their basic biological needs, such as food and shelter.
2 'The production of fresh life' (having children) through the development of social relations within family groups leads to the beginning of the most basic social organizations.
3 Men are determined by the 'means of subsistence' which they have at their disposal, such as fruit, fish or animals. These means of subsistence lead to a variety of 'modes of production', i.e. the ways in which men organize the production of the goods necessary to their subsistence.
4 In its turn, the modes of production of given societies reflect 'a definite mode of life on their part' (42). What Marx and Engels suggest here is that if we compared the lives of, say, the Inuits of Greenland and the Aborigines of Central Australia, we would soon realize the paramount influence of physical conditions on the means of subsistence, the modes of production and, ultimately, the social organization of these two distinctive groups of people.
5 The first signs of division of labour (see next section) appear with the growth of the productive forces, i.e. the number of individuals involved in the activity of production. The history of humanity is nothing but the development of man's productive capacity (50).

Going further: the influence of Hegel's dialectical method on historical materialism

Looking at the theory and method of historical materialism first outlined in *The German Ideology,* it is important to mention Marx and Engels's debt to Hegel's dialectical thought and its fundamental premiss that history is the irreversible, constant progress of mankind towards its self-realization, with labour transforming man's world in the form of activity ('historical materialism' is sometimes also called 'dialectical materialism'). However, historical materialism and its exclusive focus on the 'material life-process' 'put Hegel on his head', by contesting his claim that the development of 'Reason' alone was responsible for the formation of a particular type of society and historical epoch. For Marx and Engels, philosophy, 'as an independent branch of knowledge', becomes obsolete when its high-flying, inapplicable theories are of no use in a world defined exclusively by material conditions (48). Once detached from reality, philosophy can be used only as an ideological instrument of bourgeois domination (see THE CONCEPT OF IDEOLOGY, p. 272).

Objections

Historical materialism takes into account only the historical development of Western Europe, arguably neglecting to look at the rest of the world for other possible models of praxis (or economic activity) prevailing in non-industrial societies. In its assumption that economic relations are the key to social reality, it neglects the importance of moral or religious values constitutive of an individual's personality. Furthermore, if consciousness is *totally* determined by material forces, it is difficult to ascribe any distinctive power to reason in both its *practical* application in praxis and its *critical* role in exposing the contradictions of capitalist society.

● **KEY POINTS**

- Marx and Engels argue that material conditions determine human reality. Historical materialism is the interpretation of these material conditions throughout the ages.

- All men have to produce their material existence to survive. Man is, therefore, condemned to praxis or action.

- Physical conditions influence the means of subsistence available to man.

- The production of his means of subsistence determines man's mode of living.

- Praxis or action determines man in his totality. It defines man as man.

- We may object that historical materialism neglects the importance of moral and religious values, and neglects the power of reason.

❓ QUIZ QUESTIONS

Explain **two** differences between the Hegelian and the materialist conception of consciousness.

Explain what Marx and Engels mean by 'praxis'.

Outline and illustrate the relation between materialism and praxis.

❓ DISCUSSION QUESTION

Critically discuss Marx and Engels's materialist theory of history. (AQA, 3c, 2001, *25 marks*)

The significance of the division of labour

Any human society is composed of and determined by:

1 The economic *forces of production* or *productive forces* which consist in the combination of the means of production, such as natural resources (such as water, oil or coal), raw materials (such as cotton or wool), machines (from the simplest tools to the most sophisticated computers), but also and more importantly, the human work force or labour power of individuals.
2 The social *relations of production* (43, footnote) which concern the relations of property (industrialist and his workers), power (bourgeoisie and proletariat) and control (state and ideology or 'superstructure' versus civil society or 'base'), deriving from the various aspects of man's productive existence.

The primary *explicit* aim of the division of labour is an apparent rationalization of labour tasks leading to a higher production of goods. However, the division of labour generates private property, in the form of capital or accumulation of wealth. Private property stands for that type of ownership that has been acquired from another's labour and yet comes under the enjoyment and control of exclusive owner(s) for the specific purpose of accumulation and profit (capital). Consequently, the division of labour and the development of private property go hand in hand and are directly responsible for the creation of two distinct classes:

1 a propertied class, or *bourgeoisie*, who own the means of production; and
2 a non-propertied, or *propertyless*, class, that is the great mass of workers or *proletarians* who own only their labour force which they have no other choice but to sell to the bourgeoisie in order to survive.

Civil society and the state

This economic situation is further reinforced by the political power and ideological control held by the ruling class through the institution of the state. Marx and Engels point out the sharp distinction existing between civil society and the state. Civil society is the social stage where bourgeois and workers encounter each other in the real world of class domination, labour exploitation and alienation (57) (see THE RELATION OF THE DIVISION OF LABOUR TO ALIENATION, p. 270). The original German expression, *bürgerliche Gesellshaft*, means literally, 'bourgeois society', but it extends, here, to 'the commercial and industrial society', dominated by the bourgeoisie.

Hegel had argued that the state was the end-product of human progress and had to be obeyed as the 'absolute' representation of the collective will. By contrast, Marx and Engels contend that, far from defending the interests of all citizens, the state is determined by society, and since the economic relations of production ultimately determine the political destiny of society, the state exists only to institutionalize the hegemony of the dominant class and to perpetuate its power and ideological influence over the entire civil society (79) (see THE CONCEPT OF 'IDEOLOGY', p. 272).

The divisions resulting from the class society

The creation of distinct economic classes results in further divisions in society:

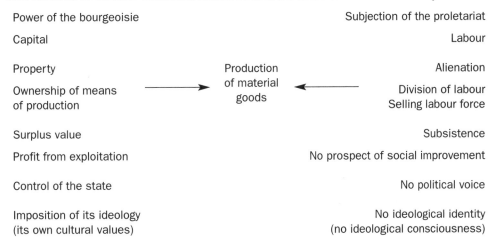

Power of the bourgeoisie		Subjection of the proletariat
Capital		Labour
Property	Production of material goods	Alienation
Ownership of means of production		Division of labour / Selling labour force
Surplus value		Subsistence
Profit from exploitation		No prospect of social improvement
Control of the state		No political voice
Imposition of its ideology (its own cultural values)		No ideological identity (no ideological consciousness)

Objections

In a modern context, the claim that the division of labour is responsible for the creation of a class society is contentious. The Victorian Marxist view of the division of society into two antagonistic classes has given way to a far more open idea of society in which social promotion is, theoretically, open to all and based exclusively on personal merit. Furthermore, the concept of 'bourgeoisie' or 'middle class' has acquired a far more flexible meaning, referring to a wide section of the population of industrialized countries, with most people having little to do with the direct accumulation of 'capital'. More significantly, the notion of 'working class' has lost its original connotations with the wane of heavy manufacturing and mining industries across Western Europe, being rapidly replaced by the service industries, such as transport, retailing and tourism. Finally, the terms 'proletarian' and 'proletariat' are now only used in the historical context of 'communist revolutions', such as the Russian Revolution.

KEY POINTS

- The division of labour and the rise of private property are inextricably linked.

- The industrial division of labour creates two conflicting classes: the bourgeoisie and the proletariat.

- Civil society is the stage where economic exploitation and ideological domination take place.

- Despite its expected impartiality, the state only represents and defends the interests of the bourgeoisie, to the detriment of the proletariat.

QUIZ QUESTIONS

Briefly explain how, according to Marx and Engels, the division of labour and the development of private property go hand in hand.

Outline the way in which the propertyless class appears in history.

Describe what Marx and Engels mean by 'civil society'.

DISCUSSION QUESTION

Critically assess the view that the division of labour creates a class society.

The historical development of the division of labour

Marx and Engels identify four distinctive forms of private property or ownership:

Tribal property

Tribal property is 'confined to landed property only. Real private property began with the ancients, as with modern nations, with movable property.—(Slavery and community)' (79). Social organization is characterized by a division of labour which 'is at this stage still very elementary and is confined to a further extension of the natural division of labour existing in the family'. Tasks are allocated according to natural or gender predispositions and mainly consist of 'hunting and fishing, the rearing of beasts or, in the highest stage, agriculture' (44). Extended tribal families follow a patriarchal model with chieftains at the top, members of the tribe below them and the first slaves at the bottom of the social structure.

Ancient communal and state property

Ancient communal and state property arises with 'the union of several tribes into a city by agreement or by conquest' (44). More institutionalized forms of slavery are present than in tribal societies; Marx and Engels have in mind the Roman Empire and the Greek city–states. Apart from slave labour, the division of labour is also intensified by the growing antagonism between the interests of the town and those of the country, while early commercial activity exacerbates potential conflicts between industry and maritime commerce. Notably, the first signs of class exploitation appear with the Roman development of private property alongside communal ownership and 'the transformation of the plebeian small peasantry into a proletariat', caught between propertied citizens and slaves (45).

Feudal property (feudalism)

Feudal property or feudalism opens a new chapter in history as, once again, new modes of production lead to new relations of production or social life. Slowly emerging from the decline of the Roman Empire and a period of barbarian military conquests (89–90), European populations divided themselves between town and country, the latter and its peasantry or serf labour force coming under the sway of the landed nobility (69).

Craftsmen and the creation of guilds

It was in towns that new economic developments started to take place with the rise of a new type of worker, viz. the craftsman. These men organized themselves into guilds in order to defend the interests of their specific trade. Serfs escaping from their original masters soon became a source of cheap labour for the guild-masters. If serfs proved unemployable by a guild, they quickly found themselves at the bottom of the medieval pecking order, as powerless day-labourers. By contrast, the journeymen and apprentices who had served their time with a guild-master could, one day, become full-fledged members of their guild (71).

The industrial and commercial expansion of towns

After a long period of limited exchange, the extension of safer means of communication between towns made possible 'the formation of a special class of merchants' (71). A new division of labour gradually took place with 'the separation of production and commerce'. The transition from the guild system to manufacture brought an entirely new dimension to economic life. Towns entered 'into relations *with one another*', local trade restrictions were lifted, inventions were shared and towns started to specialize in their own branch of industry (72).

Capitalist property (capitalism): from manufactures to big industry

Bourgeois or capitalist ownership grew out of the development of trade and manufacture between the sixteenth and nineteenth centuries. As weaving became the first main industry across Northern Europe, *manufactures multiplied*, becoming 'a refuge of the peasants from the guilds which excluded them or paid them badly' (73). At the same time, the disintegration of the feudal system and its traditional social bonds led to a period of 'vagabondage', when a rootless migrant population had to be forcibly absorbed into the new modes of production. The limited economic influence of the guilds rapidly declined as great merchants and manufacturers accumulated capital which they immediately reinvested into new lucrative ventures (74–5).

A *second phase* of the growing capitalism was, from the middle of the seventeenth until late in the eighteenth century, *the opening of a world market* alongside the exploitation of natural and human resources in newly conquered colonies. Competitive merchants and shippers were progressively gaining the upper hand over enterprising manufacturers, in both the economic and political spheres. Paper money, banks, speculations in stocks and shares were, by the eighteenth century, essential parts of economic activity (77).

The social by-product of this *universal competition* was, in a *third phase*, the rise of big industry, i.e. *the intensification of industrialization*, originally encouraged to counteract the effects of free competition between nations. Big business soon spelt the end of century-old modes of production, thus creating new relations of production and heralding full-blown capitalism. In this respect, capitalism was, from a Marxist point of view, a truly *revolutionary* historical phenomenon.

Going further: the composition of the bourgeoisie

The bourgeoisie is characterized by its enterprising spirit which can be traced back to the appearance of a merchant class during the medieval period of capitalist development. It can be divided into four distinctive categories:

1 *The industrial bourgeoisie* which controls the economic (means of production), the political (state) and cultural (ideology) life of society, along with (2);
2 *The financial bourgeoisie* which derives its capital from industrial investments;
3 *The petty bourgeoisie* composed of small, independent manufacturers, traders, shopkeepers and handicraftsmen. This section of the lower bourgeoisie enjoys a relative degree of autonomy in its working activity, but is particularly exposed to market fluctuations and always runs the risk of joining the proletarian masses. The other section of the *petty bourgeoisie* is made up of civil servants, doctors, teachers and lawyers who are essential to the smooth running of capitalist society but are not involved in its productive process.
4 *The landowners* who, as commercial farmers and employers of wage-labour, are subject to the capitalist market forces. The latter tend to be marginalized by the dominant urban bourgeoisie with which they share the same ideological values.

Objections

Marx and Engels were bourgeois thinkers who held the view that not ideas, but economic and material forces were the real driving forces of history. It is, nevertheless, on the strength of their *ideas* that they expected their readers and followers to change the material world around them. They also claimed that their method of historical interpretation was the only possible way of understanding the organization and self-contradictions of bourgeois society. They painted a history of economic development on a broad canvas with no attention paid to other important aspects of human activity. For instance, the invention of the printing press had much deeper cultural repercussions throughout Europe than the immediate economic prospect of selling many books. Furthermore, Marx and Engels never ventured outside the world of industry and trade, even though geographical, climatic or environmental factors undoubtedly played their part in the development of Western urban capitalism.

Karl Popper challenges the Marxist axiom that economic conditions are essential to social development, in the following counter-argument:

> Imagine that our economic system . . . was destroyed one day, but that technical and scientific knowledge was preserved. In such a case it might conceivably not take very long before it was reconstructed. . . . But imagine *all knowledge* of these matters to have disappeared, while the material things were preserved. This would be tantamount to what would happen if a savage tribe occupied a highly industrialized but deserted country.

Against Marx's arguments, Popper's point is that the total disappearance of knowledge, i.e. ideological production, would, on the face of it, have more far-reaching consequences than the physical destruction of all means of production and their related social forms.

KEY POINTS

- The tribal division of labour was modelled after 'the natural division of labour existing in the family'.

- The ancient division of labour was characterized by intensified slave labour and the rising antagonism between town and country.

- During the feudal phase, new economic developments, such as guilds and early manufactures, took place in towns.

- The modern industrial bourgeoisie intensified the division of labour in order to increase its capital, and the capitalist division of labour resulted in the separation between capital (bourgeois) and labour (proletariat).

- We may point out that it is contradictory for Marx and Engels to claim that material and economic forces are the real driving forces of history, while expecting their readers to change the world on the basis of their ideas, and that their theories would or could lead to revolution.

● Popper argues that knowledge is more essential to social development than economic conditions.

❓ QUIZ QUESTIONS

Outline the meaning and importance for Marx and Engels of the class of the 'bourgeoisie'. (AQA, 3b, 2002, *10 marks*)

Describe the three principal stages in the rise of the capitalist bourgeoisie.

Identify the rise of a propertyless class through the four stages of human development.

❓ DISCUSSION QUESTION

Critically discuss Marx and Engels's materialist theory of history. (AQA, 3c, 2001, *25 marks*)

The relation of the division of labour to alienation; the forms of alienation

Capitalism, through its intensified division of labour, achieves its economic goal, viz. the increased accumulation of capital, at the cost of the alienation of its proletarian work force and the ruling class itself. Marx and Engels identify its pernicious effects at the physical, psychological, economic, social and political levels:

1 The first and most disturbing sign of alienation is the individual worker's sense of loss in a world which seems and, actually is, totally beyond his control. Alienation manifests itself in the producing activity which he regards as external to him and not belonging to him. This materialist argument points out the artificial distance imposed by the division of labour between the individual and his environment, between man and nature.

2 The specialization imposed on workers is also a source of alienation, as it is impossible to change trade, or, if so, at the risk of losing one's livelihood (54).

3 On a psychological level, beyond the alienation of the activity of production and the tedious repetition of his specialized labour tasks, the worker feels alienated from himself as a free being, reduced to isolation, helplessness and want. The division of labour is a dehumanizing process (78, 84).

4 The physical exploitation of the worker is accompanied by his economic exploitation as he is systematically deprived of the legitimate fruit of his labour (this is discussed further below).

5 At the social level, under capitalism, all relations of production, outside as well as inside the workplace, are entirely determined by the demands of economic competition and

the pursuit of the accumulation of capital: 'big industry resolved all natural relationships into money relationships' (78). Human beings stop recognizing in each other their common human nature as they are transformed into interchangeable pawns in a situation beyond their understanding or control. Even 'the peculiar individuality of the various nationalities' has given way to international capitalism and the creation of a bourgeois class everywhere (78).

6 This general process of economic and social alienation takes a further political dimension with the creation of a ruling class, the bourgeoisie, which 'in all nations has the same interest and with which nationality is already dead; a class which is really rid of all the old world and at the same time stands pitted against it' (78). The social stratification imposed by the bourgeoisie finds its supreme, and political, expression in the state, which is nothing but the political voice of its interests (53).

7 Finally, the alienation suffered by the labour force is also experienced, in a more dormant way, by the bourgeoisie itself, since, despite its immediate power over the labour force, it has actually no direct influence over the constant fluctuations of 'the world market' (55), already perceived as an 'alien force' by the proletarians. Man is controlled by external economic structures instead of being the conscious master of them.

Both Marx and Engels see no foreseeable end to alienation as long as the capitalist system of production is applied with the same ruthless efficiency (see THE INEVITABILITY OF CLASS CONFLICT, p. 276).

Going further: the theory of 'surplus value'

Marx regarded his theory of 'surplus value', or value, as his most important contribution to the understanding of capitalist economic processes. Surplus value is the value added to a manufactured object by its transformation from raw material through labour. The value of the finished product, now transformed into a marketable commodity, is higher than the value of the original raw material. Therefore, it is the worker's labour which is, logically, responsible for this change in value. However, that surplus value is not enjoyed by the worker as the just reward for his *own* effort; it is, instead, cashed and turned into new capital by his employer as the exclusive owner of the means of production. The wages received by the worker in return for his physical labour are only meant to cover his basic needs and do not take into account the fact that he is constantly generating extra capital or profit for his employer. Wage labour deprives workers of their freedom, Marx argues, and he rejects the suggestion by the French socialist Pierre Proudhon that equal wages would relieve the economic alienation of the working class.

Objections

If, with Marx and Engels, we are prepared to believe in the alienation of the working class, we must assume that the proletariat is never aware of its innate freedom and its capacity for political liberation until its economic situation has become unbearable, i.e. until it acquires a 'revolutionary consciousness'. However, Sartre argued that the oppressed masses must have some degree or sense of freedom even under conditions of alienation, if they are to throw off their yoke and put an end to the division of labour. Consciousness of freedom must exist, even in a dormant state, at all times, among proletarians, if one day it is to rise to the surface and erupt into a universal revolutionary consciousness. For Sartre, whatever the degree of so-called 'ideological' or 'economic' exploitation, man is always in a position to use his freedom and change his social circumstances, through revolutionary action if need be (see Ch. 7, INTERSUBJECTIVITY, p. 303).

Second, under advanced capitalism, the intense competition imposed by the market forces on individuals is not felt as a new form of alienation but is more generally regarded as the sign of an open, free society, as well as the necessary price to pay to achieve material success. Regarding 'ideological' alienation, modern workers tend to recognize themselves in the consumers' values portrayed in the capitalist 'world ideology'. It could be argued that they are lured by the 'false consciousness' which it produces or, alternatively, that they have become more wary of its actual power of persuasion.

● **KEY POINTS**

- The proletariat experiences alienation at physical, psychological, economic, social and political levels. The ruling bourgeoisie experiences its own form of alienation.

- Big business has 'resolved all natural relationships into money relationships'.

❓ QUIZ QUESTION

Explain and illustrate Marx and Engels's theory of alienation.

❓ DISCUSSION QUESTION

Critically discuss Marx and Engels's use of the concept of alienation. (AQA, 3c, 2002, *25 marks*)

The concept of 'ideology' and its material base; its nature

It is important to make a clear distinction between the two ideologies discussed in the text. There is, first, the Hegelian, or *German*, *ideology*, discussed in its critical part. We saw how the Hegelian ideology was rejected on the ground that it failed to offer a materialist, 'practical–critical' interpretation of history (see THE CRITIQUE OF THE YOUNG HEGELIANS, p. 256 and THE METHODOLOGY OF HISTORICAL MATERIALISM, p. 258). Second, there is the *Bourgeois ideology*, analysed in the pages dedicated to capitalism or bourgeois society. Bourgeois ideology is not given the same critical treatment as its Hegelian counterpart, as Marx and Engels are primarily interested in its social and political impact on civil society. However, it is to be assumed that both share the same methodological limitations and that Hegel's ideology is, itself, the product of bourgeois society.

Marx and Engels argue that ideas are not pure intellectual entities but the products of man's material and social circumstances (47). Men may think that they have a *free* consciousness and that the religious, political or moral ideas they hold are *theirs*. But this is a profound self-delusion, as material conditions shape and dictate human thought: like an image first hits the retina upside down, so ideology must be reinterpreted and retraced back to its concrete, historical origin to be understood (45). Marx and Engels make it clear that the ascent of the capitalist bourgeois society through big industry 'destroyed all possible ideology, religion, morality, etc. and where it could not do this, made them into a palpable lie' (78). The reinforcing and guarantee by the state and its institutions of the economic domination by the bourgeoisie has been mentioned (see THE SIGNIFICANCE OF THE DIVISION OF LABOUR, p. 265). However, through ideology, the ruling class is also determined to impose on the whole of civil society its own worldview, its *own* interpretation of the human experience. Ideology is what Marx calls 'the idealistic superstructure' (57), comprising the social and intellectual phenomena which crown the economic 'base', composed of the essentially productive or material relations between the members of civil society.

To trace the source of all ideas is to look into the contents of consciousness. Marx and Engels rejected Hegel's pure subjectivism, which saw human consciousness as producing nothing less than total reality: 'What is actual is rational and what is rational is actual'. In its place, they describe consciousness as originating, like language, in the basic need to cooperate with other human beings in order to survive. At this early stage of human development, consciousness is limited to man's immediate environment. However, with the advance of the division of labour, material reality appears as a separate world and it is material conditions which condition consciousness *from without*.

Under capitalism, man is not only deprived of his physical freedom but is also denied his freedom of consciousness. In the hands of the bourgeoisie, ideology becomes an instrument of domination as its 'producers of ideas' ensure that 'their ideas are the ruling ideas of the age' (65). Marx and Engels are scathing of eighteenth-century bourgeois philosophy and its culmination in Hegel's illusory 'trick of proving the hegemony of the spirit in history' (67).

The task of the bourgeois thinkers, theorists and philosophers is to perfect 'the illusion of the [ruling] class about itself' (64) by smoothing or hiding away the true relations existing between classes and by explaining away the relations of socio-political domination and economic subordination. In this way, social relations appear, at least on the surface, harmonious, and individuals can carry out their productive tasks without any disruption.

For example, Marx and Engels criticized Bentham's theory of utility as nothing more than another deceitful ideological ploy, meant to lull the proletariat into a false sense of prevailing social justice (114).

At each stage of the historical development of mankind, new concepts have been bandied about as rallying cries for the new emerging ruling class: honour and loyalty were formative concepts of the feudal aristocratic identity; freedom and equality were central to the philosophy of the Enlightenment, paving the way to the triumphant rise of the bourgeoisie throughout Europe. When, in 1789, the representatives of the French bourgeoisie put down on paper the principles of the Declaration of Human Rights, they presented their document as a beacon of hope to all nations suffering under the yoke of a tyrannical regime. In reality, Marx and Engels argue, that declaration was only the ideological preamble to the ensuing violent overthrow of the French monarchy. But it is important for any new class that comes to be dominant in the historical state to give the impression that it presents itself, not so much as a class, as *the* representative of the whole of society, if not mankind: 'it has to give its ideas the form of universality, and represent them as the only rational, universal valid ones' (66).

Going further: the role of religion in bourgeois ideology

The existence of a dominating bourgeois ideology prevents the rise of a true 'class consciousness' among a working class blindly accepting the deceptive political and cultural ideas produced by its social betters (see REVOLUTION AND THE EMERGENCE OF THE COMMUNIST SOCIETY, p. 277). Concepts of universal 'freedom' and 'justice' mean little to exploited workers with no access to education or leisure time.

Feuerbach anticipated the complete disappearance of religion in a society run by democratic institutions and inspired by scientific progress. Marx, for his part, was indignant at the crucial role played by religion in promoting the passive acceptance of the political status quo by a working class with simplistic spiritual beliefs. As 'the opium of the people', religion is a dangerous illusion masking the real social problems to be addressed by bourgeois society.

Objections

Bourgeois ideology itself is not a *determining* historical force as it *prevents* change in order to preserve its economic interests. More generally, ideas do not necessarily require a philosophical or political form in order to change the course of history, as understood in the Marxist sense. For instance, Darwin's theory of evolution cannot be said to be the direct product of bourgeois ideology any more than it can be branded as a deliberate conspiracy to prove the social superiority of the bourgeois over his fellow-humans. The question of *truth* lies at the heart of any critical evaluation of the role of ideas in determining history. When Marx and Engels hail the proletariat as the exclusive bearer of historical truth, one may legitimately query the validity of their statement.

If to belong to a class means to see the world *only* through the eyes of one's class, then surely there is no possibility of any objective judgement and everyone is left to his own prejudiced viewpoint. How, then, did Marx and Engels manage to escape from the ideological trap of their bourgeois background? We must accept, against them, that ideas can and do transcend their class origins; the universal significance of a scientific discovery, a moral theory or the beauty of a work of art cannot be explained by or reduced to their alleged class 'content'. Was Picasso a different artist because of his support of the communist cause? The answer is 'Possibly so', but the aesthetic appeal of his works was certainly not confined to his communist admirers. There is enough factual evidence to suggest that there is no such thing as a 'truth of class' but, on the contrary, there are many universal truths accessible to all, independent of their socio-economic status.

● **KEY POINTS**

- Ideas are never neutral as they are deliberate constructs at the service of social interests and change according to the dominant class ruling society. Ideology is the imposition of the bourgeois worldview on to the dominated working class.

- Ideology is aimed at concealing the actual social contradictions created by capitalism. It presents the socio-economic domination of the ruling class as a legitimate state of affairs. In this respect, it propagates false beliefs (a 'false consciousness') about its actual intentions.

- Religion, as 'the opium of the people', contributes to the ideological alienation of the working class.

- However, we may object that

  - Not all ideas that change history take a philosophical or political form;

  - Marx and Engels do not do justice to the importance of the truth of an idea;

  - Ideas transcend their class origins.

❓ QUIZ QUESTIONS

Briefly explain what Hegelian and bourgeois ideology have in common.

Outline and illustrate how, according to Marx and Engels, ideology can be an instrument of domination.

Explain the place of religion in bourgeois ideology.

❓ DISCUSSION QUESTION

Assess Marx and Engels's theory of ideology.

The inevitability of class conflict and its place in Marx's theory

The inevitability of class conflict is treated in a broad, sketchy way in *The German Ideology* as Marx expanded his most detailed analysis of the inner contradictions of capitalism in *Capital* (1866), written twenty years later. Marx and Engels believed that historical development is dictated by observable scientific laws which point towards the cyclical replacement of an obsolete form of social existence, like feudalism, by a newer form of social organization. History, though, never repeats itself since once a class has been destroyed, it never returns: the ancient Greek and Roman world gave way to the medieval world, never to return. In its place came feudalism which eventually gave way to early industrial capitalism.

Capitalism itself was the result of previous economic and social 'revolutions', but its seemingly unchallenged supremacy is not immune to change as all social models carry within themselves the seeds of their self-destruction. The balance between big industry and labour is, by definition, a precarious one, since external competition constantly strains the economic resources of the big industrialists and, at the same time, increases the alienating conditions of the labour force. In his *Economico-Philosophical Manuscripts of 1844*, Marx criticized political economists, such as Adam Smith and David Ricardo, for ignoring the actual plight of the working class suffering under the drudgery imposed on it by the division of labour.

This process of systematic exploitation and dehumanization of the labour force is also underlined in *The German Ideology*: 'Never, in any earlier period, have the productive forces taken on a form so indifferent to the intercourse of individuals as individuals' (92). How long can this unbearable situation go on for? Central to the theory of historical determinism is the idea that the domination of one class by another necessarily leads to conflict. Marx and Engels prophesy an inevitable clash between the alienated labour force and a bourgeoisie bent on increasing industrial production along with the accumulation of capital or profit.

Two parallel phenomena can be observed in the latest stages of capitalism:

1   The economic development of capitalism is dependent upon the intensification of global competition on the world market. This competitive situation becomes 'a fetter to production' as it requires more and more important investments resulting in a drop in the rate of profit and a predictable stagnation in productivity. Such periods of insecurity will, according to Marx and Engels, generate more and more serious crises. Eventually, means of production are bound to fall into fewer and fewer hands (monopolists) and penury and want will start to spread among the working class.

2   At the same time, the social development of capitalism involves more of the proletarian population driven to harsher and harsher working and living conditions. There comes a stage in the evolution of capitalist society when 'productive forces [relations of production] and means of intercourse [social relations] cause mischief, and are no longer productive but destructive forces' (94) (in the form of intensified economic competition and unbearable alienation). Alienated labour has transformed individuals into *'abstract individuals'*, deprived of any sense of personal identity or class consciousness. It is time for the proletariat to regain its full humanity.

The latter observations were to find their full political expression in the *Manifesto of the Communist Party* (1848), in which Marx and Engels warned that the fall of the bourgeoisie and the victory of the proletariat were equally inevitable.

Objections

Marx and Engels's claim of the inevitability of class conflict is based exclusively on their economic prediction that, in the long run, due to the concentration of capital in fewer and fewer hands, the proletariat will lack the income to purchase the most basic commodities and will be driven to take the whole matter into their own hands. It is, therefore, unemployment which is the primary factor behind the expected clash between the two antagonistic classes. However, history has shown that the long periods of unemployment experienced by capitalist countries in the 1930s did not result in open class conflict nor revolution but were partly resolved by economic programmes, such as President Roosevelt's New Deal.

KEY POINTS

- Marx and Engels argued that the inner contradictions of the capitalist system of production become more acute with the intensification of global competition.

- At the same time, the working and living conditions of the proletariat become harsher and harsher.

- Sooner or later, as the conflict between the bourgeoisie and the proletariat grows, it inevitably leads to the communist revolution.

❓ QUIZ QUESTION

Outline the two parallel phenomena taking place in the latest stages of capitalism.

❓ DISCUSSION QUESTION

Assess Marx and Engels's claim of the inevitability of class conflict.

Revolution and the emergence of the communist society; the possibility of the abolition of alienation

After the critique of the Young Hegelians, *The German Ideology* oscillates between historical descriptions of the development of private property, the economic conditions obtaining under capitalism, and furtive glimpses into a future communist society inaugurating what Marx and Engels call the epoch of a 'truly human society'. It frequently describes the liberating effects of that revolution without entering into the details about how the communist society actually comes about or brings the old capitalist order to an end.

The rise of a proletarian revolutionary consciousness

As materialist thinkers, Marx and Engels are convinced that the economic 'base' of society determines the moral, religious and cultural characteristics of the 'superstructure'. The whole of civil society is, therefore, a tightly closed system, in which the working class is reduced to the paradoxical role of active producers of bourgeois capital while remaining powerless spectators of their own lives. The social norms of capitalist society are the norms dictated and decreed by the bourgeoisie whose moral, political, religious and cultural values are filtered and dispensed through institutions exclusively suited to its ideological agenda.

How can the working class, in such a hostile climate of ideological hegemony, develop a distinctive class consciousness? A universal sense of desperation is at the origin of a proletarian class consciousness. The latter would crystallize around the repressed collective frustration of the proletarians, who suddenly become aware of their potential power as the new world-historical force of revolutionary change:

> a class is called forth, which has to bear all the burdens of society without enjoying its advantages, which, ousted from society, is forced into the most decided antagonisms to all other classes; a class which forms the majority of all members of society, and from which emanates the consciousness of the necessity of a fundamental revolution, the communist consciousness (94).

Class consciousness brings home the stark reality of the working-class condition and the necessity to overcome it collectively (85). Furthermore, this class consciousness is accompanied by a sense of universal mission as the alienating conditions prevailing in one industrialized country are equally shared by all workers, in all capitalist countries, irrespective of their nationality (55).

The historical necessity of a universal communist revolution

The communist consciousness of the proletariat is the expression of historical necessity as it is entrusted with the task of transforming society in such a way that both its immediate interests and long-term objectives are preserved, and at the same time furthered, through a new dialectical movement:

> Both for the production on a mass scale of this communist consciousness, and for the success of the cause itself, the alteration of men on a mass scale is, necessary [*sic*], an alteration which can only take place in a practical movement, a *revolution* (94–5).

The main theoretical thrust of the work is that beyond the obsolete German version of idealist 'consciousness' lies a new historical consciousness rising out of the proletariat: 'Communism is for us not a state of affairs which is to be established, an ideal to which reality [will] have to adjust itself. We call communism the real movement which abolishes the present state of things' (56–7).

Marx and Engels firmly dissociate themselves from social reformers such as the 'true socialists' and their belief in an abstract, classless morality, and from the 'Utopian socialists', who failed to take into account the historical and material conditions necessary for the success of a radical social change. With *The German Ideology*, it was as if, with the benefit of hindsight, both Marx and Engels already contemplated the advent of the communist society as an unstoppable, inexorable, historical event.

A revolutionary proletarian force without a party

However, the proletariat referred to in the text is not yet organized into a revolutionary party, and its anticipated victory over the bourgeoisie seems to be the opportunistic consequence of spontaneous uprising rather than the fruit of well-planned revolutionary tactics. There is no appeal to insurrection in *The German Ideology* but what is presented, instead, are the conclusions of two historical materialists confident in the veracity of their dialectic method of analysis as opposed to the 'idealistic humbug' entertained by their German contemporaries: 'not criticism but revolution is the driving force of history, also of religion, of philosophy and all other types of theory' (59). The actual call to revolutionary action only came three years later with the publication of *The Manifesto of the Communist Party*, published in the very year (1848) that all revolutionary hopes were crushed across Europe.

Communism, the abolition of alienation and the recovery of personal freedom

If the division of labour is repeatedly condemned as the direct cause of alienation, the ultimate end of the communist revolution is, within the context of *The German Ideology*, the recovery of truly individual relations after a long period of social intercourse perverted by bourgeois exploitation and the pursuit of profit. Time and time again in their work, Marx and Engels insist upon the necessity to destroy the very forces that impede the natural development of *individuality*.

Capitalism has so successfully atomized the proletariat that its members have lost all control over their own lives. Since no social or political organization represents their interests, the only resort left to them is to 'overthrow the state' (85). Before the rise of a communist class consciousness, ignited by 'the necessity of a fundamental revolution', the proletariat participates in productive and social relations 'not as individuals but as members of a class', a class which, of course, has not yet reached any level of self-consciousness nor, for that matter, political consciousness.

In the communist society, on the other hand, individuals have regained full control of and responsibility for 'the conditions of [their] free development' (85). The overthrow of the bourgeois state is among the first revolutionary imperatives incumbent upon the revolutionary proletariat, along with the abolition of the division of labour (53, 85). With both these political and economic instruments of oppression out of the way, a genuine community of free individuals can come to life, for the first time in human history: 'Only in community [with others has each] individual the means of cultivating his gifts in all directions; only in the community, therefore, is personal freedom possible. . . . In a real community the individuals obtain their freedom in and through their association' (83).

Objections

Despite Marx and Engels's conviction that all the necessary conditions for a universal communist revolution were met in their day, such an historical development did not take place in their lifetime. If it was the case that historical materialism met the strict criteria applied to natural sciences, its fundamental laws would apply in any place and at any time, just like Newton's law of gravity. They pinned all their hopes on one and only one possible historical development, viz. the end of the class society through revolutionary action. In the pursuit of communism as 'the solution of the riddle of history', they would not even consider the growing success of democratic reform within capitalist England, through pressure groups like the enormously popular Chartist Movement or the Reform League campaigners of the 1860s.

Throwing in their lot with revolutionary socialism, Marx and Engels surprisingly refrained from clearly theorizing the political steps by which revolution would occur. During the revolution of 1848 in Germany, Marx in fact discouraged the working class from open rebellion when, for the first time in its history, it was showing clear signs of a revolutionary consciousness and was ready for action. For Marx, the inevitability of the communist revolution was something for the bourgeoisie to dread and for the proletariat to prepare for.

If the bourgeoisie was condemned to produce 'its own grave-diggers', which form of revolutionary violence was likely to be used against it? How would the communist revolution *actually* get ignited? By co-ordinated strikes? By spontaneous uprising? In which way would the proletariat seize power and take control of the state, in the first instance? These crucial questions were left unanswered by Marx and Engels. Lenin gave them a *practical* answer in a totally different historical context from the conditions prevailing in the industrial England studied by Marx and Engels.

KEY POINTS

- Marx and Engels argued that 'revolution is the driving force of history'.

- The communist revolution is only possible when the plight of the proletariat has become unbearable.

- Such a revolution is not possible without the 'communist consciousness' of the proletariat becoming aware of its historical role to liberate mankind from its economic and social alienation.

- This revolution is a 'world-historical' event as 'communism is only possible as the act of the dominant peoples [in terms of number], "all at once" and simultaneously'.

● However, the communist revolution did not happen in Marx and Engels's lifetimes, undermining the claim of historical materialism to 'scientific status'.

❓ QUIZ QUESTIONS

Outline Marx and Engels's account of the rise of a universal communist consciousness in the proletariat.

Explain Marx and Engels's theory of the division of labour and its role in producing a communist society.

❓ DISCUSSION QUESTION

Assess whether Marx and Engels were right to think that revolution is inevitable. (AQA, 3c, 2005, *25 marks*)

Liberation and positive freedom; the implicit 'ethic' of emancipation

Against 'the industrialists of philosophy' and 'the manufacturers of history', Marx and Engels are convinced that *real* liberation does not take place in sublimated 'consciousness' or idealized 'nature' but in 'the world of man' (61).

The concept of 'self-activity'

Human emancipation means, first and foremost, the end of alienated labour as experienced all around the world by the majority of individuals toiling under capitalism. It takes the form of new economic opportunities made available to each individual, thanks to the communal ownership of means of production. The positive freedom enjoyed by humanity under communism takes the form of what Marx and Engels call 'self-activity'. The latter is central to the transformation of an alienated mass of workers, dispossessed of the fruit of their labour, into autonomous individuals enjoying the recovery of their full humanity. Under capitalism, labour is 'the only possible but . . . negative form of self-activity' (93), to the extent that it has monopolized all individual energy and focused it towards the mass production of commodities. New labour relations are possible without the mediation of capitalist instruments of production or social relations marred by the division of labour (93).

The task of the communist society consists in:

1 re-apportioning the productive forces to individuals, following the abolition of private property, in order to 'turn them into free manifestations of their lives' (117); communism opens the realm of free self-activity as opposed to the former period of alienated labour; and

2 ensuring 'the necessary solidarity of the free development of all', as well as 'the universal character of the activity of individuals on the basis of the existing productive forces' (118).

Under communism, everyone will, at the same time, co-operate and be dependent on everybody else, in such a way that this total co-operation of all individuals will ensure the rounded development of each of them (55). This idea was later encapsulated in Marx's famous expression: 'To each according to his needs, from each according to his ability'.

The German Ideology offers a much-debated snapshot of what self-activity under communism will entail:

> [I]n communist society, where nobody has one exclusive sphere of activity but each can become accomplished in any branch he wishes, society regulates the general production and this makes it possible for me to do one thing today and another tomorrow, to hunt in the morning, fish in the afternoon, rear cattle in the evening, criticize [to indulge in literary criticism] after dinner, just as I have in mind, without ever becoming hunter, fisherman, herdsman or critic' (54).

The important aspect of free self-activity is not only the fact that it puts an end to imposed specialization but that it enables each individual to fully develop his talents and capacities (109).

Self-activity makes it possible for each individual to reach a level of self-expression and self-realization unknown to mankind before the advent of communism. When under big industry, workers were compelled to produce similar objects or commodities day in, day out, the same individuals, under communism, will take pride in the production of their *own* objects, reflecting their particular qualities as craftsmen. Self-activity is, therefore, the most precious aspect of personal freedom in the communist society.

It is important to note that the communist revolution does not lead to the extinction of productive activity, as both Marx and Engels have in mind the positive exploitation of the best mechanical aspects of capitalist production, but now put to the service of the communist society at large. By owning the means of production collectively and distributing productive tasks equally, communism will introduce a new conception of labour, based on voluntary co-operation. In this context, freedom can be attained only in and through the community. The degree of individuality encouraged under communism should not be mistaken for the type of wayward *individualism* defended by Max Stirner and satirized in lengthy passages of *The German Ideology*, though edited out in modern editions of the work.

The absence of a communist ethic

When it comes to the ethical aspect of communism, Marx and Engels keep their distance from moral philosophy, in the same way as they denounced the incomplete analyses and partisan conclusions of political economists. Their most significant moral comment appears in the passage in which they proclaim that the:

communists do not preach morality at all. . . . They do not put to people the moral demand: love one another [Feuerbach's injunction], do not be egoists [against Stirner's selfish stance], etc.; on the contrary, they are well aware that egoism, just as much as self-sacrifice, is in definite circumstances a necessary form of the self-assertion of individuals (104–5).

Marx and Engels refused to pose as bourgeois moralists. They believed that moral attitudes and principles are dictated by circumstances, and they accepted the fact that different circumstances demanded different forms of moral conduct. As long as society is founded on relations of exploitation, man is not free and therefore, morality as an imperative universal rule cannot apply universally. Harmonious social relations can only take place in a 'truly human society', but neither Marx nor Engels were prepared to prescribe a specific moral code to be followed by all members of a communist society.

The German Ideology stays clear of any direct appeal to ethical principles, in spite of its implicit moral condemnation of bourgeois society. Its dual purpose is the systematic demystification of false philosophical idols and the presentation of a materialist method of historical interpretation leading to the necessity of a communist revolution. The latter will free man from alienation and found a society of equals in which everyone will be able to fulfil his potential.

Objections

Marx and Engels do not claim that communist society establishes an idyllic utopia but, more prosaically, provides the best possible social conditions for human self-realization, under the form of fully accepted and fairly rewarded self-activity. However, we may note that *The German Ideology* fails to supply details about its actual implementation within the new communist organization of production. Second, we may object that communism succeeds at the price of a pacified, indistinguishable humanity, still attached to and defined by the notion of 'praxis' and 'production'. Marx and Engels continue to think in terms of 'materialist' conditions of existence in which private property may have been abolished but money has not totally disappeared. Furthermore, sociologists like Max Weber disagree with their claim that alienation was only a stage on the road to man's final emancipation, as individuals would suffer new forms of alienation under a highly regimented communist society.

● **KEY POINTS**

- The communist revolution sets itself the following tasks:
  - the abolition of the division of labour and private property;
  - the replacement of classes by a classless society;
  - the common reappropriation and share of the means of production by the communist society as a whole; and

- the opportunity for each individual to fulfil his or her potential, through 'self-activity'.

● With all these conditions satisfied, Marx and Engels claim, the communist revolution will inaugurate the era of 'a truly human society'.

● Communism makes no specific moral demands on individuals.

● However, we may object that they provide no details regarding the new means of production; and that communism produces not individuals, but indistinguishable humanity.

❓ QUIZ QUESTIONS

Outline the concept of 'self-activity'.

Explain the twofold task of the communist society.

Briefly explain Marx and Engels's meaning of 'individuality'.

Explain Marx and Engels's refusal to 'preach morality'.

❓ DISCUSSION QUESTION

Critically assess Marx and Engels's claim that the communist society will give rise to 'a truly human society'.

The scientific status of Marx's account

When assessing the scientific value of an early work, such as *The German Ideology*, we should not be prejudiced by the ensuing developments of Marx's thought nor its gradual transformation into various political movements and ideological trends. Because of its messianic role in twentieth-century history as the harbinger of a new type of humanity, Marx's thought tends to be judged in the light of the millions of victims sacrificed on the altar of Soviet and Chinese communism. Marx and Engels would have been just as horrified as we are today, by the crimes committed in the name of a murderous communist ideology which neither of them ever purported to create in the first place. Engels reported Marx exclaiming 'All I know is that I am not a Marxist!', about the distorted reception of his ideas in some European communist quarters. He also vigorously denied that he had given the world 'a historic–philosophic theory of the general path that every people is fated to tread'. However, his open-ended philosophy of history was not only to be transformed into an inflexible orthodoxy but be revered as the only possible and unsurpassable 'science of man' by communist leaders like Lenin, Stalin and Mao Tse-tung.

Engels's Marxism

A puzzling and unresolved aspect of Marx's legacy is the part played by Engels in editing, finishing or bringing up to date theoretical writings unintended for publication. Engels popularized Marxist thought but, in some cases, he also simplified it or changed it to suit his own version of the 'doctrine'. Paul Thomas argues that 'from the very beginning, Engels's Marxism – and it was Engels who "brought Marxism into existence" – had an improperly scientific aspect at variance with what we can now identify as Marx's approach, method, and subject matter'. It was Engels who drew a scientific parallel between Marx's laws of historical materialism and Darwin's law of natural selection and theory of evolution. Engels 'departed from Marx in claiming that he had found a historical law in accord, in some ultimate causal sense, with all events'. Moreover, 'by interpreting "material life" [Marx's phrase] to imply the materialism of the physical sciences, Engels glossed Marx's view of individuals and their *material* productive activity out of all recognition'.

As early practitioners of social science, Marx and Engels shared the widely held nineteenth-century conviction that human events fell under universal laws. In this respect, they were far more influenced by their Victorian intellectual way of thinking than they thought. As materialist thinkers, both men strongly believed in the emancipating character of science which unfolded the secrets of nature and enabled mankind to master and exploit its forces. After Marx's death, Engels attempted to build a bridge between historical materialism and natural science, but his *Dialectics of Nature* was never completed.

Objections

There is, therefore, a question as to how *scientific* Marx believed historical materialism to be, i.e. whether he thought that 'history is governed by necessary laws that are as immutable as natural laws'. As quoted above, he denied that he had provided a theory that determined future events; and he argued that 'men make their own history', though under circumstances determined by the past. However, many philosophers, including Karl Popper in his book *The Open Society and its Enemies*, have interpreted historical materialism to be claiming scientific status. Popper rejects this claim, arguing that the alleged scientific credentials of historical materialism are falsely derived from its deterministic claim that capitalism is doomed and that nothing can be done to prevent its final collapse. This prediction seems false (see below), and Marxism can react in two ways:

1 it can accept that it has not discovered the true scientific laws of history; or
2 it argues its laws are true, but the initial conditions have altered.

Popper rejects both. Against (2), he argues that to be scientific, a theory must be *falsifiable*, i.e. it must be possible that some evidence, in this case historical events, *could* refute it. This is the only way to test scientific laws. If a theory doesn't admit it is wrong, but just changes itself in light of new events, then it is not scientific. Against (1), he argues that not only did Marxism not discover the *true* scientific laws of history, but that we have no reason to think there are *any* genuinely *scientific* laws of history. History is simply not determined in this way.

The scientific status attached to historical materialism and its interpretation of nature – the idea that Marx and Engels discovered genuine *laws* of history that controlled the inevitable unfolding of events – cannot be defended convincingly. It appears obvious, while surveying the history of Western capitalism over the past century, that Marx and Engels's predictions have been disproved by historical facts. Since their death, capitalism has not only survived two world wars and many conjectural economic crises, but its philosophy of free enterprise has become the only 'world ideology', after the dissolution of the Soviet Union in 1991. The fact that Marx and Engels's determinist prediction has not come true may be due to their total reliance on their analysis of the critical situation of capitalism, which they were convinced was riddled with 'inner contradictions'. However, the economic 'base' and cultural 'superstructure' of capitalist society have changed in a way that both the founders of historical materialism could have never predicted.

What they regarded as the historical necessity of the collapse of capitalist society has to be reviewed in the light of the following evidence:

1 Capitalism is fully capable of successfully transcending its periodic inner crises.
2 Revolutions do not necessarily break out in the most developed countries, i.e. Cuba or Vietnam.
3 Modern factory workers (Marx's 'communist proletariat') earn wages which, comparatively, keep them well above the threshold of subsistence of Victorian times.
4 Advanced capitalism, in Western developed countries, is no longer an exploitative system as workers are invited to have a stake in their companies through shareholding.
5 Far from wanting to destroy capitalism, workers (and their families) willingly contribute to its prosperity, through their producing and consuming activities. They view their own private interests corresponding to the interests of a system of production which enables them to buy commodities at very low prices.
6 The economic revolution brought about by information technology has radically transformed the traditional notion of labour as the manufacturing of material goods into the production of immaterial ones, available on the ever expanding virtual world market (the e-economy).
7 The state, seen in *The German Ideology* as the protector of the bourgeoisie's interests, has not disappeared but has been through two momentous transformations. First, the capitalist state became an instrument of social justice when it assumed an unexpected *welfare* role, after the Second World War. With the triumph of the liberal economy, the state has lost all its powers of economic regulations but remains capable of imposing legislation defining the extent and limits of civil liberties.

● KEY POINTS

- The scientific status of Marxist thought is based on the discoveries of historical materialism, regarding the inevitable culmination of human history into the communist society.

- Engels was responsible for turning Marx's thought into the doctrine known as 'Marxism'.

- Karl Popper disputed Marx and Engels's claim that historical materialism has scientific status.

- The actual development of advanced capitalist society has cast serious doubts on Marx and Engels's view of historical change as scientifically inevitable.

❓ QUIZ QUESTION

Describe three aspects of advanced capitalism which contradict Marx and Engels's predictions.

❓ DISCUSSION QUESTION

Critically assess the scientific status of Marx and Engels's account.

7

Sartre's *Existentialism and Humanism*

UNIT 3   Jean-Marc Pascal

Quotations and page references are from the AQA recommended edition of Mairet's translation (Methuen, ISBN 0-140-44914-0).

The claim that existence precedes essence with illustrative example

The foundational principle of Sartre's existentialism is that 'existence precedes essence', meaning that, in the beginning, man is 'nothing' but a being thrown into the world by accident: 'He will not be anything until later, and then he will be what he makes of himself' (28). There is no divine plan behind the existence of man on Earth and, in the absence of God, the very concept of human nature is redundant as it has lost all meaning. Instead, man 'is what he wills' and Sartre describes this total freedom of the individual, which he calls 'subjectivity', 'the first principle of existentialism' (28).

Sartre rejects the notion of 'essence' for two reasons:

- it implies the existence of God, as divine artisan; and
- it reduces all individual experiences to a common denominator called 'human nature'.

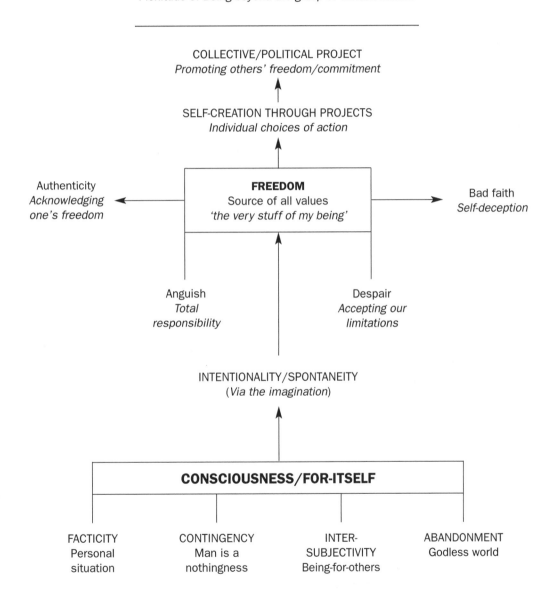

SARTREAN EXISTENTIALISM

INACCESSIBLE BEING-IN-ITSELF
Plenitude of Being beyond the grasp of consciousness

COLLECTIVE/POLITICAL PROJECT
Promoting others' freedom/commitment

SELF-CREATION THROUGH PROJECTS
Individual choices of action

Authenticity
*Acknowledging
one's freedom*

FREEDOM
Source of all values
'the very stuff of my being'

Bad faith
Self-deception

Anguish
*Total
responsibility*

Despair
*Accepting our
limitations*

INTENTIONALITY/SPONTANEITY
(*Via the imagination*)

CONSCIOUSNESS/FOR-ITSELF

FACTICITY
Personal
situation

CONTINGENCY
Man is a
nothingness

INTER-
SUBJECTIVITY
Being-for-others

ABANDONMENT
Godless world

There is, for Sartre, nothing but the world of human reality in which individuals cannot be defined in advance but can freely choose to be whoever they want to be. Therefore, as there is no God to have a conception of what human nature may be like, we all fashion our own selves, in our own way (28).

The example of the paper-knife

If, for the sake of argument, we accept the idea of human life as created by an artisan, we can say that 'production precedes existence' (27). To illustrate the unique character of human existence, Sartre uses the example of a paper-knife, although he could have chosen any type of manufactured article. The maker of a paper-knife must know, beforehand, what purpose that object is eventually going to serve. But this cannot be the case with man, who is not comparable to a manufactured object with a fixed purpose or essence, since he is his *own* designer. If we were all identical robots or perfect clones we would, indeed, fit such an essentialist (from 'essence') description of mankind. We would all be similar to Adam, the first man, just like all paper-knives are modelled after the same original paper-knife, designed with no other purpose but the one assigned to it by its maker. However, man escapes all possible definition as he cannot be labelled before his personal existence (his conscious active life) has actually begun. Consequently, the idea of an unchanging human nature, or essence, applicable to all human beings at all times, is nothing but an illusion, perpetuated, claims Sartre, by the supporters of determinism who wish to limit man's freedom for their own religious or political reasons.

The existentialist interpretation of essence

It would be wrong to assume that if 'existence precedes essence', man necessarily acquires some kind of 'essence' at the end of his 'existence'. Sartre does not imply, in any way, that we somehow acquire an 'essence' either by consciously achieving a lifelong project, such as becoming the chairman of a company, or by gaining a posthumous reputation as a 'good' friend or a 'dangerous' criminal. Essence remains, by definition, beyond the reach of human consciousness, despite its constant efforts to transcend itself. Man defines himself through his actions or 'projects' (see SUBJECTIVISM AND THE *COGITO*, p. 297). However, in death, our lives fall into the public domain and we leave to others the satisfaction of judging us for what we 'were' or 'weren't'. Only the living can defend themselves from the judgement of their peers.

Objections

When Sartre mentions 'a human universality of condition' (46) (see SARTRE'S USE OF UNIVERSALIZATION, p. 317), he is, unwittingly, very close to presenting a traditional definition of human nature. Isn't sharing the same fundamental freedom a common human essence? Sartre would argue not. If considered from the end of our life, our essence is nothing more than what we have made of our freedom through our successive projects. But man's inherent spontaneity and capacity for reinvention cannot be crystallized into a pure, immutable state. Man is never in a position to reach a semblance of 'essence' as freedom cannot, by definition, be confined to specific limits or find its ultimate realization in one final project, such as the advent of a communist society. Sartre was well aware of the contradictions between his open definition of ontological (or inherent) freedom and the expected constraints of political freedom set by Marxist thinkers (see THE CRITICISMS LAID AGAINST EXISTENTIALISM, p. 315).

Sartre's notion of 'essence' remains contentious as he claims that, for man to possess an 'essence' would necessarily imply an external agency, namely God. At the same time, he assumes that whatever constitutes the natural world, such as trees, surges into existence, already endowed with a ready-made essence (see SUBJECTIVISM AND THE COGITO, p. 298). But why should man be so different from other natural beings? For example, they equally have a genetic code.

KEY POINTS

- Sartre claims human beings are not God's creation; they are not predetermined by some human essence.

- There is no universal idea of man. There are only individuals thrown into existence.

- If there is no human essence preceding my existence, I am free to make my own essence, that is, to 'create' myself through my free choices.

- Existentialist 'essence' is man's elusive attempt to transcend himself through his projects. However, man never 'catches up' with his elusive ambition to fully realize himself. Man's 'essence' is nothing more and nothing less than the sum total of all his actions.

❓ QUIZ QUESTIONS

Explain what Sartre means by 'essence', and why he claims there is no human essence.

Briefly explain the significance of the paper-knife in Sartre's argument.

❓ DISCUSSION QUESTION

Critically discuss Sartre's claim that man's existence is not determined by an essence.

The nature of human reality in contrast with that of material objects

In contrasting the open nature of human reality with the restricted purpose of a manufactured object, Sartre attacks the view that 'Man is determined', either by social forces beyond his control, as in Marxism, or by a divine plan which limits the extent of his freedom, as asserted by Christianity. For Christians, when God created or brought into existence mankind, he already had in mind the kind of creature that man was going to be, in other words, its human nature or essence (27).

The example of the paper-knife is meant to be an easily understandable illustration of why Sartre rejects any preconception of human nature. In Sartre's play *The Flies*, Zeus, the supreme God of Greek mythology, tells Orestes that he created him free so that he might serve him. Orestes immediately retorts that, once he had been created free, he no longer belonged to his creator but was an independent creature, able to defy Zeus if he so wished. Unlike Orestes, no paper-knife could rebel against its maker by appealing to its inherent freedom! As all human beings share the same fundamental freedom, it makes, after all, no difference whether God is ultimately responsible for it or not.

Sartre sees in the universal *conception of man* entertained by the philosophers of the Enlightenment a parallel with 'the conception of man in the mind of God' (27). Eighteenth-century philosophers were critical rationalists, determined to implement the ideas extolled by *classical humanism*. It is largely thanks to this European movement that both the American and the French Revolution could proclaim the inalienable rights of mankind to life, liberty and the pursuit of happiness. These rights were regarded as innate attributes of human beings, irrespective of their racial origins or social background. Kant, who epitomized the democratic spirit of the Enlightenment, strongly believed in the notion of 'human nature', whose universal characteristics could be found in the most innocent primitive man as well as in the most refined member of a philosophical *salon*. Such a claim, despite its democratic implications, is questioned by Sartre as it implies that, for Kant, 'the essence of man precedes that historic existence which we confront in experience' (27). Sartre's point is that nobody is in a position to reduce to one universal category all sorts of distinct individual experiences.

While Sartre is very critical of classical humanism, in THE *RESPONSES (TO CRITICISM)* (p. 320), we will see that he argues that existentialism is itself a (very different) kind of humanism.

Going further: classical humanism and existentialism

Although the meaning of the word 'humanism' has evolved considerably from its Renaissance origins in fourteenth-century Italy to its modern secular forms, it always implies a deep reverence for the worth and dignity of man as the centre of a system of universal moral values. Man is portrayed as the measure of all things, as illustrated by Leonardo Da Vinci's drawing of the Vitruvian man, whose body fits perfectly into a circle and square. That highly symbolic image encapsulates the idea of a perfect creature, Man, set in a perfect cosmic order, God's Creation. Such works of art proclaim that man's essence precedes his existence and that his earthly life and actions are the predictable consequences of divine craftsmanship. Man seems reduced to nothing more than a divine artefact.

Classical humanism is, therefore, a theory which predetermines what humans, as a species, are capable of achieving, as illustrated in Cocteau's character exclaiming: 'because he is flying over mountains in an aeroplane, "Man is magnificent!"' (54). It defines human nature for once and for all, which is absurd since it is inadmissible that 'a man should pronounce judgement upon Man' (55).

The epitome of human self-gratification is to be found in the nineteenth-century French thinker Auguste Comte who announced the inevitable triumph of man in the positive Age of Science. Positivism freezes human history into predetermined periods through which mankind is meant to evolve towards its predictable self-realization. Sartre argued that Comte's conception of man was inflexible and that his views on the future scientific achievements of mankind were dangerous, as this 'cult of humanity . . . shut-in upon itself . . . ends in Fascism' (55).

Works of literature can also be influenced by their own form of determinism. Naturalist writers, under the influence of Emile Zola, reflected upon the impossibility of freeing oneself from one's genetic heritage and social environment (42).

The ontological foundations of existentialism: Being-in-Itself and Being-for-Itself

In *Being and Nothingness*, Sartre analyses the reality (or phenomenon) of Being. He distinguishes between two types of Being:

1 *Being-in-Itself:* A non-conscious material or natural entity which can be said to have an essence, such as a paper-knife or chestnut tree. Determined by their essence, Beings-in-Themselves simply exist without having to justify their existence.
2 *Being-for-Itself and its power of 'negation':* man is that conscious being, deprived of an essence but fully aware of the contingent or superfluous character of its existence, its 'nothingness'. Paradoxically, it is through his consciousness of 'nothingness' that man is capable of transcending his original situation as he can 'negate' his present situation and project himself into a different future and a different situation: a gambler may decide no longer to play cards or an alcoholic suddenly resolve to become a teetotaller. By being able to step out of our current situation, through our imagination, we are giving ourselves the power to change ourselves and avoid any categorization (see SUBJECTIVISM AND THE COGITO, p. 297).

Although this power of 'negation' is not developed in *Existentialism and Humanism*, it nonetheless underpins the positive philosophy of action defended in the lecture. As a free consciousness, and nothing else, man can 'reinvent himself', at any time, without feeling any binding attachment to his past. Consequently, man can be defined as that being who is forever in the process of inventing and reinventing himself but never achieving the self-fulfilment and plenitude of a Being-in-Itself, which has an essence.

Objections

Sartre seems to contradict himself by rejecting the fundamental principle of humanism, viz. 'man is at the centre of everything', while claiming that existentialism is, after all, a type of humanism. Second, his discussion of classical humanism shows that one can defend a human nature theory without bringing God into the equation. Third, his admission that all human beings share in a 'universal human condition' shows his difficulty in describing 'existentialist man' purely in terms of sheer spontaneity and inherent freedom.

● **KEY POINTS**

- Material objects, such as a paper-knife, are created for a specific purpose, which characterizes their fixed essence. By contrast, man has no fixed essence as he creates himself in a world of unlimited possible choices.

- Classical humanism claims that what man is capable of achieving is predetermined by his nature. In Comte's positivism, Sartre argues, this becomes a dangerous cult of humanity.

- Literature can also exhibit an idea of predetermination. Zola's naturalist novels portray characters trapped in their social environment.

- Being-in-Itself is the type of being of material objects, with an essence. But it is also the inaccessible ideal of consciousness, striving to justify its contingent, unnecessary existence, through projects.

- Being-for-Itself is the inherent characteristic of human consciousness which makes it permanently condemned to rise out of itself, in order to define itself.

- Consciousness is endowed with a power of negation which enables it to imagine new situations and to reinvent itself, at any time.

❓ QUIZ QUESTIONS

Outline and illustrate **three** contrasts between human reality and material objects.

Explain why Sartre rejects classical humanism.

Explain the difference between the idea of universal liberty, promoted by eighteenth-century philosophers, and Sartre's conception of freedom.

❓ DISCUSSION QUESTION

Critically assess Sartre's claim that there is no human nature.

God and human nature; the rejection of determinism

Although Sartre proclaims himself an atheist, he is not bent on attacking Christian beliefs with theological arguments. He admits that his intuitive atheism is an unquestioned and unexamined postulate which is fundamental to his existentialist philosophy. He regards the non-existence of God as a simple fact which requires no further explanation. He later ascribed his non-believing attitude to a natural predisposition which came to light unexpectedly when, one day, while waiting for a bus to school, he said to himself: '"You know what? God doesn't exist." And that was that: faith left, and never came back. Actually, it was a full realization of something I had sensed earlier but never completely formulated.'

Sartre states that 'existentialism is nothing else but an attempt to draw the full conclusion from a consistently atheistic position' (56). However, there is no declared hostility towards theists as Sartre asserts that the existence of God would *make no difference* whatsoever to man's existence since 'what man needs is to find himself again and to understand that nothing can save him from himself' (56).

Sartre simply rejects the determinism associated with the existence of an all-powerful God, since, for him, man has no contact whatsoever with a world ruled by divine laws or dictated by divine imperatives. Nothing stands in the way of our freedom as we are born free and carry the responsibility for our freedom throughout our lives.

KEY POINTS

Essentialism	Existentialism
God	No God, no absolute definition of man
God creates man like an artisan creates material objects	Everyone creates themselves through their own projects
God creates human nature	Everyone creates their own values
Man is determined	Everyone is free

❓ QUIZ QUESTION

Outline the reasons for Sartre's rejection of determinism.

❓ DISCUSSION QUESTION

Assess Sartre's claim that the existence of God would make no difference to man's existence.

Subjectivism and the *cogito*

Sartre follows Descartes in regarding the proposition 'I think' (known as the *cogito*) as the first proposition of certainty. However, Sartre and Descartes have different reasons for putting the 'subject' at the centre of their philosophy.

Descartes is attempting to gain an objective knowledge of the external world from the certainty of his personal *cogito*. The existence of other minds remains highly problematical in Descartes's philosophy, to the point that he was accused of 'solipsism', i.e. of denying the existence of any other reality apart from his own subjective one. Sartre's conception of consciousness, by contrast, is of a consciousness that is, at all times, engaged in an external world rather than looking back on itself in the process of self-reflection described by Descartes. Sartre understands the *cogito* in relation to the ability for consciousness to gain a changing perception of its own unique subjectivity through 'INTERSUBJECTIVITY' (p. 303), that is the realization that there exist other subjectivities. By making the existence of others part of individual consciousness, the Sartrean *cogito* dispels any potential accusation of solipsism, i.e. the total isolation of the self, reduced to interpreting the outside world through its own representations.

Furthermore, Descartes's *cogito* is discovered through a systematic process of doubt (see Ch. 5, THE WAVES OF DOUBT, p. 224, and ABSOLUTE CERTAINTY OF THE *COGITO*, p. 227), leading to the conclusion that it is the very keystone of epistemological enquiry. Sartre, by contrast, simply affirms that human subjectivity is the only absolute truth, 'easily attained and within the reach of everybody; it consists in one's immediate sense of oneself' (44).

Sartre understands consciousness in relation to the *cogito*, subjectivity, intersubjectivity, imagination and the will as follows:

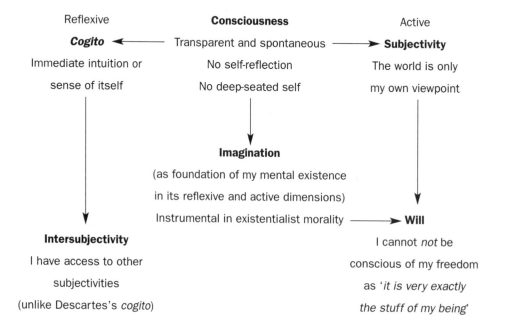

Going further: imagination and consciousness

Despite two long essays dedicated to the subject in the 1930s, Sartre does not mention in *Existentialism and Humanism*, the central role played by the imagination in the realization of the freedom of consciousness. However, understanding this role illuminates Sartre's theory:

● It is the imagination which reveals the 'nothingness' of my consciousness and enables it to project itself into future situations, 'picturing' other possibilities lying ahead. For instance, my present efforts to pass my A Level philosophy examination are only motivated by the anticipated prospect of my future success. I can just picture myself receiving the good news!

● The imagination enables me to choose my attitudes towards my life choices but also towards other people: I am free, after all, to choose to use 'bad faith' (see AUTHENTICITY AND SELF-DECEPTION, p. 313) as an excuse for my personal failures. I know that if I fail the examination, I will blame my philosophy teacher even if, deep down, I know that I could have worked harder.

● The imagination also plays a vital part in my 'inventing' new values and turning morality into an ongoing creative process (see RELATION OF CHOICE TO VALUE, p. 305): I don't see why I couldn't achieve a good grade in philosophy. From now on, I am going to give my best shot in the subject!

Going further: consciousness as pure intentionality and project

Sartre's early works demonstrate his determination to found a philosophy of man based on a direct, concrete experience of the world. His discovery of Edmund Husserl's phenomenology revealed a new way of understanding human consciousness and its relation to the world. 'Phenomenology' is a philosophical method of enquiry which studies the 'phenomena' or psychological events taking place in the conscious mind, such as sensations and emotions. By 'putting the world into brackets' and only concentrating on the analysis of the contents of consciousness, Husserl was convinced that he could reach the true nature of reality.

The philosophical revolution introduced by phenomenology was to discard the traditional view that consciousness organizes knowledge from **sense-data**. Husserl described consciousness as 'projecting itself' into the world of phenomena. This idea of consciousness constantly 'projecting itself' into the world characterizes Husserl's concept of 'intentionality', viz. 'consciousness is always conscious of something other than itself'. Sartre believes, like Husserl, that we don't discover ourselves in some rare moments of deep introspection but, on the contrary, in the hustle and bustle of human activity when we interact with other people and feel our presence in the world through their presence.

This revelation that consciousness has no core, no inside space but is condemned to look for itself outside, in the world, is the essential condition of freedom, as there can be no freedom without the ability of consciousness to rise out of itself and transcend itself in a succession of freely and voluntarily chosen actions, called 'projects'. It is in and through his projects that man chooses himself.

Going further: contingency and facticity

In *Existentialism and Humanism*, Sartre explicitly refers to four aspects of consciousness as Being-for-Itself (see THE NATURE OF HUMAN REALITY IN CONTRAST WITH THAT OF MATERIAL OBJECTS, p. 293). In the lecture, they are referred to, as ABANDONMENT (p. 307), ANGUISH (p. 310), DESPAIR (p. 312) and INTERSUBJECTIVITY (p. 303). However, both 'contingency' and 'facticity' are worth considering as substantial parts of Sartre's existentialist thought. The notion of contingency highlights the unbridgeable gap between man (Being-for-Itself) as opposed to his natural environment (Being-in-Itself). Facticity adds a personal dimension to our universal contingency.

The phenomenological experience of contingency was a crucial idea in the philosophical development of Sartre's thought. The contrast between the self-sufficient Being-in-Itself and the incomplete Being-for-Itself is best illustrated in the enlightening experience of Roquentin, the narrator of *Nausea*, while he stares at the roots of a chestnut tree, in the local park. Confronted with the black mass of the tree, the existentialist hero suddenly discovers the gratuitous character of all existence. This feeling of alienation is the realization that nothing has meaning until consciousness leaves its mark on the world, through its projects.

While contingency simply refers to my ontological status, that is, my being alive here and now, 'without rhyme or reason, necessity or justification', facticity is about the actual circumstances of my existence, such as my gender, my family background, the social and political contexts in which I find myself at birth. My for-itself, that is, the consciousness of my being, appears in a condition which it has not chosen.

With 'facticity', Sartre implies that the unchangeable bare 'facts' of my personal existence should never constitute an obstacle to my projects as I can always turn them to my advantage. However, are we always free to become what we want to be, against the will or prejudice of others? For instance, is it realistically possible to free oneself from any given social or cultural background, without experiencing open discrimination or even, among some sectarian communities, abuse and violence?

● Descartes's *cogito*, which defines his notion of consciousness, is discovered through a rational process of doubt. Sartre's *subjectivity* is immediately aware of itself through its perception of external objects.

● The imagination enables consciousness to reveal its 'nothingness' and, as pure intentionality, to project itself into future situations (or 'projects').

● There can be no freedom without the ability of consciousness to rise out of itself.

● Contingency is the realization that all human existence is fundamentally non-essential and superfluous.

● Facticity is all the external circumstances which constitute the 'facts' of my own contingency, such as my place of birth, my gender or my family background.

❓ QUIZ QUESTIONS

Outline what Sartre means by 'subjectivity'. (AQA, 4b, 2004, *10 marks*)

Explain **two** similarities and **two** differences between Descartes's and Sartre's accounts of consciousness.

Explain how Sartre answers the problem of solipsism.

❓ DISCUSSION QUESTION

Critically assess the central importance of subjectivity in existentialism.

Freedom, choice and responsibility

The concepts of freedom, choice and responsibility are at the heart of Sartre's existentialism:

1 'Man first of all exists, encounters himself, surges up in the world – and defines itself afterwards' (28). The concept of human essence pictures man as necessarily unchanging; but man is irreducible to a simplistic, static classification since he is that being which, thrown into a Godless world, fits no category or definition. Man, in his original state, is 'nothing', insofar as he has no set goal or purpose laid out in front of him; all the possibilities of human development are still open to him.

2 'Man is nothing else but that which he makes himself' (28). Subjectivity is the cornerstone of Sartrean existentialism as man is his own master and no one but himself can decide his own future. It is *my* free choices which ultimately reflect the sort of person that I am and that I want to be.

3 'Man is, before all else, something which propels itself towards a future and is aware that it is doing so' (28). Man is constantly projecting himself into the future in a

desperate attempt to justify his existence. But what part of man is projecting itself into the future? Sartre writes that man is 'aware' of his self-projection and that the latter is the result of a 'conscious decision'. He is implicitly referring to 'consciousness' as the very expression of human subjectivity. It is because my consciousness is 'condemned' to interpret the world that it is consequently 'condemned' to make up its own 'values' (see ABANDONMENT, p. 307).

4   'Thus, the first effect of existentialism is that it puts every man in possession of himself as he is, and places the entire responsibility for his existence squarely upon his shoulders' (29). Since there is no **a priori** human nature, we are without excuse and nothing but the sum total of our actions. Our fundamental freedom necessarily implies our total responsibility for ourselves. Our nature or character cannot be blamed for the positive or negative outcome of our actions since Sartre did not believe in the existence of the 'unconscious' nor in any other psychological theory taking into account the importance of external influences on a person's behaviour.

This anticipates Sartre's defence of authenticity as the pre-condition of existentialist morals since the latter is only conceivable in a world where all moral agents take full responsibility for their actions (see AUTHENTICITY AND SELF-DECEPTION, p. 313). Sartre wrote elsewhere that 'Morality is only possible if everyone is moral'.

5   Furthermore, 'in choosing for himself he chooses for all men. For in effect, of all the actions a man may take in order to create himself as he wills to be, there is not one which is not creative, at the same time, of an image of man such as he believes he ought to be' (29). This passage contains two important ideas:
   • the creative aspect of morality, which is a direct consequence of the absence of absolute moral guidance, in the guise of Christian morality or some other form of humanist ethics;
   • the inevitable responsibility attached to my absolute freedom of choice, a responsibility which goes well beyond my personal actions since every one of them sends a signal to others as to my moral *inclinations*.

Universal responsibility

The expression 'an image of man' betrays Sartre's reluctance to lay too much emphasis on a possible Kantian interpretation of his existentialist ethics (see Ch. 2, OUR AWARENESS OF WHAT IS RIGHT AND OUR DUTY TO ACT RIGHTLY IS GIVEN BY REASON, p. 75). Sartre is close to admitting here that every decision of mine reflects, in some way, a particular model which I, implicitly, would like to see adopted by other moral agents. Although he argued that none of our personal choices could become, in any sense, prescriptive as far as another person's moral choices are concerned, he claims, first, that every action of mine indicates my personal commitment to a particular way or mode of being; and second, the image which we are fashioning for ourselves 'is valid for all and for the entire epoch in which we find ourselves' (29). So, taken together, 'my action is . . . a commitment on behalf of all mankind' (30). Sartre gives several examples such as the decision to join a communist trade union, or again, the decision to marry and have children. In both cases, by choosing one particular course of action, I commit myself to political activism or family life and family values.

Since I always, like it or not, *commit* myself to one ethical type of life against another, freedom of choice is never exercised in a random, gratuitous way. From his initial metaphysical description of man as 'nothing', Sartre has reached the radical ethical conclusion that 'in fashioning myself I fashion man'.

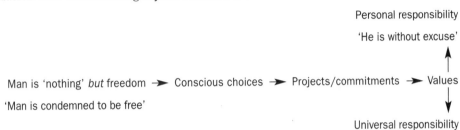

But why, we can object, should my *personal* values, derived from my *personal* choices, result in my *universal* responsibility? The answer lies in the fact noted above, that all human beings share the same condition as far as their existential experience is concerned. We are all free and each a personal contributor to the project of making man.

Going further: the different forms of responsibility

Sartre argues that there is no such thing as 'diminished responsibility' to the point that if I am conscripted to fight a war which I disapprove of, it becomes *my* war and I have no excuse whatsoever if I get killed in action or come home seriously wounded. There is always, in existentialism, the possibility to *choose* freedom, e.g. I can run away from my unit, thus showing my fellow-soldiers that desertion is one way of reacting to the present situation. 'In war time', Sartre remarked, 'there aren't innocent victims', and the only way of not becoming a willing or indirect accomplice to a conflict is to give one's life for the cause of peace. Sartre saw no justifiable alternative between complicity and martyrdom, short of living in 'bad faith' (see AUTHENTICITY AND SELF-DECEPTION, p. 313), as millions of French citizens chose to do between 1940 and 1945.

Surprisingly, Sartre steered clear of the post-war issue of *collective responsibility*, when he could have easily pointed an accusing finger at French collaborators as well as Hitler's Nazi followers. Existentialism is concerned primarily with individual responsibility, and we will see how difficult it is for existentialists to pass moral judgement on other people's actions (see THE POSSIBILITY OF MORAL CRITICISM, p. 319). However, when it came to politics, Sartre was prepared, in the name of universal freedom, to side with the victims of political oppression, whether in the form of

French colonial rule, Soviet repression in Hungary and Czechoslovakia or American military involvement in Vietnam.

Sartre does not make any exception for situations in which I may not be able to exercise my freedom at all, as in the case of addictions such as alcohol or cigarettes or when handing over my wallet to someone threatening me with a knife. To what extent can I be held 'completely responsible' for actions beyond my control? Sartre argues I am always totally responsible for *my present* situation.

Objections

Because of the moral isolation of existentialist agents, individual responsibility takes a very abstract dimension as it appears detached from the judgement or care of any moral community. Absolute responsibility is, for Sartre, the natural consequence of absolute freedom, but no moral guidance is given as to the actual management of that freedom, except the general injunction that every one of us is 'a legislator deciding for the whole of mankind'. Yet, if I have no allegiance to anyone or any group, how am I going to feel any moral obligation to the rest of mankind, when choosing to rob a bank or, instead, giving money to a beggar?

Furthermore, can everyone be expected to carry the burden of 'universal responsibility', and *at all times*? Sartre denies the power of emotions but are we always, as he assumes, masters of our psychological states, and can everyone be deemed *equally* capable of making rational, selfless decisions? In the absence of clear moral goals, existentialist morality seems to impose unspecified and unrealistic demands upon individuals. The proof of existentialist morality lies in the very moment of free decision-making; but then isn't man condemned to create his own values in a moral vacuum? (See THE POSSIBILITY OF MORAL CRITICISM, p. 319, for further discussion.)

KEY POINTS

- Man is absolutely free and, at the same time, absolutely responsible for his choices.

- We are without excuse as we are the sum total of our actions.

- By choosing for myself, I am choosing for mankind as I always commit myself and point to a particular ethical type of life.

❓ QUIZ QUESTIONS

Briefly explain how an individual becomes responsible for the whole of mankind.

Explain Sartre's claim 'in fashioning myself I fashion man'.

Outline Sartre's response to the objection that existentialist morality is prescriptive.

❓ DISCUSSION QUESTION

Critically discuss Sartre's claim that we are completely responsible for our actions. (AQA, 4c, 2004, *25 marks*)

Intersubjectivity

Between the concept of 'subjectivity', which affirms the absolute freedom of the individual, and a universal 'objectivity' of human nature, explicitly rejected by Sartre, lies 'intersubjectivity' or the world of human relations. Other people are as much part of my consciousness as I am part of them.

For Sartre, the Other is encountered at three different levels:

1 *The psychological level*, when I become aware of the existence of another consciousness as ultimately constitutive of my own identity. It is, indeed, through the 'mediation' of the Other that I am able to know and understand myself (45).
2 *The social level*, when I realize that the extent of my freedom is dependent upon the Other's freedom as much as the extent of his freedom is dependent upon mine (52).
3 *The political level* is the ultimate level of intersubjectivity, as we all share a mutual interest in bringing about a society promoting the freedom of all human beings. This is the far-reaching implication of the comment 'I cannot make liberty my aim unless I make that of others equally mine' (52). Only a common political project can counteract potentially conflicting individual projects and merge them, instead, into a single, transcending one.

Sartre never reached total satisfaction with his various treatments of human relations and his life ambition to lay the foundations of a viable existentialist ethics. There is no doubt that *Existentialism and Humanism* shows an unusually optimistic interpretation of 'intersubjectivity', a more accessible and more friendly term than the technical 'Being-for-Others' Sartre uses elsewhere. However, difficulties appear as soon as a free consciousness is confronted with an equally free consciousness, as each-for-itself is an object of consciousness (an in-itself) for another.

Going further: *In Camera* or the limits of intersubjectivity

In Sartre's play *In Camera*, the three characters, one man and two women, find themselves together in a hotel room, first unable to explain what appears to be an unfortunate misunderstanding. They have never met before but they soon decide to make the best of their predicament and accept the quiet presence of each other for the time being. Inevitably, none of the three characters can remain silent and each one of them, in turn, confesses their truth to the other two. Estelle, the seductive, innocent young woman actually killed her child to keep secret her love affair to her husband. Ines, a lesbian post-office clerk, drove her lover to suicide, out of jealousy. Finally, Garcin, the successful Brazilian journalist who allegedly gave his life for his country proves to be nothing but a coward, as he recounts to the other characters in the play how, in his former life, he was executed for desertion. During the painful exchanges that follow, one of the characters exclaims 'Hell is other people', meaning that, whatever we do, we are always subjected to other people's judgement.

The play was wrongly remembered for its memorable catch-phrase. For this reason, Sartre was determined to give a far more positive interpretation of intersubjectivity as the interdependency of human freedom in *Existentialism and Humanism* than in *Being and Nothingness*, where he discusses our problematic relations with others through attitudes like desire, love, indifference or hate.

Objections

Sartre is at pains to prove that the freedom of others is not only constitutive of my own free subjectivity but also that I must value others' freedom as much as my own. However, given the isolation of every consciousness when faced with its own moral dilemmas, the expectation of mutual respect and co-operation between individuals appears more like a matter of desirable practical necessity rather than the result of a natural empathy for one's fellow-beings. In his plays, Sartre exposes the difficulties of treating others as anything but obstacles to one's freedom or excuses for one's bad faith.

● **KEY POINTS**

- Intersubjectivity is the world in which individuals (subjectivities) interact.

- Sartre argues that 'the other is indispensable to my existence' and that others are as much dependent upon me as I am of them.

- Having elsewhere emphasized the tensions between two consciousnesses confronting each other, in *Existentialism and Humanism*, Sartre argues that individual freedom cannot flourish without mutual support and co-operation.

❓ QUIZ QUESTIONS

Outline Sartre's argument for the importance of other people to our existence.

Briefly explain and illustrate the **three** types of situations where intersubjectivity takes place.

DISCUSSION QUESTION

Critically discuss Sartre's difficulties in reconciling the pursuit of personal freedom with the respect due to other people's freedom.

Relation of choice to value

The relation of choice to value is central to existentialist ethics. Sartre argues that we come into a meaningless world, devoid of moral values and that it is our freedom alone which is able *and* compelled to forge its own values in *action*. Values are not predetermined, ideal notions informing or determining my choices. There is no moral foundation to human freedom and the potential 'moral' value attached to my actions does not derive from their corresponding to an ideal definition of morality. It is only in the exercise of his free choices that man brings values into the world. In the absence of God, 'there must be somebody to invent values' (54). Sartre comments in *Being and Nothingness* that man is never compelled to adopt one particular value as opposed to another, since *his* freedom remains, at all times, 'the unique foundation of values'. But existentialist values cannot lie dormant as passive good intentions; they can come to light only in my choice of action.

The basis of judging actions is, therefore, not on the so-called 'moral quality' of a given action but the possibility for that type of action to be taken up by other people as an inspiring 'image of man'. This again raises the issue of universal responsibility, and the 'double aspect' of existentialist *subjectivism*: 'When we say that man chooses himself, we do mean that every one of us must choose himself; but by that we also mean that in choosing for himself he chooses for all men' (29). I am never acting on my behalf but always as 'a legislator deciding for the whole of humanity' (30).

Two examples of the subjectivity of moral values

The two literary examples chosen by Sartre to illustrate the subjectivity of moral values confirm both the importance of acting 'in the name of freedom' and with a sincere, authentic adherence to one's commitment. Analysing the motivations behind both heroines' actions, it appears that, despite their clearly opposed moralities, each woman exercises her freedom with the maximum degree of responsibility.

Maggie Tulliver may appear to be a romantic person, driven by her romantic passion, but, in truth, she acts in the only selfless way she knows and is happy to embrace. La Sanseverina, for her part, could be seen as a callous schemer who uses passion to serve her own ends, but she is simply acting according to her own interpretation of freedom. For Sartre, both women are conscious of their respective situation and determined to exert their freedom in the most authentic way. Both moralities are chosen on the plane of free commitment.

Maggie Tulliver (George Eliot)	La Sanseverina (Stendhal)
Acting in good faith	Acting in good faith
Feels passion for Stephen, who is engaged	Rates 'passion' as the highest value
Chooses to sacrifice her freedom in the name of human solidarity	Prepared to sacrifice others in the name of her own freedom
'in both cases the overruling aim is freedom'	

Going further: the artistic dimension of existentialist morality

Sartre draws a parallel between art and morality, remarking that 'in both we have to do with creation and invention. We cannot decide *a priori* what it is that should be done' (49). There is no place in existentialist ethics for a Kantian faculty of practical reason, weighing the pros and cons of a decision in the light of a universal law of morality, such as the 'categorical imperative' (see Ch. 2, OUR AWARENESS OF WHAT IS RIGHT AND OUR DUTY TO ACT RIGHTLY IS GIVEN BY REASON, p. 75). Since there aren't any pre-established objective rules of morality, every new situation is to be approached not unlike a work of art, with a certain degree of imagination and inventiveness. The comparison applies only to an artist prepared to use his creative power and who refuses to be restricted or influenced by prevailing aesthetic principles. In the face of a new situation, each new decision to be taken presents itself like yet another blank canvas.

Like new shapes and colours gradually appearing on the canvas, new values are fashioned by man in the midst of action, without his feeling constrained by some **a priori** conception of what is received as *aesthetically* acceptable or not. Thus, existentialist morality shares with art the same degree of freedom and, for this very reason, Sartre refuses to bring existentialist morality under any kind of 'aesthetic' judgement. Furthermore, the personal freedom expressed in a work of art, just as in any given action, is never accidental as its coherence will eventually appear 'in the relation between the will to create and the finished work' (49).

Objections

If Sartre is right, acting 'in the name of freedom' is the only option open to man, but we may object that decisions can be morally *wrong* or *ill-advised*, in spite of their being taken in good faith and in total liberty. The artistic dimension of existentialist morality highlights the difficulties of a philosophy which, short of a moral agenda, resorts to analogies outside the moral realm. How would a young mother contemplating abortion react to the suggestion that she should act like an artist in front of a blank canvas?

Sartre leaves final moral decisions to the individual himself, in the hope that, fully aware of his universal responsibility, he will choose the best possible course of action (29). Yet, it could be argued that, choosing what is best for mankind is a virtually impossible task as no one can predict the possible adverse consequences of the best considered decisions. For example, as a heavy smoker, how would Sartre have reacted to a total ban on smoking in his favourite Paris café, knowing that his personal freedom was posing a direct threat to other customers' health? Furthermore, what does 'mankind' refer to, in this context? It is a very vague term which, apart from its implicit echo of a 'human nature', has lost its universal connotation in a post-modern context, where huge differences in moral attitudes are tolerated.

KEY POINTS

● No transcendent values exist to determine our choices and therefore it is our choices which give rise to values.

● 'Man makes himself by the choice of his morality, and he cannot but choose a morality' (50).

❓ QUIZ QUESTIONS

Outline how, for Sartre, morality is like art.

Explain why, for Sartre, Maggie Tulliver and La Sanseverina are each, in her own way, acting 'in the name of freedom'.

Explain Sartre's claim that values only come to light in human choices and actions.

❓ DISCUSSION QUESTIONS

Critically discuss Sartre's claim that freedom is the only possible criterion by which to make our choices.

Critically assess Sartre's view that we always choose what is best for mankind.

Abandonment

'Abandonment' produces the agonizing feeling that our freedom necessarily implies our total responsibility behind our decision to choose one particular course of action instead of another. It has a fundamental precedence in relation to the way we may exercise our freedom. Whereas ANGUISH (p. 310) and DESPAIR (p. 312) can be considered as part and parcel of any decision-making process, abandonment is with us at all times, as a silent reminder that there is no supernatural answer to our human situation. All choices and all decisions are taken in a context of total abandonment, as man is the only solution to man's moral dilemmas. Sartre observed candidly that 'the existentialist . . . finds it extremely embarrassing that God does not exist, for there disappears with Him all possibility of finding values in an intelligible heaven' (33). Deprived of any external guidance of any kind, 'we have neither behind us, nor before us in a luminous realm of values, any means of justification or excuse. We are left alone, without excuse' (34).

Sartre presents two stories, of a pupil of his and of a Jesuit priest, that illustrate abandonment. The young pupil and the Jesuit are faced with different situations, but they both face the same basic necessity to choose and thus define themselves through their respective choices. Neither of them can refuse to choose as their passive resignation would constitute yet another choice in itself. In other words, both individuals are free and, because of their inalienable freedom, they are condemned to act, one way or another.

The story of Sartre's pupil, or the absence of ready-made values

The context of the story is the Second World War, which makes the point more pressing. Sartre famously declared: 'We have never been so free than under the German Occupation', implying that every French citizen was faced with the inescapable dilemma of passively accepting the presence of the Nazi invaders on their soil or, instead, of risking their life in the violent struggle to restore liberty and peace in their country.

The young man of the story is showing signs of political 'commitment' to freedom: he is very tempted to join the Free French Forces in London and make his personal contribution to the fight against Nazism. However, he is faced with another option of a more personal nature: how can he leave his mother by herself when she relies entirely upon him after her repeated quarrels with her husband and the tragic death of her elder son in the German offensive of 1940? The moral dilemma is all the more desperate because no decision is likely to yield a clear, satisfactory conclusion.

Sartre carefully refrains from venturing any suggestion or opinion about the best possible course of action open to his pupil. Indeed, the anecdote can be interpreted as an indirect admission that no amount of philosophy can enable you to advise another person about the way *he* or *she* should or could conduct his or her life. The only certainty is that the pupil is condemned, at some point, to take a decision and, whatever that decision may be, it will define the kind of person he is. His dilemma lies between his patriotic and his filial duty, between his abstract attachment to the collective good and his country and, on the other hand, his concrete affection for one person, his mother.

Through this anecdote, Sartre argued the limitations of both the Christian doctrine and Kantian ethics, as neither of them can actually provide any help, here. The fact is that no final ruling can be given: 'There are no means of judging. The content is always concrete and therefore unpredictable; it always has to be invented' (52–3).

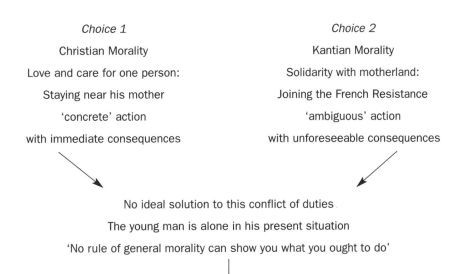

Choice 1

Christian Morality

Love and care for one person:

Staying near his mother

'concrete' action

with immediate consequences

Choice 2

Kantian Morality

Solidarity with motherland:

Joining the French Resistance

'ambiguous' action

with unforeseeable consequences

No ideal solution to this conflict of duties

The young man is alone in his present situation

'No rule of general morality can show you what you ought to do'

The young man is condemned to 'trust in his instincts'

Only by turning his final choice into action will he show

His devotion to his mother   OR   His commitment to his country

The story of the Jesuit priest, or our freedom to interpret signs

A second anecdote illustrates another aspect of abandonment, viz. our total freedom and responsibility in interpreting what we regard as *signs*, inviting us to choose one course of action in preference to another. The Jesuit is not faced with the same type of dilemma as the young man, confronted with one immediate choice of action. He is trying to find meaning to his life. He is condemned to invent himself through a subjective interpretation of his experience so far: a poor orphan, unhappy in the religious institution which awarded him a free scholarship, unlucky in love and finally, rejected by the army as he failed the entrance examination. What Sartre admires most in this story is that the Jesuit priest had the common sense or wisdom to understand that he was not cut out for a secular career but could, instead, find more personal fulfilment by joining a religious order (38).

There is no 'quietism of despair' here, and even more significantly, the choice of a religious life embraced by the Jesuit priest is not criticized from an existentialist point of view, since Sartre implies that this 'somewhat remarkable man' was not acting in bad faith (see AUTHENTICITY AND SELF-DECEPTION, p. 313), but with total sincerity and responsibility. Indeed, it could be argued that under different circumstances, the priest might have arrived at different conclusions about what to do with the rest of his life.

Sartre shows respect here for the integrity of a person holding a completely different conception of existence from his own.

KEY POINTS

- Man feels morally abandoned in a Godless world.

- Abandonment produces the agonizing feeling that our freedom necessarily implies our total responsibility. It is a constant aspect of our consciousness.

- We experience this freedom, and abandonment, in two ways: in being condemned to make choices; and in our interpretation of our experience.

❓ QUIZ QUESTIONS

Outline Sartre's example of the Jesuit priest and the conclusions he draws from it.

Briefly describe the significance of Sartre's student and its purpose. (AQA, 4b, 2003, *10 marks*)

Briefly explain why Sartre refrains from giving advice to his pupil.

❓ DISCUSSION QUESTIONS

Critically discuss Sartre's claim that moral principles cannot give final answers, so choices can legitimately be dictated by intuitions.

Critically discuss Sartre's claim that the Jesuit priest has embraced the religious life in good faith.

Anguish

We have just seen how both the young man and the Jesuit priest had to find the solution to their respective situations deep in themselves. In the face of the decision and the action to be performed, man feels the emotion of *anguish*, which increases with the degree of responsibility attached to the task being undertaken: 'Everything happens to every man as though the whole human race had its eyes fixed upon what he is doing' (32). Again, this connects to the idea of universal responsibility, that man is never choosing for himself alone but for the whole of mankind (see FREEDOM, CHOICE AND RESPONSIBILITY, p. 299). Those who disguise their anguish or try and escape from it live in bad faith (see AUTHENTICITY AND SELF-DECEPTION, p. 313).

Sartre illustrates this point in the most personal way when, in *Being and Nothingness*, he describes how, in the grip of anguish, he toys with the idea of abandoning his project of writing a book but, at the same time, discovers that he must continue with his initial project as his very freedom is at stake in this choice. He has voluntarily engaged his freedom in his writing project and it is his feeling of anguish which goads him to carry it through.

But anguish is less a moral burden here than a disguised form of moral conscience, something that Sartre would obviously deny, vehemently! Without anguish, man would be in danger of misusing his freedom, as no moral limits could be ascribed to his random spontaneity.

'The anguish of Abraham'

The first philosopher to identify anguish was Søren Kierkegaard, who identified *angst*, or 'dread', as man's feeling of dizziness when confronted with the infinite possibilities of his freedom. When Sartre refers to the existential 'anguish of Abraham', he has in mind Kirkegaard's discussion in *Fear and Trembling* of Abraham's moral isolation. Abraham is plunged into indecision by God's command to sacrifice his son Isaac as a mark of blind obedience, since it first appears to negate his very trust in divine love. His mind clouded by uncertainty, Abraham feels utterly *abandoned*, but also the anguish of being faced with an unbearable responsibility.

As a counter-example to the story of Abraham, Sartre mentions the case of a mad woman who was convinced that God gave her orders via the telephone. Irrespective of the inner or outer voices we may hear, we are still, Sartre argues, responsible for our actions. Furthermore, Sartre believes in the idea that every fully considered, genuine choice involves not only *my* freedom but other people's freedom, too. The far-reaching aspect of anguish is that it amplifies the value of my choice well beyond my personal situation: 'Who, then, can prove that I am the proper person to impose, by my own choice, my conception of man upon mankind?' (31).

KEY POINTS

- Anguish is the feeling that makes man conscious of his freedom in the face of choosing an action. And it is the realization that through my actions, I am responsible for all mankind.

- It is the inherent condition of all action. It is inescapable, except by a kind of self-deception.

❓ QUIZ QUESTIONS

Outline Abraham's moral dilemma and his anguish.

Explain why Sartre thinks that we are all, in our own way, like Abraham.

DISCUSSION QUESTION

Assess the claim that, without the feeling of anguish, man would misuse his freedom.

Despair

The second feeling associated with any choice of action is *despair*. Despair is the realization *and acceptance* that, despite our efforts, some situations are beyond our control and our very freedom is, somehow, dependent on unforeseeable events. I cannot be completely sure that my friend's train will arrive on time, just as I cannot, as a rule, bank on other people doing exactly what I expected them to do. To feel frustration, rather than despair, over circumstances beyond our control is to misunderstand the true confines of our personal freedom. That is why I should not be resigned to my fate and succumb to quietism but, on the contrary, 'I should be without illusion . . . and I should do what I can' (41).

Above all, I must not base my life on false illusions but instead accept that:

- Although I have not chosen the circumstances of my birth, which may be difficult, i.e. being born physically handicapped or being Jewish in Nazi Warsaw, there is no excuse for indulging in self-pity and resorting to irrelevant excuses or bad faith (see AUTHENTICITY AND SELF-DECEPTION, p. 313). Both situations have to be faced in the light of what can be achieved realistically. I always remain free to act on my situation in my own personal way.
- I am not indispensable, in the sense that life can and will go on without me. To think otherwise is the poor excuse of those ('the scum') who refuse to face the contingency and facticity of their own existence (see SUBJECTIVITY AND THE COGITO, p. 298) and prefer to hide behind 'the spirit of seriousness'. Again, such an attitude smacks of *inauthenticity* or bad faith.
- Other people are not responsible for my unfortunate situation and I cannot blame my parents, my teachers, my friends or any other external agency for what is my own responsibility.
- The projects which I may share with others, such as the liberation of my country from foreign invaders, will not necessarily be carried out to their full realization by others, since I have no control, from beyond the grave, over the future choices of my fellow-comrades.
- Furthermore, future generations will not necessarily share the same beliefs as my contemporaries. Indeed, as we have seen, man is always free to decide, for himself, 'what man is then to be' (40).
- I can alter only the present situation and, therefore, 'I must . . . confine myself to what I can see' (40). Yet, every situation, however dramatic or extreme, in which we find ourselves becomes 'ours'. Sartre considered that, even in the face of a death squad, a prisoner could still make a last courageous gesture.

Objections

For Sartre, consciousness *is* freedom and existentialism reveals to man his inexhaustible potential for self-realization. Yet, looking into the very structure of this seemingly transparent consciousness, we discover the predetermined ontological characteristics of abandonment, anguish and despair. Those three unmistakably *psychological* aspects of every subjectivity cast long, dark shadows over the alleged total freedom of consciousness, as they are the permanent backdrop to all our decisions. To what extent, therefore, can we be expected to make completely free choices, knowing that, condemned to invent our *own* values (abandonment), we constantly have to bear in mind the rest of mankind (anguish) and have no long-term influence on the future course of human events (despair)?

Sartre may rightly argue that existentialism is a philosophy of action and not an attitude of passive acquiescence to the world around me. However, to know that the success or failure of my projects is not entirely within my power considerably diminishes man's use of freedom. To recognize the external limits of my inherent freedom is surely to accept that my actions are, in some respect, determined by circumstances beyond my will.

● **KEY POINTS**

- Despair is the acceptance of our limited human situation, without false illusions.

- It involves the realization that, though my freedom may be unlimited, I am always dependent on probabilities beyond my control; that whatever the situation, it is always mine and I must accept it as such; and that I cannot expect my projects to be necessarily carried out by others, after my death.

❓ QUIZ QUESTIONS

Explain and illustrate Sartre's concept of 'despair'.

Explain Sartre's claim that 'I should be without illusion'.

❓ DISCUSSION QUESTION

Critically assess the view that despair can be the acceptance of a certain form of determinism.

Authenticity and self-deception (bad faith)

To regard freedom as a burden and not as an open road is a conscious, self-deceiving attitude, condemned by Sartre, not on a moral but on a logical ground: 'One can judge . . . that in certain cases choice is founded upon an error, and in others upon the truth' (50). To be in *bad faith* is to deny one's freedom and the resulting responsibility attaching to it.

Furthermore, it reveals a profound misunderstanding of what human existence is actually about. Insofar as freedom makes choices possible and is also the ground of all other values, it would be nothing short of foolish and self-contradictory to *choose* against one's freedom.

Self-deception or bad faith is one of the features of consciousness, and is closely associated with its power to *negate* the present and project itself into a different for-itself, into the future (see THE NATURE OF HUMAN REALITY IN CONTRAST WITH THAT OF MATERIAL OBJECTS, p. 293). Because consciousness is separated from the world of things by a gap, or 'nothingness', it enables us to change our situation in the world. Bad faith could be said to be a misuse of our natural power of imagining. When, for instance, someone claims that their repeated failures are due to external factors, such as a streak of bad luck or other people standing in their way to success, they are simply lying to themselves.

Sartre strongly rejected Freud's appeal to the existence of an 'unconscious' full of repressed desires and instincts as well as memories of traumatic childhood events as an influence on our action. Emotions and desires can never be used as an excuse for one's actions as we do not only control but actually *choose* our psychological states. I am never overwhelmed by fear of anger but, for Sartre, I *deliberately* choose to be afraid or angry, as a way of *being* in the world.

Sartre praises action over and above wishful thinking and regretful indecision. We make ourselves through our actions. *Reality alone is reliable* and actions speak louder than words. Sartre argues that the literary genius of Marcel Proust can be recognized in the totality of his *works*. The French writer did not simply contemplate writing *In Search of Lost Time*, but actually dedicated his life to the completion of his masterpiece (41–2).

Sartre argues against 'the spirit of seriousness' entertained by the 'scum' who choose to believe that values can exist independently of our personal choices. For Sartre, this belief is tantamount to a refusal to exercise their freedom, which constitutes, in his eyes, the highest form of existential self-betrayal.

Objections

Despite his insistence that bad faith can be disapproved of only from a logical viewpoint, Sartre is nonetheless expressing a value judgement, after arguing repeatedly for the absence of objective moral criteria. However, spotting bad faith in other people is tantamount to playing a fool's game, since a person acting in what is regarded as 'bad faith' by some external observers, may actually conceal a *good* ulterior motive, known only to that person.

To claim that it is possible to act in good faith in all situations is to assume that we never lose sight of our commitment to freedom in both its individual and universal dimensions. But then *any* decision can be justified in the name of 'good faith'. Existentialist morality is unashamedly concerned with the degree of spontaneity behind actions over and above all moral considerations. In this respect, it has little to offer about how to approach genuine moral dilemmas, such as those discussed in the text.

● **KEY POINTS**

Authentic life	Inauthentic life
Acting in good faith	Acting in bad faith
Responsibility and commitment	Self-deception
Accepting total freedom as an inescapable fact	'Cowards' hiding from freedom
'The hero makes himself heroic'	'The coward makes himself cowardly'
To will freedom for freedom's sake	To use false excuses such as determinism
Fully assuming our human situation	'Scum' denying the contingency of their lives

❓ QUIZ QUESTIONS

Outline and illustrate **three** differences between an 'authentic' and an 'inauthentic' life.

Explain Sartre's claim that bad faith is a deliberate denial of one's freedom.

❓ DISCUSSION QUESTIONS

Critically discuss Sartre's formulation and application of the concept of 'bad faith' (self-deception). (AQA, 4c, 2003, *25 marks*)

Assess Sartre's claim that it is possible to act in good faith in all situations.

The criticisms laid against existentialism

Marxist criticism

The Marxist criticism of existentialism is essentially that existentialism concentrates on the individual instead of promoting solidarity and political action. Marxist philosophy claims a clear idea of the human good and a scientific understanding of the mechanism of social cause and effect. It is, first and foremost, an instrument of political and historical change towards a better world based on universal social justice. By contrast, Sartre's existentialism seems neither practical nor scientific but *only* philosophical, i.e. estranged from the harsh reality of the oppressed working class and alien to its everyday needs and preoccupations. It is better suited to the navel-contemplating intellectuals than the majority of working-class people expecting a genuine change in their living conditions.

The Marxist Herbert Marcuse argued that Sartre is, after all, not a radical philosopher, like Karl Marx, but yet another exponent of traditional *bourgeois* philosophy, exclusively concerned with *pure subjectivity*. Sartre tells us that we are free and that the meaning of our lives depends on us. Yet he is preoccupied with the individual's *authenticity* and less concerned with the salvation of society by collective action. Existentialism is an idealistic doctrine which is part of the very ideology which it is pretending to condemn. Its radicalism is illusory, as it leaves the world as it is.

Sartre's emphasis on the individual will places man *in isolation* and leaves out of consideration the social and political side of man, and its presupposed concern for the fate of humanity. Existentialism invites one 'to dwell in quietism of despair' (23), that is, passive resignation (quietism claims that action is pointless). Sartre appears to be a *nihilist* who keeps harping on about the absurd character of existence without offering genuine practical solutions to social and political evils.

Christian criticism

Christians object to existentialism in a different way. First, they claimed, by ignoring God's commandments, it praises an absence of moral values and encourages moral anarchy and amorality. In the absence of moral barriers, everything becomes relative and 'voluntary' (24), i.e. dependent on nothing but human whim and impulse. In his atheism, Sartre also removes any hope of a possible afterlife, as well as any justification for abiding by Christian moral principles.

Second, existentialism portrays humanity in a negative, pessimistic way (23). Christians were joined by other philosophers in condemning existentialism for identifying humanity with ugliness (24). For example, Gabriel Marcel argued that Sartre's atheistic form of existentialism is nothing short of a systematic depreciation of man: 'Given that in Sartre's world, man's inherence in the universe is ignored or denied . . . it is not at all surprising that in it, man should conceive himself more and more as waste matter'. No wonder existentialism should produce the passive state of DESPAIR (p. 312).

Third, like the Marxist critics, Christians reproached Sartre for pessimistically denying the possibility of any form of human solidarity. Existentialism, they argued, deprives man of a social project and leaves him in a state of utter moral and spiritual desolation. Emmanuel Mounier objected that Sartre offers 'the lure of a haughty subjectivity tempted by a bitter isolation'. Under such circumstances, it is inevitable that man should lack any sense of moral orientation and soon become incapable of setting himself clear boundaries between what is *good* and what is *evil*.

KEY POINTS

- Marxists accuse Sartre of 'leaving out of account the solidarity of mankind and considering man in isolation' (23), thereby abandoning a concern with the fate of humanity.

- Christians accuse Sartre of abandoning morality and portraying humanity in a negative light.

❓ QUIZ QUESTIONS

Explain the phrase 'quietism of despair'.

Outline and illustrate **two** criticisms levelled at existentialism.

The implication (of existentialism) for morality; Sartre's use of universalization

Existentialism and morality

By denying the existence of God and human nature, Sartre seems to imply that we are free to do what we want. Having rejected the possibility of an unchanging 'human nature', or 'essence', Sartre must develop his existentialist ethics as a viable alternative to traditional *humanist* morals. But the task is far from easy as man cannot just act on sheer impulse, or *instinct*. However, ethics is of no use to individuals 'abandoned' to a world of subjective values. Only man can create values and this ability is the direct consequence of his freedom. ANGUISH (p. 310) is certainly a first step towards the recognition that my actions do not only affect the lives of others directly, but also create values, in their own right.

The main reason for Sartre's lecture *Existentialism and Humanism* in 1945 was to dispel the accusation of amorality attached to existentialism. He commented in the film *Sartre by Himself*: 'That was a lecture in which I articulated ideas that were not quite clearly formulated yet, ideas relating to the moral side of existentialism'. By clarifying his moral position, he hoped to make existentialism more attractive to a French generation deprived of moral guidance through the five years of German occupation: 'we can begin by saying that existentialism, in our sense of the word, is a doctrine that does render human life possible' (24).

Freedom and 'a universal condition'

Sartre argues that most of the objections to existentialism stem from a lack of understanding of its actual meaning. He tries to underline the claim that, far from encouraging moral anarchy or nihilism, existentialism is 'in truth . . . of all teachings the least scandalous and the most austere' (26).

So Sartre argues that 'freedom is the foundation of all values' (51), for 'man is free, man is freedom' (34). Man and freedom are linked inextricably. Human actions cannot be judged by some universal moral standards but they can be evaluated only according to the degree of freedom attached to them. Actions acquire their distinctive value because they have been chosen *freely* among many other possibilities of choice (32).

But Sartre develops the connection between freedom and value in the context of what he calls 'a human universality of *condition*' (46):

- Man is nothing but freedom and that freedom entails his total, unavoidable responsibility for his actions.
- Beyond all their variable historical situations, 'what never vary are the necessities of being in the world, of having to labour and to die there' (46).
- All human beings are *gratuitous* beings, thrown into the world, without any justification. We all suffer from *contingency* and *facticity* (see SUBJECTIVISM AND THE COGITO, p. 298). We all, indiscriminately, feel the same sense of ABANDONMENT (p. 307), ANGUISH (p. 310) and DESPAIR (p. 312).

This universality of condition has two important moral implications:

1 Because other human beings experience the same existential *condition* as us, along with the fact that they value freedom as much as we do, it is, therefore, possible not only to understand but to sympathize with other people's (past or present) *situation* (i.e. how they react to their immediate historical environment) and *projects* (i.e. the motivations behind their actions).

2 Importantly, because the universality of the human condition is not a kind of *human essence* in disguise, 'human universality . . . is not something given; it is being perpetually made. I make this universality in choosing myself' (47). In his own way, each human being is, through his life projects, a personal contributor to this ongoing reinvention of man: 'an existentialist will never take man as an end, since man is still to be determined' (55). This connects back to the idea of universal responsibility (see FREEDOM, CHOICE AND RESPONSIBILITY, p. 300). Sartre's interest in Marx's project of a communist society was directly linked with his deep political conviction that Marxism was the only ideology upholding both human emancipation and social justice. In his existentialism, he was prepared to join forces with Marxist philosophy in a common effort to further the cause of individual freedom and social harmony.

KEY POINTS

Sartre argues that existentialism is a viable philosophy that contains a positive moral message, namely:

- We are all absolutely free and absolutely responsible for our actions. So we can judge actions by their freedom.

- We are all *gratuitous* or 'unjustified' beings; and we all share the same human condition, as we all live, labour and die. So we can sympathize with others.

- We all, through our individual actions, participate in the ongoing reinvention of man. So we are all equally responsible actors in the human history which we make collectively.

❓ QUIZ QUESTIONS

Briefly explain and illustrate what is meant by 'a human universality of *condition*'.

Explain Sartre's claim that existentialism is 'of all teachings the least scandalous and the most austere'.

❓ DISCUSSION QUESTIONS

Assess Sartre's statement that existentialism 'is a doctrine that does render human life possible'.

Critically discuss the claim that Sartre's 'human universality of condition' is not, in fact, an account of human essence.

Critically discuss Sartre's claim that most objections to existentialism misunderstand its claims.

The possibility of moral criticism

The existentialist ethics discussed in *Existentialism and Humanism* cannot, by definition, draw on universal abstract principles, such as *utility* or *love*. In the absence of clear moral guidelines, how can we *morally* approve or disapprove of actions from an existentialist point of view? Clearly, if no action can be judged from an external standard capable of assessing its positive or negative consequences, we are left with the original motivation of the person for the action. But even here Sartre himself refrains from passing any moral judgement on the choices of the two literary heroines (see RELATION OF CHOICE TO VALUE, p. 305) or of his young pupil (see ABANDONMENT, p. 308). Mary Warnock argues that existentialism denies itself the possibility to pass *moral* judgements since 'to choose to wear red socks has as much value as the free choice to murder one's father or to sacrifice oneself for a friend'.

The one and only existentialist criterion in the evaluation of an action is *freedom* together with the degree of *authenticity* applied by the agent to his action: 'I can pronounce a moral judgement. For I declare that freedom, in respect of concrete circumstances, can have no other end and aim but itself . . . the actions of men of good faith have, as their ultimate significance, the quest of freedom itself as such' (51). This view of freedom seems close to a metaphysical interpretation if it wasn't for Sartre's insistence that we all apprehend freedom as a *subjective* value and not as an *abstract* value.

Objections

Sartre is now faced with a possible contradiction: how can he, on the one hand, uphold a person's total freedom and total responsibility when taking a particular course of action while, on the other hand, arguing that any free action must show a total commitment to a universalizable type of morality, to the freedom of everyone? This suggests that existentialist morality is prescriptive. If, on the other hand, existentialist morality cannot be systematized but has to be reinvented by each individual, it runs the risk of becoming a type of moral relativism.

KEY POINTS

- Existentialist morality refuses to appeal to traditional moral standards in order to judge choices, decisions and actions.

- Existentialist freedom is that subjective value which exclusively gives rise to all other values and by which all values can be judged.

- An action can only be judged in relation to the agent's commitment to *freedom*, together with its degree of *authenticity*.

❓ QUIZ QUESTION

Briefly explain why it is possible to criticize existentialism as advocating moral relativism.

❓ DISCUSSION QUESTIONS

Assess Sartre's claim that we cannot appeal to external moral standards to decide what to do.

Assess the claim that if there is no God and no objective morality, I can do what I want.

The responses (to criticism)

Sartre stresses that existentialism, far from being a threat to the traditional principles of humanism, is actually a form of humanism, for the following reasons:

1 'Man is himself the heart and centre of his transcendence' (55), which means that man is constantly projecting himself into new situations that define him as the person he wants to be. Sartre believes that man is the only being with the ability to *surpass* himself, i.e. to become what he is not.
2 Man is thrown into a human universe where individuals (subjectivities) compete with each other, but are also responsible for each other's freedom. Sartre insists that the only way for man to fully realize himself *as truly human* is not to live in isolation but to participate in collective projects giving him the opportunity to transcend himself and contribute to the promotion of other people's freedom (56).
3 Existentialism is about man's experience, and it values nothing more than human freedom and each individual's potential to self-realization. In this respect, it is a true humanism.

4 Existentialism is a positive philosophy which does not advocate resignation but, instead, celebrates man's freedom: 'In this sense existentialism is optimistic, it is a doctrine of action' (56).

In these respects, existentialism is a type of humanism, but without the belief in human nature or a human essence.

❓ QUIZ QUESTION

Briefly explain Sartre's responses to his critics.

❓ DISCUSSION QUESTION

Critically discuss Sartre's claim that existentialism is a type of humanism.

8

preparing for the examination

To get good exam results, you need to have a good sense of what the exam will be like and what the examiners are looking for, and to revise in a way that will help you prepare to answer the questions well. This probably sounds obvious, but in fact many students do not think about the exam itself, only about what questions might come up. There is a big difference. This chapter will provide you with some guidance on how to approach your exams in a way that will help get you the best results you can. It is divided into three sections: revision; understanding the question; and exam technique. Before continuing to read this chapter, it is worth looking back at the Introduction to see how exam questions are structured and what the Assessment Objectives are.

Throughout the chapter, I highlight revision points and exam tips, and you can find these collected together at the end of the chapter.

● REVISION: KNOWING WHAT THE EXAMINERS ARE LOOKING FOR

There are lots of tricks for memorizing information for exams. This chapter isn't about those. Revision isn't just about learning information, but also about learning how to use that information well in the exam. Being able to do this isn't a question of memory, but of directed revision and concentration in the exam. If you've been doing the exercises throughout this book, then you have been putting into practice the advice I give below.

It may sound obvious, but in order to know how best to answer the exam questions, you need to think about how they are marked. The examiners mark your answers according to three principles, known as Assessment Objectives (AOs). These are listed in the Introduction, on p. 3.

You can use these AOs to help guide your revision. AO1 leads straight to the first revision point:

R1 Learn the theories. Who said what? What terms and concepts did they use? What arguments did they use to defend their positons?

This, you may think, is challenging enough! But AO2 means that you also need to be able to *use* your knowledge. Knowing all about utilitarianism, say, won't help you if you write it all down in answer to a question about Kant. Knowing what is relevant is a special kind of knowledge, which involves thinking carefully about what you know about the theories in relation to the question asked. The best way to learn what is relevant is to practise answering questions, either exam questions or questions you make up for yourself or a friend. Try to make up questions that are similar to the exam questions, using the same *key words* (I'll talk about these in the next section). Practising answering different questions on the same topic helps keep your knowledge flexible, because you have to think of just the right bit of information that will answer the question.

R2 Practise applying your knowledge by answering questions about it. The best questions to practise with are past exam questions, but you can also make up questions for yourself.

An important part of being able to apply your knowledge is coming up with relevant examples. You can either remember good examples you have read or create your own. In either case, you should know precisely what point the example is making. An irrelevant example demonstrates that you don't really know what you are talking about.

R3 Prepare examples beforehand rather than try to invent them in the exam. If you can use your own, that's great (you'll get extra marks if they are good). But they must be short and they must make the right point – so try them out on your friends and teachers first.

What of AO3? How do you revise for *interpretation* and *evaluation*? This AO tests you on how well you can relate and compare arguments to overall theories and to other arguments. The best way to prepare for it is to spend time *thinking* about the arguments and issues. Thinking is quite different from knowing about. You might know Descartes's arguments against empirical knowledge (doubting the senses, dreaming, the evil demon), but you may never have stopped to really work out whether you think they are any good.

AO3 encourages you to do *two* things. One is to relate a particular argument to a philosopher's overall theory, to understand the relation between the parts and the whole. The second is to reflect on what a particular argument actually demonstrates, and whether there are counter-arguments that are better. Now this is what secondary sources – commentators on Plato, Descartes, etc. – try to do. So if you are working on a particular argument by Descartes, say, be guided by what the commentators have to say. Work through the arguments so that you understand for yourself the pros and cons of each viewpoint. As a minimum, be able to argue both for and against a particular view. Even if you can't come to a firm conclusion about which viewpoint is right, try to come to a firm conclusion about why the different points each seem right in their own way and why it is difficult to choose. Philosophy is not about knowing the *right* answers, it is about understanding why an answer *might* be right and why it is difficult to know.

> **R4** Think reflectively about the arguments and issues. Practise arguing for and against a particular view. Using commentators where appropriate, think about which arguments are better, and why. Think about the place and importance of arguments in a philosopher's overall viewpoint.

These first four revision points relate to taking in and understanding information. There are two more points that will help you organize the information, learn it better and prepare you for answering exam questions.

A good way of organizing your information is to create answer outlines or web-diagrams for particular issues. For example, if you are doing Unit 2 Philosophy of Religion, you could create an outline or web-diagram for the teleological (design) argument for the existence of God. Think about the essential points, and organize them, perhaps like this:

1 What is 'design'?
2 What is the classical design argument, and who has presented it?
3 What is the modern version, and how is it different?
4 Who argued against the design argument, and what did they say?
5 What are its main strengths and weaknesses? Does the modern version answer some of the criticisms of the classical version?
6 What is your conclusion, and why?

With an outline like this, you should be able to answer any question that comes up on the design argument.

> **R5** Create structured outlines or web-diagrams for particular issues. Try to cover all the main points.

Finally, once you've organized your notes into an outline or web-diagram, time yourself writing exam answers. Start by using your outline, relying on your memory to fill in the details. Then practise by memorizing the outline as well, and doing it as though it were an actual exam. You might be surprised at how quickly one hour goes by. You'll find that you need to be very focused – but this is what the examiners are looking for: answers that are thoughtful but to the point.

> **R6** Practise writing timed answers. Use your notes at first, but then practise without them.

There is one more thing important to revision that I haven't yet talked about, which is how the *structure of the questions* and how the *marks are awarded* can help you to decide what to focus on. This is what I look at next.

Understanding the question: giving the examiners what they want

The key to doing well in an exam is understanding the question. I don't just mean understanding the *topic* of the question, like 'empiricism' or Plato's theory of forms. Of course, this is very important. But you also need to understand what the question is asking you to *do*. And this is related, in a very strict way, to the three Assessment Objectives discussed above. This section is on how exam questions 'work'.

Key words

If you look at the examples of questions throughout this book, you will see that they start with different *key words*, such as 'explain', 'illustrate', 'identify', 'describe', 'outline', 'assess', 'critically discuss' and 'evaluate'. Obeying these instructions is crucially important to getting a good mark. If you are asked to 'Describe the simile of the Ship and one of its possible purposes' (Unit 3, Plato's *Republic*, AQA, June 2004), and you argue that 'Plato's simile of the ship is unpersuasive because . . .' then you will fail to gain marks. And the same is true if you are asked to 'Assess rationalism' (Unit 1, Theory of Knowledge, AQA, June 2004) and you only describe and illustrate what rationalism claims.

These different key words relate to the different AOs. The words 'describe' and 'identify' relate to AO1, *knowledge and understanding*. You are being asked simply to say what the theories say. The words 'explain', 'illustrate' and 'outline' relate to AO1 and AO2. You are being asked to demonstrate your knowledge in a way that requires *selection and application*. Explanations and illustrations are good only if they are relevant and set the points you make in a context. The words 'assess', 'evaluate' and 'critically discuss' relate to AO3, *interpretation and evaluation*. Of course, you'll have to show a lot of relevant knowledge too, but you need to go beyond this to weighing up the arguments.

The key to understanding what the question is asking, and so to getting a good mark, is to take notice of the key words.

Question structure and marks

Notice that the different key words always appear in the same parts of the question. So, in Units 1 and 2, 'describe' always appears in part (a), 'assess' always appears in part (c). This is because the marks given for each part of the question relate to a particular AO in a very strict way. You don't really need to worry about the exact correlation. If you follow the key word instructions, you won't go far wrong.

In all three AS Units, the marks for AO1 (knowledge and understanding) are distributed throughout parts (a), (b) and (c). The marks for AO2 (selection and application) are distributed in parts (b) and (c). All the marks for AO3 (interpretation and evaluation) are in part (c). In total, there are 18 marks available for AO1, 18 marks available for AO2 and 9 marks available for AO3.

Units 1, 2

(a)   6 marks for AO1
(b)   6 marks for AO1, 9 marks for AO2
(c)   6 marks for AO1, 9 marks for AO2, 9 marks for AO3.

Unit 3

(a)   (i) 2 marks for AO1; (ii) 2 marks for AO1; (iii) 4 marks for AO1, 2 marks for AO2
(b)   4 marks for AO1, 6 marks for AO2
(c)   6 marks for AO1, 10 marks for AO2, 9 marks for AO3.

Why is this important? For the same reason that the key words are important. It tells you what you should be doing. If all the marks are for AO1 (knowledge and understanding), there is no point spending any time evaluating. And if there are 9 marks for AO3 (interpretation and evaluation), then no matter how clearly you describe the theories and arguments, you cannot get a good mark for the question if you do not also evaluate them.

There is another reason why this distribution of marks is important. It can help guide your revision. There are 45 marks available in total; 18 for AO1, 18 for AO2 and 9 for AO3. So you need to have a very firm grasp of the facts about ideas and arguments, and of their relevance to any particular question. However, you will find it difficult to get an 'A' or 'B' grade unless you also know how to evaluate them well.

A note on Unit 3 Set Text examination

Part (a) of the Unit 3 exam is a special case, because it relates to a given extract of text. It is worth making three points about this question. First, notice that you only need to get the answers to part (a) out of the extract, nothing else. So it is a good idea to read part (a) of the question first, and *then* read the text extract to find the answers to the question. Second, notice that *all* of part (a) relates specifically to the extract, not just question (i). You should bear this in mind when answering (ii) and (iii) as well. Third, question (iii) often requests the development of an objection or theory. Note that this is only *development*, not evaluation. Clarity and accuracy in presenting the objection or theory is important.

Examination technique: getting the best result you can

If you've understood the question structure, and know what to expect in the exam, the exam will not seem so daunting. You'll have a good idea about how to proceed, and a sense of how the parts of the question are testing different aspects of your knowledge. This section gives you some tips on how to approach the questions when you are actually in the exam.

Exams are very exciting, whether in a good way or a bad way! It can be helpful, therefore, to take your time at the beginning, not to rush into your answers, but to plan your way. The tips I give below are roughly in the order that you might apply them when taking the exam. You might be surprised at the number of things it can be worth doing before you write anything at all.

It is important to decide carefully which question to answer, and this means reading the whole of each question before making your decision. In Unit 1 Theory of Knowledge, this just means reading both questions. In Unit 2, it means identifying the two questions which are relevant to you, and reading through them both. You might find that although you know the answer to part (a), you aren't sure about part (c). If you don't read the whole question first, but just start your answer to part (a) straightaway, you could end up wishing you had answered the other question.

In Unit 3, there is only one question which will be relevant (unless, unusually, you have studied more than one text). But you should still read the whole question first. This is because you will need to think how long to spend on each part. If you discover that you are less sure of an answer to one part, you may want to leave a little bit of extra time for tackling that section.

> **E1** Read through all the relevant questions before starting your answer. This will help you to decide which question you can answer best overall, taking into account all the parts, and will also help you to decide how long to spend on each part.

As I've already indicated, once you've decided which question to do, you need to think about how long to spend on each part. Here the marks available for each part should be your guide. You have 60 minutes for the exam, and there are 45 marks available. If you allow five minutes for making some notes at the beginning and five minutes to check over your answer at the end, then you've got just over one minute per mark. That means, for example, that in the Unit 1 exam, you should spend around 5 minutes on part (a), 15 minutes on part (b) and 30 minutes on part (c). This isn't exact, and if you find part (b) easy, you may want to spend more time on part (c), which requires the most planning. Or you may find that you know the answer to one part better than another, so you may want to leave a little more time for the part you are less sure of.

The marks also give you an idea about how much you should write. If there are just two marks, then a single precise sentence will often be enough. If there are 6 marks, then 3–4 sentences are often enough. With the longer answers, something around 500 words is good.

> **E2** The number of marks available for each part should be a rough guide to how long you spend on it and how much you should write. But allow a little extra time for the later parts and parts you find difficult.

Before you start to write your answer to any part, read the question again very closely. There are two things to look out for. First, notice the key words, and remind yourself what they are asking for. For example, the question might be 'Explain and briefly illustrate the meaning of *a priori* **and** *a posteriori* knowledge' (Unit 1 Theory of Knowledge, June 2001, *6 marks*). If you only explain, and do not provide examples, then you won't get full marks. Second, notice the precise phrasing of the question. For example, in part (c) of the same question, it asks you to 'Assess the view that all of our *concepts* are derived from experience' (*24 marks*). This is different from the question of whether all of our *knowledge* is derived from experience. Noticing this will help you keep your answer relevant.

Because an exam is exciting (good or bad), many people have a tendency to notice only what the question is about, e.g. empiricism or Descartes's views on God. They don't notice the rest of the words in the question. But the question is never 'so tell me everything you know about empiricism'! *Every word counts*. Whether you are describing, outlining or evaluating, your answer should relate not just to the issue in general, but to the *specific words* of the question.

When it comes to evaluation in part (c), it is worth noting that evaluation is more than just presenting objections and responses side-by-side. Get the objections and the theory to *talk* to each other, and try to come to some conclusion about which side is stronger. Finally, it is worth noting that one good discussion is worth more than many weak or superficial points, so choose two or three of the *most powerful* relevant objections, and discuss those in depth.

> **E3** Before starting your answer, read the question again very closely. Take note of every word, and especially the *key word* which tells you what to do.

You are now ready to start answering the question. But, especially with the longer answers – parts (b) and (c) – many people find it is worth organizing their thoughts first. What are you going to say, in what order? This is particularly important with questions that involve evaluation, since arguments require that you present ideas in a logical order. If you've memorized an outline or a web-diagram, quickly write it out at the beginning so that you note down all the points. It is very easy to forget something or go off on a tangent once you are stuck into the arguments. Having an outline or web-diagram to work from will help you keep your answer relevant and structured. It will also remind you how much you still want to cover, so it can help you pace yourself better. However, you might discover, as you develop your answer, that parts of the outline or diagram are irrelevant or just don't fit. Don't worry – the outline is only there as a guide.

> **E4** Before you start your answer, especially if it will be comparatively long, it can be worth writing out your outline or web-diagram first. This can help remind you of the key points you want to make, and the order in which you want to make them.

All the questions ask for examples at some point. Finding and using a good example is very important. Good examples are concise and relevant, and support your argument. But you need to explain why they support your argument. An example is an illustration, not an argument.

> **E5** Keep your examples short and make sure they support the point you want to make. Always explain how they support your point.

Because philosophy is about the logical relationship of ideas, there are a number of rules of thumb about presentation. Here are four important ones.

> **E6** Four rules of thumb:
>
> 1 Don't use a *technical term*, like 'the greatest happiness principle' or 'the ontological argument', without saying what it means.
> 2 Describe a theory before evaluating it. (If you have described it in answer to a previous part, you don't need to describe it again.)
> 3 Keep related ideas together. If you have a thought later on, add a footnote indicating where in the answer you want it to be read.
> 4 Don't state the conclusion to an argument before you've discussed the argument, especially if you are going to present objections to that conclusion. You can state what the argument hopes to show, but don't state it *as a* conclusion.

It is very easy to forget something, or say it in an unclear way. Leave time to check your answer at the end. You might find you can add a sentence here or there to connect two ideas together more clearly, or that some word is left undefined. These little things can make a big difference to the mark.

> **E7** Leave time to check your answer at the end. You may want to add a helpful sentence here and there.

Revision tips

R1   Learn the theories. Who said what? What terms and concepts did they use? What arguments did they use to defend their positions?

R2   Practise applying your knowledge by answering questions about it. The best questions to practise with are past exam questions, but you can also make up questions for yourself.

R3   Prepare examples beforehand, rather than try to invent them in the exam. If you can use your own, that's great (you'll get extra marks if they are good). But they must be short and they must make the right point – so try them out on your friends and teachers first.

R4   Think reflectively about the arguments and issues. Practise arguing for and against a particular view. Using commentators where appropriate, think about which arguments are better, and why. Think about the place and importance of arguments in a philosopher's overall viewpoint.

R5   Create structured outlines or web-diagrams for particular issues. Try to cover all the main points.

R6   Practise writing timed answers. Use your notes at first, but then practise without them.

Examination tips

E1   Read through all the relevant questions before starting your answer. This will help you to decide which question you can answer best overall, taking into account all the parts, and will also help you to decide how long to spend on each part.

E2   The number of marks available for each part should be a rough guide to how long you spend on it and how much you should write. But allow a little extra time for the later parts and parts you find difficult.

E3   Before starting your answer, read the question again very closely. Take note of every word, and especially the 'key word' which tells you what to do.

E4   Before you start your answer, especially if it will be comparatively long, it can be worth writing out your outline or web-diagram first. This can help remind you of the key points you want to make, and the order in which you want to make them.

E5   Keep your examples short and make sure they support the point you want to make. Always explain how they support your point.

E6   Four rules of thumb:

- Don't use a *technical term*, like 'the greatest happiness principle' or 'the ontological argument', without saying what it means.
- Describe a theory before evaluating it. (If you have described it in answer to a previous part, you don't need to describe it again.)
- Keep related ideas together. If you have a thought later on, add a footnote indicating where in the answer you want it to be read.
- Don't state the conclusion to an argument before you've discussed the argument, especially if you are going to present objections to that conclusion. You can state what the argument hopes to show, but don't state it *as* a conclusion.

E7 Leave time to check your answer at the end. You may want to add a helpful sentence here and there.

GLOSSARY OF KEY PHILOSOPHICAL TERMS

a posteriori   Knowledge of propositions that can only be known to be true or false through sense experience.

a priori   Knowledge of propositions that do not require (sense) experience to be known to be true or false.

analytic   An analytic proposition is true (or false) in virtue of the meanings of the words. For instance, 'A bachelor is an unmarried man' is analytically true, while 'A square has three sides' is analytically false.

contingent   A proposition that could be either true or false, a state of affairs that may or may not hold, depending on how the world actually is.

deductive   An argument whose conclusion is *logically entailed* by its premisses, i.e. if the premisses are true, the conclusion *cannot* be false.

empirical   Relating to or deriving from experience, especially sense experience, but also including experimental scientific investigation.

empiricism   The theory that there can be no a priori knowledge of synthetic propositions about the world (outside my mind), i.e. all a priori knowledge is of analytic propositions, while all knowledge of synthetic propositions must be checked against sense experience.

fallacy   A pattern of poor reasoning; a fallacious argument or theory is one that is mistaken in some way.

inductive   An argument whose conclusion is *supported* by its premisses, but is not logically entailed by them, i.e. if the premisses are true, the conclusion may be false, but this is unlikely (relative to the premisses); one form of inductive argument is inference to the best explanation, i.e. the conclusion presents the *best explanation* for why the premisses are true.

innate   Knowledge or ideas that are in some way present from birth.

natural law   The view that morality is known through reason, founded on what is intelligibly good, and is a matter of a principled or deontological pursuit of what is good.

necessary   A proposition that *must* be true (or if false, it must be false), a state of affairs that *must* hold.

normative   Relating to *norms*, rules or reasons for conduct.

prima facie   At first sight, correct or accepted until shown otherwise.

proposition   A declarative statement (or more accurately, what is claimed by a declarative statement), such as 'Mice are mammals'; propositions can go after 'that' in 'I believe that . . .' and 'I know that . . .'.

rationalism   The theory that there can be a priori knowledge of synthetic propositions about the world (outside my mind); this knowledge is gained by reason without reliance on sense experience.

scepticism   The view that our usual justifications for claiming our beliefs amount to knowledge (in a particular area, e.g. morality; or generally – global scepticism) is inadequate, so we do not in fact have knowledge.

self-evident   A judgement that has no other evidence or proof but its own plausibility; this doesn't necessarily mean that everyone can immediately see that it is true. 'Self-evident' is not the same as 'obvious'. However, the only way we can come to know the judgement is true is by considering it.

sense-data (singular **sense-datum**)   In perception, mental images or representations of what is perceived, *bits* of experience; if they exist, they are the immediate objects of perception.

synthetic   A proposition that is not analytic, but true or false depending on how the world is.

veridical   A proposition that is true or an experience that represents the world as it actually is.

INDEX

eBooks – at www.eBookstore.tandf.co.uk

A library at your fingertips!

eBooks are electronic versions of printed books. You can store them on your PC/laptop or browse them online.

They have advantages for anyone needing rapid access to a wide variety of published, copyright information.

eBooks can help your research by enabling you to bookmark chapters, annotate text and use instant searches to find specific words or phrases. Several eBook files would fit on even a small laptop or PDA.

NEW: Save money by eSubscribing: cheap, online access to any eBook for as long as you need it.

Annual subscription packages

We now offer special low-cost bulk subscriptions to packages of eBooks in certain subject areas. These are available to libraries or to individuals.

For more information please contact webmaster.ebooks@tandf.co.uk

We're continually developing the eBook concept, so keep up to date by visiting the website.

www.eBookstore.tandf.co.uk